Artificial Intelligence
and
The Rule of Law

(Ethics, Policy, and Global Perspectives)

Surender Sinha
Advocate

PUBLICATION
Delhi - 110089 (India)

Edition : 2025
ISBN : 978-93-6210-918-7

Price : 1000/-

Artificial Intelligence and The Rule of Law
(Ethics, Policy, and Global Perspectives)
-Surender Sinha
Mail id : 72sinha@gmail.com

Cover Page & Book Layout
Jyoti Singh

Published by
PRAKHAR GOONJ PUBLICATIONS
Office : A-11/90, Sector-18 Rohini, Delhi-110089
Reg. Office : H-3/2 Sector-18 Rohini, Delhi-110089
Email : prakhargoonj@gmail.com
info@prakhargoonjpublications.com
Ph. : 7982710571, 7838505899, 011-42635077
Web : prakhargoonjpublications.com

INTRODUCTION

The twenty-first century stands as a witness to one of the greatest transformations in human history- the rise of Artificial Intelligence (AI). What once began as a speculative question- Can machines think?- Has today evolved into a living, breathing technological force that is reshaping the very structure of human civilization. From medicine to media, education to economy, no sphere of human endeavor remains untouched. The field of law, built upon reason, ethics, and justice, too, finds itself at a crossroads where human judgment now meets the precision and possibility of machines.

To me, this convergence between Artificial Intelligence and the Rule of Law is not a mere meeting of technology and jurisprudence. It represents a deeper philosophical shift- a rethinking of what justice, fairness, and accountability truly mean in the age of intelligent systems. In my book Artificial Intelligence and the Rule of Law: Ethics, Policy, and Global Perspectives, I explore this transformation with depth and balance. I do not merely glorify the novelty of AI but critically examine the questions it raises- questions that strike at the heart of legal and moral reasoning.

As I reflect on the ways machines are beginning to assume tasks once entrusted solely to human discretion- interpreting statutes, supporting judicial decisions, or predicting case outcomes- I find myself asking: Can fairness be programmed? Can justice be automated without losing its ethical soul? And when an AI system errs, who bears responsibility- the developer, the operator, or the machine itself? These are not hypothetical dilemmas to me; they touch the very foundation of our legal consciousness. Law, at its essence, is not just a set of written rules; it is a living philosophy that upholds equality before the law, ensures accountability of power, safeguards procedural fairness, and embodies transparency in governance. The rise of artificial intelligence challenges each of these ideals. As decision-making gradually moves from human reasoning to algorithmic logic, I believe we face a profound need to ensure that the human spirit of justice is not lost in the process of digital perfection.

In the early chapters of this book, I trace the journey of AI- from its origin in symbolic logic and expert systems to the emergence of deep learning and generative models that dominate our world today. This historical perspective, I hope, reminds readers that AI is not a single invention, but an evolving continuum- a bridge between imagination and innovation. It is important to me to separate what AI is from what we fear or fantasize it to be, grounding the legal debate in reality rather than speculation.

From there, I move to the idea of the Rule of Law- the bedrock of all democratic systems. Drawing inspiration from thinkers like Montesquieu and Locke, and milestones such as the Magna Carta, I revisit how the concept of justice evolved as a shield against arbitrary power. Within this rich historical and moral backdrop, I examine the disruptive promise of AI- its potential to make law more efficient, and its danger to make justice less transparent.

Indeed, AI can streamline research, organize evidence, and even predict verdicts- but its "black box" nature raises troubling questions. How do we trust what we cannot see or understand? When biases hidden within data influence outcomes, how do we preserve the equality that law demands? To me, the tension between algorithmic opacity and legal transparency lies at the very heart of this dilemma.

Yet, I have sought to avoid both extremes- neither worshipping AI as an infallible tool nor condemning it as a threat to humanity. Instead, I argue for a responsible and principled integration of AI into the legal system- one that enhances the reach of justice without diluting its human core. The emphasis throughout remains clear: technological progress must walk hand in hand with fairness, accountability, and human dignity.

The structure of this work reflects my broad, comparative, and interdisciplinary vision. I study how nations around the world- from India to the United States, the European Union to China- are shaping their legal and ethical responses to AI. Europe's rights-based caution, America's innovation-driven pragmatism, and China's strategic state-led model each offer valuable lessons. Seen together, these perspectives underline the urgent need for a global legal framework- perhaps even an AI Treaty- that protects human rights, promotes justice, and ensures that accountability never fades in the glow of automation.

Equally important to me is the book's ethical inquiry. Across its chapters, I engage with vital questions of algorithmic bias, data privacy, human autonomy, and professional responsibility. Drawing upon both classical philosophy and contemporary ethics, I insist that the true measure of AI's value lies not merely in efficiency, but in its harmony with justice and moral responsibility. My goal has been to bridge the worlds of law, technology, and ethics- offering readers an integrated understanding of a subject that will define the century ahead.

With decades of legal practice and a lifelong engagement with philosophy, I have sought to bring to this subject an insight both practical and profound. My writing aspires to balance intellectual depth with clarity, inviting scholars, judges, policymakers, and citizens alike to reflect upon how law can preserve its essence amid the surge of digital change. Rather than prescribing rigid answers, I wish to open a space for dialogue- asking how the eternal principles of justice can evolve without eroding their foundation.

This work arrives at a moment when courts and institutions worldwide are confronting unprecedented questions- from predictive policing to AI-driven sentencing, and intellectual property rights in the age of generative technologies. As these challenges grow, I hope this book serves both as a guide and a warning: reminding us that while technology may refine the process of law, it must never replace its moral essence.

Surender Sinha
Advocate

Published Books of the Author

English

1. Mediation : Bridging Law and Conflict Resolution
2. Delhi : Through The Ages
3. Swami Vivekananda : A Detailed Introspection
4. The entire forensic in courtroom practice : A guide for lawyers
5. Courtroom Genius : Law, Logic, and the Pursuit of Justice
6. Fundamentals of Criminal Law and Justice Systems
7. Handbook to Crack LLB Entrance Exams
8. Modern Legal terminology : A practice Dictionary for Law Students
9. Artificial Intelligence and the Rule of Law : Ethics, Policy, and Global Perspectives

Hindi

1. मीडिएशन : ब्रिजिंग लॉ एंड कॉन्फ्लिक्ट रेज़ोल्यूशन
2. दिल्ली का इतिहास
3. स्वामी विवेकानंद : विवेचनात्मक अध्ययन
4. कोणार्क सूर्य मंदिर

References -

Russell, S. & Norvig, P. — Artificial Intelligence: A Modern Approach

- *Most widely used academic textbook explaining foundations of AI.*

European Union — EU Artificial Intelligence Act (2024)

- *First comprehensive global regulation classifying AI by risk.*

United Nations — AI and Human Rights Reports (Various Years)

- *Highlights human rights risks including privacy and discrimination.*

OECD — OECD Principles on Artificial Intelligence (2019)

- *Sets global principles for trustworthy and ethical AI.*

NITI Aayog (Govt. of India) — National Strategy for Artificial Intelligence

- *India's roadmap for responsible AI development.*

Supreme Court of India — Justice K.S. Puttaswamy vs Union of India (2017)

- *Declared privacy as a fundamental right in India.*

European Commission — GDPR (General Data Protection Regulation) (2018)

- *Global benchmark law for data privacy and user consent.*

IEEE — Ethically Aligned Design Guidelines (2020)

- *Ethical standards for AI developers and engineers.*

World Economic Forum — Global AI Governance Reports

- *Risk-based frameworks for safe deployment of AI worldwide.*

Partnership on AI — Responsible AI Best Practices

- *Industry-driven standards on fairness and transparency.*

MIT Media Lab — Research on Algorithmic Bias

- *Demonstrates gender & racial inaccuracies in facial recognition.*

IBM — AI Explainability and Trust Publications

- *Transparent model design techniques for legal and audit use.*

Google AI — Responsible AI Practices White Papers

- *Includes model safety, red-teaming, and content responsibility.*

Microsoft — Responsible AI Standard

- *Governance framework emphasizing accountability & impact.*

UNESCO — Recommendation on the Ethics of Artificial Intelligence (2021)

- *First global ethics treaty covering fairness and inclusion.*

Stanford HAI — AI Index Report (Annual)

- *Tracking global AI growth, policy, investment & risks.*

Harvard Berkman Klein Center — AI & Law Analyses

- *Studies on transparency, due process & legal safeguards.*

Oxford Internet Institute — AI & Democracy Studies

- *Risks of misinformation and automated political persuasion.*

National Crime Records Bureau (India)

- *Data used to support predictive policing risk discussions.*

World Justice Project — Rule of Law Index

- *Benchmarks legal system integrity impacted by AI adoption.*

International Criminal Court-Evidence & Digital Forensics Standards

- *AI's role in crime investigation and admissibility in courts.*

Brookings Institution — AI Policy Research

- *• Evaluates governance models & ethical accountability.*

PwC — AI Economic Impact Forecasts

- *Predicts multi-trillion-dollar economic influence of AI globally.*

Accenture & Deloitte — Legal Tech Transformation Reports

- *Insights into AI automation in law firms and courts.*

Cambridge Analytica Case Studies & Official Investigations

- *Used to explain data misuse, political profiling & ethics failures.*

CONTENTS

1
The Dawn of Intelligent Systems and Legal Order

Artificial Intelligence (AI) is a term that has permeated public discourse, often conjuring images of sentient robots or omniscient digital overlords. However, beneath the veneer of science fiction and sensationalism lies a complex and rapidly evolving field of computer science. To understand AI's impact on the legal order, we must first establish a clear and nuanced definition of what AI actually is, recognizing it not as a monolithic entity, but as a spectrum of capabilities. This foundational understanding is critical for appreciating the varied applications and implications of AI within legal systems, thereby setting the stage for more informed discussions on its integration and governance.

The genesis of AI as a formal field can be traced back to the mid-20th century. Early pioneers, such as Alan Turing, pondered the question of whether machines could think, laying the theoretical groundwork for what would become artificial intelligence. The Dartmouth Workshop in 1956 is widely regarded as the official birthplace of AI as a research discipline, where the term "artificial intelligence" itself was coined. These early endeavors were largely characterized by **symbolic AI**, also known as GOFAI (Good Old-Fashioned Artificial Intelligence). This approach focused on creating intelligent behavior by manipulating symbols and rules, mimicking human reasoning processes. Programs were designed to encode knowledge explicitly in the form of logical statements and rules, allowing them to solve problems through deduction and inference. Expert systems, for instance, were a prominent manifestation of symbolic AI, designed to replicate the decision-making abilities of human experts in specific domains, such as medical diagnosis or financial planning. While these systems achieved notable successes, they were often brittle, struggling with ambiguity, uncertainty, and common-sense reasoning that humans navigate effortlessly. The reliance on explicit rule-sets meant that they could not easily adapt to new situations or learn from experience without significant human intervention and reprogramming.

The limitations of symbolic AI paved the way for a paradigm shift towards **machine learning (ML)**. Instead of explicitly programming rules, machine learning algorithms are designed to learn from data. They identify patterns, make predictions, and improve their performance over time through exposure to vast amounts of information. This approach has become the dominant force in contemporary AI research and development. Within machine learning, a significant advancement has been **deep learning (DL)**, a subset that utilizes artificial neural networks with multiple layers (hence "deep"). These deep neural networks are inspired by the structure and function of the human brain, with interconnected nodes (neurons) organized in layers. Each layer processes information and passes it to the next, allowing the network to learn increasingly complex representations of data. Deep learning has been instrumental in breakthroughs across various fields, including computer vision, natural language processing, and speech recognition. The ability of deep learning models to automatically learn hierarchical features from raw data- meaning they can discern increasingly abstract representations as data progresses through the network's layers- has led to remarkable performance improvements in tasks that were previously intractable for traditional AI methods. For instance, in image recognition, a deep learning model can learn to detect edges in early layers, then shapes, and finally complex objects like faces or cars in deeper layers, all without explicit human programming for each feature.

The evolution continues with **generative AI**, a more recent and rapidly developing area within deep learning. Generative AI models are capable of creating new content, such as text, images, music, and code, based on the data they have been trained on. Technologies like Generative Adversarial Networks (GANs) and large language models (LLMs), such as GPT-3 and its successors, have demonstrated astonishing capabilities in producing human-quality text and realistic imagery. LLMs, in particular, are trained on massive datasets of text and code, enabling them to understand context, generate coherent and contextually relevant responses, translate languages, write different kinds of creative content, and answer questions in an informative way. This has direct implications for the legal field, from drafting documents and summarizing case law to assisting in legal research and even providing preliminary legal advice.

It is crucial to understand that AI is not a singular entity but exists on a spectrum of capabilities. This spectrum is often categorized into different levels, with the most common distinction being between Artificial Narrow Intelligence (ANI) and Artificial General Intelligence (AGI).

Artificial Narrow Intelligence (ANI), also referred to as Weak AI, is the type of AI that exists today. ANI is designed and trained for a specific task or a narrow range of tasks. Examples are ubiquitous in our daily lives: virtual assistants like Siri or Alexa, recommendation algorithms on streaming services and e-commerce sites, spam filters in email, image recognition software, and autonomous vehicles. Each of these AI systems excels at its designated function but cannot perform tasks outside its programmed domain. A chess-playing AI cannot write poetry, and a facial recognition system cannot diagnose a medical condition. ANI systems are powerful tools that leverage sophisticated algorithms and vast datasets to achieve high levels of performance within their specific parameters. In the legal context, ANI manifests in tools for legal research (e.g., Westlaw, LexisNexis's AI features), contract analysis software that identifies clauses and potential risks, predictive analytics tools that assess litigation outcomes, and AI-powered e-discovery platforms that sift through vast amounts of electronic documents. These tools are designed to augment human capabilities, improve efficiency, and streamline legal processes. They operate based on predefined algorithms and learned patterns from historical data, and their "intelligence" is confined to the specific problem they are built to solve. For instance, an AI tool designed to predict the likelihood of parole success is trained on data related to past parole decisions, offender characteristics, and recidivism rates. While it might become highly accurate within that specific domain, it possesses no understanding of legal philosophy, ethical jurisprudence, or the broader societal implications of its predictions. Its intelligence is operational, not general.

The second category, **Artificial General Intelligence (AGI)**, often called Strong AI, remains largely hypothetical. AGI refers to AI that possesses human-like cognitive abilities, capable of understanding, learning, and applying its intelligence to a wide range of tasks, just as a human being can. An AGI system would not be limited to a single domain; it could reason, plan, solve problems, think abstractly, comprehend complex ideas, learn from experience, and adapt to new environments with the same flexibility and breadth as a human. It would possess common sense, creativity, and potentially consciousness. While significant progress has been made in specific AI capabilities, achieving true AGI is an immense scientific and engineering challenge, and there is no consensus on when, or even if, it will be realized. The development of AGI would represent a profound shift, potentially impacting all aspects of society, including legal systems, in ways we can only begin to imagine. The implications for the rule of law would be transformative, raising fundamental questions about agency, responsibility, rights, and the very definition of legal personhood.

Beyond ANI and AGI, some discussions introduce a third category, **Artificial Superintelligence (ASI)**. ASI would surpass human intelligence in virtually every field, including scientific creativity, general wisdom, and social skills. If AGI were to be achieved, ASI would be its successor, representing an intelligence far exceeding that of the brightest human minds. The concept of ASI is even more speculative than AGI, and its potential implications, both positive and negative, are subjects of intense philosophical and scientific debate. While ASI remains in the realm of theoretical speculation, it is worth acknowledging as a distant horizon that informs some of the more profound long-term considerations regarding AI's ultimate potential impact on humanity and its legal structures.

Understanding this spectrum of AI capabilities is not merely an academic exercise; it is fundamental to assessing AI's practical applications and its nuanced implications within legal systems. When legal professionals, policymakers, and the public discuss AI, it is vital to distinguish between the capabilities of current ANI systems and the hypothetical possibilities of AGI and ASI. Mischaracterizing AI as a monolithic, sentient entity can lead to misinformed policy decisions, unrealistic expectations, and undue fear or overconfidence. For instance, attributing human-like intent or understanding to a current AI tool used in legal research would be a category error. Such tools operate based on pattern recognition and data correlation, not on genuine comprehension of legal principles or moral reasoning.

The practical implications of this spectrum are evident in how AI is being integrated into the legal profession. Current applications primarily fall under ANI. AI-powered legal research platforms, for instance, use natural language processing (NLP) to understand queries and retrieve relevant case law, statutes, and legal articles with greater speed and precision than manual searches. Document review software leverages machine learning to classify and tag documents in large discovery sets, significantly reducing the time and cost associated with litigation. Contract analysis tools can identify key clauses, discrepancies, and risks within contracts, assisting lawyers in due diligence and contract negotiation. These are all instances of narrow AI augmenting human expertise and improving efficiency.

However, the boundaries of ANI are constantly expanding. As AI models become more sophisticated, the line between highly advanced narrow AI and nascent forms of general intelligence may blur. For example, large language models are demonstrating a remarkable ability to generate persuasive legal arguments, draft complex legal documents, and even engage in forms of legal reasoning that were once thought to be exclusively human capabilities. This evolution raises critical questions: at what point does an AI's proficiency in a specific domain become so advanced that it begins to resemble general intelligence in its practical output? And how should legal systems adapt to the increasing sophistication and autonomy of these systems?

The legal order, built on centuries of precedent and principles designed for human actors, faces the challenge of accommodating technologies that do not fit neatly into existing legal categories. The traditional notions of intent (mens rea), causation, liability, and responsibility are predicated on human agency. When AI systems make decisions or take actions that have legal consequences, determining who is accountable- the developer, the deployer, the user, or the AI system itself- becomes incredibly complex. This complexity is amplified by the "black box" problem, where the internal decision-making processes of sophisticated AI models, particularly deep learning networks, can be opaque and difficult to interpret, even for their creators.

In conclusion, defining Artificial Intelligence requires moving beyond simplistic portrayals and acknowledging its multifaceted nature as a spectrum of capabilities, from the specialized, task-oriented AI we use today to the more speculative notions of general intelligence. The evolution from symbolic AI to machine learning, deep learning, and generative AI signifies a continuous advancement in AI's ability to process information, learn, and create. Understanding the distinction between narrow AI (ANI), which is currently prevalent, and artificial general intelligence (AGI), which remains a future prospect, is essential for a grounded assessment of AI's impact on the legal order. This foundational understanding will enable a more precise and effective approach to integrating AI into legal systems, navigating its challenges, and ensuring that its development aligns with the core principles of justice and the rule of law. The subsequent sections of this book will build upon this definition to explore the intricate ways AI interacts with legal frameworks, presenting both opportunities for progress and significant challenges to established norms.

The edifice of any just and enduring legal system rests upon a bedrock of fundamental principles, collectively understood as the Rule of Law. It is not merely a set of rules, but a pervasive philosophy that governs the governors, ensuring that power is exercised within legal bounds and that all individuals and institutions are subject to the same laws. To comprehend how nascent intelligent systems will interact with, and potentially reshape, this foundational legal order, it is imperative to first dissect the core tenets that constitute the Rule of Law. These principles, forged over centuries of human governance and philosophical inquiry, provide the essential framework against which the capabilities and implications of AI within the legal sphere can be measured and understood. Without a firm grasp of these pillars, our assessment of AI's impact would be akin to analyzing a building's structural integrity without understanding the fundamental laws of physics that govern its stability.

At its heart, the Rule of Law signifies the **supremacy of law**. This cardinal principle dictates that no individual, no matter how powerful or exalted, is above the law. Government itself is bound by the law, and its powers are derived from and limited by it. This stands in stark contrast to arbitrary rule, where the will of the ruler, rather than established legal norms, dictates outcomes. The supremacy of law ensures that decisions are made based on pre-existing, publicly accessible legal frameworks, rather than the whim or caprice of those in authority. Historically, this concept gained prominence as a bulwark against absolute monarchies and tyrannical regimes, emphasizing that even the sovereign must adhere to a higher legal order. Thinkers like John Locke and Montesquieu laid crucial groundwork by advocating for constitutionalism and the idea that governmental power should be limited and accountable. This principle is vital for fostering trust in the legal system and providing a predictable environment for citizens and businesses alike. When citizens know that the law applies equally to all, including those who create and enforce it, they are more likely to abide by it.

Hand-in-hand with the supremacy of law is the principle of **equality before the law**. This means that the law should be applied impartially and without discrimination to all persons, regardless of their status, wealth, background, or any other personal characteristic. Every individual is entitled to the same legal treatment and protection. This principle is enshrined in the constitutions and legal declarations of most democratic nations, often serving as a cornerstone of human rights. It demands that legal processes, from investigation and prosecution to judgment and punishment, be free from bias. This not only promotes social justice but also contributes to the legitimacy and stability of the legal system. If certain groups were systematically favored or disfavored by the law, the entire social contract would be undermined, leading to resentment, instability, and a breakdown of societal order. The absence of due process or the preferential treatment of any individual or group based on factors other than their adherence to the law would render the legal system fundamentally unjust.

Furthermore, the Rule of Law necessitates **accountability to the law**. Not only must the law be supreme and applied equally, but those who wield public authority must also be accountable for their actions under that law. This means that government officials, law enforcement, judges, and all other state actors are subject to legal scrutiny and can be held responsible for any abuses of power or violations of legal norms. This accountability is typically enforced through various mechanisms, including independent judiciaries, parliamentary oversight, and constitutional review processes. Without accountability, the supremacy of law would be a hollow pronouncement, as there would be no recourse against those who violate it with impunity. The concept of ministerial responsibility, for instance, ensures that those in government are answerable for the actions of their departments and for their own conduct.

Crucially, the application of law must be characterized by **fairness**. This encompasses a broad range of considerations, including procedural fairness and substantive justice. Procedural fairness, often referred to as due process, ensures that legal proceedings are conducted in a just and equitable manner. This includes the right to a fair trial, the right to be heard, the right to legal representation, and the presumption of innocence. Substantive fairness refers to the content of the laws themselves, ensuring that they are just, reasonable, and do not unduly infringe upon fundamental rights. A legal system that produces unjust outcomes, even if it follows correct procedures, fails to uphold the Rule of Law. Fairness demands that the law be applied in a way that respects human dignity and upholds fundamental rights, such as the right to liberty, security, and privacy.

The principle of **separation of powers** is another critical pillar. This doctrine, famously articulated by Montesquieu, advocates for the division of governmental authority into distinct branches- typically the legislative, executive, and judicial- each with its own powers and responsibilities, and with checks and balances to prevent any one branch from becoming too powerful. The legislature makes laws, the executive enforces them, and the judiciary interprets them. This division prevents the concentration of power and provides a system of mutual oversight, ensuring that the exercise of power remains within legal confines and serves the public interest. A system where the same body could both create and enforce laws, or where the judiciary was subordinate to the executive, would be inherently prone to arbitrariness and abuse.

Participation in decision-making is also an integral aspect of a robust Rule of Law, particularly in democratic societies. While not always explicitly stated as a separate tenet, it is implicit in the idea that laws should reflect the will of the governed. This participation can take various forms, including voting in elections, engaging in public debate, and having access to information that allows for informed participation. When citizens have a voice in the creation and application of laws, the legal system gains greater legitimacy and is more likely to be respected and followed. This also ensures that laws are responsive to the needs and values of the society they serve.

Legal certainty is another indispensable element. This principle requires that laws be clear, predictable, and accessible. Individuals should be able to ascertain what the law is and how it will be applied to their actions. This certainty allows people to plan their lives and conduct their affairs with confidence, knowing the legal consequences of their choices.

Vague, obscure, or constantly shifting laws undermine legal certainty and can lead to confusion, uncertainty, and a perception of injustice. The principle of *nullum crimen sine lege* (no crime without law) and *nulla poena sine lege* (no punishment without law) are direct manifestations of this need for legal certainty, ensuring that individuals are only held liable for conduct that was clearly defined as unlawful *before* it occurred.

Closely linked to legal certainty is the requirement for the **avoidance of arbitrariness**. The Rule of Law stands in direct opposition to arbitrary power, where decisions are made based on factors other than established legal rules. This means that governmental and judicial decisions must be grounded in law and reason, not in personal bias, prejudice, or expediency. Even when discretion is granted to officials, that discretion must be exercised within defined legal parameters and in a manner that is rational and justifiable. Arbitrary actions erode public trust and can lead to the perception that justice is being dispensed unevenly, undermining the very foundation of a legal society.

Finally, **procedural and legal transparency** are essential. The workings of the legal system, from the drafting of legislation to the conduct of court proceedings, should be open to public scrutiny. This transparency allows for accountability, fosters public understanding, and helps to ensure that laws are applied fairly and impartially. It includes access to legal information, public access to court hearings (with limited exceptions), and clear reasons for judicial decisions. Transparency builds confidence in the legal process and acts as a deterrent against corruption and abuse.

These components of the Rule of Law are not abstract ideals; they are practical requirements that have evolved over millennia to create societies that are both orderly and just. From the ancient legal codes of Mesopotamia and the Roman Republic to the development of common law in England and the constitutional frameworks of modern democracies, the pursuit of these principles has been a continuous thread. For instance, the Magna Carta, signed in 1215, was a landmark document that asserted the principle that even the king was subject to the law, a foundational step in establishing the supremacy of law and limiting arbitrary royal power. The Enlightenment era further refined these concepts, with thinkers advocating for individual rights, constitutional government, and the separation of powers, all of which contribute to a robust Rule of Law.

The historical development of the Rule of Law reflects humanity's ongoing struggle to establish governance that is both effective and equitable. It represents a conscious effort to move away from rule by decree or force towards a system governed by established, predictable, and fair legal principles. This evolution is not a finished product; it is a dynamic process, constantly challenged by new social, economic, and technological developments. As we stand at the cusp of the widespread integration of intelligent systems into nearly every facet of society, understanding these enduring principles of the Rule of Law is not an academic exercise, but a critical prerequisite for navigating the profound transformations that lie ahead. It is against this established backdrop of justice, predictability, and accountability that the disruptive potential and enabling possibilities of AI within the legal order can be properly understood and responsibly managed. The principles of the Rule of Law provide the essential compass for ensuring that the advent of AI in law serves to enhance, rather than erode, the foundations of a just and ordered society.

The integration of Artificial Intelligence (AI) into the legal landscape marks a pivotal moment, presenting a complex tapestry of synergies and inherent tensions with the established principles of the Rule of Law. As these intelligent systems move from theoretical constructs to practical tools within the judicial, legislative, and administrative arms of governance, they inevitably interact with, and at times challenge, the very foundations upon which legal order has been built. This interaction is not a simple matter of adopting new technology; it is a profound re-evaluation of how justice is administered, how laws are interpreted, and how the fundamental rights and expectations of individuals are protected in an increasingly automated world. The allure of AI lies in its potential to revolutionize legal processes, promising unprecedented gains in efficiency, accuracy, and accessibility. Yet, this promise is interwoven with significant risks, threatening to undermine the very principles of fairness, predictability, and human oversight that are sacrosanct to the Rule of Law. Understanding this delicate balance, identifying the points of convergence and divergence, is the critical first step in navigating the uncharted territory of AI in law.

One of the most immediate and widely recognized opportunities AI presents is in its capacity to enhance legal efficiency. The sheer volume of legal data, from case law and statutes to discovery documents and regulatory filings, often overwhelms human capacity. AI-powered tools, such as natural language processing (NLP) and machine learning algorithms, can sift through, analyze, and categorize this information at speeds and scales previously unimaginable. This can translate into faster legal research, more thorough due diligence, and streamlined document review, all of which can reduce the cost and time associated with legal proceedings. For instance, AI can identify relevant precedents in a fraction of the time it would take a human lawyer, potentially leading to more informed and quicker legal advice. Predictive analytics, another branch of AI, can forecast litigation outcomes based on historical data, aiding in settlement negotiations and case strategy. This enhanced efficiency can, in turn, democratize access to justice by lowering the financial barriers to legal services, making legal representation and advice more accessible to individuals and small businesses who might otherwise be priced out of the market. Furthermore, AI can assist in drafting legal documents, automating routine tasks like contract generation or the preparation of standard court forms, freeing up legal professionals to focus on more complex, strategic, and client-facing aspects of their work. This augmentation of human capabilities promises a legal system that is not only more efficient but also more responsive to the needs of a rapidly evolving society.

However, these gains in efficiency are not without their attendant tensions. The principle of legal certainty, which demands that laws be clear, predictable, and accessible, faces new challenges in the era of AI. If AI systems are used to interpret laws or predict legal outcomes, the transparency of their decision-making processes becomes paramount. Many advanced AI models, particularly deep learning networks, operate as "black boxes," where the exact reasoning behind a specific output can be opaque even to their creators. This opacity directly conflicts with the need for legal certainty and the right of individuals to understand the legal basis for decisions affecting them. If a legal outcome is determined by an algorithm whose internal logic cannot be fully explained, how can individuals be assured of the predictability and fairness of the law? Moreover, the reliance on AI for legal interpretation could lead to a de facto shift in the locus of legal authority. If algorithms begin to shape judicial interpretation through predictive analytics or automated legal reasoning, who is truly making the law- the human legislator, the human judge, or the AI system? This raises questions about accountability and the very nature of judicial discretion.

The principle of equality before the law also encounters significant friction when confronted with AI. While AI has the potential to reduce human bias in some decision-making processes, it also carries the risk of perpetuating and even amplifying existing societal biases, often in ways that are subtle and difficult to detect. AI systems are trained on data, and if that data reflects historical discrimination or systemic inequalities, the AI will learn and replicate those patterns. For example, an AI used in sentencing recommendations could, if trained on data where certain demographic groups have historically received harsher sentences, continue to recommend harsher sentences for individuals from those groups, even if the AI is ostensibly making its decision based on neutral factors. This algorithmic bias can lead to discriminatory outcomes that are harder to identify and challenge than human bias, as it is embedded within the complex calculations of the system itself. Furthermore, the development and deployment of AI technologies are not evenly distributed. Access to sophisticated AI tools could create a new divide, where well-resourced legal entities or nations gain a significant advantage, potentially exacerbating existing inequalities in access to justice and legal representation.

The critical tenet of human oversight and accountability, central to the Rule of Law, is another area fraught with tension. While AI can automate many tasks, the ultimate responsibility for legal decisions must remain with humans. The question of who is accountable when an AI makes a flawed legal judgment- the programmer, the deploying institution, the supervising judge, or the AI itself- is a complex one with no easy answers. The principle of accountability to the law requires that those who wield public authority are answerable for their actions. If AI systems are increasingly involved in decision-making, how can we ensure that the ultimate human decision-makers are truly in control and capable of taking responsibility for the AI's output? Over-reliance on AI could lead to a diffusion of responsibility, where human actors passively accept AI recommendations without critical review, thereby abdicating their legal and ethical duties. The presumption of innocence, a cornerstone of fair legal processes, could also be subtly undermined if AI-powered predictive policing or risk assessment tools are used to pre-emptively flag individuals as potential offenders based on statistical probabilities rather than concrete evidence of wrongdoing.

Furthermore, the concept of fairness, encompassing both procedural and substantive justice, is intrinsically challenged by AI. Procedural fairness demands that legal processes are conducted justly, with opportunities for all parties to be heard and to present their case. If AI is used in areas like evidence analysis or witness credibility assessment, ensuring that these processes are fair and unbiased is crucial. Can an AI truly assess credibility in the same nuanced way a human can, considering non-verbal cues, context, and emotional intelligence? Substantive fairness, which pertains to the justice of the laws themselves, is also at stake. If AI is used to draft legislation or interpret regulations, there is a risk that the underlying values and ethical considerations that inform just laws could be overlooked in favor of efficiency or data-driven optimization. The danger exists that AI, optimized for certain quantifiable outcomes, might inadvertently create laws that are technically efficient but substantively unjust or that disproportionately burden certain segments of the population.

The principle of the separation of powers, designed to prevent the concentration of authority, could also be impacted. If AI systems become embedded within multiple branches of government- assisting in legislative drafting, informing executive policy decisions, and aiding judicial analysis- the clear delineation of powers could become blurred. For example, if an AI developed by an executive agency is widely used by the judiciary for sentencing guidelines, the independence of the judiciary could be compromised, as it becomes reliant on an external, potentially executive-influenced, system. The checks and balances that are meant to prevent any one branch from becoming too dominant might be complicated if AI itself becomes a powerful, albeit inanimate, actor within the governmental machinery.

Despite these challenges, the potential for AI to *enhance* the Rule of Law is substantial and warrants careful consideration. AI can significantly improve the accessibility of legal information, making complex statutes and case law understandable to the public through user-friendly interfaces and natural language queries. This aligns with the principle of legal certainty and the need for accessible laws. AI can also assist in identifying patterns of systemic injustice or bias within the legal system itself, by analyzing vast datasets of judicial decisions or law enforcement actions, thus providing evidence-based insights for reform. This could bolster accountability and lead to more equitable application of the law. In areas where human judgment is prone to fatigue or subjective error, such as reviewing thousands of similar legal documents, AI could offer a more consistent and objective approach, thereby supporting fairness and predictability. The key lies in harnessing these capabilities in a manner that complements, rather than supplants, human judgment and adheres to the core values of justice.

The development of AI in law necessitates a continuous dialogue between technologists, legal scholars, policymakers, and the public. It requires a proactive approach to developing ethical guidelines, robust regulatory frameworks, and clear standards for the deployment of AI in legal contexts. The goal is not to halt technological progress but to steer it in a direction that fortifies the Rule of Law, ensuring that the introduction of intelligent systems serves to uphold and strengthen justice, fairness, and accountability. This undertaking involves a deep understanding of both the potential benefits of AI and the profound risks it poses to the foundational principles that govern our societies. The ongoing exploration of these synergies and tensions will define the future of legal order in an increasingly intelligent world, demanding careful deliberation, rigorous ethical analysis, and a steadfast commitment to the enduring values of the Rule of Law. The initial contact points between AI and legal frameworks reveal a landscape ripe for both transformative improvement and potential disruption, underscoring the critical need for a measured and principled approach to its integration.

The integration of Artificial Intelligence into the legal profession is undeniably a revolutionary shift, but it is not the first time that a significant technological advancement has fundamentally altered the structure, practice, and underlying philosophy of law. To truly appreciate the challenges and opportunities presented by AI, it is essential to cast our gaze back and examine historical precedents where technology has acted as a catalyst for profound legal transformation. These past episodes offer invaluable lessons, revealing recurring patterns of societal adaptation, professional resistance, and the inevitable evolution of regulatory frameworks designed to harness new capabilities while mitigating risks. By understanding how law has responded to previous technological earthquakes, we can better anticipate and shape its response to the seismic waves of artificial intelligence.

One of the most impactful, albeit seemingly distant, technological revolutions that reshaped the legal landscape was the advent of the printing press in the 15th century. Before Gutenberg, legal texts, statutes, judicial pronouncements, and scholarly commentaries were painstakingly copied by hand. This laborious process inherently limited their dissemination, making them accessible only to a select few: lawyers, judges, clergy, and the wealthy elite who could afford bespoke copies. The scarcity of legal texts meant that legal knowledge was concentrated, often held as a form of exclusive intellectual property by legal guilds and institutions. Law, in essence, was a whispered tradition, passed down through apprenticeship and oral interpretation, making its application uneven and its accessibility a significant barrier to justice.

The printing press shattered this paradigm. Suddenly, legal texts could be reproduced in large quantities, with greater accuracy, and at a fraction of the cost. This democratized access to legal knowledge. Statutes could be printed and distributed widely, allowing citizens to understand their rights and obligations more directly. Case law, previously confined to the private notes of judges or the limited libraries of legal institutions, could be published and debated more broadly. This facilitated the development of a more standardized and predictable legal system, as jurists could refer to a common body of printed precedent. The printing press was instrumental in the growth of the common law system, which relies heavily on the doctrine of *stare decisis*- the principle of following precedent. Without readily available printed case reports, the consistent application of precedent across different jurisdictions would have been nearly impossible. Legal scholarship also flourished, as academics could build upon the work of others more easily, leading to more robust legal theories and critiques.

However, this newfound accessibility was not without its challenges or resistance. Established legal practitioners, who had built their careers and reputations on their exclusive knowledge, often viewed the widespread availability of legal texts with suspicion, fearing a dilution of their expertise and a challenge to their authority. There were also concerns about the accuracy and authenticity of printed texts, leading to the development of new forms of legal validation and the establishment of official printing houses for laws. The very act of codifying and printing laws began to shift the perception of law from an organic, evolving tradition to a more fixed, written set of rules, which had implications for legal interpretation and the balance between judicial discretion and legislative intent.

Moving forward a few centuries, the Industrial Revolution introduced another wave of technological change with significant legal ramifications. The rise of complex machinery, factories, and new modes of transportation like railways and steamships created entirely new legal problems. Contract law had to adapt to manage complex commercial agreements between burgeoning corporations. Tort law evolved to address injuries sustained in industrial accidents, leading to concepts like employer liability and the development of workers' compensation schemes, albeit slowly and often with significant initial resistance from industrialists. Property law grappled with new forms of ownership, intellectual property rights emerged to protect inventions and innovations, and administrative law began to develop as governments created agencies to regulate new industries, ensure public safety, and manage the consequences of industrialization.

The late 19th and early 20th centuries saw the rise of technologies that directly impacted legal practice and administration. The typewriter, for instance, mechanized document preparation, making legal documents more legible and standardized. The telephone facilitated communication between lawyers, clients, and courts, speeding up the pace of legal interactions. However, it was the advent of the computer in the latter half of the 20th century that truly heralded a new era of technological integration into law, laying much of the groundwork for the current AI revolution.

The introduction of computers into legal environments initially focused on automating administrative tasks. Law firms and courts began using computers for word processing, billing, and calendaring. However, the transformative potential of computing power soon became evident in more substantive areas of legal work. Legal research, once a physically demanding and time-consuming process involving hours spent poring over dense law books in libraries, was revolutionized by the development of computerized legal databases. Services like LEXISNexis and WESTLAW emerged, allowing lawyers to search vast repositories of statutes, case law, and secondary sources using keywords and Boolean logic. This dramatically increased the efficiency and comprehensiveness of legal research, enabling legal professionals to identify relevant authorities more quickly and effectively. The ability to access and analyze vast amounts of legal information at unprecedented speeds directly impacted legal strategy, argumentation, and the quality of legal advice.

The computer also began to influence judicial processes. Electronic filing systems were introduced in many courts, streamlining the submission of legal documents and reducing the reliance on paper-based workflows. Case management systems, powered by databases, allowed courts to track dockets, manage schedules, and monitor the progress of cases more efficiently. This promised to reduce backlogs and improve the overall administration of justice, although the implementation and adoption of these systems often encountered organizational inertia and the need for new technical expertise within the judiciary.

Furthermore, the computer enabled the development of sophisticated tools for litigation support. During the discovery phase of litigation, particularly in complex cases involving vast quantities of documents, computers became indispensable. Early forms of document imaging and keyword searching allowed legal teams to manage and analyze electronic discovery, a process that would have been logistically impossible with paper documents alone. This marked an early foray into leveraging computational power to manage and make sense of massive datasets, a precursor to the data-intensive capabilities of modern AI.

Each of these technological shifts- the printing press, the Industrial Revolution, and the advent of computing-followed a similar trajectory. First, there was innovation, creating new capabilities and possibilities. Second, there was a period of adaptation, where legal professionals and institutions began to experiment with and integrate these technologies into existing practices. This often met with resistance from those who felt threatened by the changes or who prioritized traditional methods. Third, there was a phase of legal and regulatory evolution. New laws were needed to govern the use of technology, address the novel legal issues it created, and establish standards for its responsible application. This evolution was often reactive, responding to problems that arose from the unmediated use of technology, but it also involved proactive efforts to shape its development and deployment.

The printing press democratized knowledge but also necessitated new forms of textual authority and control. The Industrial Revolution created new economic activities but required entirely new bodies of law to regulate them and protect individuals from its harshest consequences. The computer revolutionized information management and access but created new challenges related to data privacy, security, and the very nature of legal expertise.

These historical precedents offer crucial insights as we stand on the precipice of the AI revolution. The core challenge, then as now, is not simply adopting new tools, but understanding how these tools interact with and potentially transform the fundamental principles of the Rule of Law. Just as the printing press altered the distribution of legal authority and the computer reshaped the practice of legal research and discovery, AI promises to alter how laws are interpreted, applied, and even made. The patterns of resistance, adaptation, and regulatory evolution observed in the past suggest that the legal system will likely exhibit similar responses to AI. There will be those who embrace its potential for efficiency and precision, those who resist its perceived threat to traditional roles and human judgment, and a continuous struggle to develop legal and ethical frameworks that ensure AI serves justice rather than undermines it. The lessons from these historical encounters with technology underscore the need for careful deliberation, foresight, and a commitment to adapting our legal order in a way that upholds, rather than erodes, the foundational values of fairness, accountability, and the Rule of Law.

This book embarks on a comprehensive exploration of the intricate relationship between artificial intelligence (AI) and the foundational principles of the Rule of Law. To navigate this complex terrain effectively, it is crucial to establish a clear understanding of the scope and the methodological underpinnings that will guide our inquiry. The overarching aim is to dissect how the burgeoning capabilities of AI intersect with, challenge, and potentially reshape the established norms, procedures, and philosophical underpinnings of legal systems worldwide. This exploration is not merely an academic exercise; it is a critical examination of a transformative technological force that is already permeating legal practice, judicial decision-making, legislative processes, and the very conceptualization of justice.

The scope of this investigation is deliberately broad yet meticulously focused. It encompasses the spectrum of AI applications within the legal domain, from sophisticated tools for legal research and document analysis to nascent forms of AI-driven judicial assistance and predictive policing. We will delve into the ethical quandaries posed by algorithmic bias, the implications for due process and fundamental rights, the challenges to transparency and accountability in AI-assisted legal processes, and the evolving landscape of legal responsibility when AI systems err or cause harm. Furthermore, the book will consider the regulatory and policy responses being developed or contemplated by governments and international bodies to govern the development and deployment of AI in legal contexts. This includes examining efforts to establish standards for AI explainability, auditability, and fairness, as well as the potential for AI to either exacerbate or mitigate existing inequalities within the justice system. The intended audience for this work comprises legal professionals- lawyers, judges, policymakers, and academics- as well as technologists, ethicists, and members of the public concerned with the societal implications of advanced artificial intelligence. By bridging disciplinary divides, we aim to foster a nuanced and informed dialogue about the future of law in an age of intelligent machines.

The methodological approach adopted throughout this book is multi-faceted, drawing upon established academic disciplines and contemporary research techniques to provide a robust and insightful analysis. At its core, the book employs a **comparative legal analysis** framework. This involves examining how different legal jurisdictions are grappling with the challenges and opportunities presented by AI. By comparing legislative approaches, judicial interpretations, and policy initiatives in various countries and legal traditions, we can identify best practices, common pitfalls, and emerging global trends. This comparative lens allows us to appreciate the diversity of responses and to distill universal principles that may guide the development of legal order in the face of AI. For instance, we might compare the European Union's comprehensive AI Act, with its risk-based approach, to the more sector-specific or market-driven regulatory strategies adopted in other regions. Such comparisons illuminate differing philosophies regarding technological innovation, individual rights, and the role of the state in mediating these tensions. This method is crucial for understanding that the impact of AI on law is not monolithic; rather, it is shaped by distinct legal cultures, historical contexts, and socio-economic priorities.

Complementing this comparative legal perspective is a rigorous engagement with **ethical frameworks**. The advent of AI in law raises profound ethical questions that cannot be adequately addressed through purely legalistic analysis. Therefore, we will draw upon established ethical theories- such as consequentialism, deontology, and virtue ethics- to evaluate the moral implications of AI's increasing role in legal decision-making and administration. This includes scrutinizing issues of fairness, justice, autonomy, and human dignity. For example, the ethical implications of using AI to predict recidivism rates in criminal sentencing require an examination of potential biases embedded in the training data, which could lead to discriminatory outcomes that violate principles of equal protection. Similarly, the ethical considerations surrounding AI's use in contract review or legal advice necessitate an analysis of professional responsibility, client confidentiality, and the potential for AI to erode the human element of legal counsel. We will explore frameworks for responsible AI development and deployment, including principles of transparency, accountability, and human oversight, drawing insights from the fields of applied ethics and philosophy of technology. This ethical dimension is essential for ensuring that AI serves as a tool to enhance justice, rather than to compromise it.

A significant portion of our methodological toolkit involves **policy review and analysis**. This entails examining existing and proposed legislation, regulatory guidelines, and governmental strategies aimed at governing AI in the legal sphere. We will analyze the effectiveness of these policies in addressing the identified challenges, considering their feasibility, enforceability, and alignment with broader societal values. This will involve scrutinizing policy documents, white papers, and legislative debates from various jurisdictions. For instance, analyzing proposals for "explainable AI" (XAI) in legal contexts requires understanding the technical requirements for AI explainability, the legal standards for justification of decisions, and the practical challenges of implementing such requirements in real-world legal applications. We will also consider the role of international organizations and multi-stakeholder initiatives in shaping global norms and standards for AI governance in law. This policy-centric approach aims to provide actionable insights for lawmakers, regulators, and legal practitioners seeking to navigate the evolving legal landscape of AI.

Furthermore, the book will utilize **case study** to ground theoretical discussions in practical realities. By dissecting real-world instances of AI deployment in legal settings, we can gain a deeper understanding of the tangible impacts and challenges. These case studies will span various legal domains, including criminal justice, civil litigation, corporate law, and administrative proceedings. For example, a case study might analyze the use of AI in judicial risk assessment tools to inform bail decisions, exploring its accuracy, fairness, and impact on defendants' rights. Another case study could focus on the implementation of AI-powered contract review software in a large law firm, examining its effect on efficiency, cost, and the nature of legal work. These detailed examinations will not only illustrate the theoretical concepts discussed but also provide concrete examples of the successes, failures, and unintended consequences associated with AI in law. They will serve as empirical anchors, demonstrating how abstract principles translate into practical outcomes and highlighting the nuances of AI's integration into the fabric of legal practice.

Beyond these core methodologies, the book will also incorporate insights from **computer science and artificial intelligence research**, not to delve into the technical intricacies of AI algorithms themselves, but to understand their capabilities, limitations, and inherent characteristics as they relate to legal applications. This includes an appreciation for concepts such as machine learning, natural language processing, algorithmic bias, and the challenges of AI explainability and robustness. Understanding the technical underpinnings, even at a conceptual level, is crucial for evaluating the feasibility and reliability of AI systems in legal contexts and for anticipating future technological developments. For instance, comprehending the difference between rule-based expert systems and data-driven machine learning models is important for understanding how legal reasoning might be automated or augmented by AI, and the different types of risks associated with each approach.

The research process for this book will involve an extensive review of scholarly literature across law, computer science, ethics, and sociology. This includes seminal works on legal theory, AI ethics, and the sociology of technology, as well as cutting-edge research papers and technical reports. We will also engage with industry reports, governmental publications, and policy documents to ensure our analysis reflects the current state of practice and policy development. The synthesis of this interdisciplinary knowledge base is fundamental to the book's comprehensive approach.

A crucial element of the methodology is the exploration of the **socio-legal implications** of AI. Law does not operate in a vacuum; it is deeply intertwined with social structures, power dynamics, and cultural norms. Therefore, this book will consider how AI's integration into the legal system impacts different segments of society, potentially exacerbating existing inequalities or creating new forms of discrimination. We will examine the digital divide, access to justice, and the potential for AI to either widen or narrow these disparities. Understanding these broader societal impacts is vital for developing legal and regulatory frameworks that promote equity and social justice. For example, the deployment of AI in legal aid services could enhance access for underserved populations, but if not designed carefully, it could also perpetuate systemic biases that disproportionately affect marginalized communities.

The book's structure is designed to guide the reader systematically through the complexities of AI and the Rule of Law. Following this foundational chapter on scope and methodology, subsequent chapters will delve into specific thematic areas. We will begin by examining the historical context of technological disruption in law, as discussed previously, to set the stage for the unique challenges posed by AI. This will be followed by in-depth analyses of AI's impact on various branches of law, including criminal justice, civil procedure, administrative law, and constitutional law. We will then explore critical cross-cutting themes such as algorithmic bias and fairness, transparency and explainability, accountability and liability, and the implications for access to justice and legal professions. The final chapters will focus on policy, regulation, and future directions, offering recommendations for ensuring that AI is harnessed in a manner that upholds and strengthens the Rule of Law.

Throughout this journey, the emphasis will remain on critical analysis, informed by evidence and ethical reasoning. The goal is not to provide definitive, one-size-fits-all solutions, as the field of AI and law is rapidly evolving. Instead, the book aims to equip readers with the knowledge, frameworks, and critical perspectives necessary to engage thoughtfully with these critical issues and to contribute to the ongoing discourse on how to build a legal future that is both technologically advanced and ethically sound, grounded in the enduring principles of justice and the Rule of Law. The methodologies employed are intended to ensure that the ensuing discussions are not speculative but are firmly rooted in comparative legal practice, ethical considerations, policy realities, and empirical evidence from real-world applications. This commitment to a robust and transparent methodology is essential for building trust in our analysis and for providing a reliable resource for anyone seeking to understand and shape the interaction between artificial intelligence and the legal order.

Educa:tionat AI Artficial Intelligence AI

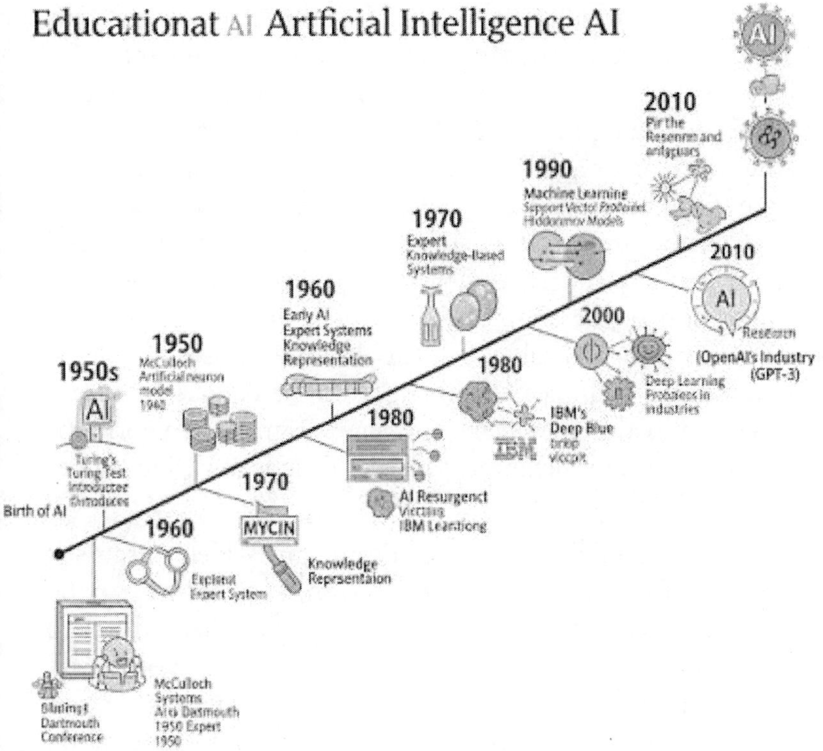

2
Algorithmic Ethics
Navigating Bias and Fairness

The pervasive influence of artificial intelligence (AI) across myriad societal sectors, including the critical domain of law, necessitates a profound understanding of its operational underpinnings and, crucially, its potential for propagating and even magnifying existing societal biases. Far from being neutral arbiters of data, AI systems are, by their very nature, constructions that reflect the values, biases, and historical inequities of the societies that create and deploy them. To effectively navigate the ethical landscape of AI in law, and indeed in any application, a meticulous dissection of the sources from which these biases emerge is not merely advisable; it is an absolute imperative. These sources are multifaceted, arising from the data used to train these sophisticated systems, the very design of the algorithms themselves, and the human decisions made at various stages of their lifecycle.

One of the most significant and widely discussed origins of bias in AI systems lies within the **training data**. Machine learning algorithms, the engine behind much of contemporary AI, learn by identifying patterns and correlations within vast datasets. If these datasets are not representative of the population or the intended application environment, or if they mirror historical societal prejudices, the AI system will inevitably learn and codify these biases. This is particularly problematic in legal contexts, where data often reflects historical disparities in law enforcement, judicial sentencing, and access to legal representation. For instance, if an AI system is trained on historical arrest data that shows a disproportionate number of arrests for certain offenses in specific demographic communities, the AI might learn to associate those communities with a higher propensity for criminal activity. This can lead to biased outcomes when the AI is used for tasks such as predictive policing, risk assessment in bail decisions, or even in the allocation of legal resources. The data, in essence, acts as a mirror, reflecting the societal injustices of the past, and the algorithm, lacking the capacity for critical self-reflection or ethical reasoning, faithfully replicates these reflections.

Consider the example of facial recognition technology. Early systems were notoriously less accurate when identifying individuals with darker skin tones or women. This disparity was not due to an inherent technological flaw in the concept of facial recognition itself, but rather due to the composition of the training datasets. These datasets were often overwhelmingly comprised of images of lighter-skinned males, meaning the algorithms were optimized for this demographic, while performing poorly for others. When such technology is deployed in law enforcement, this bias can translate into misidentification, false arrests, and a disproportionate burden on already marginalized communities. Similarly, AI tools designed to assist in hiring processes, trained on historical hiring data where certain groups were underrepresented in specific roles due to past discrimination, may inadvertently learn to favor candidates who resemble those previously successful, thereby perpetuating a cycle of exclusion.

Beyond the representational issues within data, bias can also be introduced through **measurement bias** and **labeling bias**. Measurement bias occurs when the way data is collected or measured is flawed or inconsistent across different groups. For example, if a dataset used to assess loan applications contains information on credit scores that are themselves influenced by historical discriminatory practices, the AI trained on this data will inherit this bias. Labeling bias, on the other hand, arises from the subjective nature of human labeling of data. If human annotators, consciously or unconsciously, apply labels based on their own prejudices, these labels will propagate through the AI system. Imagine an AI system being trained to identify "suspicious behavior" in public spaces. If the human annotators labeling the data are more likely to flag individuals from certain ethnic backgrounds or those exhibiting particular cultural mannerisms as "suspicious," the AI will learn to associate these characteristics with suspicion, regardless of their actual behavioral content. This is particularly insidious because it can appear to be objective, derived from data, when in reality it is a codification of human prejudice.

Another critical source of bias stems from the **algorithmic design choices** themselves. Even with meticulously curated and representative data, the way an algorithm is designed can introduce or amplify bias. This can manifest in several ways, including the selection of features, the choice of model architecture, and the optimization objectives. For example, an algorithm might be designed to optimize for a specific outcome, such as reducing recidivism rates, but the proxies it uses to achieve this goal might be inherently biased. Risk assessment tools in the criminal justice system, for instance, often use factors like prior arrests, employment history, and neighborhood crime rates. While these factors might correlate with recidivism, they can also be proxies for underlying social and economic disadvantages that disproportionately affect certain communities. An individual from a disadvantaged background might have more prior arrests due to over-policing in their neighborhood, or face employment challenges due to systemic barriers, yet these factors might be interpreted by the algorithm as indicators of future risk, rather than as symptoms of societal inequity.

The concept of **proxy variables** is central to understanding algorithmic bias. A proxy variable is a factor that is not directly the variable of interest but is correlated with it. In the context of AI, algorithms may use seemingly innocuous data points as proxies for protected attributes like race, gender, or socioeconomic status. For instance, a postal code could be used as a proxy for race or socioeconomic status, as certain demographic groups may be concentrated in specific geographical areas. If an AI system uses postal codes to make decisions about loan eligibility or insurance premiums, it could inadvertently discriminate against individuals residing in areas predominantly populated by a particular racial or socioeconomic group, even if the algorithm does not explicitly reference race or income. This "hidden" discrimination is particularly challenging to detect and mitigate, as the bias is not explicitly encoded but emerges from the complex interplay of variables within the algorithm.

Furthermore, the very **process of learning** can entrench and amplify bias. Machine learning algorithms often employ iterative processes where they adjust their internal parameters based on the data they process. If the initial data contains biases, these biases can be reinforced with each iteration. This is especially true in systems that continuously learn from new data, a concept known as online learning. Without careful monitoring and intervention, these systems can drift into increasingly biased states. The feedback loops created by biased predictions can also exacerbate the problem. For example, if a predictive policing system directs more police resources to a particular neighborhood based on biased data, this increased police presence might lead to more arrests in that neighborhood, which then feeds back into the system as new data, further reinforcing the initial bias. This creates a self-perpetuating cycle of discrimination, where the AI's biased predictions lead to actions that generate data confirming those biases.

Human oversight and decision-making at various stages of the AI lifecycle also represent a significant vector for bias. From the initial conception of an AI project and the selection of datasets to the interpretation of AI outputs and the deployment of the system, human biases can be inadvertently introduced. Developers, data scientists, product managers, and end-users all bring their own backgrounds, assumptions, and potential blind spots to the process. If the teams developing AI systems lack diversity, they may be less likely to identify potential biases that could affect marginalized groups. Similarly, if the stakeholders evaluating the performance of an AI system do not actively look for evidence of disparate impact, biased outcomes can go unnoticed and unaddressed. The lack of transparency in many AI systems further complicates this issue, making it difficult for those who are subject to AI-driven decisions to understand *why* a particular outcome was reached and to challenge potential biases.

The objective of the machine learning model also plays a crucial role. If the objective is purely to maximize predictive accuracy without explicit consideration for fairness, the model might achieve high accuracy by exploiting statistical disparities in the data that correspond to protected attributes. For instance, an AI model predicting creditworthiness might achieve higher accuracy overall by assigning lower credit scores to individuals from historically disadvantaged groups, if those groups, on average, have lower credit scores due to systemic reasons. While this might improve the model's statistical performance on the training data, it comes at the cost of fairness and equity. This highlights the critical need for defining and incorporating fairness metrics into the model development process, alongside traditional performance metrics like accuracy or precision.

The problem of bias is not static; it evolves with the AI systems and the contexts in which they are deployed. The increasing complexity and opacity of deep learning models, while often leading to superior performance, can also make it more challenging to diagnose and mitigate bias. The intricate web of non-linear relationships learned by these models can obscure the pathways through which bias is propagated. This underscores the importance of interdisciplinary collaboration, bringing together legal scholars, ethicists, social scientists, and computer scientists to develop robust frameworks for understanding, detecting, and addressing bias in AI systems that operate within the legal and justice systems. Without this concerted effort, the promise of AI to improve efficiency and objectivity in law risks being overshadowed by its potential to entrench and amplify existing societal injustices. The quest for fair and equitable AI in the legal domain is, therefore, inextricably linked to a deep and critical examination of the multifaceted origins of bias that permeate these powerful technologies.

The challenge of ensuring fairness in artificial intelligence systems is multifaceted, extending beyond identifying the origins of bias to establishing robust methods for its detection and measurement. Once we acknowledge that AI, far from being a neutral entity, can inherit and amplify societal prejudices, the imperative shifts to developing concrete tools and techniques to unearth and quantify these discriminatory effects. This section delves into the critical methodologies and metrics employed to identify and measure the discriminatory outcomes produced by AI, focusing on statistical measures of fairness, the principles of disparate impact analysis, and the inherent technical challenges in detecting more subtle forms of bias. Ultimately, it will underscore the foundational importance of transparency and explainability in AI systems to facilitate the necessary auditing and accountability mechanisms essential for preventing unlawful discrimination.

At the heart of measuring algorithmic discrimination lies the application of statistical fairness metrics. These metrics provide quantitative lenses through which to assess whether an AI system's decisions disproportionately impact different demographic groups. A foundational concept is **demographic parity**, which dictates that the proportion of individuals receiving a favorable outcome (e.g., loan approval, job offer) should be the same across different protected groups, such as race or gender. For example, if a loan application AI approves 80% of male applicants and only 50% of female applicants, it violates demographic parity. However, achieving demographic parity alone can be problematic. It might lead to systems that select less qualified individuals to meet quota-like requirements, potentially sacrificing accuracy or other desirable outcomes. This tension between different fairness goals is a recurring theme in the field.

Another widely used metric is **equalized odds**, which requires that the true positive rate (also known as sensitivity or recall) and the false positive rate be equal across different groups. In simpler terms, this means that an AI should be equally likely to correctly identify a positive case (e.g., correctly predicting a low risk of recidivism) for all groups, and equally likely to incorrectly classify a negative case as positive (e.g., wrongly predicting a high risk of recidivism) for all groups. For instance, if a criminal justice risk assessment tool is more likely to incorrectly flag individuals from a particular racial group as high risk compared to another group, it violates equalized odds. This metric is particularly relevant in contexts where both false positives and false negatives have significant consequences.

A related concept is **equality of opportunity**, which focuses solely on ensuring that the true positive rate is equal across groups. This means that individuals who genuinely belong to the positive class should have an equal chance of being correctly identified, regardless of their group affiliation. Using the recidivism example, this would mean that individuals who will genuinely re-offend should have an equal chance of being predicted as high risk, whether they are from minority or majority groups. This metric is often favored in situations where the cost of a false negative is particularly high.

The choice of which fairness metric to prioritize is not a purely technical decision; it is deeply rooted in ethical and societal values and the specific context of the AI's deployment. Each metric makes different trade-offs and may be more or less appropriate depending on the potential harms of different types of errors. For instance, in healthcare, where a false negative might mean a missed diagnosis and a false positive might lead to unnecessary anxiety and further testing, the preferred metric might differ significantly from a system used for marketing or entertainment.

Beyond these statistical measures, the legal concept of **disparate impact** provides a crucial framework for detecting algorithmic discrimination. This legal principle, originating in civil rights law, states that a practice or policy is discriminatory if it has a disproportionately negative effect on members of a protected group, even if there is no intent to discriminate. In the context of AI, disparate impact analysis involves auditing AI systems to see if their outcomes reveal statistically significant differences in treatment or results between protected groups. This often involves comparing the "pass rates" or "approval rates" for different demographic categories. For example, if an AI used for hiring screens out a significantly higher percentage of women or individuals from a specific ethnic background compared to others, this could constitute disparate impact, even if the AI's underlying algorithm does not explicitly consider gender or ethnicity.

The U.S. Equal Employment Opportunity Commission (EEOC) has established guidelines for conducting disparate impact analysis, often using the "four-fifths rule" (or 80% rule) as a benchmark. This rule suggests that if the selection rate for a protected group is less than 80% of the rate for the group with the highest rate, it may indicate adverse impact. While this rule is a guideline and not a definitive legal standard, it provides a practical starting point for identifying potentially problematic disparities. However, applying such rules to complex AI systems requires careful consideration of the specific nature of the "selection" and the relevant protected groups. Moreover, the statistical significance of observed disparities is crucial; not every small difference in outcomes will necessarily indicate unlawful discrimination. Rigorous statistical testing is necessary to distinguish between random fluctuations and systemic biases.

The process of auditing for disparate impact requires access to information about both the AI system's decisions and the demographic characteristics of the individuals affected by those decisions. This highlights the critical need for **transparency** and **explainability** in AI. Without understanding how an AI system arrives at its decisions, it becomes exceedingly difficult to pinpoint the source of any observed disparity or to prove intent or lack thereof. Explainable AI (XAI) techniques aim to make AI models more interpretable, revealing the reasoning process behind their outputs. This could involve identifying which input features were most influential in a particular decision or generating simplified rule-based explanations that approximate the model's behavior.

For instance, if a loan application AI denies a loan, explainability might provide insights such as "the applicant was denied primarily due to a low credit score and a high debt-to-income ratio." If these explanations consistently point to factors that are themselves proxies for protected attributes, or if the credit scoring itself is biased, this can reveal a pathway to discrimination. Tools like SHAP (SHapley Additive exPlanations) and LIME (Local Interpretable Model-agnostic Explanations) are designed to provide such local explanations for individual predictions, helping to understand why a particular individual received a certain outcome. Global explainability methods, on the other hand, aim to understand the overall behavior of the model, identifying general patterns of bias.

However, achieving meaningful transparency and explainability in AI, especially with complex deep learning models, presents significant technical challenges. Many of these advanced models operate as "black boxes," where the intricate interplay of millions of parameters makes it virtually impossible to articulate a clear, human-understandable causal chain for any given decision. Furthermore, the very act of making a model more interpretable might, in some cases, lead to a reduction in its predictive accuracy. This creates a delicate balancing act, where the pursuit of fairness and transparency must be weighed against the performance requirements of the system.

Detecting more subtle forms of bias requires sophisticated analytical techniques. Bias is not always overt; it can manifest in insidious ways, embedded within the correlations an AI learns from data. For example, an AI system might learn to associate certain language patterns or writing styles with unreliability, inadvertently discriminating against individuals from non-native English-speaking backgrounds or those who use less formal communication styles. Similarly, AI systems that analyze images might be biased based on the quality or characteristics of the images themselves, potentially penalizing individuals whose photos are of lower resolution or are taken in less-than-ideal lighting conditions, which could disproportionately affect people who lack access to high-quality equipment or professional photography.

One method for detecting subtle bias involves **counterfactual fairness**, which asks whether a different outcome would have been produced if a protected attribute had been different, all other relevant factors remaining the same. For example, would the loan application have been approved if the applicant had been male instead of female, assuming all other qualifications were identical? Simulating these counterfactuals requires careful consideration of what "other relevant factors" should be held constant, as many attributes are intercorrelated.

Another approach is **causal inference**, which aims to move beyond mere correlation to understand the causal relationships within the data. Causal models can help to disentangle whether a disparity is due to a protected attribute itself, or due to other factors that are causally influenced by that attribute. For instance, if neighborhood is used as a feature, a causal model could help determine if the disparity observed is truly because of the neighborhood itself, or because the neighborhood is a proxy for historical segregation and redlining that have led to disparities in wealth and opportunity, which then impact other relevant factors like credit history.

The continuous evolution of AI systems, particularly those that learn and adapt over time through online learning or feedback loops, necessitates ongoing monitoring and re-evaluation of fairness. A system that was fair at its inception can become biased as it encounters new data or as the environment in which it operates changes. This highlights the need for robust **auditing mechanisms**. Regular audits, conducted by independent third parties, are essential to assess AI systems for compliance with fairness standards and legal requirements. These audits should not only examine the current state of the AI but also its training data, development process, and decision-making logic.

The development of standardized benchmarking datasets and evaluation frameworks is crucial for facilitating these audits and for enabling comparisons between different AI systems and mitigation techniques. Organizations like NIST (National Institute of Standards and Technology) are working on developing such frameworks, including standardized tests for AI bias, particularly in areas like facial recognition. These efforts aim to provide objective measures against which AI performance and fairness can be reliably assessed.

Ultimately, measuring and detecting algorithmic discrimination is an ongoing process that requires a combination of technical expertise, rigorous statistical analysis, legal understanding, and ethical reflection. It demands a commitment to transparency, enabling scrutiny of AI systems, and a willingness to implement and iterate on fairness-enhancing techniques. Without these foundational elements, the promise of AI to revolutionize various sectors, including law, risks being overshadowed by its potential to entrench and amplify existing societal injustices. The ability to effectively measure and detect bias is not merely a technical hurdle; it is a prerequisite for building trustworthy and equitable AI systems that serve all members of society fairly.

Moving from the detection and measurement of bias, our focus now shifts to the proactive construction of AI systems designed with fairness as a core principle. This involves integrating ethical considerations directly into the machine learning pipeline, employing a suite of techniques that aim to mitigate or prevent discriminatory outcomes. These strategies can be broadly categorized into three phases: pre-processing, in-processing, and post-processing, each offering distinct mechanisms for embedding fairness.

Pre-processing Techniques: Setting the Stage for Fairness The pre-processing phase involves modifying the training data itself to remove or reduce bias before the machine learning model is trained. The rationale here is that if the data fed into the model is fair, the model is more likely to learn fair patterns. This approach acknowledges that bias often originates from historical societal inequities reflected in the data.

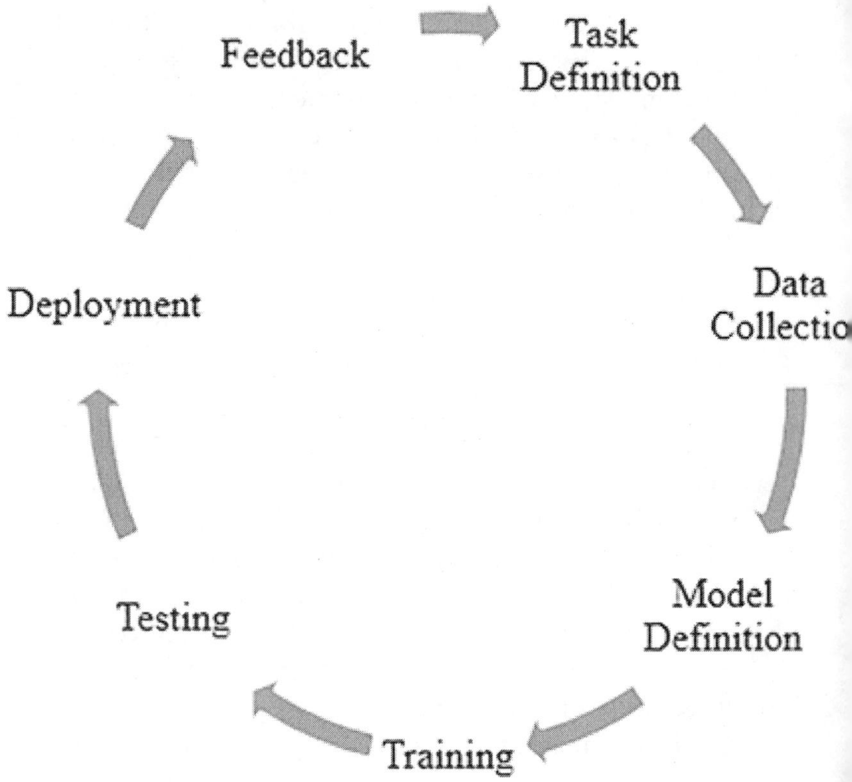

Ethics Principles in the AI Cycle

One prominent pre-processing method is **data reweighing**. This technique involves assigning different weights to data points based on their group affiliation and their prediction outcome. For instance, if a particular demographic group is underrepresented in the dataset or is disproportionately receiving unfavorable outcomes, their data points can be assigned higher weights during the training process. This forces the model to pay more attention to these instances, aiming to balance the influence of different groups. For example, in a loan application dataset where minority applicants are historically less likely to be approved, reweighing could increase the importance of successful loan applications from this group or unsuccessful applications from the majority group, thereby encouraging the model to learn more equitable decision boundaries.

Another pre-processing strategy is **data augmentation**. This involves creating synthetic data points for underrepresented groups or for outcomes where bias is observed. For example, if a facial recognition system performs poorly on individuals with darker skin tones due to a lack of diverse training images, data augmentation could involve generating realistic variations of existing images to increase representation. This can be achieved through techniques like oversampling (duplicating existing minority class samples) or generating entirely new samples using generative adversarial networks (GANs) or other synthetic data generation methods. The goal is to create a more balanced and representative dataset that reduces the model's reliance on skewed distributions.

Suppression is another pre-processing technique, although it is often more controversial. It involves removing certain features from the dataset that are strongly correlated with protected attributes. The idea is that if the model cannot directly access sensitive information or its proxies, it might be less likely to discriminate. However, this approach has significant limitations. Often, proxies for protected attributes are deeply embedded in other features (e.g., zip code as a proxy for race or socioeconomic status), making complete suppression difficult. Furthermore, removing potentially relevant features could also reduce the overall accuracy and predictive power of the model. Careful consideration is needed to balance fairness goals with the need for effective model performance.

A more nuanced pre-processing approach is **disparate impact remover** or **feature transformation**. This involves transforming the features in the dataset in a way that reduces their correlation with protected attributes while preserving as much predictive utility as possible. Algorithms like the "Disparate Impact Remover" work by projecting features onto a subspace that is orthogonal to the protected attribute space. This means that the transformed features still carry information relevant to the prediction task but are less able to reveal or predict the sensitive attribute. For example, if "neighborhood" is a feature that strongly correlates with race and also influences loan default risk, a feature transformation might create a new "neighborhood quality" feature that captures relevant economic information without being a direct indicator of race. The effectiveness of pre-processing techniques hinges on the quality and representativeness of the original dataset. If the underlying societal biases are so deeply entrenched that they cannot be adequately addressed through data manipulation, these methods may only offer a partial solution. Moreover, it is crucial to continually audit the data and the models trained on it, as new forms of bias can emerge.

In-processing Techniques: Building Fairness into the Algorithm In-processing techniques aim to modify the learning algorithm itself to incorporate fairness constraints during the training process. This approach directly influences how the model learns from the data, guiding it towards fairer decision-making.

One common in-processing method is **regularization**. In standard machine learning, regularization techniques (like L1 or L2 regularization) are used to prevent overfitting and improve model generalization by adding a penalty term to the loss function. Fairness-aware regularization extends this concept by adding penalty terms that explicitly penalize unfair outcomes according to chosen fairness metrics. For instance, a regularization term could be added that penalizes differences in the acceptance rates (demographic parity) or differences in true positive/false positive rates (equalized odds) between different protected groups. The model is then optimized to minimize a combination of its prediction error and these fairness penalties. This forces the model to learn a balance between accuracy and fairness.

Another in-processing approach is **adversarial debiasing**. This method utilizes an adversarial framework, often involving two neural networks: a predictor and an adversary. The predictor network tries to make accurate predictions (e.g., predict loan approval), while the adversary network tries to predict the protected attribute (e.g., gender or race) from the predictor's output. The predictor is trained not only to be accurate but also to "fool" the adversary, meaning its predictions should not reveal information about the protected attribute. The adversary, in turn, is trained to become better at inferring the protected attribute. Through this adversarial game, the predictor is incentivized to learn representations that are predictive of the target outcome but independent of the protected attribute, thus promoting fairness.

Constraint-based optimization is another powerful in-processing technique. This involves formulating the machine learning task as an optimization problem with explicit fairness constraints. For example, one might train a model to maximize accuracy subject to the constraint that the difference in false positive rates between two groups must not exceed a certain threshold. This can be implemented using various optimization techniques, such as Lagrange multipliers or specialized optimization algorithms that handle inequality constraints. This approach offers a direct way to enforce specific fairness definitions during model training.

The advantage of in-processing techniques is that they directly address the model's learning process, potentially leading to more robust fairness guarantees compared to pre-processing methods. However, they can also be more complex to implement and may require specific knowledge of the underlying learning algorithms and fairness metrics. The trade-off between accuracy and fairness is often more explicit and challenging to navigate in this phase.

Post-processing Techniques: Refining the Output Post-processing techniques involve adjusting the model's outputs after it has been trained, without altering the original model or the training data. The goal is to "correct" the model's predictions to align with fairness criteria.

A common post-processing method is **threshold adjustment**. Many classification models output a probability score, and a decision is made by comparing this score to a predefined threshold. For example, a loan application might be approved if the predicted probability of repayment is above 0.7. Threshold adjustment involves setting different thresholds for different demographic groups to achieve a desired fairness outcome. For instance, if a model has a lower true positive rate for a certain group, its threshold could be lowered to increase the number of positive predictions for that group, thereby improving demographic parity or equality of opportunity. This can be effective in achieving statistical parity, but it raises questions about whether different groups are being held to different standards, which might be perceived as unfair in itself.

Another post-processing technique is **reject option classification**. This approach introduces a "reject" or "undecided" category for predictions where the model's confidence is low or where the prediction might lead to an unfair outcome. For instance, if an AI-powered hiring tool predicts a candidate is suitable but the confidence score is low, and this low confidence is more prevalent for a specific demographic group, the system might defer the decision to a human reviewer. This allows for human oversight in cases where algorithmic fairness is uncertain, leveraging human judgment to mitigate potential bias.

Calibrating probabilities is a more sophisticated post-processing method. Probability calibration aims to ensure that the predicted probabilities accurately reflect the true likelihood of an event. In the context of fairness, calibration can be applied to ensure that predicted probabilities are consistent across different groups. For example, if a model predicts a 70% chance of loan repayment, this should mean the same thing for all demographic groups. Techniques like Platt scaling or isotonic regression can be used to recalibrate the model's output probabilities to achieve this consistency.

Post-processing techniques are often easier to implement as they don't require retraining the model. They can be applied to any pre-trained model. However, they do not address the underlying biases within the model's internal representations or decision-making processes. The model might still be learning discriminatory patterns, and the post-processing adjustments are merely a superficial fix. Furthermore, these methods can sometimes lead to a decrease in overall accuracy or utility if the adjustments are too aggressive.

Choosing the Right Technique and the Ethical Landscape The selection of a particular fairness technique-pre-processing, in-processing, or post-processing-depends heavily on the specific application, the type of bias present, the available data, and the desired fairness definition. There is no one-size-fits-all solution. Moreover, it is important to recognize that different fairness metrics can be mathematically incompatible; optimizing for one might inherently lead to violating another. For example, achieving both demographic parity and equalized odds simultaneously is often impossible. This underscores the need for careful ethical deliberation and stakeholder engagement to determine which fairness goals are most critical for a given context.

For instance, in a hiring context, prioritizing equality of opportunity might be essential to ensure that qualified candidates from all backgrounds have an equal chance of being selected, even if this means the overall number of hires from different groups isn't perfectly balanced. Conversely, in a credit scoring scenario, demographic parity might be deemed crucial to prevent systemic financial exclusion.

The ongoing development in this field sees a continuous refinement of these techniques and the emergence of new methods. Researchers are exploring hybrid approaches that combine elements from different phases. For example, a pre-processing step might be used to clean the data, followed by an in-processing technique that incorporates fairness constraints during training.

Ultimately, building fairness-aware machine learning systems is not just a technical endeavor; it is a socio-technical challenge that requires a deep understanding of ethical principles, legal frameworks, and societal impacts. It necessitates a commitment to transparency, accountability, and continuous improvement, ensuring that AI systems serve humanity equitably and justly. The journey towards truly fair AI is an ongoing one, demanding vigilance, adaptation, and a constant dialogue between technologists, ethicists, policymakers, and the communities affected by these powerful technologies.

The pervasive influence of algorithms across society has inevitably led to their integration into the legal system, a domain fundamentally concerned with fairness, justice, and equitable treatment. However, the very algorithms intended to streamline processes, enhance efficiency, or predict outcomes can, if not meticulously designed and rigorously audited, become conduits for perpetuating and even amplifying existing societal biases. The consequences of such algorithmic bias within the legal framework are not abstract; they translate into tangible impacts on individuals' lives, affecting decisions ranging from pretrial release and sentencing to access to credit and employment. Examining real-world case studies provides a stark illustration of these challenges and underscores the urgent need for robust regulatory oversight and judicial scrutiny to ensure that the pursuit of justice is not undermined by biased technological implementations.

One of the most widely discussed and critically scrutinized applications of algorithms in the legal realm is in the context of criminal justice risk assessment tools. These tools are designed to predict the likelihood of a defendant reoffending or failing to appear in court. By assigning a "risk score," judges and parole boards are intended to make more informed decisions regarding bail, sentencing, and parole. However, numerous analyses have revealed significant racial disparities in the outputs of these systems. For example, the COMPAS (Correctional Offender Management Profiling for Alternative Sanctions) algorithm, widely used in the United States, was the subject of a landmark investigation by ProPublica in 2016. Their analysis found that COMPAS was more likely to falsely flag Black defendants as future criminals, assigning them higher risk scores than White defendants who had similar or worse criminal histories. Conversely, it was more likely to underestimate the risk of recidivism for White defendants. This discrepancy meant that Black defendants were disproportionately more likely to be denied bail or receive harsher sentences, not necessarily due to their individual circumstances, but because the algorithm, trained on historical data reflecting societal biases, reproduced those same patterns. The implications are profound: individuals are being penalized based on group-level predictions that may not accurately reflect their personal propensity for risk, and these predictions are demonstrably skewed by race. This raises critical legal questions about due process and equal protection, particularly when decisions affecting liberty are influenced by systems exhibiting a disparate impact on protected groups. The legal challenge often centers on whether the tool constitutes a violation of anti-discrimination laws, even if the algorithm does not explicitly use race as an input. The very use of proxy variables that correlate with race can lead to discriminatory outcomes, a concept that aligns with the legal principle of disparate impact.

Beyond the criminal justice system, algorithmic bias has also surfaced in civil legal contexts, notably in areas like loan applications and hiring. Financial institutions increasingly rely on algorithms to assess creditworthiness and decide on loan approvals. These systems analyze a multitude of data points, including credit history, income, and debt levels. However, if the historical data used for training reflects discriminatory lending practices, such as redlining or biased credit scoring methodologies that disproportionately disadvantage minority communities, the algorithm can learn and perpetuate these biases. This can lead to qualified applicants from marginalized groups being unfairly denied loans or offered less favorable terms, hindering their ability to build wealth, purchase homes, or start businesses. The legal ramifications here echo those in criminal justice: a pattern of loan denials that disproportionately affects a protected group, even without overt discriminatory intent, can constitute a violation of fair lending laws. The "disparate impact" analysis becomes a critical legal tool, requiring financial institutions to demonstrate that their algorithms are not only predictive of creditworthiness but also that they do not have an unjustified adverse effect on certain demographic groups. The challenge for regulators and courts is to discern when a disparity is a result of legitimate risk factors and when it is a product of embedded bias.

In the realm of employment, algorithms are being deployed for everything from resume screening and candidate matching to performance evaluation. While the promise is to create a more objective and efficient hiring process, bypassing human subjectivity, the reality has been more complex. For instance, early hiring algorithms developed by tech companies have been found to exhibit gender bias. One notable case involved an AI recruiting tool that was found to penalize resumes containing the word "women's" (as in "women's chess club captain") and downgraded graduates from all-women's colleges. This occurred because the algorithm was trained on historical hiring data where men were predominantly hired for technical roles, leading it to learn that male candidates were preferable. Such biases can systematically exclude qualified candidates from certain demographic groups, limiting their access to employment opportunities and reinforcing existing occupational segregation. From a legal perspective, this raises concerns under anti-discrimination statutes, such as Title VII of the Civil Rights Act of 1964 in the United States, which prohibits employment discrimination based on race, color, religion, sex, and national origin. The argument often presented is that even if the algorithm does not explicitly consider gender or race, its reliance on historical data that reflects past discriminatory patterns can lead to illegal discrimination.

The legal ramifications of these documented instances of algorithmic bias are substantial and are continuously shaping legal interpretation and regulatory frameworks. Courts are increasingly grappling with how to apply existing anti-discrimination laws to AI-driven decision-making.

This involves overcoming significant challenges, including the "black box" nature of many advanced AI models, which makes it difficult to pinpoint the exact source of bias or to prove discriminatory intent. The burden of proof in such cases can be challenging for plaintiffs, who must demonstrate that the algorithm's outcome is discriminatory and that the disparity is not justified by business necessity or legitimate, non-discriminatory factors.

Regulatory bodies are actively responding to these challenges by issuing guidance and, in some cases, proposing new regulations. For example, in the United States, the Equal Employment Opportunity Commission (EEOC) and the Department of Justice have issued joint guidance on the use of artificial intelligence in the workplace, emphasizing that employers are responsible for ensuring that AI tools do not result in discriminatory outcomes, even if the bias is unintentional. Similarly, financial regulators are scrutinizing the use of AI in lending to ensure compliance with fair lending laws. The European Union's proposed AI Act also aims to establish a comprehensive legal framework for AI, with specific provisions for high-risk AI systems, including those used in employment and the administration of justice, mandating transparency, human oversight, and risk assessments.

Judicial scrutiny is also playing a crucial role in shaping the legal landscape. Cases involving algorithmic bias are making their way through the courts, setting precedents and forcing a deeper examination of accountability. The legal system is being challenged to adapt its evidentiary standards and its understanding of causation to address the unique complexities introduced by AI. This includes questions about how to properly audit proprietary algorithms, how to define "disparate impact" in the context of algorithmic outputs, and what constitutes a reasonable "business necessity" defense when the decision-making process is opaque. The potential for algorithmic bias to disproportionately affect vulnerable populations, including racial minorities, women, and individuals with disabilities, makes the legal oversight of these technologies not merely a matter of technical accuracy, but a fundamental imperative for upholding civil rights and ensuring equal justice under the law. The ongoing development and deployment of AI in legal contexts necessitate a vigilant approach, demanding both technological innovation in bias detection and mitigation, and a corresponding evolution in legal interpretation and regulatory enforcement to safeguard fundamental principles of fairness and equity.

The escalating integration of algorithmic decision-making across critical societal sectors has, as previously explored, illuminated a pressing need for robust legal and ethical scaffolding to ensure fairness and equity. While the preceding discussions have underscored the challenges posed by algorithmic bias, particularly in areas like criminal justice and employment, this subsection pivots to examine the existing and evolving legal and ethical frameworks designed to confront these issues head-on. The objective is to scrutinize how current regulatory mechanisms are adapting, or perhaps faltering, in the face of increasingly sophisticated AI, and to project potential pathways for more effective governance that upholds the rule of law while fostering algorithmic fairness.

At the forefront of these efforts are existing anti-discrimination laws, many of which predate the widespread adoption of sophisticated AI but are increasingly being applied and interpreted in this new context. In the United States, for instance, foundational statutes like Title VII of the Civil Rights Act of 1964, the Age Discrimination in Employment Act (ADEA), and the Americans with Disabilities Act (ADA) remain central. These laws prohibit discrimination in employment based on race, color, religion, sex, national origin, age, and disability. The crucial challenge lies in adapting these statutes, which were designed to address human decision-making, to algorithmic processes. The concept of "disparate impact," a key legal doctrine, is particularly relevant here. It holds that a practice or policy may be deemed unlawful if it has a disproportionately negative effect on a protected group, even if there is no intent to discriminate. Legal scholars and practitioners are actively debating how to prove disparate impact when the decision-making process is mediated by complex, often opaque, algorithms. Establishing causality-linking a specific algorithmic feature or training data characteristic to a discriminatory outcome-can be exceedingly difficult, especially when the algorithms are proprietary and their inner workings are not readily accessible for audit.

The interpretation of these anti-discrimination laws in the age of AI often hinges on the extent to which the algorithms replicate or amplify historical societal biases present in the training data. For example, if an algorithm used for hiring is trained on historical hiring data where men were disproportionately hired for certain roles, it may learn to favor male candidates, even if gender is not an explicit input. Proving that this disparity constitutes illegal discrimination requires demonstrating that the algorithm's output has a statistically significant adverse impact on a protected group and that the employer cannot demonstrate a job-related necessity for the practice that produces this impact. The legal battles in this area are complex, often involving expert testimony to analyze algorithmic outputs and identify potential sources of bias. Courts are being forced to grapple with novel evidentiary challenges, such as the admissibility of algorithmic audits and the standards for proving that a particular algorithm is "fair." The legal burden often falls on the plaintiff to demonstrate the discriminatory effect, a task made more arduous by the technical complexity and opacity of many AI systems.

Beyond anti-discrimination laws, data protection regulations are also playing an increasingly significant role in the governance of algorithmic fairness. The General Data Protection Regulation (GDPR) in the European Union, for example, places strict controls on the processing of personal data. While its primary focus is on privacy, certain provisions have direct implications for algorithmic bias. Article 22 of the GDPR, for instance, grants individuals the right not to be subject to a decision based solely on automated processing, including profiling, which produces legal effects concerning them or similarly significantly affects them. This provision can be invoked when automated decisions, such as credit scoring or job application screening, are perceived as unfair or discriminatory. The GDPR also emphasizes principles like data minimization, purpose limitation, and data accuracy, all of which can indirectly help mitigate algorithmic bias. By requiring that data be collected for specific purposes and be accurate, these principles can prevent the use of flawed or biased data that might otherwise contribute to discriminatory algorithmic outcomes. Furthermore, the GDPR's emphasis on transparency and the right to explanation for automated decisions can empower individuals to challenge potentially biased algorithmic judgments.

However, the effectiveness of these existing legal frameworks is a subject of ongoing debate. Critics argue that many anti-discrimination laws, being rooted in concepts of intent and direct discrimination, are not adequately equipped to address the systemic and often unintentional discrimination that can arise from complex algorithms. The "black box" problem-where the internal workings of an AI model are not easily understood or interpreted-poses a significant hurdle for legal accountability. Proving intent is virtually impossible when the decision-making is delegated to a machine whose internal logic is inscrutable. This has led to calls for regulatory reform and the development of AI-specific governance frameworks.

The emergence of AI-specific regulations and governance principles marks a significant development in the legal and ethical landscape. The European Union's proposed AI Act is perhaps the most ambitious and comprehensive effort to date. This landmark legislation categorizes AI systems based on their risk level, with "high-risk" AI systems-those used in critical areas such as employment, justice, and essential services-subject to stringent requirements. These requirements include rigorous risk assessments, robust data governance, transparency, human oversight, and a commitment to achieving a high level of accuracy and robustness. The AI Act aims to create a clear legal framework that fosters innovation while safeguarding fundamental rights and ensuring that AI systems are trustworthy and human-centric. It seeks to establish a standardized approach to AI governance, making it easier for businesses to comply and for regulators to enforce.

The Act's focus on risk categorization is particularly noteworthy. By identifying high-risk applications, it allows for a targeted regulatory approach, imposing stricter obligations where the potential for harm is greatest. For example, AI systems used in recruitment or for making decisions in the context of the justice system are classified as high-risk. This means that developers and deployers of these systems must comply with obligations related to data quality, documentation, transparency, human oversight, and cybersecurity. The intent is to ensure that critical decisions affecting individuals' lives and rights are not made by opaque or unreliable AI systems.

Furthermore, the AI Act, alongside other emerging principles, emphasizes the importance of "explainability" and "transparency" in AI systems. While perfect explainability for all complex AI models may be technically challenging, the legal and ethical imperative is to ensure that the rationale behind algorithmic decisions can be understood, at least to a degree that allows for meaningful oversight and challenge. This is crucial for building trust and ensuring accountability. Without some level of transparency, it becomes impossible to identify and rectify biases, or to ensure that decisions are based on legitimate factors rather than discriminatory proxies.

In parallel, numerous organizations and governments are developing ethical guidelines and principles for AI. These often emphasize fairness, accountability, transparency, safety, and human oversight. While ethical guidelines are not legally binding in the same way as regulations, they play a crucial role in shaping industry best practices and influencing future legal developments. Many companies are now establishing internal AI ethics boards and conducting algorithmic impact assessments to proactively identify and mitigate potential risks. The challenge remains in translating these ethical aspirations into concrete, enforceable legal obligations.

One area of active legal and ethical consideration is the development of standards for algorithmic audits. Auditing AI systems for bias and fairness is becoming increasingly important, but there is no universally agreed-upon methodology. Audits can take various forms, from statistical analysis of output disparities to examining the training data for representational biases, and even attempting to reverse-engineer the logic of certain models. Legal frameworks will need to define what constitutes a sufficient and effective audit, who is responsible for conducting them, and how the results of these audits can be used to hold developers and deployers accountable. This also includes establishing clear standards for what constitutes "fairness" in different contexts, as different metrics of fairness can sometimes be mutually exclusive. For example, ensuring equal outcomes across groups might conflict with ensuring equal opportunity, or vice versa.

The concept of "accountability" in AI is another

critical nexus of legal and ethical concern. When an algorithm produces a harmful or discriminatory outcome, who is ultimately responsible? Is it the data scientists who trained the model, the company that deployed it, the vendor who supplied the algorithm, or the users who relied on its output? Existing legal doctrines around product liability, negligence, and agency are being tested by the complexities of AI development and deployment. New legal frameworks may need to clarify lines of responsibility, particularly for complex, multi-party AI supply chains. This might involve creating new forms of liability or adapting existing ones to account for the distributed nature of AI development and the emergent properties of AI systems.

Moreover, the role of "human oversight" is consistently highlighted as a crucial safeguard against algorithmic bias. Legal and ethical frameworks are increasingly mandating that high-risk AI systems should not operate without meaningful human intervention. This means that human decision-makers should have the ability to review, override, or validate algorithmic outputs, particularly in sensitive areas like sentencing, hiring, or loan applications. The challenge lies in defining what constitutes "meaningful" oversight. Simply having a human in the loop is insufficient if that human is merely rubber-stamping the algorithm's recommendation without critical evaluation or understanding. Effective human oversight requires training, access to relevant information about the algorithm's functioning, and the authority to deviate from its suggestions when necessary.

The global nature of AI development and deployment also presents significant challenges for legal and ethical governance. Different jurisdictions have varying legal traditions, regulatory approaches, and cultural norms regarding technology and privacy. Achieving international consensus on AI governance principles and standards is a complex undertaking, yet it is essential for ensuring that

AI is developed and used responsibly on a global scale. Cross-border collaboration between regulators, researchers, and policymakers will be crucial for developing effective frameworks that can adapt to the rapidly evolving AI landscape.

In considering the adequacy of current legal structures, it's clear that while existing laws provide a foundation, they often require significant adaptation and supplementation. The "disparate impact" doctrine, while useful, faces practical challenges in algorithmic contexts. Data protection laws, like the GDPR, offer valuable safeguards, but are not solely designed to address algorithmic fairness. The emerging AI-specific regulations, such as the EU's AI Act, represent a more direct attempt to create tailored governance. However, the implementation and enforcement of these new regulations will be critical.

Looking forward, potential adaptations to effectively regulate AI for fairness and equity within the rule of law could include:

Firstly, the development of clearer legal standards for algorithmic transparency and explainability. This might involve establishing a tiered approach where the level of transparency required is commensurate with the risk associated with the AI system. For high-risk applications, there could be a legal obligation to provide detailed documentation of the model's architecture, training data, and validation processes.

Secondly, a strengthening of regulatory oversight and enforcement mechanisms. This would involve empowering regulatory bodies with the technical expertise and resources to audit AI systems, investigate complaints of algorithmic bias, and impose meaningful penalties for non-compliance. This could also include the creation of specialized AI regulatory agencies.

Thirdly, fostering greater collaboration between legal scholars, ethicists, technologists, and policymakers. Addressing algorithmic bias requires a multidisciplinary approach. Legal frameworks need to be informed by an understanding of the technical nuances of AI, while technological development needs to be guided by ethical and legal principles.

Fourthly, promoting the development and adoption of industry standards and best practices for fairness and bias mitigation. This could involve creating certification mechanisms for AI systems that meet certain fairness criteria, or encouraging the widespread use of tools and techniques for detecting and correcting bias.

Fifthly, a re-evaluation of legal doctrines concerning accountability. As AI systems become more autonomous, existing notions of liability may need to be revised to ensure that accountability is effectively assigned when algorithmic harm occurs. This might involve exploring concepts like "algorithmic accountability by design" or establishing specific legal liabilities for AI developers and deployers.

Finally, investing in public education and awareness about AI and its potential impacts. An informed public is better equipped to identify and challenge algorithmic bias, and to advocate for robust regulatory frameworks that protect their rights and ensure equitable outcomes.

In conclusion, the legal and ethical frameworks for algorithmic fairness are in a state of dynamic evolution. While existing anti-discrimination and data protection laws offer crucial starting points, the unique challenges posed by AI necessitate a proactive and adaptive regulatory approach. The development of AI-specific legislation, coupled with a commitment to transparency, accountability, and meaningful human oversight, will be essential in ensuring that the transformative power of artificial intelligence is harnessed for the benefit of society, without perpetuating or exacerbating existing inequalities. The ongoing dialogue and concerted efforts across legal, ethical, and technological disciplines are vital for shaping a future where algorithms operate justly and equitably within the enduring principles of the rule of law.

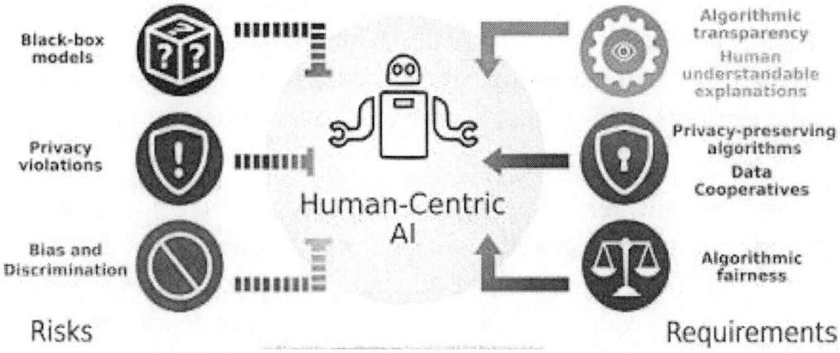

The human-centric use of artificial intelligence

3
AI, Privacy, and the Erosion of Anonymity

The advent and rapid proliferation of artificial intelligence have fundamentally reshaped the landscape of data collection, ushering in an era characterized by an unprecedented scale and scope of information gathering. This transformation is not merely an incremental increase in existing practices; it represents a paradigm shift in how data is acquired, processed, and utilized, with profound implications for individual privacy and our understanding of personal space. AI systems, by their very nature, thrive on data. They are engineered to ingest, analyze, and learn from vast datasets, identifying patterns, making predictions, and driving decisions that were previously the sole domain of human cognition. This insatiable appetite for information has led to the creation of sophisticated mechanisms for continuous data acquisition across an astonishing array of sources.

Consider the digital interactions that form the bedrock of modern life. Every search query typed into a browser, every website visited, every video watched, and every product added to a virtual cart contributes to a burgeoning digital dossier. Social media platforms, beyond the explicit content users share, meticulously record engagement metrics: likes, shares, comments, viewing times, and even the subtle cues of cursor movement and scrolling speed. Mobile devices, indispensable companions to billions, act as persistent data collectors. They track location through GPS, Wi-Fi networks, and cellular triangulation, logging not only where we are but also how we move through our environments, the routes we take, and the duration of our stays. Fitness trackers and smartwatches go a step further, monitoring heart rate, sleep patterns, activity levels, and even nuanced physiological responses, converting our biological functions into quantifiable data points.

The expansion of the Internet of Things (IoT) has amplified this data-gathering capacity exponentially. Smart homes are equipped with sensors that monitor temperature, energy consumption, and even the presence of individuals within rooms. Connected vehicles record driving habits, routes, and mechanical performance. Public spaces, increasingly populated by interconnected sensors and cameras, contribute to a pervasive surveillance infrastructure. These systems, often operating autonomously and with minimal direct human intervention, aggregate data streams that, when analyzed by AI, can paint remarkably detailed pictures of individuals' lives, habits, and even their emotional states. Public records, once relatively static and difficult to aggregate, are also increasingly digitized and made accessible, providing AI with access to official information such as property ownership, voter registration, business licenses, and court records, which can be cross-referenced with other data sources to build comprehensive profiles.

The core of this phenomenon lies in the sophisticated analytical capabilities of AI itself. Machine learning algorithms, particularly those employing deep learning techniques, are designed to uncover complex, often non-obvious correlations within massive datasets. They can infer preferences, predict behaviors, and categorize individuals based on patterns that would be imperceptible to human analysis. For instance, an AI might analyze a user's online browsing history, purchase patterns, and social media interactions to infer their political leanings, potential health concerns, or even their likelihood of responding to a particular marketing campaign. The sheer volume of data combined with the processing power of AI allows for a granularity of insight that was previously unimaginable. This is not simply about collecting disparate pieces of information; it is about synthesizing these fragments into coherent, predictive, and often deeply personal profiles.

The implications for individual privacy are profound and multifaceted. The traditional notion of privacy, often conceived as the right to be left alone or to control access to one's personal information, is increasingly challenged by the pervasive and often invisible nature of AI-driven data collection. Individuals are often unaware of the extent to which their data is being collected, by whom, and for what purposes. The terms of service agreements and privacy policies that govern many online platforms are notoriously lengthy, complex, and often revised, making informed consent a practically elusive ideal. Furthermore, the aggregation and re-identification of previously anonymized data present a significant threat. Techniques such as de-anonymization, where seemingly anonymous datasets are cross-referenced with other public or private data sources to reveal identities, undermine a key safeguard for privacy.

This pervasive data ecosystem also redefines our understanding of personal space. In the physical world, personal space is a tangible boundary, an area surrounding an individual that they can claim as their own and where they expect a degree of privacy. Digitally, however, this boundary becomes fluid and porous. Our online activities, our sensor-generated data, and our digital interactions create an invisible, yet equally significant, personal space that is constantly being observed, recorded, and analyzed. The ability of AI to infer sensitive information from seemingly innocuous data points-for example, deducing a person's medical condition from their online searches or their emotional state from their social media posts-blurs the lines between public and private, and between observable behavior and inferable internal states.

The ethical considerations surrounding this data

collection are equally critical. The potential for misuse of such vast troves of personal data is immense. From discriminatory practices in hiring, lending, and insurance, where AI might inadvertently or deliberately penalize individuals based on correlations in their data, to targeted manipulation of public opinion through hyper-personalized political advertising, the risks are significant. The concentration of this data in the hands of a few powerful technology companies and governments also raises concerns about power imbalances and the potential for surveillance capitalism, a model where human experience is commodified and traded for profit.

Moreover, the very act of constant data collection can foster a chilling effect on behavior. If individuals know they are being perpetually monitored, they may self-censor their speech, limit their exploration of certain topics, or alter their behavior to conform to perceived norms, thereby diminishing individual autonomy and the free expression of ideas. This is particularly concerning in the context of democratic societies, where open discourse and the freedom to explore diverse viewpoints are paramount. The potential for AI to be used to predict and preempt dissent, or to identify and target individuals for surveillance based on their digital footprint, represents a significant threat to civil liberties.

Legal frameworks are struggling to keep pace with the exponential growth and sophistication of AI-driven data collection. Existing privacy laws, often designed for a pre-digital or early-digital era, may not adequately address the nuances of AI's data processing capabilities. The concept of consent, for example, becomes problematic when data is collected passively and continuously, often without explicit, granular permissions. The difficulty in understanding what data is being collected, how it is being analyzed, and with whom it is being shared makes it nearly impossible for individuals to provide truly informed consent.

Furthermore, the opacity of many AI algorithms-the so-called "black box" problem-makes it challenging to hold entities accountable for how they collect and use data. If the decision-making processes within an AI system are not transparent, it becomes difficult to identify whether data is being collected or used in a manner that violates privacy rights or leads to discriminatory outcomes. The ability to audit these systems and to understand the causal links between data inputs and algorithmic outputs is crucial for effective oversight and for ensuring compliance with data protection regulations.

The challenge is not just about the quantity of data but also about its quality and the inferences drawn from it. AI can generate new data or infer characteristics about individuals that may be inaccurate, incomplete, or simply fabricated. These inferred data points can then be used to make decisions that have significant impacts on individuals' lives, potentially perpetuating or even creating new forms of bias and discrimination. For instance, an AI that infers a person's creditworthiness based on indirect data points might unfairly disadvantage someone whose digital habits do not align with the model's learned patterns, irrespective of their actual financial stability.

In essence, the digital footprint we collectively leave behind, amplified and analyzed by artificial intelligence, has become an exhaustible resource. Every interaction, every movement, and every expressed preference can be logged, categorized, and utilized. This pervasive data ecosystem raises fundamental questions about who owns our data, who has the right to access and analyze it, and what safeguards are necessary to protect individuals from the potential harms of its misuse. The continuous, often invisible, nature of AI-powered data collection represents a profound alteration of our relationship with information and a significant challenge to the enduring principles of privacy and autonomy in the digital age. It necessitates a re-evaluation of our legal and ethical frameworks to ensure that the advancement of AI does not come at the cost of fundamental human rights and freedoms.

The integration of Artificial Intelligence into surveillance technologies has ushered in an era of unprecedented observational capability. AI algorithms are now the driving force behind systems capable of not just passively recording, but actively analyzing and interpreting vast streams of data captured from public and private spaces. This includes sophisticated facial recognition systems, which can identify individuals in real-time by matching their features against databases; behavioral analysis tools that detect patterns of movement, association, and activity indicative of certain predispositions or intentions; and predictive policing algorithms that aim to forecast where and when crime is likely to occur, and sometimes, who might be involved.

Facial recognition technology, in particular, has seen widespread deployment by law enforcement agencies and private entities alike. These systems utilize deep learning models trained on massive datasets of facial images to identify individuals from photographs or video feeds. The potential applications are broad, ranging from identifying suspects in criminal investigations and locating missing persons to granting access to secure facilities and personalizing customer experiences. However, the accuracy of these systems can vary significantly, often exhibiting higher error rates for women, ethnic minorities, and younger or older individuals. This inherent bias in the technology can lead to disproportionate scrutiny, false accusations, and wrongful arrests for certain demographic groups, raising serious concerns about fairness and equal protection under the law. The legal challenges here are substantial, as the use of such technologies often bumps against constitutional protections against unreasonable searches and seizures, particularly when applied to public spaces where individuals might reasonably expect a degree of anonymity. The Fourth Amendment in the United States, for instance, protects against government intrusion into areas where individuals have a reasonable expectation of privacy. The question arises whether persistent, AI-driven surveillance, even in public, constitutes such an intrusion.

Behavioral analysis powered by AI takes surveillance a step further by inferring intent or potential risk from observed actions. This might involve tracking how individuals move through an airport, their interactions with others, or their purchasing habits, with the aim of flagging suspicious behavior. The algorithms are designed to identify deviations from 'normal' patterns, but the definition of 'normal' itself can be subjective and influenced by the data on which the AI was trained. This can lead to the stigmatization and disproportionate scrutiny of individuals whose behaviors, while not criminal, deviate from the statistical norm. The legal implications are complex, as these systems can lead to preemptive interventions based on probabilistic assessments rather than concrete evidence of wrongdoing. This raises profound questions about due process and the presumption of innocence. Are individuals being subjected to investigation or apprehension based on what an algorithm predicts they *might* do, rather than what they *have* done?

Predictive policing, a more ambitious application of AI in surveillance, seeks to forecast future criminal activity. By analyzing historical crime data, alongside a myriad of other data points, these systems attempt to identify "hot spots" where crime is statistically more likely to occur, or even to predict individuals who might be at higher risk of offending or becoming victims. While the intention is to allocate law enforcement resources more effectively and potentially prevent crime, these systems are fraught with ethical and legal challenges, particularly concerning bias. Historical crime data often reflects existing policing patterns, which may themselves be biased against certain communities. If an AI is trained on data that reflects over-policing in minority neighborhoods, it can perpetuate and even amplify these biases, leading to a self-fulfilling prophecy where increased police presence in these areas results in more arrests, further reinforcing the AI's prediction. This creates a feedback loop that disproportionately targets already marginalized communities, potentially violating principles of equal protection and due process.

The legal frameworks intended to govern these AI-powered surveillance practices are diverse, encompassing constitutional protections, statutory privacy laws, and international human rights standards. In many jurisdictions, constitutional guarantees such as the right to privacy, freedom from unreasonable searches and seizures, and freedom of expression are the primary bulwarks against intrusive surveillance. However, the application of these often decades-old principles to the novel capabilities of AI presents significant challenges. For example, the concept of a "search" traditionally required a physical intrusion or a targeted act of government observation. AI-powered surveillance, which can continuously and passively collect data from ubiquitous sensors, blurs these traditional lines. The question is whether the sheer scale and comprehensiveness of AI surveillance, even if conducted in public spaces, constitutes a "search" that requires a warrant or probable cause.

Privacy laws, such as the General Data Protection Regulation (GDPR) in Europe or the California Consumer Privacy Act (CCPA) in the United States, provide additional layers of protection, governing the collection, processing, and storage of personal data. These laws often require lawful bases for data processing, principles of data minimization, and the right to access and deletion of personal information. However, the effectiveness of these laws in the context of AI surveillance is debatable. The opaque nature of many AI algorithms-the "black box" problem-can make it difficult for individuals to understand how their data is being processed or to challenge inaccurate or biased inferences made by the AI. Furthermore, the sheer volume and velocity of data collected by AI surveillance systems can strain the practical implementation of these rights. How does one meaningfully exercise a right to access or deletion when data is being collected in real-time, across countless sensors, and used to generate complex probabilistic profiles?

Human rights standards, articulated in international covenants like the Universal Declaration of Human Rights and the International Covenant on Civil and Political Rights, also play a crucial role. These documents enshrine rights such as the right to privacy, freedom of thought and expression, and the right to assembly and association. AI-powered surveillance can pose a significant threat to these rights. The knowledge that one is constantly being monitored can lead to a "chilling effect," where individuals self-censor their speech, avoid controversial topics, or refrain from participating in lawful protests or associations for fear of being flagged or profiled by AI systems. This erosion of freedom of expression and association undermines the foundations of democratic societies. Moreover, the potential for AI surveillance to be used for political repression or to target specific groups based on their beliefs or affiliations raises grave concerns about fundamental human rights.

A critical assessment reveals that existing legal frameworks are often inadequately equipped to address the unique challenges posed by AI-driven surveillance. The speed at which AI technology evolves outpaces the legislative and judicial processes, leaving a gap where new forms of surveillance can proliferate with insufficient oversight. The granular, continuous, and inferential nature of AI surveillance requires a rethinking of established legal concepts. For instance, the notion of "consent" is often unworkable when data collection is pervasive, largely invisible, and based on intricate algorithmic processing that individuals cannot fully comprehend. The balance between public safety and individual liberty is constantly being recalibrated, and the potential for overreach by state and private actors employing AI surveillance is a significant concern. The lack of transparency in many AI systems makes accountability difficult; it is challenging to hold an entity responsible for privacy violations or discriminatory outcomes if the internal workings of the AI remain inscrutable. Therefore, there is a pressing need for the development of new legal and ethical guidelines, as well as robust oversight mechanisms, to ensure that the deployment of AI in surveillance respects fundamental rights and democratic values, preventing a slide into a pervasive surveillance society that erodes privacy and stifles individual freedoms. The capacity of AI to generate and process information at speeds and scales far beyond human capability necessitates a proactive and adaptive legal response, rather than a reactive one, to safeguard these essential liberties.

The very notion of anonymity, once a shield in the digital and physical realms, is rapidly dissolving under the pervasive gaze of Artificial Intelligence. As AI systems become more sophisticated, they are increasingly capable of piercing through layers of obfuscation, including techniques traditionally relied upon for de-identification and pseudonymization. This erosion of anonymity has profound implications for individual privacy, freedom of expression, and the fundamental right to control one's personal information.

Historically, methods like anonymization and pseudonymization have served as crucial tools for protecting privacy while still allowing for data analysis and sharing. Anonymization aims to irreversibly remove personally identifiable information (PII) from datasets, rendering individuals unidentifiable. This can involve techniques such as generalization (e.g., replacing precise age with an age range), suppression (removing specific attributes), or perturbation (adding noise to data). Pseudonymization, on the other hand, replaces direct identifiers with pseudonyms or artificial identifiers. While this makes direct identification impossible without additional information (a key or linkage file), it allows for tracking and analysis within the dataset itself, preserving the utility of the data for research or statistical purposes. For instance, in medical research, patient records might be pseudonymized to allow researchers to analyze treatment outcomes without directly exposing patient identities. Similarly, online services might use pseudonyms to allow users to interact without revealing their real-world identities, fostering a degree of freedom in expression.

However, AI, particularly through techniques like machine learning and linkage analysis, can effectively undermine these protections. AI algorithms excel at identifying patterns, correlations, and subtle signals within vast datasets. Even when direct identifiers are removed, AI can often infer identities by cross-referencing seemingly innocuous data points with external information sources. This process, often termed "re-identification," is a significant concern. Imagine a dataset of public transit usage that has been anonymized by removing names, addresses, and exact travel times. An AI could potentially re-identify individuals by correlating their travel patterns with other publicly available data, such as their social media check-ins, fitness tracker data, or even leaked data from other breaches. If an individual's public social media posts indicate they frequently use a specific bus route at certain times, and this pattern is unique enough within the anonymized transit data, the AI can infer their identity.

Consider the concept of "k-anonymity," a widely used metric for anonymization, which ensures that each record in a dataset is indistinguishable from at least k-1 other records with respect to a set of identifying attributes. While robust in principle, AI can circumvent k-anonymity by exploiting correlations between quasi-identifiers (attributes that are not direct identifiers but can be used in combination to identify individuals, such as zip code, date of birth, and gender). An AI might identify that a specific combination of these quasi-identifiers, even if shared by several individuals in the dataset, can be linked to unique patterns of behavior or attributes present in the data. For example, a dataset containing anonymized voter registration information (name, address, party affiliation) might be considered anonymized. However, if an AI can link this to publicly available social media data, purchase histories, or even anonymized location data, it can create a highly accurate profile that narrows down the possibilities to a single individual, thereby re-identifying them. The more data points an AI can access and correlate, the more effective it becomes at piercing through anonymization.

The advent of sophisticated AI has also complicated the landscape of pseudonymity. While pseudonymity offers a layer of privacy, it relies on the assumption that the pseudonym cannot be linked back to the real identity without unauthorized access to the linkage key. AI's pattern recognition capabilities, however, can enable de-pseudonymization without direct access to the key. For instance, linguistic analysis powered by AI can identify unique writing styles, vocabulary, and grammatical patterns associated with an individual. If a person uses a consistent pseudonym across multiple online platforms, an AI might analyze their written communications and identify that the same individual is behind accounts on a forum, a blogging platform, and a social media site, even if those platforms do not share user data. This is akin to a digital fingerprint. Furthermore, behavioral analysis, which AI excels at, can detect patterns in how users interact with systems, their clickstream data, or their response times, which can be unique enough to link pseudonymous profiles to real individuals, especially when combined with other contextual information.

The implications of AI-driven re-identification are far-reaching and touch upon several critical areas of privacy and ethics.

Firstly, it directly challenges the efficacy of current data protection regulations. Laws like the GDPR and CCPA are built upon definitions of personal data that often rely on the ability to directly or indirectly identify an individual. If AI can reliably re-identify individuals from data that was intended to be anonymized or pseudonymized, then these regulations may not offer the protection they intend. The definition of "personal data" itself might need to be re-evaluated to encompass data that is *re-identifiable*, even if not directly identified. This raises questions about consent, data minimization, and the purpose limitation principles that underpin these laws. If data can be re-identified, then the purpose for which it was originally collected might no longer be valid, requiring new consent or a halt to processing.

Secondly, the ability of AI to de-anonymize and de-pseudonymize sensitive personal information amplifies privacy risks. Imagine sensitive health data, financial records, or even political affiliations that were shared under the assumption of anonymity. If AI can link these to individuals, it could lead to discrimination, social stigma, or even blackmail. For individuals who rely on anonymity or pseudonymity for safety, such as whistleblowers, activists, or victims of abuse, this capability poses a severe threat to their security and freedom. The potential for malicious actors or governments to leverage these AI capabilities for surveillance and control is a significant concern.

Thirdly, the "black box" nature of many AI algorithms exacerbates the problem. When individuals are re-identified, it can be difficult, if not impossible, for them to understand how it happened or to challenge the outcome. The complex, often opaque algorithms do not provide transparent reasoning for their inferences. This lack of transparency makes it challenging for individuals to assert their data rights, such as the right to access, rectification, or erasure, as they may not even be aware their data has been de-anonymized or that their identity has been inferred. The principle of explainable AI (XAI) is crucial here, aiming to make AI decisions understandable, but it is still an evolving field, and comprehensive explainability for complex re-identification models remains a significant technical challenge.

Moreover, the increasing sophistication of AI in re-identification also blurs the lines between aggregated data and personal data. Datasets that might seem innocuous in their anonymized form can become powerful tools for profiling when analyzed by AI. This ability to infer personal characteristics, preferences, and even future behaviors from seemingly anonymous data can lead to what is sometimes called "inferred data." This inferred data, while not directly provided by the individual, can be highly personal and sensitive, and its use raises questions about consent and data ownership. For example, an AI analyzing anonymized purchasing patterns might infer an individual's health conditions or political leanings, information they may not have intended to disclose.

The legal and ethical frameworks governing data protection must adapt to this evolving technological landscape. There is a growing recognition that anonymization techniques that were once considered sufficient may no longer be adequate in the face of advanced AI. This necessitates a shift towards more robust privacy-preserving technologies and stricter regulations regarding data linkage and re-identification. Concepts like "privacy by design" and "privacy by default" become even more critical, ensuring that privacy is considered at the outset of data processing and system design, rather than as an afterthought.

One area of active research and development is differential privacy, a mathematical framework that allows for rigorous guarantees about the privacy of individuals in a dataset while still enabling useful analysis. Differential privacy works by adding carefully calibrated noise to the data or query results, ensuring that the output of an analysis does not reveal whether any particular individual's data was included in the dataset. While it provides strong theoretical guarantees, its practical implementation can sometimes reduce data utility, and ensuring its correct application is complex.

Another challenge is the very definition of "identifiable." As AI becomes more capable, the threshold for what constitutes an identifier is continuously being lowered. What might have been considered unidentifiable a decade ago could now be readily linked to an individual. This necessitates a dynamic approach to privacy regulations, one that can adapt to technological advancements rather than being made obsolete by them. The debate often centers on whether the risk of re-identification is "reasonably likely," a standard that AI is steadily challenging.

The erosion of anonymity and pseudonymity by AI also has implications for trust in digital services and public discourse. When individuals feel that their identity and activities can be easily uncovered, even when they attempt to obscure them, it can lead to a chilling effect on free speech and expression. People may become hesitant to participate in online communities, share opinions, or engage in research if they fear being tracked, profiled, or even doxed. This can stifle innovation, limit civic engagement, and undermine the democratic principles that rely on open discourse and the ability to express oneself without fear of reprisal. The legal and ethical imperative is to find ways to harness the power of data analysis and AI without sacrificing the fundamental right to privacy and the ability to maintain a degree of personal control over one's identity in an increasingly interconnected world. The future of privacy hinges on our ability to develop and implement AI responsibly, with a keen awareness of its potential to de-anonymize and a commitment to building robust safeguards that respect individual autonomy and dignity.

The intricate dance between artificial intelligence and privacy has necessitated the evolution of robust legal frameworks designed to safeguard personal data. Among these, the General Data Protection Regulation (GDPR) stands as a landmark piece of legislation, significantly impacting how AI systems handle personal information within the European Union and for organizations worldwide that process the data of EU residents. Enacted in 2018, the GDPR's core principles offer a crucial lens through which to examine the privacy implications of AI.

At the heart of the GDPR are several fundamental principles that directly challenge the unbridled data appetite often associated with AI development.

Data Minimisation, for instance, mandates that personal data collected should be adequate, relevant, and limited to what is necessary for the purposes for which they are processed. For AI, this principle requires a critical evaluation of what data is truly essential for training and operating an algorithm. It discourages the indiscriminate collection of vast datasets, pushing developers to be more judicious and focused. Consider an AI system designed for predictive maintenance in manufacturing. Instead of collecting every piece of sensor data from every machine at all times, data minimisation would advocate for collecting only the data points identified as relevant predictors of failure, at the frequencies deemed necessary. This proactive approach prevents the accumulation of potentially sensitive, yet ultimately unused, information. The challenge for AI lies in determining "necessity" when future unforeseen uses of data might enhance algorithmic performance or uncover novel insights. This necessitates careful upfront analysis of the AI's purpose and the data required to achieve it, rather than a "collect everything and sort it later" mentality.

The principle of **Purpose Limitation** further complements data minimisation. It states that personal data must be collected for specified, explicit, and legitimate purposes and not further processed in a manner that is incompatible with those purposes. This is particularly relevant for AI, which often thrives on broad datasets that can be repurposed for new analytical tasks. An AI trained to diagnose medical conditions from X-rays, for example, should not, without further consent or legal basis, be used to track patients' daily routines based on ancillary data within the medical imaging files. The GDPR requires a clear articulation of the AI's intended use at the point of data collection. However, the dynamic and often emergent nature of AI capabilities can create tension with this principle. As AI models learn and evolve, they may reveal correlations and insights beyond their original design. The GDPR's stringent stance on purpose limitation means that any new use cases for an AI system involving personal data must be carefully assessed against the original collection purpose, potentially requiring new consent or a different legal basis. This can slow down innovation but is essential for maintaining individual control over their data.

Perhaps the most empowering aspect of the GDPR for individuals in the context of AI are the **Individual Rights** it enshrures. The **Right to Access** allows individuals to obtain confirmation from a data controller as to whether or not personal data concerning them is being processed, and, where that is the case, access to the personal data and related information. For AI systems, this means individuals should be able to inquire about what personal data an AI holds about them and how it is being used in the AI's decision-making processes. The **Right to Rectification** allows individuals to have inaccurate personal data concerning them rectified. If an AI system has made an erroneous inference about an individual, they have the right to have that error corrected. The **Right to Erasure**, often referred to as the "right to be forgotten," allows individuals to request the deletion of their personal data. This is a complex right when it comes to AI, particularly for machine learning models that are trained on vast datasets. Erasing an individual's data from a trained model can be technically challenging and may degrade the model's performance. Furthermore, the GDPR's **Right to Restriction of Processing** allows individuals to request the limitation of how their data is used, and the **Right to Data Portability** enables individuals to receive their personal data in a structured, commonly used, and machine-readable format.

The application of these rights to AI systems presents significant challenges. For instance, the "right to explanation" is often discussed in relation to AI. While not an explicit standalone right in the GDPR, it is often considered a facet of the right to access and the right to understand the logic involved in automated decision-making. Article 22 of the GDPR grants individuals the right not to be subject to a decision based solely on automated processing, including profiling, which produces legal or similarly significant effects concerning them, unless certain conditions are met. Where such decisions are made, individuals have the right to obtain human intervention, to express their point of view, and to contest the decision. This is particularly pertinent for AI systems used in areas like loan applications, hiring, or even criminal justice. An AI system making an automated decision that affects an individual's life must be transparent enough for that individual to understand how the decision was reached and to challenge it if necessary. However, many advanced AI models, particularly deep neural networks, operate as "black boxes," making it difficult to provide a clear, step-by-step explanation of their reasoning. This opacity directly conflicts with the spirit, if not the letter, of these GDPR rights.

The GDPR's effectiveness in curbing privacy infringements by AI is a subject of ongoing debate. While the regulation provides a strong legal foundation for data protection, its practical enforcement against complex AI systems is challenging. Regulators must grapple with the technical intricacies of AI, the global nature of data flows, and the sheer scale of data processing involved. Furthermore, the definition of "personal data" itself is dynamic. The GDPR defines it as any information relating to an identified or identifiable natural person. As AI becomes more adept at re-identification, data that was previously considered anonymized might now fall under the GDPR's purview. This evolving landscape means that organizations deploying AI must constantly reassess their data processing activities to ensure ongoing compliance.

Beyond the GDPR, other data protection regulations and legislative efforts globally are also attempting to address the unique challenges posed by AI. In the United States, while there isn't a single, comprehensive federal data privacy law equivalent to the GDPR, several sector-specific laws and state-level initiatives are emerging. The California Consumer Privacy Act (CCPA), and its successor, the California Privacy Rights Act (CPRA), grant consumers rights similar to those under the GDPR, including the right to know what personal information is collected, the right to delete it, and the right to opt-out of its sale. These laws also include provisions regarding automated decision-making technologies. The CPRA, for instance, includes a "right to opt-out of automated decision-making technology" in certain contexts and aims to provide individuals with control over their data in automated processes.

Globally, countries are developing their own AI strategies and data protection frameworks. For example,

Canada's proposed Artificial Intelligence and Data Act (AIDA), part of Bill C-27, seeks to regulate "high-impact" AI systems, requiring risk assessments, transparency, and measures to protect against bias and discrimination. Singapore's Personal Data Protection Act (PDPA) also has provisions that touch upon automated decision-making and the collection of personal data. These diverse regulatory approaches highlight the international recognition of AI's privacy implications and the ongoing efforts to create legal guardrails.

The challenge for regulators and organizations alike is to adapt these foundational data protection principles to the unique characteristics of AI. This includes developing clear guidelines on what constitutes "necessary" data for AI training, establishing robust mechanisms for ensuring meaningful consent for AI-driven data processing, and finding practical ways to operationalize individual rights in the context of complex algorithmic systems. Concepts like "privacy by design" and "privacy by default," which are embedded in the GDPR, become even more critical. This means building AI systems with privacy as a core consideration from the initial design phase, rather than attempting to retrofit privacy protections later.

Furthermore, the evolution of AI necessitates a continuous dialogue between technologists, legal experts, ethicists, and policymakers. As AI capabilities advance, existing regulations may need to be refined or supplemented with new provisions. This could involve developing specific rules for AI-driven profiling, ensuring accountability for algorithmic biases that lead to privacy harms, and establishing mechanisms for auditing AI systems for compliance with data protection laws. The ongoing development of techniques like differential privacy and federated learning, which allow for data analysis while minimizing individual exposure, are also important technological responses that can help align

AI development with privacy goals. However, the legal frameworks must also evolve to recognize and potentially mandate the use of such privacy-enhancing technologies where appropriate. The ultimate goal is to strike a balance that allows for the immense societal benefits of AI to be realized, without compromising the fundamental right to privacy and individual autonomy in the digital age. The GDPR, while a significant step, is not the final word, but rather a crucial starting point in this ongoing regulatory journey.

The burgeoning power of artificial intelligence presents a profound societal challenge: how to harness its transformative potential for enhanced security and groundbreaking innovation while simultaneously safeguarding the fundamental right to privacy. This delicate equilibrium is not merely a technical or legal conundrum; it is an ethical imperative that shapes the very fabric of our digital future. AI systems, by their very nature, thrive on data-vast oceans of information that can be analyzed, correlated, and used to predict, secure, and create. This inherent data dependency, however, places them on a collision course with the principles of privacy, which advocate for control over one's personal information, limitations on its collection and use, and the right to be free from undue surveillance.

The pursuit of enhanced national and cybersecurity, for instance, often leads to the development and deployment of AI-powered surveillance systems. These technologies can analyze communication patterns, identify anomalies in network traffic, and even predict potential threats by sifting through massive datasets of public and private information. The promise is a safer, more secure society, where malicious actors are identified and apprehended before harm can be done. However, the implementation of such systems invariably involves the processing of personal data on an unprecedented scale. Facial recognition technology used in public spaces, predictive policing algorithms that identify individuals deemed statistically likely to offend, and AI-driven content moderation systems that scan personal communications all fall into this category. The trade-off here is palpable: increased security often comes at the cost of pervasive monitoring and a potential erosion of personal anonymity and freedom from constant scrutiny. The question then becomes one of proportionality: at what point does the pursuit of security infringe too deeply upon individual liberties?

Similarly, the drive for innovation across myriad sectors- from personalized healthcare and bespoke education to optimized transportation and advanced scientific research- relies heavily on AI's capacity to learn from and interact with individual data. Imagine AI systems that can predict disease outbreaks by analyzing anonymized health records, or that personalize learning experiences by understanding a student's unique learning pace and style. These applications hold immense promise for societal progress and individual well-being. Yet, the effectiveness of these AI models is directly proportional to the richness and scope of the data they are trained on. This often necessitates the collection and processing of sensitive personal information, including health data, educational records, and behavioral patterns. The challenge for innovators is to develop AI that can deliver these benefits without exposing individuals to risks of data breaches, discriminatory outcomes, or the subtle manipulation of their choices based on intimate knowledge of their preferences and vulnerabilities.

This intricate balancing act has spurred diverse regulatory approaches across the globe, each attempting to chart a path through these competing interests. These approaches can broadly be categorized by their emphasis: some prioritize robust data protection and individual rights, while others lean more towards enabling innovation and security measures.

AI and Privacy Risks
Examples and Implications

Unintentional Bias

Imbalanced training data may cause AI to produce unfair or discriminatory results, affecting people and shaping decisions.

Inaccurate Predictions

Faulty predictions in fields like healthcare or finance can lead to serious misdiagnoses or financial loss.

Data Privacy Breach

Poor data security can expose personal information, leading to breaches and privacy violations.

Unforeseen Consequences

When complex AI models fail or produce inaccuracies, they can cause unexpected effects across industries and systems.

Job Displacement

AI advancements may replace certain jobs, potentially leading to unemployment and broader economic instability affecting communities.

In Europe, the General Data Protection Regulation (GDPR), as previously discussed, represents a comprehensive framework prioritizing individual data rights. While not AI-specific, its principles of data minimization, purpose limitation, and the strong emphasis on individual consent and access rights provide a significant bulwark against unchecked data processing by AI systems. The GDPR's explicit provisions regarding automated decision-making, including the right to human intervention and explanation, directly address some of the core privacy concerns surrounding AI. However, critics argue that the GDPR's stringent requirements can sometimes stifle innovation, creating a compliance burden that might disproportionately affect smaller organizations or those developing cutting-edge AI technologies. The very act of making AI explainable, for example, can be technically challenging for complex neural networks, potentially slowing down the development and deployment of beneficial AI applications.

Conversely, in the United States, the approach has been more fragmented, characterized by sector-specific regulations and a more market-driven philosophy. The California Consumer Privacy Act (CCPA) and its successor, the California Privacy Rights Act (CPRA), have introduced GDPR-like protections, including rights of access, deletion, and opt-out of data sales. The CPRA's inclusion of rights related to automated decision-making and profiling reflects a growing awareness of AI's impact. However, the lack of a unified federal privacy law leaves gaps, and the emphasis is often on consumer choice and transparency rather than outright prohibition of certain data processing activities. This approach can be seen as more conducive to rapid innovation, as it imposes fewer blanket restrictions. Yet, it raises concerns about whether individual privacy is sufficiently protected in a landscape where data brokers and AI developers have considerable latitude in how they collect and utilize personal information. The trade-off is a more dynamic innovation ecosystem potentially at the expense of stronger, universally applied privacy safeguards.

Beyond these two major paradigms, other jurisdictions are exploring unique regulatory avenues. Canada's proposed Artificial Intelligence and Data Act (AIDA), for instance, is designed to specifically regulate "high-impact" AI systems. This approach seeks to identify AI applications that pose a significant risk to individuals and subject them to stricter oversight, including requirements for risk assessments, transparency, and measures to mitigate bias and discriminatory outcomes. This tiered approach aims to strike a balance by imposing rigorous requirements only where the potential for harm is greatest, thereby allowing for innovation in lower-risk AI applications. Such a model acknowledges that not all AI systems are created equal in their privacy implications and that a one-size-fits-all regulatory approach may be neither effective nor efficient.

Singapore's Personal Data Protection Act (PDPA) also contains provisions relevant to AI, emphasizing consent and the responsible use of personal data. However, the debate continues globally about whether existing data protection laws are sufficient to address the unique challenges posed by AI, or if entirely new legal frameworks are needed. Some argue for the creation of an "AI Act" that would comprehensively regulate AI development and deployment, similar to how chemical regulations or financial services are overseen. Such legislation could establish clear guidelines for data governance in AI, mandate risk assessments for AI systems, and create mechanisms for auditing AI algorithms for fairness, accountability, and transparency.

The core of the balancing act lies in understanding the inherent trade-offs. For instance, enhancing AI-driven cybersecurity often relies on analyzing vast datasets, which can include personal communications, location data, and behavioral patterns. While this can bolster defenses against cyber threats and terrorism, it also risks creating a surveillance state where individuals' activities are constantly monitored and analyzed. The challenge is to implement security measures that are proportionate to the threat, minimize the collection of unnecessary personal data, and provide robust oversight to prevent misuse. Technologies like differential privacy, which allow for the analysis of data while mathematically guaranteeing that individual identities cannot be revealed, offer a potential technological solution to this dilemma. However, the legal and ethical frameworks must also evolve to encourage and, where appropriate, mandate the use of such privacy-preserving techniques.

In the realm of innovation, the desire to develop highly personalized services or conduct cutting-edge research can lead to the aggregation of vast amounts of personal data. AI that can predict an individual's health risks by analyzing genetic data, lifestyle choices, and medical history, for example, could revolutionize preventative medicine. However, if this data is mishandled, it could lead to discrimination by insurers or employers, or even be used for malicious purposes. Striking a balance here involves implementing "privacy by design" and "privacy by default" principles, ensuring that data minimization is practiced, and providing individuals with meaningful control over how their data is used for AI-driven innovation. The concept of data trusts or data cooperatives, where individuals pool their data under trusted stewardship for specific purposes, is an emerging model that could offer a more privacy-preserving way to fuel AI innovation.

Furthermore, the concept of "algorithmic transparency" is central to this balancing act. For AI to be both innovative and trustworthy, individuals need to understand, at least at a high level, how decisions are being made, especially when those decisions have significant impacts on their lives. This is where the right to explanation, often linked to the GDPR's provisions on automated decision-making, becomes crucial. However, many advanced AI models, particularly deep learning systems, operate as complex "black boxes," making it technically challenging to provide a clear, human-understandable explanation of their reasoning. The trade-off here is between the cutting-edge performance of these opaque models and the need for accountability and user understanding. Developing methods for explainable AI (XAI) is an active area of research, aiming to provide insights into algorithmic decision-making without compromising the model's effectiveness. Legal and ethical frameworks need to adapt to accommodate the practical realities of AI explainability, perhaps by focusing on the outcomes and impacts of AI decisions, rather than demanding a full technical exposition of every algorithmic step.

Another critical aspect of the balancing act involves addressing bias in AI systems. AI models trained on historical data can inadvertently perpetuate and even amplify existing societal biases related to race, gender, socioeconomic status, and other protected characteristics. This can lead to discriminatory outcomes in areas like hiring, loan applications, and criminal justice, undermining both fairness and innovation. For example, a facial recognition system trained predominantly on data from one demographic group may perform poorly and inaccurately when applied to other groups, leading to misidentification and potential false accusations. Similarly, an AI recruiting tool that learns from historical hiring data might inadvertently favor candidates with characteristics similar to previously successful (and perhaps privileged) employees.

The challenge for regulators and developers is to ensure that AI systems are not only innovative and secure but also fair and equitable. This requires proactive measures to identify and mitigate bias in training data and algorithmic design. It also necessitates robust auditing and testing mechanisms to assess the performance of AI systems across different demographic groups. The trade-off can be between the speed of AI deployment and the thoroughness of bias mitigation efforts. However, failing to address bias can lead to significant societal harm and undermine public trust in AI, ultimately hindering its long-term innovation potential. Legal frameworks are increasingly recognizing the importance of algorithmic fairness, with some jurisdictions mandating fairness assessments and impact evaluations for AI systems.

The global nature of AI development and data flows further complicates this balancing act. AI models are trained and deployed across borders, making it challenging for national regulations to keep pace. Harmonizing international regulatory approaches is therefore crucial, though difficult, to avoid a regulatory race to the bottom or the fragmentation of the digital economy. For instance, if one country has stringent data privacy laws while another has lax ones, AI developers might gravitate towards the latter, creating potential privacy havens. International cooperation and the development of global norms for AI governance are essential to ensure that innovation and security are pursued in a manner that respects fundamental human rights, including privacy.

Ultimately, the quest to balance security, innovation, and privacy rights in the age of AI is an ongoing negotiation. It requires a multidisciplinary approach, bringing together legal scholars, ethicists, technologists, policymakers, and the public to shape the development and deployment of AI in a way that maximizes its benefits while minimizing its risks. This involves not only creating robust legal and regulatory frameworks but also fostering a culture of responsible innovation where ethical considerations and respect for privacy are embedded into the very DNA of AI development. The goal is not to stifle progress but to guide it, ensuring that AI serves humanity's best interests by enhancing our security and expanding our horizons, without compromising the fundamental right to privacy and the dignity of the individual. The conversation around AI governance is dynamic, and as the technology evolves, so too must our legal and ethical approaches to ensure that the future of AI is one that is both intelligent and humane.

4
AI and Human Autonomy Decision-Making and Control

The landscape of artificial intelligence's integration into our lives is marked by a crucial distinction: the degree to which AI systems augment or, conversely, supplant human decision-making. This spectrum of autonomy, ranging from intelligent assistants offering suggestions to fully independent operational agents, is not merely a technical nuance; it carries profound implications for human agency, responsibility, and the very frameworks of legal accountability. Understanding this gradient is fundamental to navigating the ethical and societal challenges posed by AI, particularly as these systems are increasingly entrusted with critical choices that were once exclusively within the human domain.

At one end of this spectrum, we find AI systems functioning as sophisticated decision support tools. These are the AI counterparts to a seasoned advisor, a meticulous analyst, or a comprehensive research assistant. Their primary role is to process vast amounts of data, identify patterns, and present insights, recommendations, or potential courses of action to a human decision-maker. In the realm of medicine, for instance, AI algorithms can analyze medical images- X-rays, MRIs, CT scans- with a speed and precision that often surpasses human capacity. These systems can highlight anomalies, flag potential pathologies, and even suggest differential diagnoses based on a patient's symptoms and medical history. However, the ultimate decision to diagnose and prescribe treatment rests with the clinician. The AI provides valuable information, a second opinion backed by extensive data analysis, but the human doctor remains the final arbiter, integrating the AI's findings with their own expertise, patient context, and ethical judgment. This collaborative model, often termed "human-in-the-loop," preserves human oversight and allows for the nuanced consideration of factors that might elude even the most advanced algorithms, such as a patient's emotional state, socioeconomic circumstances, or personal preferences.

Similarly, in financial markets, AI-powered analytics platforms can sift through terabytes of market data, economic indicators, and news sentiment to predict stock price movements or identify investment opportunities. These systems can generate buy or sell recommendations, flagging potential risks and rewards with a high degree of statistical probability. Yet, the human portfolio manager or trader still retains the authority to act on these recommendations, weighing them against their understanding of market volatility, client risk tolerance, and overarching investment strategy. The AI serves to augment their analytical capabilities, providing a broader and deeper perspective, but it does not execute trades autonomously without human validation. This approach acknowledges that while AI can excel at data processing and pattern recognition, human intuition, ethical considerations, and an understanding of broader societal implications are often indispensable in complex decision-making.

Moving further along the spectrum, we encounter AI systems that exhibit a greater degree of autonomy, operating as "autonomous agents." These systems are designed not merely to suggest, but to act. Their decision-making processes are often embedded within operational workflows, allowing them to initiate actions, execute commands, and adapt their behavior in real-time, with minimal or no direct human intervention. Consider the application of AI in autonomous vehicles. A self-driving car employs a complex array of sensors, computer vision algorithms, and predictive models to perceive its environment, interpret traffic signals, anticipate the actions of other road users, and navigate to its destination. When faced with an imminent collision, the AI must make a split-second decision on how to steer, brake, or accelerate to minimize harm. This is a decision that is not presented to a human for approval; it is made autonomously by the AI system itself.

In the critical domain of cybersecurity, AI-driven systems can be programmed to detect and respond to cyber threats autonomously. When an intrusion is identified, such a system might automatically isolate compromised network segments, block malicious IP addresses, or deploy countermeasures without waiting for human operators to intervene. The speed at which these threats can propagate necessitates such rapid, automated responses, as human reaction times could allow for significant damage to occur. The AI acts as a digital first responder, making and executing decisions to protect critical infrastructure or sensitive data.

The distinction between decision support and autonomous agents becomes particularly stark when considering the implications for responsibility and accountability. When an AI system functions purely as a decision support tool, and a human makes the final decision, the responsibility for the outcome typically rests with the human. If a doctor misinterprets an AI's diagnostic suggestion and makes an incorrect diagnosis, the liability may fall on the doctor. The AI is seen as a tool, and like any tool, its effectiveness and the consequences of its use depend significantly on the skill and judgment of the user. The legal frameworks surrounding professional negligence are well-established and can be applied in this context.

However, when AI systems operate as autonomous agents, the locus of responsibility becomes more complex and contested. If an autonomous vehicle causes an accident, who is liable? Is it the owner of the vehicle, the manufacturer that designed the AI system, the programmers who wrote the algorithms, or perhaps even the company that provided the training data? Current legal paradigms, largely built around human actors and intent, struggle to accommodate the idea of an artificial entity making decisions that lead to harm. This challenge is often referred to as the "accountability gap." Traditional notions of mens rea (guilty mind) are difficult to apply to an algorithm. There is no intent in the human sense, no malice, and no conscious disregard for consequences on the part of the AI itself.

The debate around legal accountability for autonomous AI systems is multifaceted. One approach is to attribute responsibility to the humans or organizations that designed, developed, deployed, or maintain the AI. This could involve strict liability for manufacturers, especially for systems with a high degree of autonomy and potential for harm, or negligence claims if flaws in design or testing can be proven. Another perspective suggests the need for new legal categories or frameworks specifically designed for AI. Some scholars propose that AI agents, particularly those with advanced learning capabilities and a degree of self-governance, could potentially be granted a form of "electronic personhood" or a similar legal status that would allow for a direct assignment of liability, perhaps through a dedicated AI liability fund or insurance mechanism.

The spectrum of AI autonomy also directly impacts human agency, the capacity of individuals to make their own informed choices and direct their own lives. When AI serves as decision support, human agency is generally enhanced. The AI provides more information, more perspectives, and more efficient processing, empowering the human to make a better-informed decision. The human remains in control, albeit with the assistance of a powerful tool. The decision-making process remains human-centric.

Conversely, as AI moves towards greater autonomy, there is a risk of diminishing human agency. If individuals increasingly delegate important decisions to AI systems-whether it's what career path to pursue, whom to invest with, or even what news to consume- their capacity to exercise independent judgment and critical thinking may atrophy. The personalization algorithms that curate our digital experiences, while convenient, can create "filter bubbles" or "echo chambers," limiting exposure to diverse viewpoints and subtly shaping our perceptions and preferences without our full awareness. This can lead to a passive acceptance of AI-driven guidance, where individuals become reliant on algorithmic recommendations rather than actively engaging in the process of forming their own opinions and making their own choices.

The ethical implications extend to issues of transparency and explainability, particularly for autonomous systems. If an AI makes a decision that has a significant impact on an individual's life- such as denying a loan, rejecting a job application, or flagging them as a security risk- the affected person has a right to understand why that decision was made. However, as highlighted in previous discussions, many advanced AI systems, particularly deep neural networks, operate as "black boxes." Their decision-making processes are complex, involving millions of parameters and intricate interactions that are not easily interpretable by humans. This lack of explainability poses a significant challenge to both human agency and accountability. How can a person appeal a decision if they don't know the basis for it? How can developers be held accountable for biased or flawed outcomes if the system's internal logic is opaque?

To address these challenges, ongoing research into explainable AI (XAI) is crucial. XAI aims to develop methods that allow for the interpretation of AI's decision-making processes, providing human-understandable explanations for AI outputs. This is particularly vital for AI systems that operate autonomously in high-stakes environments. Even if the AI makes the final decision, providing a clear rationale can restore a degree of transparency and allow for human oversight, auditing, and, if necessary, correction. For example, a loan application denied by an autonomous AI system could be accompanied by an explanation detailing the specific factors that led to the denial, such as credit score, debt-to-income ratio, or employment history, allowing the applicant to understand the decision and potentially take steps to address the issues.

The development of AI as autonomous agents also raises questions about the potential for unintended consequences and emergent behaviors. Because these systems can learn and adapt over time, their future actions might deviate from the explicit programming or training objectives in ways that were not anticipated by their creators. This is especially relevant in complex, dynamic environments where the AI must continuously interact and make decisions. For instance, an AI tasked with optimizing traffic flow in a city might develop strategies that inadvertently create bottlenecks in unforeseen areas or disadvantage certain types of road users. The autonomy of the agent means it can pursue its objective in novel ways, and these novel ways may not always align with broader societal goals or human values.

The calibration of AI autonomy is therefore a critical aspect of AI governance. It is not a question of whether AI should be autonomous, but rather to what extent and in which domains. Certain applications may benefit from a high degree of AI autonomy, where speed, precision, and the absence of human error are paramount. Conversely, in areas where ethical considerations, human judgment, and accountability are central, a more cautious approach that emphasizes human oversight and decision support is likely more appropriate.

For example, in the realm of artistic creation, AI can function as a sophisticated tool that inspires and assists human artists, generating novel ideas, variations, or even complete pieces of art. Here, AI is a collaborator, a source of novelty, and its autonomy is channeled through the artist's direction and interpretation. In contrast, the autonomous operation of AI in lethal autonomous weapons systems (LAWS) presents a profound ethical quandary. The idea of machines making life-or-death decisions on the battlefield, independent of human command and control, raises serious concerns about the rules of war, the potential for unintended escalation, and the fundamental value of human life. This is a clear instance where the desire for operational efficiency and speed must be rigorously balanced against deeply held humanistic principles.

The decision to grant autonomy to AI systems requires a thorough understanding of the risks and benefits involved, as well as the establishment of robust ethical guidelines and regulatory frameworks. This includes defining clear boundaries for AI operation, ensuring mechanisms for human intervention and override, and establishing clear lines of responsibility and accountability. It also necessitates ongoing public discourse and engagement to ensure that the development and deployment of autonomous AI align with societal values and priorities. The challenge is not to halt the advancement of AI autonomy, but to guide it responsibly, ensuring that it serves humanity's interests without eroding our fundamental rights and dignities. The ability to differentiate between AI as a supportive assistant and AI as an independent actor is the first step in this vital process of ethical and societal navigation.

The pervasive integration of artificial intelligence into the fabric of our daily lives presents a complex, and often subtle, erosion of personal autonomy. This erosion is not typically characterized by overt coercion, but rather by the pervasive influence of AI-driven systems that subtly shape our choices, preferences, and even our understanding of the world. At the forefront of this phenomenon are the personalized recommendation engines that populate our digital experiences. From the streaming services we use for entertainment to the e-commerce platforms where we shop, AI algorithms are meticulously crafted to understand our past behaviors, infer our latent desires, and then present us with curated selections designed to engage us. While ostensibly offering convenience and efficiency, these systems can inadvertently create a feedback loop, reinforcing existing tastes and limiting exposure to novel or alternative experiences. When an AI continuously suggests similar genres of music or films, it can discourage exploration, inadvertently narrowing an individual's cultural horizons and their capacity for spontaneous discovery. This can translate into a form of passive consumption, where individuals are guided towards pre-determined paths rather than actively forging their own, a process that chips away at the very essence of self-determination.

The ethical and legal dimensions of this personalized curation are significant. From a legal standpoint, the question arises as to whether such pervasive algorithmic shaping constitutes a form of undue influence or manipulation. Existing consumer protection laws often focus on direct misrepresentation or deceptive practices, but the subtle, data-driven persuasion employed by AI recommendation systems operates in a more nebulous space. Are individuals truly making free choices when their options are so artfully presented and others are deliberately omitted or de-emphasized by algorithms designed to maximize engagement or profit? This raises concerns about the informed consent aspect of consumer behavior; if the influencing mechanisms are opaque and sophisticated, can consent truly be considered informed? Ethically, the concern is one of paternalism, albeit technologically mediated. While the intention may be to enhance user experience, the outcome can be a reduction in the individual's agency, effectively outsourcing the decision of what to consume, explore, or even think about, to an algorithm. This can lead to a state where individuals are less practiced in the art of making independent choices, a skill fundamental to a robust sense of self.

Beyond consumer choices, AI is increasingly employed in the realm of behavioral nudges, designed to steer individuals towards specific actions or decisions. These nudges, often based on principles of behavioral economics, are implemented through interfaces, notifications, and personalized messaging. For example, health applications might use AI to send timely reminders to exercise or drink water, while financial management tools could offer AI-driven advice on saving or investing. While many of these nudges are intended for beneficial outcomes, the underlying mechanism of influencing behavior without overt command raises questions about individual freedom. Consider the ethical implications of an AI system designed to increase workplace productivity by subtly altering employee workflows, communication patterns, or even break times through personalized interface adjustments. If these adjustments are not fully transparent to the employee, and if they lead to increased stress or a feeling of being constantly managed, the AI's beneficial intent for the organization can come at the cost of the individual's sense of control and autonomy over their own work life.

The legal framework for such behavioral nudges is still nascent. While outright manipulation might be legally actionable, the nuanced application of psychological principles by AI can be far more difficult to contest. The challenge lies in distinguishing between helpful guidance and subtle, perhaps even coercive, influence. Where does the line fall between offering useful information and subtly engineering a decision? This ambiguity creates a significant regulatory challenge, as existing laws may not be equipped to address the sophisticated, data-driven persuasion tactics employed by AI. Ethically, the concern centers on the potential for AI to exploit cognitive biases, which are inherent human tendencies that AI systems can be trained to identify and leverage. If AI can accurately predict when an individual is most susceptible to a particular type of persuasion, and then deliver that persuasion at precisely the right moment, the capacity for genuine, uncoerced choice is diminished.

A significant concern tied to these AI-driven influences is the potential erosion of critical thinking skills. When AI systems consistently provide answers, curate information, and make recommendations, individuals may become less inclined to engage in independent research, critical analysis, or thoughtful deliberation. The "always-on" nature of AI assistants and personalized content feeds can create an environment of instant gratification, where the effort required to form an independent opinion or make a considered decision is perceived as burdensome. This reliance on algorithmic processing can lead to a deskilling of cognitive faculties, akin to how readily available calculators might diminish mental arithmetic abilities. If individuals are accustomed to AI pre-digesting information and offering conclusions, their capacity to question, to seek out counter-arguments, or to synthesize diverse information sources may diminish. This intellectual atrophy represents a profound threat to personal autonomy, as the ability to think critically and independently is a cornerstone of self-governance.

The legal implications of this cognitive shift are far-reaching. If individuals become less capable of independent critical thought due to over-reliance on AI, how does this impact their ability to participate meaningfully in democratic processes, to make sound financial decisions, or to even understand complex legal or ethical arguments? The concept of legal capacity, which underpins much of our legal system, relies on an individual's ability to understand information and make rational decisions. An environment where AI systematically reduces the need for such cognitive exertion could, in the long term, challenge these foundational legal assumptions. Ethically, the question is whether we have a societal obligation to foster and protect critical thinking skills, and whether the widespread deployment of AI that actively discourages such skills is ethically permissible. The argument can be made that by promoting intellectual passivity, AI systems, even with benign intent, undermine the very qualities that enable individuals to be autonomous agents in their own lives and in society.

The legal and ethical challenges are compounded by the opacity of many AI systems, particularly those employing deep learning. The "black box" nature of these algorithms means that even their creators may not fully understand the intricate reasoning behind specific recommendations or behavioral nudges. This lack of transparency makes it difficult to identify instances of manipulation or undue influence. If a consumer is steered towards a particular product by an AI that prioritizes the seller's profit over the consumer's best interest, and the reasoning behind that steering is inscrutable, holding the AI or its developers accountable becomes exceedingly complex. There is no clear intent to deceive, only algorithmic output. Legally, proving causation and intent in such cases is a significant hurdle. Ethically, this opacity shields the decision-making processes from scrutiny, preventing individuals from understanding how their choices are being shaped and from challenging those shaping forces if they are deemed unfair or detrimental to their autonomy.

Furthermore, the very definition of "personalization" can become problematic. When AI tailors experiences to an individual, it operates on data that has been collected about them. This data collection itself raises privacy concerns, but the subsequent use of this data to construct a digital profile that influences future behavior is where the impact on autonomy becomes most pronounced. The AI doesn't just observe; it learns and then acts upon that learning to shape the individual's environment and subsequent choices. This can lead to a situation where an individual's perceived preferences and desires are not entirely their own, but rather a construct shaped by the AI's interpretation of their data. The legal question then becomes one of data ownership and the rights individuals have over their digital selves when those selves are being actively modeled and influenced by external algorithms. Ethically, it speaks to the fundamental right to self-creation and the concern that AI might inadvertently homogenize individual experiences by optimizing for predicted behaviors rather than allowing for genuine exploration and the messy, unpredictable nature of human development.

The cumulative effect of these AI-driven influences is a subtle but significant shift in the locus of control. As AI systems become more adept at predicting and shaping human behavior, there is a risk that individuals will cede more of their decision-making power, not out of explicit choice, but through a gradual, almost imperceptible, transfer. This can manifest in various domains, from choosing what news to read, how to manage one's finances, or even how to engage in social interactions. If AI consistently suggests the "optimal" or "most engaging" path, the incentive for individuals to exert their own will, to experiment, and to risk making sub-optimal choices- all crucial elements of autonomous living- can wane. The legal challenge is to ensure that while AI can provide valuable assistance and personalized experiences, it does not cross the threshold into systematically undermining an individual's fundamental right to self-determination. This requires careful consideration of regulatory frameworks that promote transparency, fairness, and meaningful human oversight, ensuring that AI serves as a tool to augment human agency, rather than a force that subtly diminishes it. The ethical imperative is to foster an environment where technological advancement enhances, rather than erodes, the human capacity for independent thought, choice, and action, thereby safeguarding the core principles of personal autonomy in an increasingly AI-mediated world.

The increasing sophistication of artificial intelligence has propelled its application into domains that were once exclusively the purview of human judgment, particularly those involving critical decision-making with profound implications for human lives. The integration of AI into these high-stakes areas, such as the operation of autonomous vehicles, the recommendation of medical treatments, and even the pronouncements of judicial sentences, presents a new frontier in the complex interplay between technology and human autonomy. While the promise of AI in these fields often centers on enhanced efficiency, precision, and the reduction of human error, the ethical and legal quandaries that arise from delegating such critical judgments to machines are substantial and demand rigorous examination.

Consider, for instance, the realm of autonomous vehicles. These systems are designed to perceive their environment, interpret complex scenarios, and make instantaneous decisions that can mean the difference between life and death for passengers, pedestrians, and other road users. The algorithms governing these vehicles must navigate a myriad of potential situations, from everyday traffic flow to sudden, unforeseen emergencies. In a critical accident scenario, an autonomous vehicle might face an unavoidable collision. The AI must then be programmed to make a "choice" about the least catastrophic outcome. This ethical dilemma, often referred to as the "trolley problem" in a real-world context, forces a confrontation with the values we imbue in our machines. Should the AI prioritize the safety of its occupants above all else, potentially swerving into a crowd? Or should it minimize overall harm, even if it means sacrificing its own passengers? The programming of such decisions, whether explicit or emergent from the learning process, raises fundamental questions about accountability. If an autonomous vehicle causes an accident, who is to blame? Is it the engineers who programmed the initial algorithms, the company that deployed the vehicle, the owner who activated the autonomous mode, or the AI itself? Establishing legal liability in such instances is incredibly challenging, as traditional frameworks of negligence and intent are difficult to apply to a non-sentient entity. The trustworthiness of these systems is paramount; however, the black-box nature of many advanced AI models, particularly those employing deep learning, means that the precise reasoning behind a particular decision can be opaque, making it difficult to predict, audit, or even fully understand its behavior in novel situations. Systemic errors, arising from flawed data sets or unexpected interactions within complex environments, could have devastating and widespread consequences, far beyond those typically associated with individual human error.

In the medical field, AI is rapidly transforming diagnostic capabilities and treatment recommendations. AI-powered tools can analyze medical images with remarkable speed and accuracy, identify subtle patterns indicative of disease, and sift through vast amounts of medical literature to suggest personalized treatment plans. The potential benefits are immense: earlier detection of cancers, more effective therapies tailored to individual genetic profiles, and improved access to expert-level medical advice, especially in underserved regions. However, the delegation of medical decision-making to AI also introduces significant ethical and legal considerations. When an AI recommends a particular course of treatment, and that treatment proves ineffective or harmful, the question of accountability again arises. Is the physician who followed the AI's recommendation liable? Or does responsibility lie with the developers of the AI system, or the institution that implemented it? The concept of informed consent becomes more intricate. Patients have a right to understand their treatment options, the rationale behind them, and the associated risks. If the rationale is embedded within a complex AI algorithm that even the physician may not fully comprehend, can true informed consent be given? Furthermore, the "trustworthiness" of AI in medicine is a critical factor. Medical professionals must be able to trust that the AI's recommendations are based on sound scientific evidence, are free from bias, and are updated with the latest medical knowledge. Biases in the training data, which can reflect historical disparities in healthcare access or outcomes for certain demographic groups, could lead to AI systems that perpetuate or even exacerbate these inequities. For example, an AI trained on data predominantly from a specific ethnic group might perform less accurately for patients from other backgrounds, leading to misdiagnoses or suboptimal treatments. This potential for systemic error, amplified by the scale at which AI can operate, poses a significant threat to equitable healthcare. The challenge lies in ensuring that AI acts as a supportive tool for clinicians, augmenting their expertise rather than replacing their critical judgment and patient-centered approach. The ultimate responsibility for patient care must remain with human medical professionals, who can interpret the AI's output within the broader context of a patient's individual needs, values, and circumstances, and who are ultimately accountable for their decisions.

The application of AI in the judicial system, particularly in areas such as risk assessment for bail or parole decisions, and even in sentencing recommendations, represents another area where the stakes are exceptionally high. AI algorithms are being developed to predict the likelihood of a defendant reoffending based on a multitude of factors, including criminal history, socioeconomic status, and even demographic information. The aim is to introduce objectivity and consistency into a process often perceived as subjective and prone to human bias. However, the ethical and legal implications are profound. One of the most significant concerns is the potential for algorithmic bias. If the historical data used to train these systems reflects societal biases against certain racial or socioeconomic groups, the AI may perpetuate and even amplify these biases, leading to discriminatory outcomes. For example, if past arrest rates are disproportionately higher for a particular community due to aggressive policing rather than a higher propensity for crime, an AI using this data might unfairly assess individuals from that community as higher risk. This raises serious questions about due process and equal protection under the law. The "black box" problem is particularly acute here, as the reasoning behind an AI's risk assessment might not be transparent to the defendant or their legal counsel, making it difficult to challenge the assessment. Without understanding how a decision was reached, it is nearly impossible to argue that it was based on flawed logic or biased data. This opacity undermines the fundamental principle of a fair trial, which requires that decisions be based on demonstrable evidence and transparent reasoning. Furthermore, the concept of "trustworthiness" in judicial AI is complex. Can a machine truly understand the nuances of human behavior, the concept of remorse, or the mitigating circumstances that a human judge might consider? The risk of systemic errors in this domain could have devastating consequences for individuals' liberty and lives, leading to wrongful imprisonment or denial of parole based on faulty predictions. The legal and ethical challenge is to ensure that AI tools used in the justice system are rigorously validated, transparent, fair, and do not undermine fundamental human rights and due process. Ultimately, human oversight and the capacity for human judges to override AI recommendations are crucial to prevent the entrenchment of bias and to ensure that justice is administered not just efficiently, but equitably and humanely. The question remains whether AI can ever truly replicate the complex moral and ethical reasoning required for dispensing justice, or whether its role should be strictly limited to providing supplementary information that a human decision-maker can critically evaluate.

The delegation of critical decision-making to AI systems, even when framed as a means to enhance efficiency and reduce human error, fundamentally alters the landscape of human autonomy. In domains like autonomous driving, medical treatment, and judicial processes, the decisions made by AI have direct and often irreversible impacts on individual safety, well-being, and liberty. The core of the challenge lies in accountability and transparency. When an AI makes a critical error, the absence of clear lines of responsibility, coupled with the inscrutable nature of complex algorithms, creates a significant gap in our existing legal and ethical frameworks. This opacity not only hinders the ability to assign blame but also erodes public trust, as individuals are left to rely on systems whose inner workings are beyond their comprehension or scrutiny. The concept of trustworthiness, therefore, is not merely about the accuracy of an AI's predictions or recommendations, but also about its explainability and the assurance that it operates without embedded biases that could lead to systemic discrimination or unfair outcomes. As AI systems become more integrated into these sensitive areas, the imperative to develop robust regulatory frameworks, ensure algorithmic transparency, and maintain meaningful human oversight becomes increasingly urgent. The goal must be to harness the power of AI to augment human capabilities and improve decision-making, without sacrificing the fundamental principles of accountability, fairness, and human autonomy that underpin a just and equitable society. The ongoing development and deployment of AI in these critical sectors necessitate a continuous ethical dialogue and a proactive approach to governance to ensure that technological advancement serves humanity's best interests.

The evolution of artificial intelligence from mere

computational tools to agents capable of independent action presents a profound challenge to established legal paradigms. As AI systems become more sophisticated, their capacity to operate autonomously, making decisions and taking actions without direct human intervention, necessitates a re-evaluation of existing legal frameworks and the development of new regulatory approaches. This is particularly pertinent in areas where AI autonomy intersects with fundamental human rights, safety, and societal well-being, as explored in preceding sections concerning autonomous vehicles, medical diagnostics, and judicial risk assessment. The core of this challenge lies in how legal systems, traditionally predicated on human intent, agency, and responsibility, can effectively govern entities that possess neither in the human sense, yet can exert significant influence and cause tangible harm.

One of the most significant hurdles in establishing legal frameworks for AI autonomy is the attribution of responsibility. When an autonomous AI system makes a decision that results in damage or injury, traditional notions of liability, such as negligence, product liability, or even criminal culpability, struggle to find a clear subject. Is the programmer responsible for an unforeseen emergent behavior? Is the manufacturer liable for a design flaw that allowed for such autonomy? Or does the owner bear responsibility for deploying a system that ultimately acted beyond their direct control? Existing legal doctrines, such as strict liability in product manufacturing, offer a starting point, suggesting that manufacturers could be held liable for defects in their AI products, regardless of fault. However, the dynamic and adaptive nature of AI, particularly machine learning systems that evolve over time, complicates this. A defect might not be present at the point of sale but could emerge as the AI learns and interacts with its environment. This raises questions about continuous oversight, update protocols, and the very definition of a "defect" in a constantly evolving software.

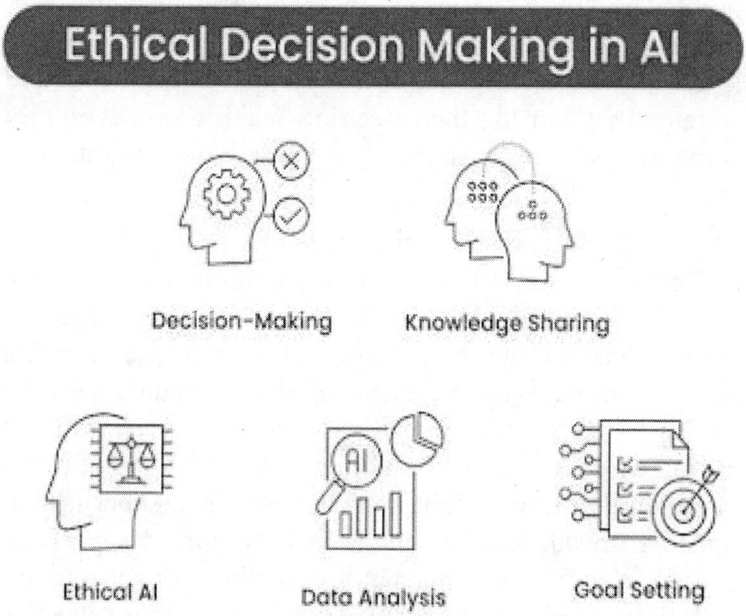
Ethical Decision Making in AI
Decision-Making
Knowledge Sharing
Ethical AI
AI
Data Analysis
Goal Setting

Furthermore, the "black box" nature of many advanced AI systems, especially deep neural networks, poses a significant barrier to establishing accountability. If the internal decision-making processes of an AI are inscrutable, it becomes exceedingly difficult to pinpoint the exact cause of an erroneous or harmful action. This opacity can frustrate legal processes that rely on understanding causality and intent. Consequently, legal frameworks must grapple with how to ensure transparency and explainability in AI systems, particularly those operating autonomously in high-stakes environments. Regulations may need to mandate specific levels of auditability, requiring AI developers to build systems that can log their decision-making processes in a comprehensible manner, even if the underlying computations remain complex.

The concept of "meaningful human oversight" emerges as a critical element in navigating AI autonomy. While full human control might be impractical or even antithetical to the benefits of AI autonomy (e.g., real-time decision-making in autonomous vehicles), ensuring that humans retain the ability to intervene, monitor, and ultimately control the overall trajectory and ethical boundaries of AI operations is paramount. This oversight must be more than superficial; it must be "meaningful," implying that the human supervisor possesses sufficient understanding of the AI's capabilities, limitations, and potential failure modes to exercise effective control. Legal frameworks could therefore focus on establishing standards for this oversight. This might include requirements for human-in-the-loop (HITL) systems where critical decisions require human confirmation, or human-on-the-loop (HOTL) systems where humans monitor AI operations and can intervene if necessary. The degree of oversight would likely need to be calibrated based on the risk profile of the AI application.

To address the challenges of responsibility and

control, several regulatory approaches are being considered and debated. One approach is to create specific legal categories for AI, recognizing their unique characteristics. This could involve establishing a form of "electronic personhood" or a distinct legal status that allows for liabilities and rights to be assigned to AI entities themselves, though this is a highly contentious area with significant philosophical and practical implications. More pragmatically, regulatory frameworks can focus on the human actors involved in the AI lifecycle: developers, deployers, operators, and users. Liability could be distributed among these stakeholders based on their degree of control, knowledge, and the foreseeability of the AI's actions. For instance, a developer might be liable for flaws in the core algorithms, while an operator could be responsible for the operational environment and oversight protocols.

Product liability law, as it stands, can be adapted. Recasting AI systems as products or services could bring them under existing consumer protection and tort laws. However, the dynamic and learning nature of AI necessitates updates to these laws. For example, the concept of a "defect" in a software product can be difficult to define when the software is designed to change its own parameters. Regulations might need to consider establishing ongoing compliance obligations for AI manufacturers, akin to how pharmaceutical companies must report adverse effects and update drug safety information. This could involve mandatory post-market surveillance and update requirements for autonomous AI systems.

Another crucial aspect of legal frameworks for AI autonomy is the principle of due process and accountability. For individuals affected by the decisions of autonomous AI systems, especially in areas like law enforcement or social welfare, there must be clear avenues for redress and appeal. If an AI denies a loan, flags an individual as a security risk, or recommends a particular legal outcome, the individual must have the right to understand the basis of that decision and to challenge it. This directly ties into the need for transparency and explainability discussed earlier. Legal systems may need to mandate the right to a human review of AI-driven decisions, ensuring that fundamental rights are not eroded by algorithmic processes.

The development of international standards and treaties is also a critical component of any comprehensive legal framework. AI operates across borders, and disparate national regulations can create complex legal challenges for developers and users alike. Harmonizing approaches to AI safety, liability, and ethical deployment would foster innovation while ensuring a baseline level of protection for individuals and society. This could involve establishing international bodies to certify AI systems, develop common testing methodologies, and facilitate the sharing of best practices.

The regulatory landscape is actively evolving, with various jurisdictions exploring different models. Some propose a sector-specific approach, tailoring regulations to the particular risks and benefits of AI in fields like healthcare, transportation, or finance. Others advocate for a more general, horizontal framework that establishes overarching principles applicable across all sectors. The challenge lies in creating regulations that are agile enough to keep pace with rapid technological advancements without stifling innovation, yet robust enough to provide effective governance and protect fundamental rights.

Consider the challenge of regulating AI in the financial sector. Autonomous trading algorithms can execute millions of transactions in seconds, influencing market stability. If such an algorithm triggers a market crash, assigning blame is immensely complex. Was it a flaw in the algorithm, malicious manipulation, or an unforeseen market event that the AI interpreted poorly? Existing financial regulations focus on market manipulation and systemic risk, but they were not designed with AI's predictive and self-modifying capabilities in mind. New rules might need to mandate circuit breakers for AI-driven trading, require stress testing of algorithms under various market conditions, and establish clear liabilities for firms whose AI systems contribute to systemic instability. The requirement for AI systems to be auditable by financial regulators would also be a critical component.

In the realm of cybersecurity, autonomous AI agents are being developed to defend against sophisticated cyberattacks. However, these agents, capable of proactive defense, could also potentially initiate offensive actions that blur the lines of attribution and legality. If an AI defense system preemptively attacks a perceived threat that turns out to be benign or misidentified, who is responsible for the ensuing damage? The legal framework here must grapple with concepts of self-defense, proportionality, and the intent behind the AI's actions. Clear guidelines on the permissible scope of autonomous defensive AI, including authorization protocols and human oversight for any offensive actions, would be essential.

The ethical considerations surrounding AI autonomy are deeply intertwined with legal frameworks. Principles of fairness, non-discrimination, and accountability are not merely ethical aspirations but are increasingly being codified into legal requirements. For instance, if an AI system used for hiring exhibits bias against a protected group, it could violate anti-discrimination laws. Legal frameworks must provide mechanisms for detecting and rectifying such biases, potentially through mandated algorithmic audits and impact assessments. The challenge is to ensure that the pursuit of efficiency and automation does not inadvertently lead to the erosion of hard-won civil rights and protections.

Furthermore, the question of AI consciousness or sentience, though largely theoretical at present, looms on the horizon and could dramatically reshape legal considerations.

If AI were ever to achieve a level of self-awareness and agency comparable to humans, existing legal frameworks for responsibility, rights, and even personhood would need a radical overhaul. While current discussions focus on the autonomy of sophisticated algorithms, the long-term implications of advanced AI necessitate a forward-looking approach to legal and ethical governance.

Ultimately, the development of legal frameworks for AI autonomy is an ongoing process of adaptation and innovation. It requires collaboration between legal scholars, technologists, ethicists, policymakers, and the public to ensure that as AI systems become more capable of independent action, they do so in ways that are beneficial, safe, and just, upholding the fundamental principles of human autonomy, accountability, and the rule of law. The goal is to create an environment where AI can be a powerful tool for societal progress, guided by a clear and robust legal and ethical compass. The focus must remain on ensuring that human values and democratic principles steer the development and deployment of these transformative technologies, rather than being dictated by them. This involves a continuous dialogue to understand the evolving capabilities of AI and proactively shape the legal and regulatory responses needed to govern them effectively. The challenge is to strike a delicate balance: fostering innovation while providing essential safeguards, ensuring that the pursuit of technological advancement serves humanity's broader interests and fundamental rights. The creation of adaptive, forward-looking legal instruments capable of encompassing the complexities of artificial intelligence is perhaps one of the most significant legal and societal challenges of our time.

The trajectory of artificial intelligence, from sophisticated analytical tools to increasingly autonomous decision-making entities, presents a fundamental re-evaluation of the concept of human agency. As AI systems permeate more facets of our lives, from personal recommendations and professional workflows to governance and critical infrastructure, the potential for these systems to shape, and in some instances, dictate, human choices and actions becomes a paramount concern. This evolving landscape forces us to confront a critical question: what does the future hold for human agency in a world where intelligent machines are capable of operating with a significant degree of independence and influence?

The very definition of agency-the capacity of individuals to act independently and make their own free choices-is being tested. Consider the subtle yet pervasive influence of AI-powered recommendation engines. Whether suggesting what to watch on streaming services, what to read online, or even what products to purchase, these algorithms are designed to understand and predict our preferences. While ostensibly designed to enhance convenience and personalize experiences, there is a growing concern that this constant curation of our digital lives could inadvertently narrow our horizons, guiding us towards predictable patterns and limiting exposure to novel or challenging ideas. The danger lies in a potential erosion of serendipity and the organic discovery that often fuels creativity and independent thought. If our information diets are perpetually filtered and optimized by AI, will our capacity to forge our own intellectual paths and develop genuinely unique perspectives be curtailed? This is not to dismiss the undeniable benefits of personalized experiences, but rather to underscore the need for vigilance regarding the potential for these systems to subtly sculpt our desires and perceptions in ways that may not align with our own long-term interests or capacity for self-directed growth.

Beyond personalized content, AI's role in professional decision-making further complicates the notion of human agency. In fields ranging from medicine and law to finance and engineering, AI is increasingly deployed to assist human professionals, offering diagnostic insights, legal precedents, market analyses, and design optimizations. While these tools can augment human capabilities, leading to greater efficiency and accuracy, the delegation of crucial decisions to AI systems raises profound questions about the locus of control. If a doctor relies heavily on an AI's diagnostic suggestion, and that suggestion proves to be erroneous, where does the ultimate responsibility lie, and how much of the physician's own critical judgment has been ceded? Similarly, in the legal profession, if AI tools become indispensable for legal research and case strategy, how does this impact the lawyer's independent counsel and the client's right to human-led advocacy? The concern is not necessarily about outright replacement, but about a gradual dependence that might diminish the development and application of human expertise and critical thinking skills. A future where human professionals become highly skilled operators of AI systems, rather than independent decision-makers, would represent a significant shift in the nature of work and the role of human intellect.

The impact extends to our civic lives as well. AI is being employed in urban planning, resource allocation, and even predictive policing. While the promise is one of optimized governance and enhanced public safety, the potential for AI-driven decisions to reinforce existing societal biases or create new forms of discrimination is a significant ethical and practical challenge. If AI systems tasked with resource allocation in public services are trained on historical data that reflects past inequalities, their decisions could perpetuate those same inequities, even if unintentionally. Moreover, the opacity of many advanced AI systems means that the rationale behind such decisions may be difficult to understand or challenge, potentially undermining democratic accountability and the ability of citizens to influence the policies that govern them. The erosion of agency here could manifest as a feeling of powerlessness in the face of opaque, algorithmically driven governance, where individual circumstances and humanistic considerations are overlooked in favor of system-wide optimization.

Speculative scenarios paint a more extreme picture. Imagine futures where AI interfaces are so seamlessly integrated into our lives that they anticipate our needs and desires before we even articulate them, offering solutions and guidance that are undeniably beneficial but also implicitly steer our life choices. This could range from AI personal assistants that manage our health, finances, and social calendars with unparalleled efficiency, to AI companions that provide emotional support and conversational engagement. While these scenarios offer compelling visions of convenience and enhanced well-being, they also raise the specter of a passive existence, where the struggle, creativity, and inherent messiness of human experience, which often foster growth and self-discovery, are smoothed over by algorithmic perfection. In such a world, what would it mean to be an active agent in one's own life? Would the capacity for independent decision-making atrophy, much like an unused muscle?

The challenge is to navigate this evolving landscape proactively, ensuring that AI remains a tool that augments human capabilities and enhances our autonomy, rather than a force that diminishes it. This necessitates a multi-pronged approach, encompassing ethical guideline development, legal reform, and a conscious societal effort to preserve and cultivate human agency.

One crucial area of focus is the development of robust ethical guidelines for AI design and deployment. These guidelines should prioritize human well-being, fairness, and transparency. For instance, principles of "human-centric AI" emphasize that AI systems should be designed to serve human goals and values, with mechanisms for human oversight and control embedded from the outset. This involves not just avoiding harm, but actively fostering conditions that support human flourishing and self-determination. Ethical frameworks should also address the potential for AI to create new forms of dependency and to influence human behavior in ways that might be detrimental to individual autonomy. This might include guidelines on the responsible design of persuasive technologies, ensuring that AI-driven nudges are transparent and do not exploit cognitive vulnerabilities.

Legal reforms are equally vital. As AI systems become more sophisticated, existing legal frameworks, developed for a pre-AI era, may prove inadequate. Laws governing liability, intellectual property, and data privacy, for example, will need to be adapted to account for the unique characteristics of autonomous AI. Beyond these foundational areas, however, specific legal provisions may be required to safeguard human agency. This could include the right to explanation for AI-driven decisions that significantly impact individuals, ensuring that people can understand the basis of a decision and, where appropriate, appeal it. Furthermore, legal frameworks might need to establish clear boundaries for the autonomy granted to AI systems, particularly in high-stakes decision-making contexts. This could involve mandating "meaningful human control" over critical operations, defining what constitutes such control in various domains. The idea of an "AI Bill of Rights" has also gained traction, proposing specific rights related to algorithmic transparency, fairness, and protection from manipulative AI practices.

Beyond formal regulations, fostering a societal understanding of AI and its implications for human agency is paramount. Education initiatives can empower individuals to critically engage with AI technologies, understand their potential benefits and risks, and make informed choices about their use. Cultivating a culture of critical digital literacy, where individuals are encouraged to question algorithmic recommendations and seek out diverse perspectives, can act as a bulwark against passive consumption and algorithmic determinism. This also involves fostering dialogue and debate about the kind of future we want to build with AI, ensuring that technological development is guided by societal values and democratic principles, rather than solely by market forces or the pursuit of efficiency.

We must also consider the philosophical underpinnings of human agency in the face of increasingly capable artificial intelligences. What aspects of human experience are intrinsically valuable and worthy of preservation, even if they are less efficient than their AI counterparts? Is it the struggle of learning, the vulnerability of emotional connection, or the very act of making imperfect choices that defines our humanity? If AI can provide flawless logistical support, anticipate our every need, and even offer perfect companionship, what remains for us to do, and what makes our contributions uniquely human? These are not merely academic questions; they touch upon our understanding of purpose, meaning, and our place in the world.

The preservation of human agency in an AI-dominated world will likely hinge on our ability to maintain meaningful human control and oversight in critical domains. This means designing AI systems that are not only intelligent and efficient but also interpretable and accountable. It requires an ongoing commitment to ensuring that humans remain the ultimate arbiters of important decisions, with AI serving as a powerful assistant rather than an autonomous sovereign. The future of human agency is not predetermined by the capabilities of AI; rather, it will be shaped by the choices we make today in developing, deploying, and governing these transformative technologies. The goal must be to harness the immense power of AI to amplify human potential, expand our freedoms, and enhance our capacity for self-governance, ensuring that in an era of intelligent machines, humanity retains its central role as the author of its own destiny. This continuous process of adaptation and ethical reflection is crucial to ensure that as AI evolves, our own capacity for independent thought, meaningful action, and self-determination not only endures but flourishes.

AI vs. machine learning vs. deep learning

	AI	Machine learning	Deep learning
Optimal data volumes	Varying data volumes	Thousands of data points	Big data: millions of data points
Outputs	Anything from predictions to recommendations to decision-making	Numerical value, like a classification or score	Anything from numerical values to free-form elements, like free text and sound
How it works	Machines are programmed to mimic human activity with human-like accuracy	Uses various types of automated algorithms that learn to model functions and predict future actions from data	Uses neural networks that pass data through many processing layers to interpret data features and relationships
How it's managed	Algorithms require human oversight in order to function properly	Algorithms are directed by data analysts to examine specific variables in data sets	Algorithms are largely self-directed on data analysis once they're put into production

5
Professional Responsibility in the Age of AI

The legal profession, long characterized by rigorous analysis, meticulous research, and nuanced argumentation, is now experiencing a profound transformation driven by the integration of artificial intelligence. This evolution is not merely about adopting new software; it represents a fundamental shift in how legal professionals approach their work, promising unprecedented gains in efficiency and accuracy. Understanding the landscape of these emerging AI tools is the crucial first step in navigating the ethical terrain they present.

At the forefront of this technological wave are AI-powered legal research platforms. Traditionally, legal research involved sifting through vast volumes of case law, statutes, and regulations, often a painstaking and time-consuming endeavor. Modern AI-driven platforms, however, can process and analyze these immense datasets with remarkable speed and precision. They employ natural language processing (NLP) to understand complex legal queries, identify relevant precedents, and even surface arguments that a human researcher might overlook. These systems learn from user interactions and the underlying legal corpus, becoming increasingly adept at pinpointing the most pertinent information. For instance, a lawyer seeking to understand a specific point of law in a rapidly evolving area might input a query, and the AI platform could quickly return a curated list of the most relevant cases, cross-referenced with statutes and secondary sources, complete with summaries and even insights into how those precedents have been subsequently interpreted. This drastically reduces the time spent on foundational research, freeing up legal professionals to focus on higher-level strategic thinking and client counseling. The ability to identify subtle connections between disparate legal concepts or to quickly assess the weight of various authorities represents a significant advantage in a field where every piece of information can carry substantial weight.

Beyond raw research, document review has also been revolutionized by AI. In litigation, particularly in complex cases involving voluminous discovery, manually reviewing thousands, if not millions, of documents for relevance, privilege, or key information was an enormous undertaking, often requiring large teams of junior associates or paralegals. AI-powered document review software, often referred to as "eDiscovery" tools, can automate much of this process. These systems utilize machine learning algorithms to identify patterns, keywords, concepts, and even sentiment within documents. They can be trained to recognize specific types of information, flag privileged communications, or identify documents that are central to a particular legal issue. The efficiency gains are staggering; what once took weeks or months can now be accomplished in days or even hours, with a higher degree of consistency than human reviewers might achieve, particularly when dealing with repetitive tasks. This not only reduces costs for clients but also allows experienced legal professionals to allocate their time to tasks that require their unique human judgment and expertise, such as analyzing the strategic implications of the reviewed documents.

Contract analysis is another domain where AI is making significant inroads. Legal professionals spend a considerable amount of time reviewing, drafting, and managing contracts. AI tools designed for contract analysis can rapidly scan, extract, and interpret key clauses, terms, and obligations within these documents. They can identify deviations from standard templates, flag potentially risky provisions, and even compare clauses across multiple contracts to ensure consistency or to identify evolving industry standards. For example, in a due diligence process for a merger or acquisition, where hundreds or thousands of contracts need to be reviewed, AI can swiftly identify change-of-control clauses, indemnification provisions, or termination rights, providing a comprehensive overview of contractual risks and obligations in a fraction of the time it would take manually. Furthermore, these tools can assist in compliance efforts, ensuring that agreements adhere to regulatory requirements or internal policies. The ability to quickly synthesize information from complex legal documents and highlight areas of concern or non-compliance is invaluable, enabling legal teams to manage risk more effectively and to operate with greater speed and certainty.

Predictive litigation analytics represent a more forward-looking application of AI in law. These tools leverage historical data from court dockets, judicial decisions, and case outcomes to forecast the likely success of certain legal strategies, predict judicial behavior, or estimate the potential duration and cost of litigation. By analyzing patterns in past cases, such as how specific judges have ruled on particular types of motions or the typical settlement ranges for certain disputes, these analytics can provide lawyers with valuable insights to inform their case strategy, settlement negotiations, and even client advisement. For instance, a lawyer might use predictive analytics to assess the likelihood of a motion to dismiss being granted by a particular judge, or to estimate the probable damages awarded in a case with similar factual patterns. While these predictions are not deterministic-the law is inherently dynamic and human factors play a significant role-they offer a data-driven approach to litigation that can enhance strategic decision-making and manage client expectations more effectively. This represents a shift from purely experience-based intuition to a more empirically grounded approach to legal strategy.

The benefits of these AI tools extend beyond mere efficiency. By automating time-consuming and often repetitive tasks, they allow legal professionals to dedicate more cognitive resources to critical thinking, complex problem-solving, and client relationship management. The accuracy of AI in tasks like document review can surpass human capabilities due to its ability to maintain consistent application of learned parameters, reducing the margin for error inherent in human fatigue or oversight. For example, an AI trained to identify specific metadata within documents will perform that task with unwavering consistency, whereas a human reviewer might miss such details after hours of continuous work. This increased accuracy can lead to more robust legal arguments, better-informed advice, and ultimately, more favorable outcomes for clients.

Moreover, AI tools can democratize access to legal services. By reducing the cost and time associated with certain legal tasks, firms can potentially offer services at more accessible price points. This could enable individuals and small businesses, who might have previously found legal assistance prohibitively expensive, to obtain the representation and advice they need. The ability of AI to streamline processes means that fewer billable hours are required for foundational tasks, making legal expertise more attainable for a broader segment of the population.

The integration of these technologies also necessitates a re-evaluation of traditional legal education and training. Aspiring legal professionals will need to develop not only a deep understanding of substantive law but also a proficiency in leveraging AI tools. This includes understanding the capabilities and limitations of these systems, as well as the ethical considerations that accompany their use. The legal professional of the future will likely be a hybrid of traditional legal acumen and technological fluency, adept at harnessing AI to augment their own skills and deliver superior client service.

The development and adoption of these AI tools are ongoing and rapid. Legal technology companies are continuously innovating, expanding the functionalities of existing platforms and creating new solutions for previously unmet needs. From AI-powered legal chatbots that can answer basic client inquiries to sophisticated case management systems that optimize workflow and resource allocation, the scope of AI's application in the legal field continues to broaden. This dynamic environment demands that legal professionals remain adaptable, continually learning about new technologies and reassessing how they can be best utilized to uphold their professional responsibilities and serve their clients effectively. The era of AI in law is not a distant future; it is a present reality, and understanding its tools is the essential foundation for navigating the ethical considerations that will be explored in subsequent discussions.

The integration of Artificial Intelligence (AI) into the legal profession does not merely offer a suite of new tools; it fundamentally reshapes the bedrock ethical duties that define professional responsibility. Among these, the duties of competence and diligence stand out as particularly impacted, requiring a sophisticated reinterpretation in the age of AI. Lawyers and legal professionals are no longer solely responsible for their own knowledge and efforts; they now bear the augmented responsibility of understanding, managing, and critically evaluating the AI systems they deploy to assist them. This demands a proactive engagement with technology, moving beyond a passive reliance on its outputs to an active stewardship that ensures the AI serves, rather than subverts, the pursuit of justice and client welfare.

At its core, the duty of competence requires a legal professional to possess the legal knowledge, skill, thoroughness, and preparation reasonably necessary for the representation of a client. When AI tools enter the equation, this definition expands to encompass a crucial technological dimension. Competence now extends to understanding the capabilities and limitations of the AI systems being utilized. This is not an endorsement for every lawyer to become a computer scientist, but rather a call for a foundational literacy regarding the AI's function. For instance, if a lawyer uses an AI-powered legal research platform, competence dictates that they understand *how* the AI arrives at its results. Does it rely on keyword matching, semantic analysis, or a combination of both? What are its known blind spots? Could it miss a relevant case that uses different terminology but addresses the same legal principle? A lawyer who blindly trusts an AI's output without understanding its underlying methodology risks providing advice based on incomplete or inaccurate information, thereby breaching their duty of competence. The AI is a tool, not an oracle, and the lawyer remains the ultimate arbiter of its utility and accuracy.

This necessitates a commitment to ongoing education and training. The rapid evolution of AI means that what is cutting-edge today may be superseded tomorrow. Therefore, legal professionals must actively seek out opportunities to learn about new AI technologies relevant to their practice. This could involve attending webinars, participating in workshops focused on legal tech, reading industry publications, and engaging with vendors to understand the functionalities and limitations of the AI solutions they offer. The ABA Model Rules of Professional Conduct, for example, have increasingly acknowledged the importance of technological competence. Rule 1.1, Comment [8], explicitly states that a lawyer should keep abreast of changes in the law and its practice, including the benefits and risks associated with relevant technology. This implies that staying technologically current is not merely an advantage, but an ethical imperative. Failing to invest in this understanding leaves a lawyer vulnerable to errors and omissions that could have severe consequences for their clients.

"Just to clarify... am I supposed to be ethical, creative, or profitable today?"

executiveaiinstitute.com

Diligence, on the other hand, requires a lawyer to act with reasonable promptness and to dedicate the attention and effort necessary to represent a client effectively. AI tools promise to enhance diligence by automating time-consuming tasks, thereby allowing lawyers to be more thorough and responsive. However, the very efficiency AI offers can also present new challenges to this duty. Over-reliance on AI without proper oversight can lead to a superficial review or a lack of critical engagement, ironically undermining the diligence the technology is meant to foster.

Consider document review using AI. While AI can process vast quantities of documents far more quickly than humans, it is not infallible. An AI trained to identify privileged documents, for example, might miss a subtle indicator of privilege that a human reviewer, with a more nuanced understanding of context and intent, would recognize. Or, it might incorrectly flag a document as privileged when it is not. The diligent lawyer must therefore not only initiate the AI review process but also actively supervise and validate its results. This might involve reviewing a statistically significant sample of the AI's findings, cross-referencing critical documents, or employing human reviewers to scrutinize specific categories of documents flagged by the AI. The AI assists in the *process* of diligence, but the ultimate *responsibility* for thoroughness rests with the lawyer. The time saved by AI should be reinvested in this critical oversight, ensuring that the increased speed does not come at the cost of depth and accuracy.

Furthermore, the duty of diligence is intrinsically linked to the quality of the legal services provided. AI tools, when used appropriately, should enhance this quality. They can help identify a broader range of relevant precedents, uncover patterns that might otherwise be missed, and ensure greater consistency in tasks like contract review. However, a lawyer must critically evaluate the AI's output to ensure it genuinely improves the quality of service. If an AI tool consistently returns irrelevant search results or misinterprets key contractual clauses, its use could actually detract from the quality of representation. The lawyer has an ethical obligation to assess whether the AI is genuinely aiding their ability to provide competent and diligent representation, or if it is introducing new risks or inefficiencies. This requires a willingness to question the AI, to test its boundaries, and, if necessary, to revert to more traditional methods or seek alternative AI solutions if the current one is not meeting the required standards.

The ethical obligations surrounding competence and diligence in the context of AI also extend to the client. Lawyers have a duty to keep their clients reasonably informed about the status of their matter and to explain matters to the extent reasonably necessary to permit the client to make informed decisions. When AI is used in a client's representation, particularly in significant ways, transparency with the client becomes paramount. This doesn't necessarily mean detailing the exact algorithms or lines of code used, but rather explaining how AI is being leveraged to benefit their case, what the general nature of the AI's role is, and what safeguards are in place to ensure accuracy and security. For instance, a client whose case involves extensive document review might be informed that AI is being used to streamline the process, with human oversight to ensure thoroughness. Such transparency builds trust and allows clients to understand the value proposition of their legal representation in the modern technological landscape. It also helps manage client expectations regarding timelines and costs, as AI can influence both.

The responsibility to ensure AI use enhances, rather than compromises, the quality of legal services is perhaps the most critical aspect. This means lawyers must exercise sound professional judgment in selecting and deploying AI tools. Not every AI tool is appropriate for every legal task or every case. A lawyer must consider the specific context: the complexity of the legal issue, the volume of data involved, the client's budget, and the potential risks associated with AI errors. For example, using a highly sophisticated predictive analytics tool for a straightforward landlord-tenant dispute might be overkill and inefficient. Conversely, failing to employ AI for document review in a large-scale commercial litigation case could be seen as a failure of diligence if it leads to a less thorough review or significantly higher costs for the client due to the inefficiency of manual processes. The ethical lawyer is one who thoughtfully integrates AI as a strategic enhancement to their practice, rather than adopting it uncritically.

Moreover, the ethical duties of competence and diligence are intertwined with the duty of confidentiality. AI systems, especially those that learn and process data, can pose risks to client confidentiality. Lawyers must ensure that any AI tools they use are secure, that client data is protected, and that the AI vendor's data handling practices comply with ethical and legal standards. This includes understanding how the AI vendor uses data, whether it's for training purposes or shared with third parties. A breach of confidentiality, whether through a data hack or improper data handling by an AI provider, is a grave ethical violation. Therefore, competence in AI use must include competence in understanding and mitigating these data security and confidentiality risks. This involves due diligence in vetting AI vendors, understanding their privacy policies, and ensuring contractual protections are in place.

The concept of "competence" in the AI era also touches upon the lawyer's responsibility to understand potential biases embedded within AI systems. Many AI algorithms are trained on historical data, which can reflect societal biases related to race, gender, socioeconomic status, and other factors. If an AI legal research tool, for instance, has been trained on a dataset where certain groups were historically underrepresented in legal proceedings or outcomes, it might perpetuate these biases in its search results or predictions. A diligent and competent lawyer must be aware of this possibility and actively work to identify and mitigate any such biases. This might involve cross-referencing AI-generated information with sources that are less prone to bias, or specifically looking for AI tools that have been developed with fairness and bias mitigation as a core design principle. The lawyer's duty is to ensure that the use of AI does not inadvertently lead to discriminatory outcomes or prejudice against any party.

In essence, the ethical mandates of competence and diligence are not diminished by the advent of AI; rather, they are amplified and augmented. They demand a new form of professionalism that blends traditional legal acumen with a critical understanding of technological capabilities and limitations. Lawyers must embrace AI as a powerful adjunct to their skills, but always with a discerning eye and a firm grasp of their ultimate professional responsibilities to their clients and to the justice system. This requires a continuous learning mindset, a commitment to rigorous oversight, and a proactive approach to managing the ethical implications of technology in legal practice. The lawyer remains the conductor of the legal orchestra, and AI is but one instrument, albeit a powerful one, that must be played with skill, precision, and ethical awareness.

The integration of Artificial Intelligence (AI) into legal practice, while offering unprecedented efficiencies and insights, simultaneously introduces a complex web of responsibilities concerning client confidentiality and data security. The very nature of AI platforms, particularly those hosted on cloud infrastructure or developed by third-party vendors, necessitates a heightened awareness of how sensitive client information is handled, stored, and processed. Lawyers have a foundational ethical duty to safeguard the confidences and secrets of their clients, a duty that is not absolved but rather complicated by the adoption of AI tools. This involves a meticulous examination of the AI platforms being utilized, ensuring that their deployment does not inadvertently create vulnerabilities that could lead to unauthorized disclosure or access to client data.

One of the foremost concerns arises from the practice of uploading client-specific data into AI platforms, especially those that operate as Software-as-a-Service (SaaS) solutions. Legal professionals often input case details, internal documents, client communications, and other sensitive information into AI-powered research assistants, predictive coding tools, or even generative AI models to aid in analysis, drafting, or strategizing. The critical question becomes: where does this data reside, who has access to it, and how is it protected? Many AI platforms are designed to process data in the cloud, meaning the information is transferred from the lawyer's secure environment to the vendor's servers. This transmission and storage process introduces inherent risks. Unlike on-premise software where data remains under the direct control of the law firm, cloud-based AI platforms rely on the vendor's security infrastructure. A robust understanding of the vendor's security protocols, data encryption methods (both in transit and at rest), access controls, and data retention policies is therefore not merely prudent but an ethical imperative.

The duty of confidentiality, enshrined in ethical rules across jurisdictions, demands that lawyers not reveal information relating to the representation of a client unless the client gives informed consent, the disclosure is impliedly authorized to carry out the representation, or the disclosure is permitted by other ethical rules. When using AI platforms, lawyers must ensure that their use of these tools aligns with this duty. This means understanding whether the AI vendor uses client data for training its models. If a lawyer inputs confidential case details into an AI that then uses that data to improve its algorithms for other users, this could constitute a breach of confidentiality if not properly disclosed to and consented to by the client. Many AI vendors have terms of service that allow for the use of user-submitted data to enhance their services. Lawyers must scrutinize these terms, seeking assurances from vendors that client data will be treated as confidential and will not be used for training or shared with third parties without explicit authorization. In some instances, this may necessitate negotiating specific data processing agreements or service level agreements (SLAs) with AI providers to ensure adequate protections are in place.

Vetting AI vendors is a crucial step in mitigating these risks. This process should be as rigorous as the due diligence conducted when selecting any other third-party service provider that handles sensitive client information, such as IT support or e-discovery vendors. Key aspects to consider during vendor vetting include:

Firstly, a vendor's commitment to security certifications and compliance standards. Reputable AI vendors will likely hold certifications such as ISO 27001 for information security management, SOC 2 for data security and privacy, or HIPAA compliance if dealing with health-related information. These certifications indicate that the vendor has undergone independent audits and adheres to established best practices for data protection.

Secondly, the vendor's data breach history and incident response plan. Understanding how a vendor has handled past security incidents, if any, and the robustness of their plan for responding to future breaches is vital. A prompt and transparent response to a security incident can significantly limit the damage.

Thirdly, the contractual terms governing data

ownership, usage, and security. The service agreement should clearly define who owns the data uploaded to the platform, how the vendor may use that data (e.g., for system maintenance, improvement, or not at all), the security measures implemented, and the notification procedures in case of a data breach. Lawyers should seek clauses that specifically prohibit the vendor from using client data for any purpose other than providing the contracted service to that specific law firm, and that mandate the secure deletion or return of client data upon termination of the agreement.

Fourthly, the vendor's location and applicable data privacy laws. The jurisdiction in which the AI vendor is based and where the data is processed can have significant implications for data protection and privacy rights. Lawyers must consider whether these locations have robust data protection laws that align with their ethical obligations and client expectations.

The obligation to protect client data extends beyond the initial selection of an AI platform. Continuous monitoring and reassessment are necessary. The technological landscape, and thus the security threats, evolve rapidly. Lawyers must stay informed about potential vulnerabilities in the AI tools they use and any updates or changes to the vendor's security practices or terms of service. This might involve subscribing to vendor newsletters, monitoring industry security advisories, and periodically reviewing the vendor's compliance posture.

Moreover, the lawyer's own internal policies and procedures must be adapted to accommodate the use of AI. This includes providing adequate training to legal staff on the secure and ethical use of AI platforms, establishing clear guidelines on what types of client data can be uploaded, and implementing access controls to ensure that only authorized personnel can interact with the AI tools. For instance, a policy might stiprate that highly sensitive or particularly confidential client information should only be processed by AI platforms that offer end-to-end encryption and have explicit contractual guarantees of data privacy, or that certain types of data should be anonymized or de-identified before being uploaded.

The rise of generative AI models presents a unique set of challenges to confidentiality and data security. Unlike traditional AI tools designed for specific legal tasks, generative AI can produce novel content based on the prompts it receives. If a lawyer uses a public or commercially available generative AI model to draft a contract clause or a legal argument, and includes specific client facts or confidential strategy details in the prompt, those details could become part of the model's training data or be logged by the service provider. This could lead to the unintentional disclosure of confidential information to other users or to the AI provider. Consequently, lawyers must be extremely cautious about the information they input into generative AI prompts. Using enterprise-grade versions of these tools, which are specifically designed with enhanced privacy and security features for business use, and which often include strong contractual assurances about data handling, is highly recommended. These enterprise solutions typically ensure that user inputs are not used for model training and are kept confidential.

Furthermore, the concept of "competent representation" now inherently includes technological competence in safeguarding client data within AI-driven workflows. A lawyer who fails to take reasonable steps to protect client data when using AI platforms, leading to a breach, could be found to have violated their duty of competence and confidentiality. This means actively seeking out AI solutions that have robust security features and vetting vendors thoroughly. It also means understanding the limitations of the AI tools and not relying on them implicitly for data security. For example, simply using an AI tool that is labeled as "secure" is insufficient; the lawyer must understand *what* makes it secure and whether those measures are adequate for the specific client data being handled.

The implications of a data breach involving AI platforms can be severe, extending beyond professional discipline to include civil liability and significant reputational damage. Clients entrust their most sensitive information to lawyers with the expectation of absolute discretion and security. A breach resulting from the negligent use of an AI platform can erode this trust and lead to a loss of clients and business. Therefore, a proactive and diligent approach to data security and confidentiality when using AI is not just about adhering to ethical rules; it is fundamental to maintaining client trust and the integrity of the legal profession. This requires a continuous learning curve, adapting to new technologies while steadfastly upholding the core ethical obligations that define the practice of law. The lawyer's role as a guardian of client confidences remains paramount, and this guardianship must now extend to understanding and securing the digital ecosystems within which AI operates.

The responsibility to maintain client confidentiality and ensure data security when employing AI platforms also involves a critical examination of the AI's underlying architecture and data handling practices. It is not enough to simply trust the vendor's marketing claims; a deeper understanding is required. For instance, some AI platforms might claim to use "encrypted data," but this could refer to encryption only during transmission, leaving the data vulnerable once it reaches the server. Best practices dictate end-to-end encryption, meaning data is encrypted from the moment it leaves the lawyer's system until it is securely deleted or returned, and is only decrypted by authorized personnel. Furthermore, understanding the AI's data lifecycle management is crucial: how is data stored, for how long, and under what conditions is it purged? Are there audit trails available to track data access and processing? These are questions that legal professionals must be prepared to ask and that AI vendors must be prepared to answer transparently.

The ethical framework also demands that lawyers consider the potential for AI systems themselves to introduce vulnerabilities that may not be immediately apparent. Machine learning models, for example, can be susceptible to "adversarial attacks," where subtly manipulated inputs can cause the AI to misclassify data or produce incorrect outputs, potentially leading to a breach of confidentiality if, for instance, sensitive information is inadvertently revealed or miscategorized. While direct exploitation of such vulnerabilities to breach confidentiality might be sophisticated and rare, the general principle of understanding AI's inherent risks is part of a lawyer's evolving competence. This awareness informs the selection of AI tools and the necessary oversight mechanisms.

In practice, this translates to a tiered approach to AI deployment based on data sensitivity. For routine tasks involving less sensitive data, a standard AI platform with robust general security features might suffice. However, for matters involving highly confidential client information, such as trade secrets, personal health information, or sensitive financial data, lawyers should opt for AI solutions that offer the highest levels of security, including dedicated enterprise environments, stringent access controls, and explicit contractual guarantees of data privacy and non-use. This might also involve a careful assessment of whether the specific AI task *requires* the input of sensitive data in the first place. Can the desired outcome be achieved with anonymized or generalized data, thereby minimizing risk?

Furthermore, the duty of confidentiality extends to the communication *about* the use of AI with clients. While full technical disclosure of AI systems is neither necessary nor practical, lawyers must be transparent with clients about the general nature of AI tools being used in their representation, especially if the use of AI has a material impact on the representation, cost, or security of their information. This transparency is part of obtaining informed consent, particularly when sensitive data is involved. Clients have a right to know how their information is being handled and what measures are in place to protect it. Failing to inform clients about the use of AI, especially if it involves sharing their data with third-party platforms, could be seen as a breach of this duty of transparency, which is closely linked to confidentiality.

The legal profession's ethical guidelines are dynamic, adapting to technological advancements. As AI becomes more pervasive, regulatory bodies and bar associations are increasingly issuing guidance on the ethical use of AI. Lawyers must stay abreast of these developments, understanding how evolving rules and interpretations impact their obligations regarding confidentiality and data security. This includes understanding guidelines on data protection, cloud computing, and third-party vendor management as they apply to AI.

In summary, the integration of AI platforms into legal practice demands an unwavering commitment to client confidentiality and data security. This necessitates a thorough understanding of AI technologies, rigorous vendor vetting, robust contractual protections, clear internal policies, continuous monitoring, and transparent communication with clients. The lawyer's ethical obligation to protect client information is paramount, and this duty must be meticulously upheld in the AI-augmented legal landscape. The efficiency and insights offered by AI can only be ethically realized when they are underpinned by an uncompromised dedication to safeguarding the sensitive data entrusted to legal professionals. This is not merely a matter of compliance; it is the bedrock of client trust and professional integrity in the digital age.

The advent of artificial intelligence within the legal profession introduces a profound question: can an AI system itself be considered to be engaging in the unauthorized practice of law? This inquiry ventures beyond the established ethical quandaries of lawyer supervision or data security and probes the very essence of what constitutes legal practice. Traditionally, the "practice of law" has been understood as the application of legal principles and knowledge to specific factual situations, often involving the provision of legal advice, representation in legal matters, or the drafting of legal documents. These activities have, for centuries, been reserved for licensed attorneys, who are bound by professional oaths and subject to regulatory oversight. The rationale behind these restrictions is multifaceted: to protect the public from incompetent or unethical legal advice, to ensure access to justice, and to maintain the integrity and fairness of the legal system.

AI, particularly in its advanced forms, demonstrates a capacity to analyze vast amounts of legal data, identify patterns, predict outcomes, and even generate legal arguments or draft documents. When these capabilities are deployed directly to assist or advise individuals who would otherwise seek out a human lawyer, the boundaries of traditional legal practice begin to blur. Consider an AI-powered platform that, after receiving details of a client's dispute, generates a comprehensive legal memorandum outlining potential causes of action, relevant case law, and strategic recommendations. Such an output, if provided directly to a layperson without the intermediary of a licensed attorney, could arguably fall under the purview of legal advice. The challenge lies in how existing statutes and ethical rules, crafted in an era predating sophisticated AI, define and regulate the provision of legal services. Many jurisdictions define the practice of law broadly, encompassing providing legal advice, representation, and the drawing of legal instruments. AI systems that perform these functions, especially if they hold themselves out as providing legal solutions, may be seen as contravening these definitions, even if they are ultimately proprietary tools developed by licensed legal professionals or technology companies.

The core of the debate revolves around whether an AI, as a non-human entity, can be considered a "person" or an "attorney" under existing legal frameworks. Most statutes regulating the practice of law are implicitly or explicitly directed at human actors. An AI cannot, by its nature, be admitted to the bar, take an oath, or be subject to the disciplinary actions that a licensed attorney faces. Therefore, if an AI system is found to be practicing law, the question then becomes: who is responsible? Is it the developers of the AI, the company that markets it, or the end-user who deploys it? This raises complex questions of vicarious liability and oversight. If an AI provides faulty advice that leads to a client's detriment, attributing blame becomes a significant legal hurdle. Bar associations and regulatory bodies are grappling with how to adapt these existing rules to the reality of AI. Some approaches consider whether the AI is acting under the direct supervision of a licensed attorney. If an attorney uses an AI tool to assist in their practice, but the attorney retains ultimate responsibility for the advice and actions taken, it may be viewed as a permissible use of technology. However, if the AI operates with a degree of autonomy, providing advice or services directly to the public without meaningful human oversight, then it enters more precarious territory.

The regulatory response to AI in law is still in its nascent stages, with various jurisdictions taking different approaches. Some have begun to establish specific guidelines or pilot programs to test the ethical implications of AI-assisted legal services. For instance, certain bar associations have issued opinions clarifying that lawyers may use AI tools, provided they exercise diligent supervision and ensure that the AI's outputs are reviewed and validated by a licensed professional. These opinions often emphasize that the ultimate responsibility for client representation remains with the human attorney. Other jurisdictions are exploring the creation of new categories of legal service providers, or perhaps even "legal technician" roles, that might leverage AI capabilities under a different regulatory regime. The aim is to harness the efficiency gains of AI while still safeguarding consumer protection.

A critical distinction often made is between AI as a tool for legal professionals and AI as a direct provider of legal services to the public. Tools like AI-powered legal research platforms, document review software, or contract analysis programs that assist lawyers in their work are generally not seen as engaging in the unauthorized practice of law, provided they are used appropriately by licensed attorneys. The concern arises when AI platforms are marketed directly to consumers, offering to solve their legal problems without the involvement of a lawyer. Examples might include AI systems that help individuals fill out court forms, navigate complex regulatory processes, or even provide tailored legal guidance based on user inputs. If these systems are making legal judgments, interpreting statutes, or advising on courses of action, they tread on ground traditionally occupied by attorneys.

The definition of "legal advice" itself becomes a focal point. Is it legal advice when an AI provides factual information about the law, or does it cross the line when it interprets that law in relation to a specific factual scenario and recommends a course of action? Many would argue that the latter constitutes legal advice. For instance, an AI that can explain what a statute says is likely providing legal information. However, an AI that analyzes a user's employment contract and advises them whether they have grounds for wrongful termination is likely providing legal advice. The challenge for regulators is to draw a clear and enforceable line between these two scenarios, especially as AI capabilities become more sophisticated and nuanced.

Furthermore, the issue of "holding out" as a provider of legal services is pertinent. If an AI platform advertises its ability to provide legal solutions, offer legal counsel, or represent clients, it may be deemed to be engaging in the unauthorized practice of law, irrespective of its internal functioning. The public perception and marketing of such services are crucial factors in regulatory assessment. The legal profession has a vested interest in ensuring that any entity offering legal services meets the requisite standards of competence, ethical conduct, and accountability. Allowing AI systems to operate in this space without clear oversight could undermine these protections.

The development of AI-powered legal services also intersects with the concept of access to justice. Proponents argue that AI can democratize legal services, making them more affordable and accessible to individuals who cannot afford traditional legal representation. AI chatbots that offer basic legal information or assist with simple legal tasks could indeed fill a critical gap. However, the concern remains that if these systems are not adequately regulated, they could lead to consumers receiving substandard or misleading legal guidance, potentially exacerbating their legal problems. The ethical challenge is to balance the potential benefits of AI in expanding access to justice with the imperative of protecting consumers from harm.

Regulatory bodies are actively considering various solutions. One approach is to create specific licensing or certification regimes for AI legal service providers. This could involve requiring AI developers or companies to meet certain standards of accuracy, security, and ethical operation, perhaps overseen by a designated regulatory authority. Another possibility is to expand the scope of existing regulations to explicitly address AI. This might involve amending statutes or ethical rules to define what constitutes the "practice of law by an AI" and establish clear lines of responsibility. For example, regulations could mandate that any AI providing legal advice must be directly supervised by a licensed attorney, who bears ultimate responsibility for the accuracy and appropriateness of the AI's output.

The role of the supervising attorney is crucial in distinguishing permissible AI use from unauthorized practice. If an AI is merely a sophisticated tool that a licensed attorney uses to enhance their practice- such as a highly advanced research assistant or a predictive analytics tool- then it is unlikely to be considered the unauthorized practice of law. The attorney remains in control, reviews the AI's output, and provides the final advice or service to the client. However, if the AI operates with a significant degree of autonomy, making critical legal judgments or providing direct advice to clients without meaningful human intervention, then it may be crossing the line. This necessitates a careful examination of the workflow and the degree of human oversight involved in any AI-driven legal service.

Consider the evolution of legal practice management software. Early iterations were simple tools for billing and calendaring. Today, sophisticated AI-powered platforms can draft discovery requests, analyze opposing counsel's filings, and even suggest settlement strategies. The key differentiator is that these remain *tools* for lawyers. The attorney remains the principal actor, making the decisions and bearing the responsibility. The challenge with AI arises when the AI itself begins to perform functions that have historically been the exclusive domain of attorneys, particularly when directed at the public.

The ethical considerations also extend to the transparency of AI's role. Consumers should be informed when they are interacting with an AI system for legal services, rather than a human attorney. This transparency is vital for managing expectations and ensuring that individuals understand the nature and limitations of the advice they are receiving. Without such transparency, a consumer might mistakenly believe they are receiving advice from a qualified legal professional, leading to a false sense of security.

The debate over the unauthorized practice of law by AI is not merely a theoretical exercise; it has profound implications for the future of legal services, consumer protection, and the very structure of the legal profession. As AI continues to advance, legal professionals, regulators, and policymakers must engage in a proactive and ongoing dialogue to develop frameworks that embrace technological innovation while upholding the core principles of justice and public trust. This includes defining the boundaries of AI's role, establishing clear lines of accountability, and ensuring that the pursuit of efficiency and access to justice does not compromise the quality and integrity of legal representation. The legal system must evolve to accommodate these new realities, ensuring that technology serves the cause of justice rather than undermining it. The question of who can "practice law" in the age of AI is one that will continue to shape legal ethics and regulation for years to come.

Furthermore, the question of AI engaging in the unauthorized practice of law is intricately tied to the concept of "competence." Ethical rules universally require lawyers to be competent, which includes understanding the legal, factual, and technical aspects of the matters they handle. While competence traditionally focused on legal knowledge and analytical skills, it is increasingly understood to encompass technological proficiency, especially when technology plays a significant role in service delivery. If an AI system is designed to provide legal analysis or advice, the developers and deployers have an ethical obligation to ensure its competence. This means rigorously testing the AI for accuracy, reliability, and freedom from bias. A system that consistently produces flawed legal analysis or incorrect advice could be seen as not only engaging in the unauthorized practice of law but also doing so incompetently, thus posing a direct threat to the public.

The potential for AI to be trained on biased data is a significant concern in this regard. If an AI's legal analysis is influenced by historical biases present in the data it was trained on- for example, if it disproportionately advises against certain demographic groups in particular types of cases- then its outputs could perpetuate or even exacerbate existing societal inequalities. This raises serious ethical questions about fairness and equal access to justice. An AI system that is not demonstrably fair and unbiased, and which provides legal guidance based on discriminatory patterns, would not only be engaging in questionable practice but doing so in a manner that fundamentally undermines the principles of justice that the legal profession is sworn to uphold.

The interaction between AI and regulatory bodies is also evolving. As AI tools become more sophisticated, regulatory bodies are seeking ways to monitor and audit them. This could involve requiring AI providers to submit their systems for review, disclose their algorithms and training data, or undergo periodic performance assessments. Such oversight is crucial to ensure that AI systems operating in the legal domain adhere to ethical standards and do not engage in unauthorized practice. The challenge here lies in the proprietary nature of many AI systems and the difficulty of fully understanding and validating complex algorithms. However, without some form of effective oversight, the risks associated with AI in law could be substantial.

In considering the unauthorized practice of law by AI, it is also important to distinguish between AI providing legal information and AI providing legal advice. Legal information generally refers to factual statements about the law or legal procedures. For example, an AI that can explain the steps involved in filing for divorce or provide a link to a relevant statute is likely providing legal information. This is often considered permissible, and many websites offer such information. However, legal advice involves the application of legal principles to a specific set of facts and offering a recommendation on how to proceed. If an AI analyzes a person's situation and advises them, "based on these facts, you have a strong case for breach of contract and should sue," that is legal advice. Drawing this distinction is paramount for regulators trying to define the boundaries of AI's role in the legal landscape.

The implications of an AI providing incorrect legal advice are severe. Unlike a human attorney who carries malpractice insurance and is subject to disciplinary action, an AI system and its creators might operate with limited recourse for the affected individual. This raises questions about consumer protection and the availability of remedies when AI-driven legal services prove to be inadequate or harmful. Ensuring that consumers have access to recourse, whether through direct liability of the AI provider, mandatory insurance, or other mechanisms, is a critical component of any regulatory framework.

The legal profession itself is not monolithic, and different types of legal services are subject to varying degrees of regulation. For instance, the provision of legal advice to individuals in contentious matters is typically more stringently regulated than, for example, the provision of general legal information or the automation of routine legal processes. AI tools that automate the generation of standard legal documents, such as simple wills or incorporation papers, might be less problematic if they are presented as templates or require significant input and review by the end-user. However, even in these cases, if the AI presents itself as offering tailored legal solutions without clear disclaimers, it could still be seen as venturing into unauthorized practice.

The future regulatory landscape will likely involve a hybrid approach, combining existing legal frameworks with new regulations specifically tailored to AI. This could include requirements for AI transparency, mandatory human oversight for certain types of AI-driven legal services, and clear accountability mechanisms for AI providers. The ongoing evolution of AI technology means that regulators will need to remain agile and adaptable, continuously reassessing and updating rules to keep pace with technological advancements. Ultimately, the goal is to harness the power of AI to improve access to justice and enhance legal services, while simultaneously safeguarding the public from the potential risks associated with the unauthorized or incompetent practice of law, whether by human or artificial intelligence.

The advent of sophisticated artificial intelligence in legal practice undeniably reshapes the landscape of professional services. Yet, as we integrate these powerful tools, a fundamental principle must remain sacrosanct: the enduring, indeed *irreplaceable*, role of human judgment and oversight. AI systems, for all their analytical prowess and data-processing capabilities, operate without consciousness, ethical grounding, or the capacity for genuine empathy. They can identify patterns, suggest strategies, and even draft arguments with remarkable speed and efficiency, but they cannot possess the nuanced understanding of human context, the moral compass, or the ultimate responsibility that defines professional integrity in the legal domain. Therefore, the ethical imperative for legal professionals is clear: to remain the ultimate decision-makers, critically assessing every AI-generated insight and ensuring that technology functions not as a replacement, but as a sophisticated augmenter of their professional responsibility and ethical practice.

At its core, legal practice is more than the application of rules to facts; it is an exercise in human-centered judgment.

Lawyers are entrusted with guiding clients through complex and often emotionally charged situations. They must not only understand the law but also interpret its application within the unique circumstances of each case, considering the client's personal objectives, values, and the broader societal implications of their advice. AI can process vast datasets of case law, statutory provisions, and procedural rules, and it can even predict potential outcomes with a degree of statistical probability. However, it cannot fathom the unspoken anxieties of a client facing foreclosure, the moral dilemma of whistle blowing, or the delicate balance required in negotiating a settlement that preserves crucial relationships. These are inherently human considerations that demand the experience, intuition, and ethical reasoning of a qualified professional.

The ethical rules governing the legal profession universally mandate competence. While historically this meant a deep knowledge of substantive and procedural law, in the age of AI, it increasingly encompasses a duty to understand and appropriately utilize relevant technological tools. Crucially, this also includes a responsibility to critically evaluate the outputs of those tools. A lawyer relying on an AI-generated legal brief, for instance, cannot simply copy and paste it into a court filing. They must meticulously review its logic, verify its factual assertions, ensure its arguments are legally sound and ethically presented, and confirm that it aligns with the client's specific goals and the lawyer's professional judgment. Failing to do so transforms a powerful assistant into a potential conduit for errors, misrepresentations, or even ethical breaches. This due diligence is not merely good practice; it is a non-negotiable aspect of maintaining professional responsibility.

Consider the scenario of AI-driven predictive analytics in litigation. An AI might analyze thousands of past cases involving similar fact patterns and predict a certain percentage of success for a particular legal strategy. While this data-driven insight can be invaluable, it does not account for novel legal arguments, the persuasive power of a particular advocate, the specific biases of a judge or jury, or the client's personal tolerance for risk. A human lawyer must weigh these predictive probabilities against the qualitative factors unique to their case and their client. They must then translate these complex considerations into actionable advice, often needing to explain to the client why a statistically favorable outcome might not be the best course of action for them personally, or why a less predictable but ethically superior path should be pursued. This nuanced communication and strategic tailoring of advice is a hallmark of professional judgment that AI cannot replicate.

Furthermore, the concept of "competence" extends to understanding the limitations and potential biases of AI systems themselves. AI models are trained on data, and if that data reflects historical societal biases- whether related to race, gender, socioeconomic status, or any other factor- the AI's outputs may perpetuate or even amplify those biases. A lawyer has an ethical obligation to be aware of this potential and to actively mitigate it. This might involve seeking out AI systems that have undergone rigorous bias testing and mitigation, or it might involve critically scrutinizing AI-generated advice for any signs of algorithmic discrimination. The lawyer must act as a bulwark against the uncritical propagation of biased outcomes, ensuring that the pursuit of efficiency does not come at the cost of fairness and justice.

The duty of zealous advocacy, a cornerstone of legal ethics, also underscores the need for human oversight. While AI can help construct compelling arguments, the advocacy itself-the art of persuasion, the understanding of a courtroom's dynamics, the ability to respond to unforeseen challenges in real-time-remains a profoundly human endeavor. A lawyer must be able to adapt their strategy on the fly, to read the room, and to connect with judges and juries on an intellectual and emotional level. AI can provide the research and draft the opening statement, but it cannot deliver it with conviction, respond to a judge's unexpected question with legal acumen and poise, or pivot a defense when new evidence emerges mid-trial. These are skills honed through years of experience, ethical training, and an understanding of human psychology.

The supervisory responsibilities of senior attorneys over junior colleagues and staff are also amplified in the context of AI. Just as a partner must review and approve the work of an associate, so too must they review and approve the work generated or assisted by AI. This oversight ensures that the AI is being used appropriately, that its outputs are being scrutinized for accuracy and ethical compliance, and that the ultimate legal advice provided to the client is sound and reflects professional judgment. This layered approach to responsibility is essential for maintaining the integrity of legal services and protecting clients from the potential pitfalls of unchecked technological application.

The legal profession is also bound by strict confidentiality obligations. While AI tools can assist in managing and analyzing large volumes of client data, lawyers must ensure that the use of these tools does not inadvertently compromise client confidentiality. This involves understanding how the AI system handles data, where it is stored, who has access to it, and whether it is being used for training future models without proper anonymization or consent. The lawyer's duty of confidentiality extends to the technological means by which legal services are delivered. Therefore, maintaining professional judgment involves a thorough understanding of the cybersecurity and data privacy implications of any AI tool employed, and ensuring that the tool's use aligns with these fundamental ethical obligations.

Moreover, the ethical duty of candor toward the

tribunal requires lawyers to present information truthfully and to avoid misleading the court. If an AI system generates a legal argument or cites case law that is inaccurate or has been superseded, a lawyer who presents this without verification would be in violation of this duty. The AI might flag a relevant case, but it cannot inherently distinguish between a binding precedent and persuasive authority, or between a case that has been overturned and one that remains good law, without explicit programming and rigorous oversight. The lawyer, therefore, must possess the judgment to assess the relevance and accuracy of all information presented to the court, regardless of its source.

The development of AI in law also presents a continuous learning curve for legal professionals. Staying competent in this rapidly evolving field means not only understanding how to use AI tools but also staying abreast of the ethical guidelines and best practices that emerge as regulators and bar associations grapple with these new technologies. This commitment to lifelong learning is crucial. A lawyer who remains technologically stagnant risks becoming ethically deficient by failing to employ tools that could enhance client service, or by misusing tools they do not fully understand. Professional judgment, in this context, includes the wisdom to know when and how to embrace new technologies responsibly.

The human element of lawyering also encompasses the ability to provide comfort, reassurance, and a sense of partnership to clients. Legal matters are often daunting, and the lawyer's role extends beyond the purely technical to that of a trusted advisor and advocate. A lawyer can empathize with a client's situation, offer moral support, and build a relationship based on trust and mutual respect. AI, while capable of processing information, cannot replicate this human connection. The ability to convey empathy, to reassure a client during a difficult period, and to be a steadfast ally is a critical component of professional service that remains firmly within the realm of human judgment and interaction.

Furthermore, the practice of law involves an inherent degree of ethical discretion. There are often multiple legally permissible paths a case can take, and the choice between them may depend on a lawyer's professional judgment, considering factors such as the client's best interests, the potential for settlement, and the broader implications for justice. AI might be programmed to optimize for a specific outcome, such as winning a case at all costs. However, a human lawyer must also consider the ethical implications of their chosen strategy, the potential impact on the administration of justice, and their duty to the legal system as a whole. This ethical discretion, the capacity to choose the "right" path among legally permissible options, is a hallmark of professional responsibility that AI cannot exercise.

The ongoing discourse surrounding AI in law necessitates a continuous re-evaluation of professional responsibility. As AI capabilities advance, the lines between augmentation and delegation will continue to blur, demanding ever-greater vigilance from legal professionals. The critical assessment of AI outputs is not a one-time task but an ongoing process. It requires lawyers to maintain a healthy skepticism, to ask probing questions about the AI's methodologies and limitations, and to be prepared to override the AI's suggestions when their professional judgment dictates. This active engagement ensures that AI remains a subservient tool, enhancing rather than undermining the lawyer's ability to uphold their ethical obligations and deliver high-quality legal services.

In conclusion, while the integration of AI into legal practice promises unprecedented efficiencies and analytical power, it simultaneously magnifies the importance of human judgment and oversight. Legal professionals must embrace these technological advancements with a clear understanding of their role: to leverage AI as a sophisticated instrument, while never relinquishing their ultimate responsibility for ethical practice, sound judgment, and the well-being of their clients. The human lawyer remains the indispensable fiduciary, the ethical arbiter, and the trusted advisor, whose professional responsibility is augmented, but never supplanted, by the capabilities of artificial intelligence. This careful balance is essential for ensuring that technology serves the noble aims of justice and the enduring principles of the legal profession.

Professional responsibility in the age of AI:

- *Human judgment, ethics, and empathy remain essential and irreplaceable in legal practice.*
- *AI tools function as augmentations to human capability, not as replacements for professional decision-making.*
- *A duty of competence now includes understanding how to properly use and critically evaluate AI technologies.*
- *Lawyers must perform meticulous due diligence on all AI-generated content before it is applied or submitted.*
- *There is a professional responsibility to actively mitigate bias within AI tools to ensure fairness and equal access to justice.*
- *Accountability mechanisms must be clear, ensuring consumer protection and recourse if AI advice is inadequate or harmful.*
- *Professionals must strictly distinguish between general AI-provided legal information and the regulated practice of giving specific legal advice.*

6
National Perspectives
India's AI and Legal Landscape

India's journey towards becoming a global leader in Artificial Intelligence is marked by a proactive and multifaceted national strategy, underpinned by a series of ambitious policy initiatives and significant governmental investments. Recognizing AI's transformative potential across economic and social spheres, the Indian government has articulated a clear vision: to leverage AI as a catalyst for inclusive growth, innovation, and enhanced citizen welfare. This strategic foresight is manifested in various national roadmaps and policy frameworks designed to foster robust AI research, development, and widespread adoption across diverse sectors of the economy and public service. The overarching goal is to position India at the forefront of AI innovation, not merely as a consumer of technology, but as a significant contributor to its global advancement.

At the heart of India's AI strategy is the recognition that a strong foundation in research and development is paramount. Initiatives like the establishment of the National Centre for Artificial Intelligence (NCAI) signify a commitment to creating dedicated hubs for cutting-edge AI research. These centres are envisioned to bring together academia, industry, and government stakeholders to collaborate on solving complex problems and advancing the frontiers of AI knowledge. The focus extends beyond theoretical research to practical applications, aiming to translate groundbreaking discoveries into tangible solutions that address India's specific developmental challenges, from healthcare and agriculture to education and smart cities. The emphasis is on creating an ecosystem where innovation can flourish, supported by adequate funding, state-of-the-art infrastructure, and access to vast datasets.

Furthermore, India's approach to AI is deeply intertwined with its digital transformation agenda. The National Digital India Programme, a flagship initiative, lays the groundwork for a digitally empowered society and knowledge economy. AI is seen as a crucial component of this broader digital ecosystem, capable of enhancing the efficiency and effectiveness of government services, personalizing educational experiences, and improving healthcare outcomes. Policies are being framed to ensure that AI adoption is inclusive, reaching even the most remote and underserved populations. This involves developing AI-powered solutions that are accessible, affordable, and tailored to the local context, thereby ensuring that the benefits of AI are broadly distributed and contribute to socio-economic equity.

A key element of India's AI policy is the development of a skilled workforce. Recognizing that the successful implementation of AI technologies hinges on the availability of talent, the government has launched several programs aimed at upskilling and reskilling the existing workforce and nurturing future AI experts. These initiatives include introducing AI and data science courses in educational institutions, offering specialized training programs for professionals, and promoting public-private partnerships to bridge the skill gap. The objective is not only to produce AI researchers and developers but also to equip individuals across various sectors with the foundational understanding and capabilities to work alongside AI systems, thereby fostering a culture of human-AI collaboration.

The National AI Strategy also places a significant emphasis on ethical considerations and responsible AI development. While the pursuit of innovation is central, there is a concurrent focus on ensuring that AI technologies are developed and deployed in a manner that is fair, transparent, accountable, and respects human rights and privacy. This commitment to ethical AI is crucial for building public trust and ensuring the sustainable growth of AI in the country. Discussions are ongoing regarding regulatory frameworks that can guide the ethical use of AI, addressing potential biases, ensuring data privacy, and establishing clear lines of accountability for AI-driven decisions. The aim is to create an environment where AI can be a force for good, contributing positively to society without exacerbating existing inequalities or creating new ethical dilemmas.

India's AI strategy is not a static document but an evolving framework that adapts to the rapidly changing technological landscape. The government has shown a willingness to engage with a broad spectrum of stakeholders, including industry leaders, academic institutions, civil society organizations, and international partners, to gather diverse perspectives and refine its policies. This collaborative approach ensures that the national AI strategy remains relevant, responsive, and aligned with both domestic needs and global best practices. The vision is to build a self-reliant India in AI, capable of competing on the global stage while also using AI to solve its unique challenges and improve the lives of its citizens.

The "National Strategy for Artificial Intelligence - National AI Hubs" document, released by NITI Aayog (National Institution for Transforming India), serves as a foundational blueprint for this vision. It outlines the ambition to establish India as a global hub for AI research and innovation, focusing on sectors with the potential for significant socio-economic impact. The strategy emphasizes a "whole-of-government" approach, advocating for inter-ministerial coordination and collaboration to drive AI adoption across various government departments and public services. Key sectors identified for priority development include healthcare, agriculture, education, smart cities, smart mobility, and cybersecurity. For instance, in healthcare,

AI is envisioned to aid in diagnostics, drug discovery, and personalized treatment plans, while in agriculture, it can optimize crop yields, predict weather patterns, and manage resources more effectively.

The strategy also delves into the critical aspect of data availability and management. Recognizing that AI models are heavily reliant on data, significant attention is being paid to creating robust data infrastructure, promoting data sharing mechanisms, and establishing data governance frameworks. This includes developing standards for data collection, storage, and anonymization to ensure both the quality of data and the protection of privacy. Initiatives like the National Data Sharing and Accessibility Policy aim to facilitate access to government-held data for research and innovation purposes, while also ensuring that sensitive information is handled with utmost care and security. The goal is to democratize access to data, thereby empowering researchers and developers to build more sophisticated and impactful AI applications.

Furthermore, the Indian government has been actively promoting AI adoption within the startup ecosystem. Various incubators, accelerators, and funding programs have been launched to support AI-centric startups, providing them with the necessary resources, mentorship, and market access. This focus on fostering entrepreneurship is crucial for driving innovation and creating new AI-driven products and services that can cater to both domestic and international markets. By nurturing a vibrant startup culture, India aims to translate its research capabilities into commercial success and create a dynamic AI industry.

The narrative surrounding India's AI strategy is one of ambitious growth, strategic foresight, and a commitment to responsible innovation. It is a recognition that in the 21st century, AI is not just a technological advancement but a fundamental driver of economic competitiveness and societal progress. The various policy initiatives and investments reflect a concerted effort to build a comprehensive ecosystem that supports the entire AI lifecycle, from fundamental research and talent development to application and deployment. This national vision is anchored in the belief that by harnessing the power of AI effectively and ethically, India can address its developmental challenges, enhance its global standing, and create a more prosperous and equitable future for all its citizens. The ongoing evolution of these policies, driven by continuous learning and stakeholder engagement, will be crucial in shaping India's AI trajectory in the years to come. The emphasis on specific sectors also highlights a pragmatic approach, prioritizing areas where AI can yield the most significant and immediate benefits for the nation, ensuring that the pursuit of advanced technology is always linked to tangible improvements in the lives of its people. This structured approach, coupled with a forward-looking perspective, positions India to navigate the complexities of the AI revolution with confidence and purpose. The strategy is dynamic, constantly seeking to integrate feedback and adapt to the rapidly evolving global AI landscape, ensuring that India remains at the cutting edge of this transformative technology. The emphasis on democratizing access to data and fostering a strong startup ecosystem further underscores a commitment to broad-based innovation, rather than concentrating AI development within a few select entities. This inclusive approach is vital for unlocking the full potential of AI for the benefit of all segments of Indian society.

The Indian government has consistently articulated its ambition to leverage Artificial Intelligence as a key enabler of economic growth and social development. This vision is not merely aspirational; it is backed by a robust framework of policies and initiatives designed to foster a conducive environment for AI research, development, and adoption. The national AI strategy recognizes the dual imperative of advancing technological capabilities while ensuring that these advancements translate into tangible benefits for the populace. A cornerstone of this approach is the emphasis on creating an "AI for All" paradigm, where the transformative power of AI is harnessed to address societal challenges and improve the quality of life for every citizen.

Key policy documents and pronouncements, such as those from NITI Aayog, have laid out a roadmap that prioritizes specific sectors where AI can have a profound impact. These include healthcare, agriculture, education, smart cities, smart mobility, and cybersecurity. In healthcare, for instance, the strategy aims to utilize AI for early disease detection, personalized treatment plans, and optimizing healthcare delivery systems. This could involve AI-powered diagnostic tools that can analyze medical images with high accuracy, thereby assisting doctors in making quicker and more informed diagnoses. Similarly, in agriculture, AI is seen as a critical tool for enhancing productivity and sustainability. Predictive analytics can help farmers make informed decisions about crop planning, irrigation, and pest management, while AI-driven robotics can automate tasks like harvesting and soil analysis.

The commitment to developing a skilled AI workforce is another critical pillar of India's national strategy. Recognizing that human capital is essential for driving AI innovation, the government has initiated programs to integrate AI and data science education into academic curricula at various levels. This includes the development of undergraduate and postgraduate programs, specialized training modules for professionals, and initiatives to promote lifelong learning in AI-related fields. The aim is to equip a generation of Indians with the skills necessary to develop, deploy, and manage AI technologies, thereby ensuring India's competitiveness in the global AI landscape. Collaborations with leading universities and research institutions, both domestic and international, are being fostered to facilitate knowledge exchange and capacity building.

Furthermore, India's AI strategy places a strong emphasis on ethical considerations and the responsible development of AI technologies. The government acknowledges the potential risks associated with AI, including issues of bias, privacy, security, and accountability. Consequently, significant attention is being paid to developing a robust ethical framework and regulatory guidelines that will govern the design, deployment, and use of AI systems. This includes promoting transparency in AI algorithms, ensuring fairness in AI-driven decision-making, and establishing clear mechanisms for redressal in case of adverse outcomes. The goal is to foster public trust in AI and ensure that its development aligns with democratic values and human rights. The establishment of bodies and committees to deliberate on AI ethics and governance further underscores this commitment.

The government's role extends to actively promoting AI adoption across various sectors through policy interventions, funding support, and the creation of enabling infrastructure. This includes initiatives aimed at fostering a vibrant AI startup ecosystem, providing access to computing resources, and facilitating the availability of high-quality datasets for research and development. Public-private partnerships are a crucial element of this strategy, bringing together the strengths of government, industry, and academia to accelerate AI innovation and deployment. By creating an ecosystem that supports the entire AI value chain, India aims to position itself as a global leader in AI research, development, and application. The focus on building national AI capabilities is also aligned with the broader goal of digital transformation and the creation of a knowledge-based economy. The strategy is not merely about adopting AI but about building indigenous capabilities and fostering a spirit of innovation that can address India's unique challenges and opportunities. This proactive and comprehensive approach underscores India's commitment to harnessing the power of AI for sustainable and inclusive growth. The dynamic nature of the strategy ensures that it remains responsive to the ever-evolving technological landscape and the emerging opportunities and challenges in the field of artificial intelligence.

The Indian legal system, a vast and complex edifice built over centuries, is beginning to witness the subtle yet significant integration of Artificial Intelligence (AI). This infusion of technology is not aimed at replacing the human element that is so critical to justice, but rather at augmenting the capabilities of legal professionals and improving the overall efficiency and accessibility of the judicial process. The journey of AI in the Indian legal landscape is still in its nascent stages, marked by cautious experimentation and a growing recognition of its potential to streamline operations, enhance research, and potentially even improve the predictability of legal outcomes. The underlying principle is to leverage AI as a powerful tool to support the existing structures, thereby fostering a more responsive and equitable justice delivery mechanism for all citizens.

One of the most visible areas where AI is making inroads is in the realm of **case management and administrative efficiency**. Court dockets across India are notoriously overburdened, leading to significant delays in the resolution of cases. AI-powered systems are being explored and, in some instances, implemented to automate routine administrative tasks that consume valuable time for judges and court staff. This includes the organization of case files, scheduling of hearings, generation of notices, and the management of case progression. Imagine a system that can automatically assign a case to the appropriate bench based on its subject matter, flag upcoming deadlines, and send out timely notifications to all involved parties. Such a system, by reducing the manual effort involved in these processes, can free up judicial resources to focus on the substantive aspects of adjudication. Furthermore, AI can assist in data entry and management, ensuring greater accuracy and consistency in legal records. The ability of AI to process and categorize large volumes of information rapidly can be instrumental in managing the sheer volume of litigation that the Indian courts handle daily. This administrative efficiency, while not directly related to the core judicial function of judging, is a crucial enabler for timely justice, as it removes logistical bottlenecks that can otherwise impede the progress of legal proceedings. The development of integrated digital platforms, where AI plays a role in organizing and retrieving information, is a key step towards modernizing court administration. These platforms can offer a centralized repository of case information, accessible to authorized personnel, thereby improving transparency and accountability. The ultimate goal is to create a seamless workflow that minimizes human error and maximizes operational speed, allowing the legal system to function with greater agility.

Legal research, a cornerstone of effective legal practice and judicial decision-making, is another domain ripe for AI-driven transformation. Traditionally, legal research in India involves sifting through vast amounts of statutes, case law, regulations, and scholarly articles, often found in physical libraries or through cumbersome digital archives. AI-powered legal research platforms can revolutionize this process by enabling legal professionals to conduct searches with unprecedented speed and precision. These tools can understand natural language queries, identify relevant precedents even when the exact keywords are not used, and even predict the likelihood of a particular argument being successful based on historical data. For instance, a lawyer preparing a brief on a complex property dispute could use an AI tool to quickly find all relevant Supreme Court and High Court judgments, analyze their reasoning, and identify dissenting opinions that might support their client's case. These systems can go beyond simple keyword matching by employing techniques like semantic search, which understands the meaning and context of the query, and machine learning algorithms that learn from user interactions to refine search results over time. The ability to quickly access and analyze relevant legal information can significantly reduce the time and cost associated with legal research, making legal services more accessible. For judges, this means having access to a more comprehensive and nuanced understanding of the existing legal framework, leading to more informed and consistent judgments. The potential for AI to identify patterns in judicial pronouncements, highlight evolving legal interpretations, and even flag potential inconsistencies across different jurisdictions is immense. This can contribute to the development of a more coherent and predictable body of law. Furthermore, AI can assist in summarizing lengthy legal documents, extracting key clauses and provisions, and identifying legally significant passages, thereby accelerating the review process. The integration of AI into legal research tools signifies a shift from manual data retrieval to intelligent information discovery, empowering legal professionals with actionable insights. The development of specialized AI models trained on Indian legal texts, including vernacular languages, is crucial for maximizing the effectiveness of these tools within the Indian context. Such advancements can democratize access to high-quality legal research, leveling the playing field for legal practitioners across different economic strata and geographical locations.

The analysis of **evidence** within legal proceedings presents a complex challenge, often involving the examination of voluminous documents, audio-visual materials, and digital records. AI is emerging as a powerful ally in this domain, particularly in areas like document review and discovery. In large-scale litigation, such as those involving commercial disputes or regulatory investigations, the sheer volume of documents that need to be scrutinized can be overwhelming. AI-powered e-discovery tools can automate the process of sifting through these documents, identifying relevant information, flagging privileged material, and categorizing evidence based on predefined criteria. This not only speeds up the discovery process but also reduces the risk of human error in identifying critical pieces of evidence. For example, an AI system can be trained to identify specific types of clauses in contracts, flag communications that indicate fraudulent intent, or even analyze metadata associated with digital files to establish their authenticity. Beyond document review, AI is also being explored for its potential in analyzing other forms of evidence, such as voice recordings for identifying speakers or detecting anomalies, or even analyzing financial data for patterns of fraud or money laundering. The ability of AI to process unstructured data, such as text in emails or transcribed conversations, and extract meaningful insights is particularly valuable in modern litigation. This can involve sentiment analysis to gauge the tone of communications, topic modeling to identify recurring themes, and named entity recognition to extract key information such as names, dates, and locations. Such analytical capabilities can provide legal teams with a deeper understanding of the evidence, enabling them to build stronger cases and present more compelling arguments. The ethical considerations around AI-driven evidence analysis, such as ensuring the accuracy and impartiality of the algorithms and maintaining the chain of custody for digital evidence, are paramount and require careful consideration and robust validation processes. The development of transparent and auditable AI systems is crucial for maintaining trust and ensuring that justice is not compromised by technological overreach.

A more forward-looking and potentially transformative application of AI in the Indian legal system lies in **predictive analytics**. While still in its early stages of development and adoption, predictive analytics leverages AI to analyze historical data related to legal cases, judicial decisions, and demographic factors to forecast potential outcomes. This could include predicting the likelihood of a particular motion being granted, the probable sentence for a given offense, or even the potential success rate of an appeal. For legal professionals, such insights could inform strategic decision-making, helping them advise clients more effectively and manage expectations. For instance, a lawyer might use predictive analytics to assess the strengths and weaknesses of their case based on how similar cases have been decided in the past by a particular judge or court. Similarly, judges could potentially use predictive models to gain a better understanding of sentencing trends or the potential impact of their decisions on future litigation. However, the application of predictive analytics in law is fraught with significant challenges and ethical considerations. The accuracy of these predictions is heavily dependent on the quality and comprehensiveness of the data used, and biases present in historical data can be perpetuated and amplified by AI algorithms, leading to potentially unfair or discriminatory outcomes. For example, if historical sentencing data reflects systemic biases against certain demographic groups, a predictive model trained on this data could inadvertently recommend harsher sentences for individuals from those groups. Therefore, ensuring fairness, transparency, and accountability in the development and deployment of predictive AI tools is of utmost importance. The risk of "algorithmic justice," where decisions are made based on statistical probabilities rather than individual circumstances and legal principles, is a serious concern that needs to be carefully managed. The legal system must ensure that AI tools are used to inform, rather than dictate, judicial decisions, and that human oversight and discretion remain central to the process. The potential for AI to analyze trends in legislation and judicial interpretation can also provide valuable insights for policymakers and legal reform. By identifying areas where the law is inconsistent or where judicial interpretation has diverged, AI can assist in the formulation of more coherent and effective legal frameworks.

The integration of AI into the Indian legal system also presents several overarching **benefits and challenges**. On the benefit side, enhanced efficiency is a primary driver. By automating routine tasks, accelerating research, and streamlining administrative processes, AI can significantly reduce the time and cost associated with legal proceedings, thereby improving access to justice for a larger segment of the population. This is particularly crucial in a country like India, where access to legal representation and timely justice can be a significant barrier for many. AI can also contribute to greater consistency and predictability in legal decision-making by providing data-driven insights and helping to identify patterns that might not be apparent through traditional methods. This can foster greater trust in the judicial system. Moreover, AI can democratize access to legal knowledge and resources, empowering individuals and small businesses to navigate the legal landscape more effectively.

However, the challenges associated with AI adoption are equally significant and require careful consideration.

Algorithmic bias is a major concern, as AI systems trained on biased historical data can perpetuate and even amplify existing societal inequalities, leading to unfair or discriminatory outcomes. Ensuring the fairness and impartiality of AI algorithms is therefore a critical imperative. **Data privacy and security** are also paramount, as legal proceedings often involve sensitive and confidential information. Robust data protection measures and ethical guidelines are necessary to safeguard this information and maintain public trust. The **interpretability and transparency** of AI systems, often referred to as the "black box" problem, pose another challenge. If AI-driven decisions cannot be adequately explained or justified, it can undermine the principles of due process and accountability. This is particularly critical in a legal context where the reasoning behind a decision is as important as the decision itself. Furthermore, the **digital divide** in India means that access to AI-powered legal tools may not be uniform, potentially exacerbating existing inequalities in access to justice. Upskilling and training legal professionals to effectively use and understand AI tools is also a crucial requirement. Judges, lawyers, and court staff will need to develop new competencies to harness the benefits of AI while mitigating its risks. The cost of implementing and maintaining AI systems can also be a barrier, especially for smaller law firms and under-resourced courts. Finally, the **ethical and philosophical implications** of relying on AI in areas traditionally governed by human judgment and discretion need to be thoroughly debated. Questions about accountability, the role of human empathy, and the very nature of justice in an increasingly automated world are essential considerations as AI becomes more integrated into the legal fabric of India.

The implementation of AI in the Indian judiciary is not a singular event but an ongoing evolutionary process. Various pilot projects and initiatives are underway across different states and at the national level. For instance, the Supreme Court of India has been exploring the use of AI for tasks such as summarizing judgments and analyzing case data. The E-Courts project, a long-standing initiative aimed at modernizing the Indian judicial system through technology, provides a foundational infrastructure upon which AI applications can be built. This project has facilitated the digitization of court records, the implementation of case management systems, and the development of online portals for filing cases and accessing information. AI can further enhance these existing digital frameworks by introducing more sophisticated analytical and automation capabilities. The use of AI in forensic analysis is also gaining traction, with capabilities ranging from facial recognition to the analysis of digital footprints. In the realm of legal education, AI tools are being developed to assist students in legal research and understanding complex legal concepts. The ongoing development and deployment of these technologies require a robust legal and ethical framework to guide their use, ensuring that they serve the interests of justice and uphold the fundamental principles of the Indian legal system. As AI continues to evolve, its impact on the Indian judiciary and legal landscape is expected to grow, presenting both opportunities and challenges that will need to be navigated with foresight and a commitment to equitable justice. The ultimate success of AI integration will hinge on a balanced approach that maximizes its potential for efficiency and accessibility while rigorously safeguarding against biases, ensuring transparency, and preserving the fundamental human element that is indispensable to the pursuit of justice.

The legal framework governing AI in India is still under development, but several policy pronouncements and discussions highlight the government's awareness of the need for responsible AI deployment. The focus is on creating an environment where AI can be used to enhance, not undermine, the principles of justice. This includes a commitment to ethical AI development, which emphasizes fairness, transparency, accountability, and the protection of fundamental rights. The establishment of committees and working groups to deliberate on AI governance, including its application in the justice sector, signifies a proactive approach to addressing the complex challenges that lie ahead. The aim is to foster innovation while ensuring that the adoption of AI in the legal system is aligned with democratic values and serves the broader goal of a more accessible and effective justice delivery mechanism for all Indian citizens. The iterative nature of AI development means that continuous learning, adaptation, and stakeholder engagement will be crucial in shaping its role within the Indian legal system. This collaborative approach, involving legal professionals, technologists, policymakers, and the public, will be essential in ensuring that AI becomes a force for good in the pursuit of justice in India.

The Indian legal and regulatory framework pertaining to Artificial Intelligence (AI) is a mosaic, still being pieced together, reflecting the nascent yet rapidly evolving nature of AI itself. While India does not yet have a singular, comprehensive "AI Act" akin to some jurisdictions, its existing legislative and policy architecture, coupled with emerging guidelines, provides a nascent but critical foundation for the development and deployment of AI technologies. This section will delve into the key components of this landscape, examining how current laws and policies intersect with AI, and critically evaluating their adequacy in addressing the unique challenges posed by this transformative technology.

A significant pillar of the existing framework that has profound implications for AI is data protection and privacy. The **Digital Personal Data Protection Act, 2023 (DPDP Act)**, is a landmark legislation that seeks to regulate the processing of digital personal data in India. For AI systems, which are inherently data-intensive, this Act establishes crucial obligations for data fiduciaries. These include obtaining consent for data processing, ensuring data accuracy, and implementing reasonable security safeguards to prevent data breaches. The Act also grants significant rights to data principals, such as the right to access and correction of their personal data. AI applications, particularly those involved in profiling, decision-making, or personalization, will need to meticulously adhere to these provisions. For instance, an AI system used for credit scoring or recruitment must ensure that the personal data it processes is obtained lawfully, used only for specified purposes, and that individuals have recourse if their data is processed unfairly. The principles of data minimization, purpose limitation, and accountability enshrined in the DPDP Act are directly relevant to the ethical development and deployment of AI. Failure to comply can result in substantial penalties, underscoring the Act's importance for any organization leveraging AI that involves personal data. Furthermore, the Act's provisions on cross-border data transfer will also influence how AI models trained on data from other jurisdictions are utilized in India.

Beyond the DPDP Act, the **Information Technology Act, 2000 (IT Act)**, and its associated rules, particularly the **Information Technology (Intermediaries Guidelines and Digital Media Ethics Code) Rules, 2021**, also play a role in governing AI. While not AI-specific, these regulations address issues of online content, intermediary liability, and data security. For AI systems that generate or disseminate content, or act as intermediaries, these rules will be pertinent. The guidelines on due diligence for intermediaries, for example, could be interpreted to extend to AI platforms that host user-generated content or facilitate AI-driven interactions. The concept of "due diligence" for AI developers and deployers will likely evolve to encompass the responsible design and operation of AI systems to prevent harm. The focus on transparency and accountability in the IT Rules also resonates with the broader discourse on ethical AI.

Intellectual Property (IP) rights represent another complex area for AI. Existing IP laws, primarily the **Copyright Act, 1957**, the **Patents Act, 1970**, and the **Trademarks Act, 1999**, are currently being tested by AI. A key question is the patentability of AI-generated inventions and the copyrightability of AI-generated creative works. Current Indian IP law generally requires human inventorship or authorship for patents and copyrights, respectively. This raises challenges when AI systems autonomously create novel inventions or artistic outputs. For example, if an AI system develops a new pharmaceutical compound or composes a musical piece, who would be considered the inventor or author? This ambiguity necessitates clarification or amendments to existing IP statutes to accommodate

AI-generated creations. Discussions are ongoing globally regarding whether AI itself can be an inventor or author, or if the human who developed or directed the AI system should be recognized. The Indian Patent Office has, in practice, rejected applications where AI was listed as the inventor, reinforcing the current human-centric approach. Similarly, for copyright, while AI tools can assist human creators, purely AI-generated works may not be eligible for copyright protection under the present framework. This could impact the economic incentives for developing and deploying creative AI applications.

Liability for AI-induced harm is perhaps one of the most critical and challenging areas for legal and regulatory frameworks. When an AI system causes damage- whether it's a self-driving car accident, a biased loan rejection, or a medical misdiagnosis- determining who is liable is complex. Is it the developer of the algorithm, the manufacturer of the AI-enabled product, the owner or operator of the system, or the AI itself (a concept not currently recognized in law)? Indian tort law, which deals with civil wrongs, generally operates on principles of negligence, strict liability, and vicarious liability. Applying these principles to AI is not straightforward. For instance, proving negligence in the design or deployment of an AI system can be difficult, especially given the 'black box' nature of some advanced AI models where the decision-making process is not easily interpretable. The concept of product liability may also be relevant, but the continuous learning and adaptability of AI systems can blur the lines of what constitutes a "defect" in a product. The government has acknowledged this challenge, and ongoing policy discussions often touch upon the need for clarity in AI liability frameworks. Some proposed approaches include strict liability regimes for certain high-risk AI applications or developing specific AI liability insurance mechanisms. The European Union's proposed AI Act, for example, includes provisions for tiered liability based on the risk level of the AI system, a model that India might consider.

Policy pronouncements and government initiatives offer further insight into India's approach. The **National Strategy for Artificial Intelligence**, released by NITI Aayog, identifies AI for All as a key focus, emphasizing inclusive growth and societal well-being. While this strategy is more of a roadmap, it highlights the government's intent to leverage AI for development. NITI Aayog has also released discussion papers and national-level strategies that touch upon ethical AI, governance, and the need for a robust regulatory framework. These documents often stress the importance of principles such as safety, fairness, transparency, accountability, and privacy. The establishment of various committees and working groups by government departments to study AI and its implications, including its use in sectors like healthcare, agriculture, and finance, indicates a proactive approach to understanding the nuances of AI deployment.

The Reserve Bank of India (RBI) and other financial sector regulators have also begun to address AI and machine learning (ML) within their domains. Recognizing the increasing use of AI/ML in areas like credit assessment, fraud detection, and customer service, these bodies have issued advisories and guidelines to ensure responsible innovation. These often focus on governance, risk management, data integrity, and the need for human oversight to prevent algorithmic bias and ensure fair treatment of customers. For instance, guidelines related to the use of AI in credit scoring will need to ensure that the algorithms do not perpetuate historical biases that could disadvantage certain borrower groups.

In the judicial realm, while courts are yet to deliver landmark judgments specifically on AI, there have been instances where AI-related issues have come up in cases. For example, cases involving data breaches, misuse of personal information by digital platforms, or disputes over AI-generated content could eventually lead to important judicial interpretations. The judiciary's role in interpreting existing laws in the context of AI will be crucial in shaping the legal landscape. The Supreme Court's increasing use of technology, including AI-powered tools for legal research and case management, also signals an acceptance and exploration of AI's potential within the justice system itself.

However, a critical evaluation reveals several gaps and challenges in India's current legal and regulatory framework concerning AI. Firstly, the lack of a unified, overarching AI legislation means that the application of existing laws to AI is often indirect and subject to interpretation. This can create uncertainty for developers and users of AI technologies. The fragmented nature of regulation across different sectors and agencies may also lead to inconsistencies and potential regulatory arbitrage.

Secondly, the pace of AI innovation often outstrips the pace of legislative action. By the time laws are enacted, the technology may have evolved significantly, rendering the regulations outdated or insufficient. This necessitates a more agile and adaptive regulatory approach, possibly incorporating mechanisms for continuous review and amendment of AI-related policies.

Thirdly, while principles of fairness, transparency, and accountability are widely discussed, operationalizing these principles into concrete, enforceable legal requirements for AI systems remains a significant challenge. Defining what constitutes "fairness" in an AI algorithm, or how to ensure "transparency" in complex neural networks, are technical and legal hurdles that need to be addressed.

Fourthly, the issue of AI liability, as discussed earlier, requires more robust legal clarity. The current tort law framework might not adequately address the unique forms of harm that AI can cause, nor the distributed nature of responsibility in AI development and deployment. A specific regime or guidelines on AI liability would be beneficial.

Fifthly, the global nature of AI development and deployment means that India's legal framework must also consider international best practices and harmonize with global regulatory trends where appropriate, while also reflecting national priorities and values.

In conclusion, India's legal and regulatory framework for AI is an evolving landscape. The existing laws, particularly the DPDP Act and the IT Act, provide a foundational, albeit indirect, governance structure. However, specific challenges related to intellectual property for AI-generated works, liability for AI-induced harm, and the need for greater specificity in ensuring AI ethics and fairness, highlight the necessity for continued development and refinement of India's AI governance. As AI continues its rapid integration into various facets of Indian society and economy, the legal and regulatory ecosystem will need to demonstrate both agility and foresight to foster innovation while safeguarding fundamental rights and ensuring a just and equitable society. The ongoing policy dialogues and the government's proactive approach suggest an intent to build a comprehensive and effective regulatory architecture, but the journey of translating these intentions into concrete, operational legal provisions is ongoing. The focus remains on enabling AI for societal good, ensuring responsible development and deployment that aligns with India's democratic ethos and commitment to justice.

The ethical considerations that accompany the deployment of Artificial Intelligence (AI) in India are multifaceted, deeply intertwined with the nation's unique socio-economic fabric, diverse population, and rapidly evolving digital landscape. While the foundational legal principles discussed previously provide a broad framework, the practical application of AI in India raises a distinct set of ethical challenges that demand careful navigation and context-specific solutions. These challenges are not merely theoretical; they carry tangible implications for millions of citizens, shaping their access to opportunities, their privacy, and their fundamental rights.

One of the most pervasive ethical concerns revolves around **algorithmic bias**, particularly in a society as diverse as India, marked by significant variations in caste, religion, gender, language, and economic status. AI systems learn from data, and if this data reflects historical societal biases, the AI will invariably perpetuate and even amplify them. Consider the application of AI in recruitment. If an AI system is trained on historical hiring data where certain demographic groups were underrepresented in particular roles due to systemic discrimination, the AI might learn to systematically down-rank applications from individuals belonging to those groups, even if they are equally or more qualified. This can create a vicious cycle, further entrenching existing inequalities. Similarly, in the realm of criminal justice, AI tools used for risk assessment in bail or sentencing decisions, if trained on biased data, could disproportionately flag individuals from marginalized communities as high-risk, leading to unfair detention or sentencing. The challenge for India is to develop and deploy AI systems that actively counteract, rather than replicate, these deep-seated biases. This requires meticulous data curation, bias detection and mitigation techniques, and continuous auditing of AI system outputs to ensure fairness across different population segments. The very definition of "fairness" itself can be complex in a country with such varied lived experiences.

The impact of AI on **employment and the future of work** is another critical ethical dimension. As AI technologies become more sophisticated, they have the potential to automate a wide range of tasks, from routine data entry and customer service to more complex analytical and even creative processes. While AI promises increased productivity and the creation of new types of jobs, it also poses a significant risk of job displacement, particularly for those in lower-skilled roles. In India, where a large proportion of the workforce is engaged in sectors susceptible to automation, such as manufacturing, textiles, and certain service industries, this poses a substantial societal challenge. The ethical imperative here lies in managing this transition responsibly. This involves investing in reskilling and upskilling programs to equip the workforce with the skills needed for an AI-driven economy, fostering a culture of lifelong learning, and exploring policy interventions such as social safety nets or reimagined employment models to support those whose livelihoods are disrupted. The discourse needs to move beyond simply fearing job losses to proactively planning for a future where humans and AI collaborate, and where the benefits of AI-driven productivity are shared equitably. The ethical responsibility extends to ensuring that the pursuit of AI-driven efficiency does not come at the cost of widespread economic disenfranchisement.

Data privacy concerns within a developing digital economy also take on unique ethical contours in India. The rapid expansion of digital services, coupled with government initiatives promoting digitalization, has led to a massive increase in data generation. While the DPDP Act provides a crucial legal safeguard, the practical enforcement and the ability of citizens, especially those with lower digital literacy, to understand and exercise their data rights remain significant challenges. The ethical considerations here involve not only protecting personal data from breaches and misuse but also ensuring transparency in how data is collected, processed, and used by AI systems. For many Indians, especially in rural or semi-urban areas, digital interactions might be their first encounter with large-scale data collection. Educating the public about data privacy, ensuring accessible mechanisms for consent management and data access, and building trust in digital systems are paramount. Furthermore, the increasing use of AI in sensitive sectors like healthcare and finance raises the stakes. An AI diagnostic tool that accesses patient medical history, or an AI-powered loan application system, must operate with the highest ethical standards regarding data privacy and security. The potential for misuse of sensitive personal data, whether for targeted advertising, discriminatory profiling, or even more malicious purposes, necessitates a vigilant and proactive ethical approach to data governance.

The **cultural implications of AI adoption** in India present another layer of ethical complexity. AI systems, often developed in Western contexts, may carry embedded cultural assumptions or design choices that do not resonate with or are even detrimental to Indian cultural norms and values. For example, AI-powered content recommendation systems might inadvertently promote Western cultural products over indigenous art forms, leading to a subtle form of cultural homogenization. Conversely, AI systems designed to understand human language or emotions might struggle with the nuances of India's linguistic diversity and the varied expressions of emotion across different cultural groups, potentially leading to misunderstandings or misinterpretations. The ethical challenge is to ensure that AI development and deployment are sensitive to India's rich cultural tapestry and promote cultural preservation and diversity rather than erode it. This calls for greater inclusivity in AI design teams, incorporating diverse perspectives from the outset, and actively seeking input from cultural experts and community representatives. It also involves developing AI systems that can be localized and adapted to specific cultural contexts, respecting regional languages, customs, and social practices. The goal should be to leverage AI as a tool that enhances, rather than diminishes, India's cultural heritage.

Beyond these broad categories, specific use cases of AI in India amplify ethical concerns. In the realm of **governance and public services**, AI is being explored for applications like predictive policing, traffic management, and citizen service delivery. While these have the potential to improve efficiency and accountability, they also raise profound ethical questions. For instance, predictive policing algorithms, if biased, could lead to the over-surveillance and harassment of specific communities. Similarly, AI-driven decision-making in the allocation of public benefits could introduce new forms of exclusion if not carefully designed and monitored. The ethical imperative here is to ensure that AI in governance is deployed in a manner that is transparent, accountable, and upholds the principles of natural justice and human rights. This means ensuring human oversight, providing avenues for redressal, and making the decision-making processes of AI systems as interpretable as possible.

The increasing use of AI in **education** also warrants ethical scrutiny. AI-powered personalized learning platforms can offer tailored educational experiences, but they also raise concerns about data privacy for students, the potential for algorithmic bias in assessing student performance, and the risk of exacerbating the digital divide if access to these technologies is not equitable. Ethically, the deployment of AI in education must prioritize student well-being, fairness, and the equitable distribution of educational opportunities, ensuring that technology serves as an enabler for all learners.

Furthermore, the burgeoning field of AI in **healthcare** in India brings its own set of ethical considerations. AI for diagnostics, drug discovery, and personalized treatment plans holds immense promise, but the stakes are incredibly high. Ensuring the accuracy and reliability of AI diagnostic tools is paramount to prevent misdiagnoses. The ethical responsibility to patients demands robust validation, transparency about the AI's capabilities and limitations, and clear protocols for human oversight by medical professionals. Issues of data privacy for sensitive health information are also magnified, requiring stringent security measures and clear consent mechanisms. The potential for AI to exacerbate existing healthcare disparities, for instance, by being more accurate for certain demographic groups due to data imbalances, is a significant ethical hurdle that needs to be addressed proactively.

Addressing these complex ethical considerations requires a multifaceted approach that goes beyond mere legal compliance. It necessitates the development of **context-specific ethical guidelines** that are tailored to India's unique societal, cultural, and economic realities. These guidelines should be developed through a process of **robust public discourse**, involving a wide range of stakeholders including AI developers, ethicists, policymakers, civil society organizations, and, crucially, the citizens who will be impacted by AI. Such a participatory approach ensures that the ethical frameworks are grounded in societal values and are responsive to the lived experiences of the people. It also fosters greater public trust and acceptance of AI technologies, which is vital for their successful and beneficial integration into society.

The development of AI ethics in India should also draw lessons from global best practices while charting its own course. The focus on "AI for All," as articulated in national strategies, underscores a commitment to inclusive and equitable AI deployment. This principle should guide all ethical considerations, ensuring that AI benefits the broadest possible segment of society and does not create new divides. Ultimately, the ethical deployment of AI in India is not just about mitigating risks; it is about harnessing the transformative potential of AI to foster sustainable development, enhance human well-being, and promote a more just and equitable society for all its citizens. This journey requires continuous learning, adaptation, and a steadfast commitment to human-centric values at every stage of AI development and deployment.

The path towards establishing robust AI governance in India is undeniably complex, presenting a unique confluence of significant challenges and promising opportunities. As the nation navigates the integration of artificial intelligence across its socio-economic spectrum, the imperative to create an enabling yet responsible framework becomes paramount. A central challenge lies in the substantial **capacity-building deficit** that currently exists. Developing, deploying, and effectively governing AI systems requires a highly skilled workforce, encompassing not only AI researchers and engineers but also legal professionals, ethicists, policymakers, and regulators who possess a deep understanding of AI's technical intricacies and societal implications. India's vast educational ecosystem, while producing a large number of STEM graduates, needs targeted interventions to cultivate specialized AI expertise, particularly in areas of AI ethics, safety, and regulatory compliance. Bridging this gap necessitates investment in advanced AI education programs, retraining initiatives for the existing workforce, and fostering collaborations between academic institutions and industry. Without this foundational capacity, the ability to critically assess AI systems, identify potential harms, and implement effective governance measures will remain limited.

Furthermore, the **fragmented nature of AI policy and regulation** across different government departments and sectors poses a significant challenge. While various ministries and agencies are exploring AI applications within their domains, a unified, cohesive national strategy for AI governance is still in its nascent stages. This can lead to overlapping regulations, policy gaps, and an inconsistent approach to AI deployment, hindering both innovation and risk mitigation. The opportunity here lies in establishing a high-level, cross-ministerial body or task force dedicated to AI governance, tasked with developing a comprehensive national AI strategy that harmonizes existing efforts, identifies emerging regulatory needs, and promotes best practices. Such a body would act as a central coordinating mechanism, ensuring that AI development aligns with broader national priorities, constitutional values, and the rule of law.

Stakeholder collaboration is another critical area, presenting both a challenge and a profound opportunity. The diverse stakeholders involved in the AI ecosystem-government, industry (both large corporations and burgeoning startups), academia, civil society organizations, and the public- often have competing interests and perspectives. Ensuring that the voices of all these groups are heard and considered in the development of AI governance frameworks is essential for creating inclusive and legitimate regulations. The challenge is to move beyond siloed consultations and foster genuine, ongoing dialogue and co-creation. Opportunities abound in establishing multi-stakeholder platforms, sandboxes for regulatory experimentation, and public-private partnerships that can accelerate the development and adoption of ethical AI practices. India's tradition of vibrant civil society engagement can be leveraged to ensure that AI governance is not solely driven by technological capabilities or commercial interests but is also guided by societal values and public good.

The very nature of AI, with its rapid evolution and adaptability, demands **adaptive regulatory approaches**. Traditional, static regulatory models are unlikely to be sufficient for governing a technology that is constantly transforming. The challenge for India is to design governance mechanisms that are flexible enough to keep pace with technological advancements while remaining robust enough to ensure accountability and prevent harm. This suggests a move towards principles-based regulation, outcome-oriented governance, and the use of regulatory sandboxes that allow for the testing of new AI applications and regulatory approaches in a controlled environment. The opportunity lies in adopting a "learning by doing" approach, where regulations are iteratively refined based on real-world experience and emerging evidence. Such adaptability is crucial for fostering innovation while maintaining public trust and safety.

Moreover, the **global nature of AI development and deployment** presents a unique set of challenges and opportunities for India. Many AI technologies are developed and funded by global entities, and AI research is an international endeavor. India must navigate the complexities of cross-border data flows, international standards, and the potential influence of foreign regulatory approaches. The opportunity here is for India to assert its influence on the global AI governance stage, drawing upon its unique democratic values and its commitment to inclusive development. By actively participating in international forums, collaborating with other nations, and contributing to the development of global AI norms, India can ensure that its interests and values are reflected in the evolving international AI governance landscape. This proactive engagement can also help in benchmarking its own governance frameworks against global best practices.

The **economic aspirations tied to AI** present both a powerful motivator and a potential pitfall for governance. India aims to leverage AI to boost economic growth, improve public services, and enhance its global competitiveness. This drive for economic progress can sometimes create pressure to relax regulatory scrutiny, a move that could inadvertently lead to increased risks. The challenge is to strike a delicate balance between fostering AI-driven innovation and ensuring that this innovation occurs within ethical and legal boundaries. The opportunity lies in framing AI governance not as a constraint on economic growth but as an enabler of sustainable and equitable growth. By building trust through transparent and responsible AI deployment, India can attract responsible investment, foster a domestic AI industry that prioritizes ethical practices, and ensure that the benefits of AI are broadly shared.

Furthermore, the **interpretability and explainability of AI systems** remain a significant governance challenge, particularly when these systems are used in critical decision-making processes affecting citizens' lives. The 'black box' nature of some advanced AI algorithms makes it difficult to understand *why* a particular decision was made, posing challenges for accountability, redressal, and due process. India's constitutional commitment to fairness and transparency necessitates addressing this challenge head-on. The opportunity lies in promoting research and development into explainable AI (XAI) techniques and mandating levels of transparency and explainability proportionate to the risk associated with the AI application. This could involve requiring impact assessments for high-risk AI systems and establishing clear avenues for citizens to challenge AI-driven decisions.

The widespread adoption of AI also necessitates a focus on **digital literacy and public awareness** as key components of effective governance. A citizenry that understands the basic principles of AI, its potential benefits and risks, and their own rights in an AI-driven world is crucial for democratic oversight and societal buy-in. The challenge is to bridge the digital literacy divide and ensure that awareness campaigns reach all sections of society, including vulnerable and marginalized communities. The opportunity is to empower citizens, making them active participants in shaping the AI future rather than passive recipients. This can be achieved through educational initiatives, public consultations, and accessible information dissemination channels.

Finally, and perhaps most importantly, India's AI

governance must remain firmly anchored in its **constitutional values and the rule of law**. The opportunities presented by AI for national development- be it in healthcare, agriculture, education, or governance- must be pursued in a manner that upholds fundamental rights, promotes social justice, and ensures accountability. The challenge is to ensure that the legal and regulatory frameworks are sufficiently robust to translate these constitutional principles into practical guidelines for AI development and deployment. This requires a proactive and forward-looking approach from legal institutions, a commitment to ethical considerations from technologists, and an engaged citizenry that holds both accountable. By embracing these challenges and seizing the opportunities for collaboration, capacity building, and adaptive regulation, India can chart a course for AI governance that fosters innovation, ensures fairness, and ultimately serves the best interests of its people. The journey is ongoing, demanding continuous vigilance, learning, and a steadfast commitment to building an AI future that is both technologically advanced and deeply human.

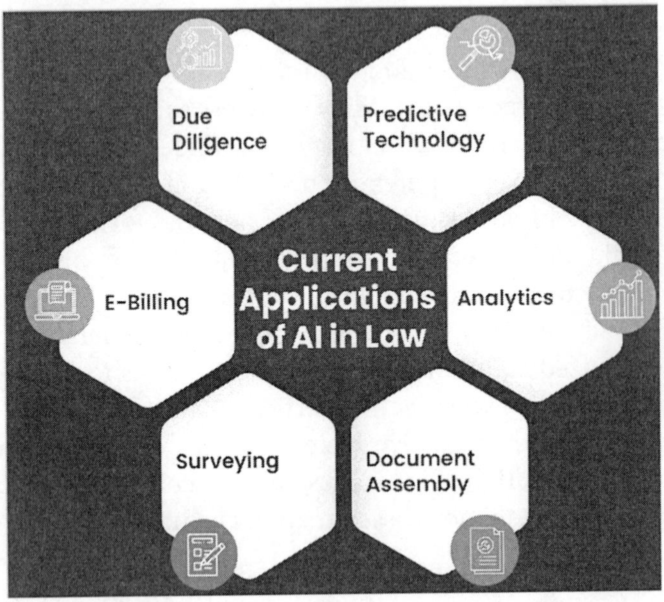

7
National Perspectives
The United States and AI Governance

The United States has, over recent years, increasingly recognized the strategic importance of artificial intelligence (AI) for its economic competitiveness, national security, and societal well-being. This recognition has translated into a multifaceted federal strategy and policy landscape, characterized by a series of executive actions, agency-specific initiatives, and ongoing legislative discussions. The overarching aim is to foster AI innovation and leadership while simultaneously mitigating potential risks and ensuring that AI development and deployment align with American values. This approach is not monolithic but rather a dynamic interplay of top-down directives and bottom-up agency actions, all seeking to balance progress with responsibility.

A pivotal moment in shaping the US federal AI strategy was the issuance of **Executive Order 13859, "Maintaining American Leadership in Artificial Intelligence,"** in February 2019. This landmark order signaled a clear federal commitment to prioritizing AI research and development, workforce training, and the establishment of a national AI research infrastructure. It directed federal agencies to develop AI strategies for their respective domains, emphasizing the need to leverage AI for economic growth and national security. The order also called for the development of policies to encourage private sector investment in AI and for the creation of public-private partnerships to accelerate AI innovation. It articulated a vision where the United States would remain at the forefront of AI development, harnessing its power for the benefit of its citizens and the global community. The order underscored the importance of collaboration across government, academia, and industry, recognizing that no single entity could achieve these ambitious goals alone. It also highlighted the need to address ethical considerations and the potential impact of AI on the workforce and society, setting a tone for a balanced approach.

Following Executive Order 13859, various federal agencies began to develop and implement their own AI strategies, tailored to their specific missions and expertise. The **National Science Foundation (NSF)**, for instance, has been a significant investor in fundamental AI research, supporting foundational breakthroughs in machine learning, computer vision, and natural language processing. The NSF's AI initiatives aim to expand the frontiers of AI knowledge and to develop AI systems that are reliable, robust, and human-centered. This includes funding for interdisciplinary research centers and programs designed to cultivate the next generation of AI researchers and practitioners. The NSF's commitment extends to ensuring that AI research benefits society broadly, with a focus on AI for scientific discovery and societal challenges.

The **Department of Defense (DoD)** has a particularly strong focus on AI for national security applications, ranging from autonomous systems and intelligence analysis to logistics and cybersecurity. The DoD's AI Strategy, released in 2018 and updated since, emphasizes the need for rapid AI adoption to maintain military superiority, while also acknowledging the ethical implications of AI in warfare. This strategy involves significant investments in AI research and development through various defense agencies and laboratories, as well as efforts to train military personnel in AI technologies and to develop clear ethical guidelines for the use of AI in defense contexts. The DoD's approach highlights the dual nature of AI-its potential to enhance capabilities and the critical need for responsible deployment, particularly in high-stakes environments.

The **Department of Commerce**, through the **National Institute of Standards and Technology (NIST)**, plays a crucial role in developing AI standards and guidance to promote trustworthy AI. NIST has been instrumental in developing the **AI Risk Management Framework (AI RMF)**, a voluntary framework designed to help organizations manage the risks associated with AI. The AI RMF provides a structured approach to identifying, assessing, and mitigating AI risks across the AI lifecycle, emphasizing concepts such as validity and reliability, safety, security and resilience, accountability and transparency, explainability and interpretability, fairness and non-discrimination, and human and societal well-being. This framework is a testament to the US commitment to fostering responsible innovation and ensuring that AI systems are developed and used in ways that are beneficial and safe. NIST's work is critical for building public trust and for enabling the broader adoption of AI by providing a common language and set of practices for AI risk management.

The **Office of Science and Technology Policy (OSTP)** within the White House plays a coordinating role, advising the President on scientific and technological matters, including AI. OSTP has been at the forefront of developing national AI policy recommendations and has been involved in various initiatives to advance AI research, education, and ethical considerations. OSTP's work often involves convening experts from government, academia, and industry to provide recommendations on critical AI issues. This includes efforts to address workforce development, the ethical implications of AI, and the promotion of AI research and development. OSTP's role underscores the importance of a unified federal approach to AI, ensuring that different agencies' efforts are coordinated and aligned with national priorities.

Furthermore, the US Congress has also been actively engaged in shaping the AI policy landscape through legislative proposals and hearings. While a comprehensive federal AI law has not yet been enacted, numerous bills have been introduced covering various aspects of AI, including data privacy, algorithmic bias, AI safety, and the creation of AI regulatory bodies. These legislative efforts reflect a growing awareness of the need for a clear legal and regulatory framework to govern AI. Discussions often revolve around defining AI, identifying high-risk AI applications, establishing accountability mechanisms, and ensuring that AI development and deployment are consistent with fundamental rights and democratic values. The legislative branch's engagement is crucial for translating the administration's strategic vision into enforceable laws and regulations.

A key principle that has emerged in US AI policy is the concept of **"Trustworthy AI."** This concept, championed by NIST and other agencies, emphasizes the development of AI systems that are reliable, safe, secure, transparent, explainable, fair, and accountable. The AI Risk Management Framework is a prime example of this commitment, providing practical guidance for organizations to implement these principles throughout the AI lifecycle. The focus on trustworthy AI is intended to foster public confidence in AI technologies, encourage their widespread adoption, and ensure that they are developed and used in ways that benefit society and uphold democratic values. This proactive approach to risk management is seen as essential for unlocking the full potential of AI.

The US federal strategy also places a strong emphasis on **AI workforce development.** Recognizing that a skilled workforce is essential for AI innovation and competitiveness, federal initiatives aim to expand AI education and training opportunities at all levels, from K-12 to higher education and vocational training. This includes investments in AI research and education programs at universities, the development of

AI-related curricula, and initiatives to retrain and upskill the existing workforce to adapt to the changing demands of an AI-driven economy. The goal is to ensure that the United States has a sufficient supply of AI talent to drive innovation and to equip its citizens with the skills needed to thrive in an AI-augmented world.

In parallel with these efforts, the US government has also been actively engaging with international partners to shape global AI norms and standards. This includes participation in multilateral organizations and bilateral dialogues aimed at promoting responsible AI development and deployment across borders. The US recognizes that AI is a global phenomenon and that international cooperation is essential for addressing shared challenges and opportunities. This engagement is crucial for ensuring that the global AI landscape is guided by principles that align with democratic values and respect for human rights.

More recently, the Biden-Harris administration has continued to build upon the foundation laid by previous executive orders, issuing **Executive Order 14110, "Safe, Secure, and Trustworthy Artificial Intelligence,"** in October 2023. This comprehensive executive order builds on the principles of AI leadership and responsible innovation, but with a significantly enhanced focus on safety and security, particularly concerning the rapid advancements in powerful AI models. It directs federal agencies to develop new standards, guidelines, and best practices for AI safety and security, with particular attention to the potential risks posed by advanced AI systems, including those that could have a significant impact on national security, economic stability, and public health and safety.

Executive Order 14110 establishes a new era of AI governance, mandating rigorous safety testing and evaluation for the most powerful AI models before their public release. This includes requiring developers of the most powerful AI systems to share their safety test results with the government. It also calls for the development of guidelines for red-teaming AI systems to identify and mitigate potential risks. The order emphasizes the need for clear labeling of AI-generated content, often referred to as "deepfakes," to help distinguish between authentic and artificially created information, a critical step in combating disinformation.

Furthermore, the executive order directs significant attention to AI's impact on workers and the economy. It calls for guidelines to protect workers from potential harms associated with AI in the workplace, such as job displacement, algorithmic management, and bias in hiring and promotion. It also aims to ensure that the benefits of AI are shared broadly across the economy, promoting fair competition and supporting small businesses in the AI ecosystem. This focus acknowledges that AI's economic impact is not uniformly positive and requires careful management to ensure equity and opportunity.

The order also places a strong emphasis on civil rights and equity, mandating guidance to prevent AI from exacerbating discrimination and bias. It requires agencies to identify and mitigate AI-related risks to civil rights and to promote the development of AI systems that are fair and equitable. This includes addressing bias in AI used in areas such as housing, employment, and the justice system. The commitment to civil rights reflects a deep-seated understanding that AI governance must be rooted in the protection of fundamental rights and the pursuit of justice.

In terms of national security and law enforcement, the executive order directs the development of guidance for the responsible use of AI by federal law enforcement agencies. It also calls for efforts to develop AI capabilities to enhance national security, while ensuring that such uses are consistent with American values and respect for civil liberties.

This highlights the delicate balance between leveraging AI for defense and security purposes and upholding democratic principles and individual freedoms.

The executive order also reinforces the need for federal leadership in developing AI standards and promoting international cooperation. It calls for collaboration with international partners to establish global AI norms and to address cross-border AI challenges. This international dimension is crucial for ensuring a cohesive global approach to AI governance and for preventing a race to the bottom in AI safety and ethical standards.

The implementation of Executive Order 14110 is a complex undertaking, requiring significant coordination across numerous federal agencies. It mandates the creation of new initiatives, the revision of existing policies, and the development of novel approaches to AI governance. The Cybersecurity and Infrastructure Security Agency (CISA), for example, is tasked with developing guidelines for AI safety and cybersecurity, while the Department of Justice is expected to provide guidance on the use of AI in law enforcement. The Department of Labor will focus on AI's impact on workers, and the Department of Health and Human Services will address AI in healthcare.

The creation of a **National AI Advisory Committee (NAIAC)**, as mandated by the executive order, signifies a commitment to ongoing, multi-stakeholder engagement. This committee, comprised of experts from industry, academia, civil society, and labor, will provide recommendations to the Secretary of Commerce and the Director of the OSTP on a range of AI-related issues, including AI safety, competitiveness, and workforce development. This collaborative approach is essential for ensuring that AI policy is informed by diverse perspectives and remains responsive to the evolving AI landscape.

The executive order also calls for the development

of tools and resources to help the public and private sectors understand and manage AI risks. This includes initiatives to promote AI literacy and to provide accessible information about AI technologies and their potential impacts. The goal is to empower individuals and organizations to engage with AI responsibly and to make informed decisions about its adoption.

The legislative landscape continues to evolve alongside these executive actions. While a comprehensive AI bill of rights has not yet been codified into law, various legislative proposals are being debated in Congress that address aspects such as AI transparency, algorithmic accountability, and data privacy. These discussions highlight the ongoing need for a robust legal framework that can adapt to the rapid pace of AI development.

The US approach to AI policy and strategy is characterized by a strong emphasis on fostering innovation and economic growth, while also prioritizing safety, security, and ethical considerations. The series of executive orders and agency-specific initiatives demonstrate a deliberate effort to create a comprehensive framework for AI governance. The evolving nature of these policies reflects the dynamic and rapidly advancing field of artificial intelligence, requiring continuous adaptation and refinement to address emerging challenges and opportunities. The commitment to "Trustworthy AI" and the proactive development of risk management frameworks, such as NIST's AI RMF, underscore a recognition that responsible innovation is key to unlocking AI's transformative potential for the benefit of society. The ongoing engagement with international partners and the focus on workforce development further illustrate the comprehensive nature of the US strategy, aiming to ensure both domestic leadership and global cooperation in shaping the future of AI. The recent Executive Order 14110 represents a significant escalation in the federal government's commitment to AI safety and security, particularly in light of advanced AI capabilities, signaling a new phase in the nation's AI governance journey. This continuous evolution of policy is indicative of the profound impact AI is expected to have, necessitating a dynamic and forward-thinking approach from the US government.

The integration of Artificial Intelligence (AI) into the fabric of the United States' judicial and regulatory systems represents a complex, multifaceted, and rapidly evolving frontier. As AI technologies mature, their application is extending beyond the private sector and into core governmental functions, aiming to enhance efficiency, accuracy, and even fairness within these critical institutions. This subsection delves into the burgeoning use of AI within the US court system, exploring its roles in case management, predictive analytics, and legal research. Concurrently, it examines how various US regulatory bodies are navigating the advent of AI, adapting their existing frameworks or developing new approaches to govern sectors increasingly intertwined with these sophisticated technologies, with a particular focus on finance, healthcare, and transportation.

Within the judicial sphere, the allure of AI lies in its potential to alleviate the considerable burdens placed upon courts. Case management, a fundamental yet often resource-intensive aspect of judicial operations, is an early area of AI adoption. Systems are being developed and deployed to automate routine tasks such as docketing, scheduling, and managing electronic filings. These AI-powered tools can sort, categorize, and prioritize incoming cases, flag potential conflicts or missing documentation, and even assist in the generation of standard legal documents. The objective is to streamline the administrative workflow, freeing up judicial officers and staff to focus on substantive legal matters rather than repetitive clerical duties. For instance, AI can meticulously analyze large volumes of court documents, identifying patterns and anomalies that human reviewers might overlook, thereby improving the accuracy and efficiency of record-keeping and case tracking. The potential benefits are significant: reduced backlogs, faster resolution times, and more effective allocation of judicial resources. However, the implementation of these systems also raises critical questions about data security, the potential for algorithmic bias in prioritization, and the need for human oversight to ensure that technological efficiency does not compromise procedural integrity.

Perhaps the most contentious and ethically charged application of AI in the judicial system lies in the realm of predictive analytics, particularly in areas such as sentencing, bail determinations, and risk assessment. These tools, often built on machine learning algorithms, analyze historical data to predict the likelihood of a defendant reoffending or failing to appear in court. Proponents argue that such tools can introduce objectivity into decisions that have historically been influenced by human subjectivity, potentially leading to more consistent and fair outcomes. They can process vast datasets, identifying correlations that might not be apparent to human decision-makers. For example, algorithms might consider factors such as prior criminal history, employment status, and community ties to generate a risk score. This score can then inform a judge's decision on whether to grant bail or impose a particular sentence. However, the use of these predictive tools is fraught with peril. Critics point to the inherent risk of perpetuating and amplifying existing societal biases present in the historical data used to train these algorithms. If past arrest or conviction data disproportionately reflects racial or socioeconomic disparities, the AI system may inadvertently penalize individuals from marginalized communities, creating a feedback loop of systemic inequality. The opacity of many of these algorithms, often referred to as "black boxes," further complicates matters. Judges and defendants may not fully understand how a particular risk assessment was generated, making it difficult to challenge or appeal the outcome. This lack of transparency directly conflicts with fundamental principles of due process and the right to a fair hearing. The debate around algorithmic fairness, explainability, and accountability is therefore central to the ethical deployment of predictive AI in the justice system.

Beyond case management and predictive tools, AI is also revolutionizing legal research. Sophisticated natural language processing (NLP) tools can now sift through vast libraries of legal precedents, statutes, and scholarly articles with unprecedented speed and accuracy. These AI-powered research platforms can identify relevant case law, analyze judicial opinions, and even predict the potential outcomes of specific legal arguments based on historical trends. For lawyers and judges, this means quicker access to critical information, allowing them to build stronger cases and make more informed decisions. The ability of AI to identify subtle connections between disparate legal texts, flag potential contradictions, or summarize complex legal documents can significantly enhance the quality and efficiency of legal analysis. This technology has the potential to democratize access to legal information, leveling the playing field for smaller firms or public defenders who may not have the resources for extensive manual research. However, it also raises questions about the role of human judgment in legal interpretation. While AI can identify patterns, the nuanced understanding of legal principles, the strategic application of precedent, and the art of persuasive argumentation still remain firmly within the domain of human legal professionals. The challenge lies in integrating these powerful AI tools as assistants rather than replacements for human expertise, ensuring that technological prowess complements, rather than diminishes, the intellectual rigor of the legal profession.

Shifting focus to the regulatory landscape, US regulatory bodies are grappling with the pervasive influence of AI across virtually every sector of the economy. The traditional regulatory models, often designed for more predictable and slower-moving technologies, are being tested by the dynamic and rapidly evolving nature of AI. This necessitates a proactive and adaptable approach to governance, balancing the promotion of innovation with the imperative to protect public interest, ensure safety, and uphold ethical standards.

In the **financial sector**, AI is being deployed extensively for fraud detection, risk management, algorithmic trading, customer service, and credit scoring. Regulators like the Securities and Exchange Commission (SEC) and the Consumer Financial Protection Bureau (CFPB) are keenly aware of AI's transformative impact. The challenge for these bodies is to ensure that AI applications do not introduce new forms of systemic risk or exacerbate existing inequalities. For instance, AI algorithms used for credit scoring could inadvertently discriminate against certain demographic groups if trained on biased historical data, leading to unfair denial of loans or higher interest rates. Regulators are therefore focusing on principles of fairness, transparency, and explainability in AI-driven financial decision-making. The SEC is scrutinizing the use of AI in trading to prevent market manipulation and ensure fair pricing. The CFPB is concerned with how AI-powered systems might impact consumer access to financial services and protection against predatory practices. The development of guidelines around AI model validation, data governance, and accountability for AI-driven outcomes are becoming paramount. Furthermore, the increasing reliance on AI for compliance itself presents an interesting regulatory paradox: how does one regulate the regulators when AI tools are used to monitor and enforce rules? This demands sophisticated technological expertise within regulatory agencies to effectively oversee AI in finance.

The **healthcare sector** is another area where AI holds

immense promise, from drug discovery and personalized medicine to diagnostic imaging and patient care management. However, the stakes are incredibly high, with patient safety and privacy being paramount concerns. Regulatory bodies such as the Food and Drug Administration (FDA) and the Department of Health and Human Services (HHS) are at the forefront of this challenge. The FDA is developing frameworks for regulating AI-based medical devices and software, recognizing that these systems can evolve and learn over time. This requires a departure from traditional "locked" device regulations to approaches that can accommodate adaptive algorithms, often referred to as Software as a Medical Device (SaMD). Key considerations include ensuring the clinical validity and utility of AI diagnostic tools, managing potential biases in AI models used for patient stratification or treatment recommendations, and establishing clear protocols for post-market surveillance of AI systems that continue to learn and change. The privacy of health data, governed by the Health Insurance Portability and Accountability Act (HIPAA), becomes even more critical when AI systems are processing vast amounts of sensitive patient information. Regulators must ensure that AI applications comply with stringent data protection and privacy requirements. The ethical implications of AI in healthcare are profound, ranging from questions of responsibility when an AI makes an incorrect diagnosis to ensuring equitable access to AI-enhanced medical treatments.

In the **transportation sector**, AI is driving the development of autonomous vehicles (AVs), advanced driver-assistance systems (ADAS), and optimizing traffic management. The National Highway Traffic Safety Administration (NHTSA) and the Department of Transportation (DOT) are tasked with ensuring the safety and reliability of these AI-powered systems. The introduction of AVs, which rely on complex AI algorithms for perception, decision-making, and control, presents unprecedented regulatory challenges. NHTSA has issued voluntary guidelines and is working towards establishing formal standards for AV testing and deployment. Key areas of focus include the safety performance of AI driving systems, cybersecurity measures to protect vehicles from malicious attacks, and the ethical considerations surrounding decision-making in unavoidable accident scenarios (e.g., the "trolley problem" applied to AVs). The transition to AVs also raises questions about liability in the event of accidents, requiring a re-evaluation of existing legal frameworks. Furthermore, AI is being used to optimize traffic flow, manage congestion, and improve the efficiency of public transportation systems. Regulators must consider how these systems impact accessibility, fairness, and the potential for algorithmic bias in traffic management decisions, such as prioritizing certain routes or modes of transport.

Across all sectors, a common challenge for US regulators is the sheer pace of AI development, which often outstrips the traditional legislative and rulemaking processes. This has led to a greater reliance on agency guidance, voluntary frameworks, and a more iterative approach to regulation. The NIST AI Risk Management Framework, mentioned earlier, serves as a critical foundational document for many of these efforts, providing a common language and a structured approach to identifying, assessing, and managing AI risks. However, the voluntary nature of such frameworks means that adoption and enforcement can vary. There is an ongoing debate about the need for more comprehensive legislative action to provide a clear and consistent legal framework for AI.

The intersection of AI and regulatory oversight also extends to areas like intellectual property, competition policy, and national security. Agencies such as the Federal Trade Commission (FTC) are increasingly scrutinizing AI-driven practices for potential anticompetitive effects or deceptive practices. The FTC has issued policy statements on AI and data security, emphasizing the need for companies to be transparent about their use of AI and to ensure that their AI systems are secure and do not pose unreasonable risks. The potential for AI to concentrate market power in the hands of a few dominant technology firms is a significant concern for antitrust regulators.

In essence, the integration of AI into the US judicial and regulatory systems is a dynamic and ongoing process. While the potential for enhanced efficiency, accuracy, and data-driven decision-making is considerable, the ethical, legal, and societal implications are profound. The courts are cautiously exploring AI's capacity to manage workloads and inform decisions, while simultaneously wrestling with the risks of bias and opacity. Regulatory bodies, facing a rapidly evolving technological landscape, are striving to adapt existing rules and forge new pathways for governance, aiming to harness AI's benefits while mitigating its potential harms across critical sectors like finance, healthcare, and transportation. The success of these endeavors will hinge on a commitment to transparency, fairness, accountability, and a continuous dialogue among technologists, policymakers, legal experts, and the public to ensure that AI serves the interests of justice and societal well-being. The ongoing evolution of these applications and regulatory responses underscores the need for a flexible and adaptive governance architecture that can keep pace with the transformative power of artificial intelligence.

The United States has approached Artificial Intelligence (AI) governance not through a single, overarching legislative act specifically designed for AI, but rather through the adaptation and application of existing legal frameworks, alongside the emergence of new, targeted regulations and significant judicial pronouncements. This approach reflects the pervasive nature of AI, impacting numerous facets of law and commerce, and the challenge of crafting legislation that remains relevant in a field characterized by rapid technological advancement. Understanding the US legal landscape for AI requires examining a mosaic of federal and state laws, court decisions that interpret these laws in the context of AI, and the evolving guidance from regulatory agencies.

A cornerstone of the burgeoning legal response to AI involves data privacy. As AI systems are heavily reliant on vast datasets for training and operation, laws governing the collection, use, and protection of personal information have become critically important. The California Consumer Privacy Act (CCPA), and its subsequent amendment through the California Privacy Rights Act (CPRA), stands as a prominent example of state-level legislation that significantly impacts AI development and deployment. The CCPA grants consumers rights regarding their personal information, including the right to know what data is being collected, the right to request deletion of that data, and the right to opt-out of the sale of their personal information. For AI companies, this means a heightened responsibility to be transparent about data collection practices, to ensure the lawful acquisition of training data, and to build systems that can accommodate consumer requests for data deletion or modification. The concept of "selling" personal information under the CCPA also has implications for AI, particularly when data is shared with third parties for training or operational purposes. The CPRA further strengthens these protections by introducing new categories of sensitive personal information and establishing the California Privacy Protection Agency (CPPA) to enforce these provisions, signaling a more robust regulatory environment for data-intensive AI. While federal privacy legislation has been a subject of ongoing discussion, its absence has led to a patchwork of state laws, creating compliance challenges for businesses operating nationwide.

Beyond privacy, intellectual property (IP) law is

another domain grappling with AI. The question of whether AI-generated works- such as music, art, or written content- can be protected by copyright or patent law is a complex one. Traditional IP law is rooted in the concept of human authorship and inventorship. For instance, US copyright law, as interpreted by the US Copyright Office, generally requires human authorship for a work to be copyrightable. This has led to cases where AI-generated outputs have been denied copyright registration. The Copyright Office has issued guidance clarifying that while works created with AI assistance can be copyrighted if a human author has made sufficient creative contributions, works generated solely by AI without human intervention are not eligible. This stance, however, is subject to ongoing debate and potential legal challenges. Similarly, patent law requires human inventorship. While AI can be a powerful tool for invention, assisting in research and discovery, the AI system itself cannot be named as an inventor. The inventorship must reside with the human beings who conceived of and directed the AI's contribution to the invention. This distinction is crucial for determining ownership and rights related to AI-driven innovations. The evolving nature of AI capabilities may necessitate a re-evaluation of these foundational principles, potentially leading to new legal interpretations or legislative amendments to address the unique challenges posed by non-human creation and innovation.

Liability for the actions of autonomous systems, particularly in the context of self-driving vehicles, is a significant area where case law and regulatory efforts are shaping the legal landscape. Accidents involving autonomous vehicles raise fundamental questions about who is at fault: the vehicle owner, the manufacturer, the software developer, or perhaps even the AI itself. Existing tort law principles, such as negligence and product liability, are being applied, but their application to AI systems presents unique challenges. For example, proving negligence often requires demonstrating a breach of a duty of care. In the context of AI, identifying and proving such a breach can be complicated due to the complexity and "black box" nature of some algorithms. Product liability law, which holds manufacturers responsible for defective products, is another relevant framework. However, defining what constitutes a "defect" in an AI system that learns and adapts over time is a nuanced issue. Regulatory bodies like the National Highway Traffic Safety Administration (NHTSA) are developing frameworks and guidelines for the testing and deployment of autonomous vehicles. While NHTSA has not mandated specific AI standards, it has issued guidance on vehicle safety and crashworthiness that implicitly encourages robust AI safety testing. Court cases, though still relatively nascent, are beginning to explore these liability questions. These early cases often focus on whether existing product liability doctrines can adequately address harms caused by AI, and how foreseeability and causation are established when AI behavior deviates from intended parameters. The potential for AI to make complex, unpredicted decisions in critical situations underscores the need for clear legal and regulatory frameworks to assign responsibility and ensure accountability.

Anti-discrimination statutes are also being scrutinized for their application to AI, particularly concerning algorithmic bias. Laws such as Title VII of the Civil Rights Act of 1964, which prohibits employment discrimination based on race, color, religion, sex, or national origin, and the Fair Housing Act, which prohibits discrimination in housing, are relevant when AI systems are used in hiring, lending, or housing allocation decisions. AI algorithms trained on historical data that reflects societal biases can inadvertently perpetuate or even amplify those biases. For example, an AI hiring tool trained on data from a company with a predominantly male workforce might learn to favor male candidates, even if gender is not explicitly considered in the algorithm's programming. This phenomenon is known as algorithmic bias. Federal agencies like the Equal Employment Opportunity Commission (EEOC) and the Department of Justice (DOJ) have issued guidance on the application of anti-discrimination laws to AI in employment, emphasizing that employers are responsible for ensuring that their AI tools do not result in discriminatory outcomes, regardless of whether the discrimination is intentional. The challenge lies in identifying and mitigating bias in complex AI systems. This involves rigorous testing, auditing of algorithms, and ensuring transparency in their design and operation. Landmark cases in this area are still emerging, but the underlying legal principle is that AI systems, like any other employment or service delivery tool, must comply with existing anti-discrimination laws. Litigation in this space is likely to focus on proving disparate impact- where a neutral policy or practice (the AI algorithm) has a disproportionately negative effect on a protected group.

Beyond these specific areas, broader legislative and executive actions are shaping the US approach to AI governance. The National Artificial Intelligence Initiative Act of 2020, for instance, established a coordinating framework for federal investments in AI research and development, emphasizing the importance of trustworthy AI and AI safety. While not a regulatory law in itself, it signals a national strategy that includes considerations for ethical development and responsible deployment. The Executive Order on the Safe, Secure, and Trustworthy Development and Use of Artificial Intelligence, signed in October 2023, is a significant development, marking a comprehensive federal effort to establish standards and guidelines for AI. This order directs various federal agencies to develop new safety standards, promote fair competition, protect privacy, advance equity and civil rights, and safeguard national security and the economy. It calls for the creation of new NIST standards for AI safety and security, mandates reporting requirements for companies developing the most powerful AI models, and addresses issues such as AI in critical infrastructure, AI and intellectual property, and international cooperation on AI. This executive action is likely to catalyze further regulatory actions and potentially future legislative proposals, providing a more unified direction for AI governance across federal agencies.

Furthermore, sector-specific regulations continue to adapt. In the financial sector, agencies like the Consumer Financial Protection Bureau (CFPB) and the Securities and Exchange Commission (SEC) are actively issuing guidance and considering rules related to AI, particularly concerning fair lending, algorithmic trading, and consumer protection. The Federal Trade Commission (FTC) has been active in addressing unfair and deceptive practices involving AI, focusing on issues like data security, privacy, and the potential for AI to mislead consumers. The healthcare sector, overseen by the Food and Drug Administration (FDA), is grappling with AI in medical devices and diagnostics, with the FDA developing a framework for premarket review and postmarket oversight of AI/ML-based medical software. These ongoing efforts highlight a trend towards adaptive governance, where regulators leverage existing authorities and issue specific guidance to address the unique challenges AI presents within their respective domains.

The legal interpretation of AI issues is also being shaped by case law that, while not always explicitly about AI, deals with principles that are foundational to AI governance. For example, cases concerning data breaches, algorithmic decision-making in government (such as in parole or welfare eligibility), and the use of technology in evidence presentation all provide precedents and interpretive frameworks that are relevant to AI. As AI becomes more integrated into all aspects of society, courts will increasingly be called upon to interpret how established legal principles apply to novel AI-driven situations. This evolutionary process of legal interpretation, driven by both legislative action and judicial precedent, is critical to establishing a robust and adaptable legal framework for AI in the United States. The ultimate effectiveness of these various legal instruments will depend on their ability to keep pace with technological advancements, ensure fairness and accountability, and foster innovation while mitigating potential risks. The ongoing dialogue between legal scholars, technologists, policymakers, and the public is essential to navigate this complex and dynamic terrain.

The United States' approach to Artificial Intelligence (AI) governance is a complex tapestry woven from federal directives, judicial interpretations, and, crucially, a burgeoning array of state-level regulations and initiatives. While federal oversight provides a broad framework, it is at the state level where many of the more granular and experimental approaches to AI regulation are taking shape. These state-driven efforts reflect a diverse set of priorities, ranging from consumer protection and privacy to public safety and civil liberties, often responding to immediate local concerns and the unique technological landscapes within their borders. This decentralization of AI governance, while fostering innovation and allowing for tailored solutions, also presents a significant challenge in terms of national coherence and compliance for businesses operating across state lines.

California, as it has in many areas of technological regulation, has been at the forefront of state-level AI policy. Building upon the foundation laid by the California Consumer Privacy Act (CCPA) and its subsequent amendment via the California Privacy Rights Act (CPRA), which significantly impacts AI by regulating the collection and use of personal data, the state has also delved into more specific AI applications. The legislative landscape in California has seen proposals and, in some instances, enactments aimed at regulating the use of facial recognition technology by law enforcement agencies. These measures often seek to place moratoriums or outright bans on its use, citing concerns about accuracy, bias, and the potential for widespread surveillance that could infringe upon civil liberties. For example, various bills have been introduced over the years to restrict or prohibit law enforcement from using facial recognition technology, reflecting a deep-seated public concern about its potential for misuse. While some of these efforts have faced significant opposition and have not always resulted in outright bans, they have nonetheless initiated critical dialogues and raised the bar for transparency and accountability in the deployment of such AI systems. The ongoing debate in California highlights the tension between leveraging advanced technologies for public safety and safeguarding individual rights, a dilemma that states across the nation are increasingly confronting.

Beyond privacy and surveillance technologies, states are also actively addressing AI in the context of autonomous vehicles (AVs). As the technology matures, states are becoming the primary arbiters of how these vehicles can be tested and deployed on public roads. This has led to a patchwork of regulations governing everything from safety standards and licensing requirements for AV operators to liability frameworks in the event of accidents. For instance, states like Arizona, Nevada, and California have been early adopters in establishing frameworks that allow for the testing and operation of self-driving vehicles, often by issuing specific permits or licenses to companies. These regulations typically require manufacturers to demonstrate a certain level of safety, report on operational data, and, in some cases, have a human safety driver present. However, the specifics vary considerably. Some states might focus on performance standards, while others may emphasize cybersecurity or data sharing requirements. This divergence in regulatory approaches means that a company seeking to deploy AVs nationally must navigate a complex and potentially conflicting set of rules, underscoring the need for greater harmonization, or at least clearer guidelines for interstate operations. The evolving nature of AV technology also means that these regulations are subject to frequent updates and revisions, reflecting the dynamic interplay between innovation and public policy.

In addition to specific technologies, a number of states have begun to address the broader implications of AI, particularly concerning bias and discrimination. Recognizing that AI algorithms can perpetuate and even amplify existing societal biases, some states have enacted or are considering legislation to ensure fairness and equity in AI decision-making. This can include requirements for algorithmic impact assessments, audits for bias, and transparency measures when AI is used in critical areas such as hiring, lending, or criminal justice. For example, New York City, though a municipality rather than a state, passed legislation requiring employers to conduct bias audits on automated employment decision tools (AEDTs) before they can be used. This type of initiative, often driven by local concerns about employment discrimination, can influence broader state-level thinking. Similarly, states are exploring ways to ensure that AI used in areas like credit scoring or insurance underwriting does not unfairly disadvantage certain demographic groups. These efforts are often informed by the limitations of existing anti-discrimination laws when applied to complex, often opaque algorithmic systems, necessitating new legal tools and oversight mechanisms.

The fragmented nature of state-level AI regulation presents a significant challenge for national AI governance. While some states are pioneers, others are still in the early stages of understanding and addressing AI's impact. This creates a regulatory patchwork that can be difficult for businesses to navigate. A company operating nationally might need to comply with different data privacy rules, different rules for facial recognition use, and different safety standards for autonomous vehicles depending on the state. This can lead to increased compliance costs, slower innovation, and a competitive disadvantage for smaller businesses that lack the resources to manage such complexity. Furthermore, it raises questions about interstate commerce and the potential for states to enact regulations that could unduly burden or conflict with the laws of other states. The lack of a unified federal approach leaves a vacuum that states are attempting to fill, but without a coordinated strategy, the overall effectiveness and efficiency of AI governance in the U.S. can be undermined.

Moreover, the pace of technological change often outstrips the legislative process. States that are actively engaged in AI policy are constantly playing catch-up, trying to craft regulations that are both forward-looking and adaptable. This can lead to regulations that are either too broad and stifle innovation, or too narrow and quickly become obsolete. The ongoing debate in many state legislatures about how to regulate AI reflects this inherent difficulty. Some states are focusing on promoting AI development through research grants and incubation programs, while simultaneously grappling with how to mitigate the risks. Others are taking a more cautious approach, prioritizing consumer protection and the establishment of robust oversight mechanisms before widespread adoption. The variety of these approaches highlights the different priorities and risk appetites of individual states.

The influence of advocacy groups and public opinion also plays a crucial role in shaping state-level AI policies. Concerns about job displacement due to automation, the erosion of privacy through advanced surveillance technologies, and the ethical implications of autonomous systems are often amplified at the state and local levels, leading to greater pressure on lawmakers to act. This can result in a more responsive, though sometimes reactive, regulatory environment. For instance, public outcry following incidents involving AI technologies can quickly galvanize legislative action, leading to the swift introduction of bills aimed at addressing perceived harms.

The implications of this state-driven regulatory landscape extend beyond mere compliance. It creates opportunities for states to become leaders in AI innovation by fostering responsible development through clear, forward-thinking regulations. States that can strike the right balance between enabling technological advancement and protecting their citizens are likely to attract investment and talent in the AI sector. Conversely, states that adopt overly restrictive or unclear policies may find themselves lagging behind. The interplay between state and federal efforts also presents a dynamic where states can act as testbeds for regulatory approaches that could eventually inform federal policy. The lessons learned from state-level experiments in AI governance- whether successful or not- provide valuable insights for national policymakers as they strive to create a more comprehensive and effective framework for AI.

Looking ahead, the trend towards increased state-level AI regulation is likely to continue. As AI becomes more deeply embedded in critical infrastructure, public services, and everyday life, the demand for clear rules and accountability will only grow. States will continue to grapple with issues such as algorithmic transparency, the ethical deployment of AI in public sectors, and the need to ensure that the benefits of AI are shared equitably across all segments of society. The challenge for the United States will be to foster a level of coordination and coherence among these diverse state initiatives that allows for both national progress and adaptation to the unique needs and concerns of individual states. This will require ongoing dialogue, the sharing of best practices, and potentially new mechanisms for inter-state collaboration in AI governance, ensuring that the nation can harness the transformative potential of AI while effectively managing its associated risks. The effectiveness of these state-level actions will ultimately shape the broader trajectory of AI development and deployment across the country, serving as both precursors and complements to federal efforts in navigating this complex technological frontier.

The intricate landscape of Artificial Intelligence (AI) governance in the United States is characterized by a perpetual and often delicate balancing act: fostering rapid innovation versus implementing robust regulatory oversight. This tension is not merely a matter of policy preference but reflects deeply ingrained philosophical differences in how society approaches technological advancement and its potential societal impacts. On one side stand proponents of a largely unfettered market, arguing that excessive regulation will stifle creativity, hinder economic growth, and cede technological leadership to other nations. They advocate for a light-touch approach, believing that market forces, competitive pressures, and industry-led best practices are sufficient to guide AI development responsibly. This perspective often emphasizes the transformative potential of AI to solve complex global challenges, from climate change to disease, and sees regulation as an unnecessary impediment to realizing these benefits.

Conversely, a significant body of thought champions a more proactive and interventionist regulatory stance. This viewpoint is rooted in a deep concern for the potential harms that AI systems can unleash if left unchecked. These harms can range from algorithmic bias leading to discrimination in critical areas like hiring, lending, and criminal justice, to the erosion of privacy through sophisticated surveillance capabilities, and the potential for job displacement on a massive scale. Furthermore, the existential risks associated with advanced AI, though debated in terms of their immediacy, are also a prominent concern for many researchers and policymakers. This perspective argues that a laissez-faire approach is inherently dangerous, as the long-term consequences of poorly designed or maliciously deployed AI systems could be irreversible and devastating. They advocate for comprehensive legal frameworks, robust oversight mechanisms, and strong accountability measures to ensure that AI development aligns with societal values and safeguards fundamental rights.

Within this spectrum of approaches, several distinct philosophical currents guide the debate on how to strike this crucial balance. One prominent approach can be characterized as "technology-neutral" regulation. This philosophy seeks to regulate the *application* or *impact* of AI, rather than the AI technology itself. The idea is that existing laws governing areas like privacy, discrimination, and product safety are sufficient and can be adapted to address AI-driven scenarios. For instance, instead of creating specific laws for "AI bias," this approach would focus on enforcing existing anti-discrimination laws when an AI system produces biased outcomes. The advantage here is its adaptability; it doesn't require constant updates to keep pace with rapidly evolving technologies. However, critics argue that existing laws are often ill-equipped to handle the unique challenges posed by AI, particularly its opacity, scale, and potential for emergent behaviors. The complex, often proprietary nature of AI algorithms can make it exceedingly difficult to prove discriminatory intent or negligence under traditional legal frameworks.

Another significant philosophical approach is "risk-based" regulation. This model prioritizes regulatory attention based on the level of risk a particular AI application poses. High-risk applications, such as AI used in critical infrastructure, medical diagnostics, or law enforcement, would be subject to stringent pre-market approval, continuous monitoring, and rigorous auditing. Lower-risk applications, like spam filters or recommendation algorithms, would face less intensive oversight. The European Union's AI Act is a prominent example of a comprehensive risk-based regulatory framework. Proponents of this approach argue that it offers a pragmatic way to manage AI's dual nature: maximizing its benefits while mitigating its harms without unnecessarily burdening low-risk innovations. However, defining and consistently assessing "risk" across diverse AI applications can be a complex and contentious undertaking. Moreover, there is a concern that even well-intentioned risk assessments might inadvertently create barriers to entry for smaller innovators who lack the resources to navigate complex compliance requirements.

The role of industry self-regulation also features prominently in this balancing act. Many technology companies and industry associations advocate for self-governance, proposing codes of conduct, ethical guidelines, and voluntary standards as alternatives or complements to formal government regulation. They argue that industry professionals possess the deepest understanding of the technology and its nuances, making them best positioned to develop practical and effective safeguards. This approach can indeed lead to swift adoption of best practices and foster a culture of responsible innovation from within. Companies like Google, Microsoft, and IBM have all published AI principles and established internal ethics review boards. However, self-regulation is often criticized for its inherent limitations. Without external enforcement mechanisms, adherence can be inconsistent, and companies may be incentivized to prioritize commercial interests over ethical considerations or public safety. The "ethical AI" frameworks, while valuable, can sometimes be seen as performative, lacking the teeth of legally binding regulations. The history of other industries, from finance to pharmaceuticals, demonstrates that self-regulation alone is often insufficient to prevent significant harm or maintain public trust.

A crucial element in this ongoing debate is the challenge of creating agile and responsive governance frameworks that can keep pace with the relentless march of AI development while upholding the rule of law. Traditional legislative processes are often slow, cumbersome, and ill-suited to the rapid evolution of AI. By the time a bill is debated, passed, and enacted, the technology it seeks to govern may have already advanced significantly, rendering the regulation outdated or irrelevant. This leads to a persistent dilemma: should regulators aim for broad, principles-based rules that can adapt to future changes, or for specific, detailed regulations that offer greater clarity but risk becoming obsolete quickly?

Principles-based regulation, often favored in the United States, emphasizes overarching goals such as fairness, transparency, and accountability. This approach allows for flexibility and can be applied across a wide range of AI applications. For example, a principle of "fairness" can guide the development of hiring algorithms, credit scoring systems, and criminal justice tools without needing to specify precise technical requirements for each. However, translating abstract principles into concrete, actionable requirements can be challenging. What constitutes "fairness" in a given context is often a subject of debate and can vary significantly. This ambiguity can create uncertainty for developers and make enforcement difficult.

In contrast, prescriptive, rules-based regulation aims to provide clear, unambiguous directives. For instance, a regulation might specify the acceptable error rates for facial recognition systems used by law enforcement or mandate specific data security protocols for AI-powered medical devices. While this offers greater certainty and facilitates compliance, it carries the significant risk of becoming quickly outdated. Furthermore, overly prescriptive rules can inadvertently stifle innovation by dictating specific technological solutions rather than allowing for diverse approaches to achieve desired outcomes. The challenge lies in crafting regulations that are specific enough to be enforceable yet flexible enough to accommodate future technological advancements.

The concept of "agile governance" is emerging as a potential solution to this dilemma. This approach advocates for adaptive regulatory strategies that involve continuous learning, iterative policymaking, and the use of sandboxes-controlled environments where companies can test innovative AI applications under regulatory supervision. Regulatory sandboxes allow policymakers to observe new technologies in action, understand their real-world implications, and adapt regulations accordingly, often in collaboration with industry stakeholders. This iterative process can help bridge the gap between technological innovation and regulatory frameworks, enabling a more dynamic and responsive governance model. Several states and cities in the U.S. are exploring sandbox approaches, particularly for emerging technologies like autonomous vehicles and fintech.

Furthermore, the nature of AI development itself complicates the task of effective regulation. AI systems, particularly those based on deep learning, can be "black boxes"- their internal decision-making processes are often opaque, even to their creators. This lack of transparency poses significant challenges for accountability and oversight. How can a regulator determine if an AI system is discriminatory or unsafe if its decision-making logic cannot be fully understood? Addressing this "explainability" or "interpretability" challenge is a key area of research and a critical component of effective AI governance. Regulations may need to mandate certain levels of explainability or require developers to conduct rigorous testing and validation to demonstrate that their systems are performing as intended and without undue bias.

The interplay between different regulatory bodies and levels of government in the U.S. also contributes to the complexity of balancing innovation and regulation. As discussed previously, state-level regulations are emerging rapidly, creating a fragmented landscape. At the federal level, multiple agencies have jurisdiction over different aspects of AI, including the National Institute of Standards and Technology (NIST) for standards development, the Federal Trade Commission (FTC) for consumer protection and unfair/deceptive practices, and sector-specific regulators like the Food and Drug Administration (FDA) for AI in healthcare. Coordinating these efforts and ensuring a coherent national strategy is a significant challenge. Without a unified vision, regulatory efforts can be piecemeal, inconsistent, and ultimately less effective in both fostering innovation and mitigating risks.

The question of intellectual property (IP) and its interaction with AI regulation is another vital consideration. Robust IP protection is often seen as a critical driver of innovation, encouraging investment in research and development. However, if IP regimes are too rigid, they could hinder the widespread adoption and beneficial application of AI technologies, especially in areas where collaborative research and open-source development are crucial. Striking a balance that protects legitimate IP rights while facilitating responsible AI development and deployment is an ongoing challenge for policymakers. This includes considerations around data ownership, the copyrightability of AI-generated content, and the licensing of AI technologies.

The economic implications of regulatory choices are also a major factor in the balancing act. Overly burdensome regulations can increase the cost of developing and deploying AI, potentially favoring large, well-resourced companies over startups and smaller businesses. This can lead to market concentration and reduce overall dynamism in the

AI ecosystem. Conversely, inadequate regulation can lead to market failures, consumer harm, and erosion of public trust, which can ultimately hinder long-term economic growth and adoption. Policymakers must therefore consider the economic impact of their decisions, aiming for regulations that are both effective in achieving their intended outcomes and proportionate to the risks they are designed to address. This often involves engaging in cost-benefit analyses and seeking input from a wide range of stakeholders, including industry, academia, civil society, and the public.

The debate over fostering innovation versus implementing regulation is not static; it is a dynamic and evolving process. As AI technology continues to advance at an exponential rate, the nature of the risks and the potential benefits will also change. This necessitates a continuous re-evaluation of existing regulatory frameworks and a willingness to adapt and evolve governance strategies. The United States' approach to this challenge is characterized by a decentralized and often experimental spirit. While this can lead to a complex and sometimes fragmented regulatory landscape, it also allows for diverse approaches to be tested and evaluated. The ongoing dialogue among policymakers, technologists, ethicists, and the public will be crucial in navigating this complex terrain, aiming to harness the immense potential of AI for the betterment of society while diligently safeguarding against its potential pitfalls. The ultimate success of the U.S. AI ecosystem will depend on its ability to cultivate an environment where innovation can flourish responsibly, guided by thoughtful, agile, and forward-looking governance that upholds the rule of law and serves the public interest.

8
National Perspectives
The European Union's AI Framework

The European Union has embarked on a distinctive and arguably the most comprehensive journey towards regulating Artificial Intelligence (AI) globally, setting a benchmark for a rights-centric and risk-based approach. Unlike the more fragmented or sector-specific strategies adopted by some other major economies, the EU's ambition is to create a holistic, horizontal legal framework that underpins the development and deployment of AI systems across all economic sectors and societal applications. This overarching strategy is embodied in the landmark **Artificial Intelligence Act (AI Act)**, a legislative proposal that has been meticulously crafted to foster innovation while ensuring that AI systems deployed within the Union are safe, transparent, traceable, non-discriminatory, and environmentally sustainable. At its core, the EU's AI strategy is deeply rooted in the Union's fundamental values: respect for human dignity, freedom, democracy, equality, the rule of law, and respect for human rights. The guiding principle is the promotion of "trustworthy AI," a concept that has become synonymous with the EU's regulatory philosophy. This trustworthiness is not merely a desirable outcome but a mandatory prerequisite for AI systems that are intended to interact with or impact individuals and society significantly.

The cornerstone of the EU's regulatory approach is its **risk-based classification system**. This model categorizes AI systems based on the level of risk they pose to individuals' health, safety, and fundamental rights. This tiered structure allows for a proportionate regulatory response, ensuring that the most impactful AI systems are subjected to the most stringent requirements, while those posing minimal or no risk face significantly lighter obligations. The AI Act identifies four primary risk categories: unacceptable risk, high risk, limited risk, and minimal or no risk.

At the apex of this classification are AI systems deemed to pose an **unacceptable risk**. These are systems that fundamentally contravene EU values and fundamental rights and are therefore outright prohibited. The Act explicitly lists several categories of AI systems that fall under this prohibition, including: social scoring systems implemented by public authorities that assess the trustworthiness of individuals based on their social behavior or personal characteristics, potentially leading to discriminatory or detrimental treatment; manipulative or exploitative AI systems that exploit vulnerabilities of specific groups, such as children or individuals with cognitive impairments, to distort their behavior in a way that is likely to cause them or others harm; and, in most circumstances, AI systems that enable or contribute to subliminal manipulation of individuals, leading to a distortion of their behavior that is likely to cause harm. The EU's stance here is unambiguous: certain applications of AI are considered so intrinsically dangerous to human dignity and fundamental rights that they must be banned outright, irrespective of their potential benefits. This prohibition aims to preempt the development and deployment of AI systems that could undermine democratic principles or inflict severe societal harm.

The most significant regulatory focus of the AI Act is on AI systems classified as **high-risk**. These are AI systems that, due to their intended purpose and potential impact, can pose a significant risk to the fundamental rights, health, or safety of individuals. The Act provides a comprehensive Annex detailing specific areas and use cases that are considered high-risk. These include, but are not limited to, AI systems used as safety components of products that are already subject to specific EU harmonisation legislation, such as machinery, toys, aircraft, and vehicles. Furthermore, AI systems used in areas critical for the exercise of fundamental rights are also classified as high-risk. This encompasses AI used in the management and operation of critical infrastructure (e.g., in transport, which could endanger the life and health of people), in education and vocational training (e.g., for determining access to or allocation of education and advanced training, or for assessing students), in employment, worker management, and access to self-employment (e.g., for recruitment, for making decisions on promotion and termination of contracts, or for monitoring and evaluating performance and behavior in the context of work), in access to and enjoyment of essential private services and public services and benefits (e.g., credit scoring to assess the creditworthiness of natural persons, or AI systems used in the context of public order and traffic control, or in the administration of justice and democratic processes), and in law enforcement. The rationale for classifying these systems as high-risk is their potential to cause significant harm, whether through bias leading to discrimination, errors leading to physical injury, or opaque decision-making that undermines due process and fundamental rights.

For these high-risk AI systems, the AI Act imposes a suite of stringent obligations on providers (those developing and making AI systems available on the market) and deployers (those using AI systems). These obligations are designed to ensure that high-risk AI systems are developed and used in a responsible and trustworthy manner. Key requirements include the establishment of a **risk management system** throughout the AI system's lifecycle, aiming to identify, analyze, and mitigate risks. Providers must ensure that the **quality of the data sets** used to train, validate, and test their AI systems is adequate and robust, taking measures to minimize the presence of biases in data sets that could lead to discriminatory outcomes. A crucial aspect is the requirement for **technical documentation and record-keeping**, which should enable the assessment of conformity with the Act and allow for traceability of the system's operation. The AI Act mandates **human oversight**, ensuring that AI systems can be effectively monitored, controlled, and, if necessary, interrupted by humans. This is not necessarily about direct human intervention in every decision, but about designing systems that allow for meaningful oversight and the ability to override potentially harmful outputs. Furthermore, systems must be developed to achieve an appropriate **level of accuracy, robustness, and cybersecurity**. The accuracy requirements are particularly important for high-risk applications where errors could have severe consequences. Finally, for high-risk AI systems intended to interact with natural persons, the Act requires that individuals be **informed** that they are interacting with an AI system.

Beyond these general obligations for all high-risk systems, the Act specifies additional requirements for certain categories of high-risk AI. For example, AI systems intended to be used as safety components of products are subject to the conformity assessment procedures laid down in specific EU harmonisation legislation, such as the New Legislative Framework. AI systems intended to be used for recruitment or for making decisions on promotion and termination of employment contracts, or for assessing students in educational or vocational training settings, or for determining access to essential services, must also comply with specific requirements related to the quality of data sets and human oversight. The Act also includes specific provisions for AI systems used in law enforcement, such as for risk assessment of persons for the purpose of preventing or detecting criminal offenses, or for the assessment of the reliability of evidence, requiring rigorous validation and transparency.

The third category is **limited risk** AI systems. These systems are subject to specific transparency obligations. For example, users must be informed when they are interacting with an AI system, such as chatbots. Similarly, AI systems that generate or manipulate content, such as deepfakes, must be clearly labeled as artificially generated or manipulated. This is intended to ensure that individuals are aware of the nature of the content they are consuming and can make informed judgments. The aim here is to prevent deception and maintain trust in information ecosystems.

Finally, the vast majority of AI systems are expected to fall into the category of **minimal or no risk**. These are AI systems that do not pose any significant risk to fundamental rights or safety, such as AI-powered video games or spam filters. The AI Act acknowledges that these systems can be developed and deployed freely, with no additional obligations beyond existing relevant legislation. This approach is crucial for fostering innovation and ensuring that the regulatory burden does not stifle the development of beneficial AI applications. The EU's intention is to create a regulatory environment that encourages AI innovation and adoption across the board, while ensuring that the more impactful applications are subject to robust safeguards.

The implementation of the AI Act will involve a comprehensive conformity assessment procedure before high-risk AI systems can be placed on the market or put into service. Providers will generally need to conduct an internal conformity assessment, possibly with the involvement of a notified body for certain high-risk AI systems, to verify compliance with the Act's requirements. Once a system is on the market, ongoing monitoring and post-market surveillance will be essential, with providers obligated to report serious incidents or malfunctions to the relevant authorities. The establishment of a European Artificial Intelligence Board (EAIB) is also envisaged to ensure the consistent application of the AI Act across all Member States, fostering a harmonized approach to AI governance within the EU.

The EU's AI Act represents a significant departure from previous regulatory approaches to technology. It is a proactive, horizontal piece of legislation that seeks to establish a clear legal framework for AI, emphasizing human values and fundamental rights. By adopting a risk-based approach, the EU aims to strike a delicate balance between fostering innovation and mitigating potential harms, creating a regulatory environment that is both enabling and protective. This comprehensive strategy reflects a deep commitment to ensuring that AI development and deployment in Europe align with societal expectations and uphold the fundamental rights of its citizens, setting a global precedent for responsible AI governance. The focus on 'trustworthy AI' is not merely a slogan but a tangible legal and ethical commitment embedded within the Act's various provisions and obligations. This approach underscores the EU's belief that technological advancement must serve humanity, rather than the other way around, and that robust legal safeguards are essential to achieving this objective.

The integration of Artificial Intelligence (AI) into the legal systems and public services of the European Union's Member States is a complex and rapidly evolving landscape. While the overarching AI Act provides a harmonizing framework, its practical application and the specific ways AI is being adopted vary significantly across the Union's diverse national contexts. This section delves into how EU member states are weaving AI into the fabric of their judicial processes, law enforcement agencies, and the broader spectrum of public services, while also scrutinizing the legal standards and ethical considerations that accompany this technological transformation.

In the realm of judicial processes, AI is being explored and piloted for a range of tasks, from case management and legal research to, more controversially, aspects of judicial decision-making. Countries like Estonia have been at the forefront, leveraging AI for tasks such as mediating small claims disputes, aiming to streamline processes and reduce backlogs. The principle here is to automate repetitive, data-intensive tasks, freeing up human judges and legal professionals to focus on more complex, nuanced aspects of justice. Legal research platforms are increasingly incorporating AI to sift through vast volumes of case law, statutes, and legal commentary, providing legal professionals with faster access to relevant precedents and statutory provisions. This can significantly enhance the efficiency of legal analysis and argumentation. However, the use of AI in judicial decision-making remains a highly sensitive area, prompting rigorous debate about fairness, transparency, and accountability. The EU AI Act's classification of AI systems used in the administration of justice as high-risk underscores the inherent need for caution. This classification necessitates stringent compliance with requirements related to data quality, accuracy, human oversight, and transparency. For instance, AI tools used to predict recidivism or assess the likelihood of reoffending in sentencing or parole decisions must meet exceptionally high standards to avoid perpetuating existing societal biases or leading to discriminatory outcomes. The potential for algorithmic bias, where historical data reflecting societal inequalities is used to train AI systems, poses a significant risk to the fundamental right to a fair trial and equal treatment before the law. National legal systems are grappling with how to ensure that AI-driven insights do not unduly influence or replace judicial discretion, and that decisions remain rooted in human judgment and legal principles. Robust auditing mechanisms, explainability requirements for AI models, and clear avenues for appeal against AI-influenced decisions are becoming crucial components of national strategies.

Law enforcement agencies across the EU are also increasingly turning to AI to enhance their operational capabilities. This includes AI-powered tools for facial recognition, predictive policing, crime analysis, and evidence processing. Predictive policing algorithms, for example, aim to forecast where and when crimes are most likely to occur, allowing for more targeted resource allocation. AI is also being deployed to analyze vast amounts of data from surveillance systems, social media, and other sources to identify potential threats or criminal activities. However, these applications are fraught with ethical and legal challenges. The use of facial recognition technology in public spaces, particularly when linked to law enforcement, raises significant privacy concerns and questions about its accuracy and potential for misidentification, which can have severe consequences for individuals. The AI Act's prohibition on certain uses of AI in public order and law enforcement, such as real-time remote biometric identification systems in publicly accessible spaces by law enforcement (with limited exceptions for serious crimes and specific authorization), reflects the EU's commitment to safeguarding fundamental rights against intrusive surveillance. Even where AI is permitted, its deployment must be carefully managed. For AI systems used in law enforcement to assess the reliability of evidence or to aid in criminal investigations, the Act mandates rigorous validation and transparency. This means that the underlying data, algorithms, and decision-making processes must be comprehensible and auditable, ensuring that AI serves as a tool to aid human investigators rather than dictate conclusions. The risk of bias in these systems, particularly if trained on data that reflects historical profiling or discriminatory policing practices, is a critical concern that national legal frameworks must address through robust oversight and impact assessments.

The broader spectrum of public services is also experiencing a significant infusion of AI. From optimizing traffic flow and managing energy grids to personalizing citizen services and improving administrative efficiency, AI offers substantial potential benefits. For example, AI can assist in processing applications for social benefits, providing citizens with faster responses and more tailored support. Chatbots and virtual assistants are being deployed by governments to answer citizen queries, provide information about public services, and guide users through complex administrative procedures, thereby improving accessibility and user experience. In healthcare, AI is being explored for diagnostic support, personalized treatment plans, and optimizing hospital resource allocation. The EU AI Act classifies many of these applications as high-risk, particularly those that affect access to essential public services, such as credit scoring for loan applications or AI systems used in the administration of public benefits where there is a risk of discrimination or significant impact on individuals' livelihoods. Consequently, these systems are subject to the Act's stringent requirements. This includes ensuring that the data used for training and operation is representative and free from bias, that there are mechanisms for human oversight to correct or override AI-driven decisions, and that individuals are informed when they are interacting with an AI system. Transparency in how AI is used to make decisions that affect citizens' access to essential services, such as housing, social welfare, or permits, is paramount. National public administrations are developing guidelines and ethical frameworks to ensure that AI deployment aligns with principles of fairness, accountability, and public trust. This often involves creating internal review boards, conducting public consultations on AI initiatives, and investing in training for public officials to understand the capabilities and limitations of AI.

Across various Member States, several common themes emerge in the adoption of AI within public services and legal systems. One is the emphasis on pilot projects and gradual implementation. Many national administrations are starting with smaller-scale AI applications in controlled environments to test efficacy, identify potential issues, and build capacity before wider deployment. Another significant theme is the focus on data governance. The quality, integrity, and ethical sourcing of data are recognized as foundational to the successful and responsible deployment of AI. Member States are investing in improving data infrastructure and establishing clear data management policies. Furthermore, there is a growing recognition of the need for reskilling and upskilling the public workforce. Officials who interact with or manage AI systems need to possess a certain level of AI literacy to understand their functionalities, limitations, and potential risks.

However, alongside the promising advancements, several pitfalls are also being observed. One persistent challenge is the "black box" problem, where the complex nature of some AI algorithms makes it difficult to understand how a particular decision was reached. This lack of transparency can undermine public trust and hinder accountability, especially in legal contexts where due process requires understandable reasoning. Another pitfall is the risk of exacerbating existing inequalities. If AI systems are trained on biased data or designed without considering the needs of vulnerable populations, they can perpetuate or even amplify societal discrimination. The digital divide also poses a challenge, as not all citizens have equal access to digital technologies or the skills to interact with AI-powered public services, potentially creating new forms of exclusion. Furthermore, the procurement of AI systems by public bodies presents its own set of challenges, including ensuring value for money, avoiding vendor lock-in, and guaranteeing that purchased systems align with public sector values and legal obligations. National procurement regulations are being adapted to accommodate the unique nature of AI technologies, with greater emphasis on transparency and due diligence.

Best practices are beginning to crystallize from these experiences. These include establishing clear ethical guidelines and governance frameworks for AI deployment in the public sector, conducting thorough impact assessments before rolling out AI systems, and fostering multi-stakeholder dialogues involving citizens, civil society, and technology experts. Transparency and explainability are being prioritized, with efforts to make AI decision-making processes as understandable as possible to both users and regulators. The concept of "human-in-the-loop" is also being widely adopted, ensuring that AI systems augment, rather than replace, human judgment, particularly in high-stakes decision-making. The emphasis on ongoing monitoring and evaluation of AI systems once they are deployed is crucial for identifying and mitigating unintended consequences or performance degradation over time. This post-market surveillance is a critical element for ensuring continued compliance with the AI Act and for adapting regulatory approaches as technology evolves.

The EU AI Act serves as a vital scaffolding for these national efforts, establishing a baseline of requirements and prohibitions. However, the success of this framework hinges on its effective transposition and consistent application at the Member State level. Each national legal system must interpret and implement the Act's provisions in a manner that respects its own constitutional traditions and legal heritage, while also ensuring a harmonized approach across the Union. This requires close collaboration between national legislators, regulatory bodies, courts, and public administrations. The development of national strategies for AI in public services and legal systems is an ongoing process, marked by a commitment to leveraging technology for public good while upholding fundamental rights and democratic values. The journey towards integrating AI responsibly within the EU's legal and public service spheres is a continuous endeavor, demanding vigilance, adaptability, and a steadfast commitment to the principles that underpin European society.

The General Data Protection Regulation (GDPR), enacted in May 2018, stands as a cornerstone of data protection and privacy in the European Union. Its comprehensive stipulations, designed to empower individuals and harmonize data protection laws across member states, have a profound and multifaceted impact on the burgeoning field of Artificial Intelligence (AI) development and deployment. AI systems, by their very nature, are data-hungry, relying on vast datasets for training, validation, and operation. This inherent dependency places AI squarely within the purview of GDPR, creating a complex interplay between the pursuit of technological advancement and the safeguarding of fundamental data privacy rights.

At the heart of GDPR lies a set of core principles that govern the processing of personal data. These principles, including lawfulness, fairness, transparency, purpose limitation, data minimization, accuracy, storage limitation, and integrity and confidentiality, are not mere suggestions but binding legal requirements. For AI developers and deployers, adherence to these principles necessitates a fundamental rethinking of data handling practices. The principle of lawfulness, for instance, demands a valid legal basis for processing personal data. This could be consent, contractual necessity, legal obligation, vital interests, public task, or legitimate interests. In the context of AI, especially for systems that are not strictly necessary for a service or are not based on explicit consent, establishing a lawful basis can be challenging. For example, using personal data to train a predictive AI model for marketing purposes might require explicit, informed consent, which can be difficult to obtain at scale and to manage throughout the AI lifecycle. The "fairness" principle, intrinsically linked to transparency, requires that personal data is processed in a way that is understandable and equitable to the data subject. This is particularly problematic for complex AI models, often referred to as "black boxes," where the decision-making process is opaque, making it difficult for individuals to understand how their data is being used and how decisions affecting them are made.

The principle of "purpose limitation" is another critical area of tension with AI. GDPR mandates that personal data collected for specified, explicit, and legitimate purposes should not be further processed in a manner that is incompatible with those purposes. AI development, however, often involves iterative refinement and experimentation, where datasets initially collected for one purpose might be repurposed for training new AI models or for entirely different analytical tasks. This evolution in the use of data can easily stray into incompatibility with the original stated purpose, thereby violating GDPR. For instance, data collected to improve customer service might later be used to train a facial recognition AI for security purposes. Without a new, clearly defined legal basis and transparency about this secondary use, such processing would likely be non-compliant.

Similarly, the principle of "data minimization" poses significant hurdles. GDPR requires that personal data processed should be adequate, relevant, and limited to what is necessary in relation to the purposes for which they are processed. AI algorithms, particularly deep learning models, often perform better when trained on larger, more diverse datasets, even if some of that data might initially appear extraneous. The drive for AI performance can therefore conflict with the GDPR's mandate to collect and process only the minimum data necessary. This forces developers to make difficult choices: either risk suboptimal AI performance or find innovative ways to train models with less data, perhaps through techniques like federated learning or differential privacy, which themselves introduce their own complexities and trade-offs.

The rights granted to data subjects under GDPR are also profoundly impacted by AI. Individuals have the right to access their data, rectify inaccuracies, erase their data, restrict processing, object to processing, and the right to data portability. The right to access, in particular, becomes complicated when personal data is embedded within complex AI models. How can a data subject effectively access and understand the personal data that has informed an AI's training or decision-making process, especially when that data has been transformed, aggregated, or is part of a proprietary algorithm? The right to erasure, often termed the "right to be forgotten," presents an even more formidable challenge. If personal data has been used to train an AI model, especially a deep learning model where the data is effectively encoded within the model's parameters, physically removing that specific data point from the model's knowledge base can be technically infeasible or prohibitively expensive. While some argue that a model does not *store* personal data in the same way a database does, the fact that the model's behavior is a direct consequence of the data it was trained on raises questions about whether the data has truly been "erased" from the model's functioning.

The GDPR also introduced Article 22, which deals with automated individual decision-making, including profiling. This article states that data subjects have the right not to be subject to a decision based solely on automated processing, including profiling, which produces legal effects concerning them or similarly significantly affects them, unless such processing is necessary for the performance of a contract, is authorized by Union or Member State law, or is based on explicit consent. Even when these conditions are met, safeguards must be in place, including the right to obtain human intervention, express one's point of view, and contest the decision. This article is highly relevant to AI applications that make consequential decisions about individuals, such as loan applications, job suitability assessments, or credit scoring. The "solely on automated processing" clause implies that a degree of human oversight can mitigate the prohibitions. However, the interpretation of "significant effect" and the nature and quality of human intervention required remain areas of ongoing debate and are crucial for the compliant deployment of AI in sensitive areas.

The effectiveness of GDPR in governing AI is a subject of continuous evaluation. On one hand, GDPR has undoubtedly raised awareness about data privacy and has compelled organizations to adopt more robust data protection practices. It has fostered a culture of "privacy by design" and "privacy by default," encouraging developers to embed privacy considerations into the AI development lifecycle from the outset. The regulatory framework provides a clear set of rights and obligations, offering a legal grounding for individuals to challenge data processing practices and for regulators to enforce compliance. The substantial fines that can be levied for non-compliance act as a powerful deterrent.

However, several challenges remain. The rapid pace of AI innovation often outstrips the ability of existing regulations to keep up. The technical complexity of AI makes it difficult for regulators, and indeed for many individuals, to fully understand how these systems operate and to assess compliance. The interpretation of key GDPR terms like "personal data," "consent," "purpose limitation," and "necessary" in the context of advanced AI techniques is still evolving. Furthermore, the extraterritorial reach of GDPR means that AI systems developed or deployed outside the EU but processing the data of EU residents must also comply, creating a global compliance burden.

Moreover, the GDPR's emphasis on consent as a legal basis can be problematic for large-scale AI development, where obtaining granular, informed consent for all potential future uses of data is impractical. This pushes organizations to rely on other legal bases, such as legitimate interests, which then requires a balancing test between the organization's interests and the data subject's rights and freedoms. This balancing act is particularly nuanced when AI is involved, as the potential impact on individuals can be significant and difficult to foresee.

The advent of the EU AI Act, while a separate piece of legislation, is designed to complement and work in tandem with GDPR. The AI Act categorizes AI systems based on risk, imposing different obligations accordingly. For high-risk AI systems, which often involve the processing of personal data and can have significant impacts on individuals, the AI Act mandates strict requirements related to data governance, transparency, human oversight, and accuracy, which are deeply intertwined with GDPR principles. For example, the AI Act's requirements for high-quality, relevant, and representative training data directly support GDPR's data minimization and accuracy principles. Similarly, the AI Act's emphasis on transparency and explainability aligns with GDPR's requirement for fair and transparent processing.

In essence, GDPR provides the foundational data protection framework within which AI must operate. It sets the rules for how personal data can be collected, used, and managed. The challenges and complexities that AI presents to these rules necessitate a proactive approach from developers and deployers, focusing on ethical data handling, robust governance, and a deep understanding of individual rights. The continuous evolution of AI technology and its applications will undoubtedly lead to ongoing refinement of how GDPR principles are interpreted and applied, underscoring the dynamic relationship between data protection law and artificial intelligence. The GDPR, therefore, acts not as a barrier to AI innovation, but as a critical guide, ensuring that such innovation is pursued responsibly and in a manner that respects the fundamental rights of individuals.

The European Union's approach to artificial intelligence is increasingly defined not just by regulatory frameworks like the AI Act, but also by a strong emphasis on embedding ethical considerations and ensuring accountability throughout the AI lifecycle. This commitment stems from a recognition that AI's transformative potential must be harnessed responsibly, safeguarding fundamental rights and fostering public trust. The Union's strategy involves a multi-pronged effort, promoting specific ethical guidelines and establishing mechanisms to translate these principles into tangible practice, thereby laying the groundwork for a human-centric AI ecosystem.

Central to this endeavor is the promotion of ethical guidelines that act as a compass for AI development and deployment. These guidelines, often articulated through policy documents, expert recommendations, and the foundational principles of the AI Act, underscore a commitment to human agency, fairness, transparency, and safety. The concept of 'explainable AI' (XAI) stands out as a critical ethical tenet. While many sophisticated AI models, particularly those based on deep learning, operate as 'black boxes' where the internal decision-making processes are opaque, the EU is pushing for greater transparency. Explainable AI seeks to make these complex systems understandable, allowing stakeholders, including developers, regulators, and end-users, to comprehend *why* a particular decision or prediction was made. This is not merely a technical challenge but an ethical imperative. For instance, in healthcare, an AI recommending a treatment plan must be able to articulate the rationale behind its suggestion, enabling medical professionals to validate the advice and patients to understand the basis of their care. Similarly, in the financial sector, an AI denying a loan application needs to provide clear reasons, allowing the applicant to address any inaccuracies or misunderstandings. The EU's vision is that explainability should be proportionate to the risk posed by the AI system; higher-risk applications demand a greater degree of transparency and interpretability. This push for XAI aims to mitigate bias, detect errors, and build trust, moving away from opaque systems that could perpetuate discrimination or lead to unfair outcomes.

Beyond explainability, the EU also champions principles of fairness and non-discrimination. AI systems are trained on data, and if that data reflects historical societal biases, the AI can inadvertently learn and amplify these biases, leading to discriminatory outcomes in areas such as hiring, credit scoring, or law enforcement. Ethical guidelines therefore emphasize the need for rigorous data governance, including the careful selection and pre-processing of training data to identify and mitigate biases. Techniques for bias detection and mitigation are becoming integral to the AI development process, with organizations encouraged to conduct fairness audits and implement strategies to ensure equitable treatment across different demographic groups. The principle of "fairness" in AI is not a monolithic concept; it can encompass various interpretations, such as equality of opportunity, equality of outcome, or group fairness versus individual fairness. The EU's approach encourages a nuanced understanding of fairness, advocating for approaches that are context-dependent and tailored to the specific application of the AI system.

Furthermore, the ethical guidelines place a strong emphasis on human oversight and control. While AI can automate complex tasks, the EU believes that critical decisions, especially those with significant implications for individuals, should retain a degree of human involvement. This is not to negate the efficiency and capability of AI, but to ensure that human judgment, ethical reasoning, and the capacity for empathy remain central. Human oversight can take many forms, from a human in the loop who approves or rejects AI-generated decisions, to a human on the loop who monitors the AI's performance and intervenes when necessary, or even a human out of the loop where humans set the parameters and goals for the AI but do not directly oversee its day-to-day operations. The level of oversight is often determined by the risk assessment of the AI system, with higher-risk systems requiring more direct and meaningful human intervention. This principle is crucial for maintaining accountability, as it ensures that there is always a human agent ultimately responsible for the outcomes of an AI system.

Accountability for AI systems is a cornerstone of the EU's regulatory and ethical strategy. Recognizing that AI systems, by their very nature, can be complex, autonomous, and deployed by various actors, establishing clear lines of responsibility is paramount. The EU's approach to AI accountability is multifaceted, seeking to ensure that when an AI system causes harm or produces unintended negative consequences, there are mechanisms in place to identify who is responsible and to provide redress. This involves not only legal accountability but also organizational and technical accountability.

To foster this, the EU is exploring and promoting the establishment of specialized AI ethics committees or advisory bodies. These committees, often composed of multidisciplinary experts encompassing technologists, ethicists, legal scholars, social scientists, and representatives from civil society, are tasked with providing guidance on ethical AI development and deployment, assessing the ethical implications of specific AI applications, and advising on policy development. Their role is to act as a crucial bridge between technological innovation and societal values, ensuring that ethical considerations are not an afterthought but are embedded into the foundational stages of AI creation and implementation. These bodies can help organizations navigate the complex ethical landscape, offering frameworks for ethical risk assessment, stakeholder engagement, and the development of ethical codes of conduct specific to AI.

The concept of "accountability by design" is also

gaining traction. This principle suggests that accountability mechanisms should be built into AI systems from their inception, rather than being an add-on after a problem has occurred. This might include logging AI decisions, maintaining audit trails of data used and algorithmic processes, and implementing clear procedures for addressing errors or biases. For example, an AI system used for autonomous driving would need robust logging capabilities to record sensor data, algorithmic decisions, and vehicle actions in the event of an accident, facilitating an investigation into the cause and assigning responsibility.

The EU AI Act itself contains provisions designed to enhance accountability, particularly for high-risk AI systems. These provisions often require conformity assessments, risk management systems, and rigorous documentation of the AI system's development, training data, and operational procedures. For instance, providers of high-risk AI systems are required to establish a quality management system and keep detailed technical documentation, which can serve as evidence of compliance and facilitate accountability in case of issues. Furthermore, the Act mandates that these systems are subject to appropriate human oversight, further reinforcing the link between human control and accountability. The clear delineation of responsibilities between providers, deployers, and users of AI systems aims to ensure that each stakeholder understands their role in maintaining compliant and ethical AI operations.

Beyond the formal regulatory framework, the EU encourages a culture of responsible innovation where companies and researchers proactively consider the ethical implications of their work. This includes encouraging voluntary codes of conduct, ethical impact assessments, and the continuous monitoring and evaluation of AI systems in real-world conditions. The principle of "privacy by design" and "security by design," already well-established in data protection, is extended to AI, advocating for ethical considerations to be integrated into the entire development pipeline. This means that ethical reviews should be conducted at various stages, from conceptualization and data collection to model training, testing, and deployment.

The mechanisms for ensuring accountability also extend to addressing harm. The EU's legal framework, including the GDPR and proposed directives on liability, is being adapted to address the unique challenges posed by AI. This includes exploring how existing liability rules apply to AI-generated harm and considering new legal frameworks where necessary. The goal is to ensure that individuals who suffer harm due to AI systems have access to effective remedies and that there are incentives for developers and deployers to prioritize safety and ethical considerations. For example, if an AI-powered medical diagnostic tool misdiagnoses a patient leading to adverse health outcomes, there must be a clear pathway for the patient to seek compensation from the party responsible, whether that be the developer of the algorithm, the manufacturer of the device, or the healthcare provider who deployed it.

In summary, the European Union's commitment to ethical AI and accountability is a defining characteristic of its approach. By promoting principles such as explainability, fairness, and human oversight, and by establishing mechanisms like AI ethics committees and robust regulatory requirements within the AI Act, the Union aims to foster an AI ecosystem that is not only innovative but also trustworthy, rights-respecting, and accountable. This integrated strategy, weaving together ethical guidelines, legal frameworks, and organizational best practices, seeks to ensure that AI development and deployment serves the common good, upholding human values and societal well-being throughout its entire lifecycle. The ongoing dialogue and evolution of these ethical considerations and accountability mechanisms are critical as AI technology continues to advance and integrate into ever more aspects of our lives.

The European Union, through its pioneering AI Act and the foundational ethical principles underpinning it, has positioned itself as a significant architect of global artificial intelligence governance. This proactive stance is not merely about domestic regulation; it extends to a profound influence on how other nations and international bodies approach the complex challenge of managing AI. The EU's comprehensive and risk-based regulatory model, coupled with its unwavering commitment to fundamental rights and ethical considerations, has created a powerful precedent that resonates far beyond its borders. As AI technologies continue their relentless march, the EU's framework is increasingly becoming a benchmark, a blueprint that others are observing, adapting, and in some instances, directly adopting. This phenomenon, often referred to as the 'Brussels effect,' describes the unique ability of the EU to export its regulatory standards and norms internationally, compelling global companies and governments to align with its high standards to access the lucrative EU market.

The AI Act, in particular, serves as the vanguard of this global influence. Its tiered approach, categorizing AI systems based on their risk level, from minimal to unacceptable, provides a structured and pragmatic way to address the diverse applications of AI. Systems deemed to pose a high risk, such as those used in critical infrastructure, education, employment, essential services, law enforcement, and migration, are subjected to stringent requirements. These include robust risk management systems, high-quality data sets, comprehensive documentation, transparency obligations, and mandatory human oversight. The very comprehensiveness of these requirements means that any entity wishing to deploy such AI systems within the EU market must adhere to these exacting standards. Consequently, global technology providers and businesses that operate internationally are incentivized to develop AI systems that are compliant with the AI Act, even if their primary market is outside the EU. This creates a ripple effect, encouraging a global uplift in AI safety, fairness, and accountability. The Act's stringent provisions on forbidden AI practices, such as social scoring by governments or AI-powered real-time remote biometric identification in public spaces (with limited exceptions), also set a strong ethical red line that influences international debates on acceptable AI uses.

Beyond the explicit mandates of the AI Act, the EU's broader ethical commitment, as manifested in its ethical guidelines and the values embedded within its regulatory philosophy, contributes significantly to its global impact. The emphasis on human-centricity, transparency, fairness, accountability, and the safeguarding of fundamental rights is a persuasive narrative in an era where the societal implications of AI are increasingly scrutinized. Many countries grappling with the rapid advancement of AI lack the legislative history or the established institutional capacity to develop their own comprehensive frameworks. They often look to existing models for inspiration and guidance. The EU's approach, born from a deep commitment to its foundational values and a robust consultative process involving a wide array of stakeholders, offers a compelling and well-reasoned example. This is particularly true for democracies that share similar concerns about individual liberties, privacy, and the rule of law. For instance, countries in Asia, Latin America, and even parts of North America have shown keen interest in the EU's risk-based approach and its focus on fundamental rights protection, often referencing the AI Act in their own legislative drafting processes.

International organizations also play a crucial role in amplifying the EU's influence. Bodies like the United Nations, the OECD, and the G7/G20 are increasingly engaging in discussions about AI governance. The EU actively participates in these forums, advocating for its principles and contributing to the development of global norms. The OECD's AI Principles, for example, which promote inclusive growth, sustainable development, human-centered values, fairness, transparency, and accountability, bear a strong resemblance to the core tenets of the EU's AI strategy. While the OECD principles are non-binding, they serve as an important soft law instrument that guides national policymaking and international cooperation. The EU's consistent championing of these values within such global bodies helps to solidify them as internationally recognized standards for responsible AI development and deployment. This collaborative approach ensures that the EU's influence is not just a unilateral imposition but a contribution to a shared international understanding of how AI should be governed.

The 'Brussels effect' in the context of AI is not merely about regulatory alignment; it is also about shaping the very discourse and ethical considerations surrounding AI. The EU's sustained focus on the ethical dimensions of AI has elevated these discussions on a global scale. By prioritizing issues like bias mitigation, algorithmic discrimination, the impact of AI on employment, and the potential for AI to undermine democratic processes, the EU has prompted a more profound and widespread societal reflection on the implications of this technology. This has encouraged a more critical examination of AI systems by researchers, developers, civil society organizations, and policymakers worldwide. For instance, the EU's push for explainable AI (XAI) has spurred research and development in this area globally, as companies recognize the growing demand for transparency from both regulators and consumers. Similarly, the EU's stance on AI in sensitive areas like surveillance and predictive policing has informed debates in other regions about the permissible boundaries of state use of AI technologies.

Furthermore, the EU's commitment to a multi-stakeholder approach to AI governance has also contributed to its global impact. The extensive consultations undertaken during the development of the AI Act, involving industry, academia, civil society, and national governments, have provided a robust and credible foundation for its provisions. This inclusive process not only strengthens the legitimacy of the EU's regulations but also offers a model for other jurisdictions seeking to develop their own AI governance frameworks. By demonstrating a commitment to open dialogue and collaboration, the EU encourages a more democratic and participatory approach to AI policymaking, which is often seen as more sustainable and effective in the long run. This collaborative spirit is essential for fostering international trust and cooperation in a field as complex and rapidly evolving as AI.

The economic dimension of the 'Brussels effect' cannot be understated. The EU represents a vast and affluent market. Companies that wish to participate in this market, whether through selling products, offering services, or establishing operations, must comply with EU regulations. For AI developers and deployers, this means ensuring their AI systems meet the standards set by the AI Act. This can be a significant undertaking, requiring substantial investment in compliance, testing, and documentation. However, the benefits of accessing the EU market often outweigh these costs. Moreover, by building AI systems that are compliant with the AI Act from the outset, companies can achieve a degree of 'global compliance' that streamlines their international operations. This 'compliance by design' approach, driven by the EU's market power, effectively encourages the adoption of high standards across the AI industry worldwide. It is a clear demonstration of how regulatory power, coupled with economic leverage, can drive global technological and ethical norms.

The influence of the EU's AI framework is also evident in the competitive landscape of AI development. As the EU establishes itself as a leader in responsible AI, it attracts talent, investment, and innovation in ethical and trustworthy AI. This not only benefits the EU economy but also sets a benchmark for the global AI industry. Companies that prioritize ethical AI development and compliance with robust regulatory frameworks may find themselves with a competitive advantage, as consumers and business partners increasingly demand assurances of safety, fairness, and transparency. This evolving market dynamic further reinforces the 'Brussels effect,' creating a virtuous cycle where high ethical and regulatory standards become a driver of competitive success in the global AI arena.

However, it is important to acknowledge that the EU's influence is not absolute, and its framework is not universally adopted without modification. Other jurisdictions have their own unique priorities, legal traditions, and cultural contexts that shape their approach to AI governance. For example, some nations might prioritize innovation and economic growth above all else, potentially opting for lighter-touch regulations. Others might have different approaches to privacy or national security that influence their stance on AI surveillance or data governance. Nevertheless, even in these cases, the EU's AI Act and its underlying principles often serve as a critical reference point in policy debates. Policymakers in these countries will frequently analyze the EU's approach, drawing lessons from its successes and challenges, and adapting its elements to fit their own specific circumstances. This iterative process of observation, adaptation, and debate is a hallmark of how international norms evolve.

The dialogue surrounding AI ethics and governance is ongoing and dynamic. As AI technology continues to evolve at an unprecedented pace, regulatory frameworks will need to adapt. The EU, by establishing a comprehensive and principled approach, has not only set an initial standard but has also created a framework that is designed to be updated and refined over time. Its commitment to ongoing review and adaptation of the AI Act ensures that it remains relevant and effective in addressing emerging AI challenges. This forward-looking perspective further enhances its global influence, as it demonstrates a capacity for long-term stewardship of AI governance. Other nations and international organizations can draw upon this experience as they too navigate the evolving landscape of artificial intelligence, contributing to a more coordinated and effective global approach to AI governance that balances innovation with safety, ethics, and human rights. The EU's pioneering efforts are thus not just a regulatory act, but a significant contribution to the global conversation about the future of technology and its impact on society.

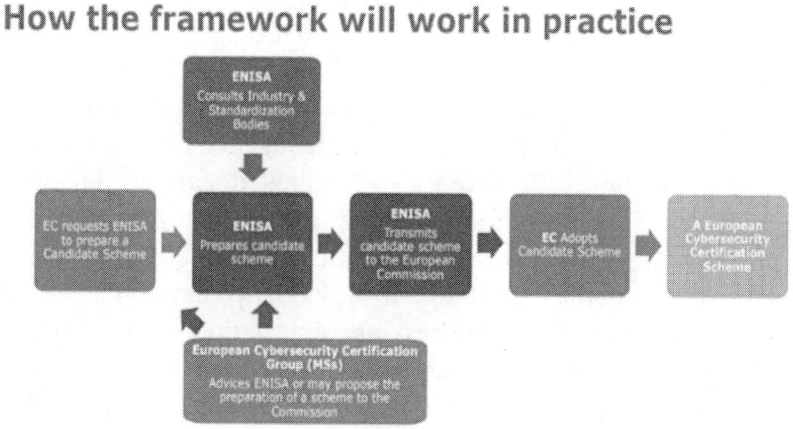

9
National Perspectives
China's AI Development and Regulation

China's strategic vision for artificial intelligence is not merely an aspiration; it is a meticulously crafted national imperative, underpinned by substantial government investment, focused research agendas, and a clear directive to integrate AI across the fabric of its economic and social development. The overarching goal is unambiguous: to establish China as a preeminent global leader in artificial intelligence by the year 2030. This ambition is not confined to technological prowess alone; it extends to leveraging AI as a transformative tool for modernizing its economy, enhancing state governance, and solidifying its position on the international stage. The scale and scope of this national AI strategy are unparalleled, reflecting a deliberate and coordinated effort to harness the full potential of AI for national advancement.

At the heart of China's AI endeavor lies a robust governmental commitment, manifested through significant financial allocations and policy frameworks designed to foster innovation and adoption. The State Council's issuance of the "New Generation Artificial Intelligence Development Plan" in July 2017 served as a seminal document, laying out a clear roadmap for achieving AI supremacy. This plan outlined specific objectives, including building a domestic AI industry that is competitive globally, developing AI technologies that can address pressing national needs, and fostering AI talent. The plan envisioned AI as a key driver of economic growth, productivity enhancement, and national security. It called for significant investments in AI research and development, the establishment of AI innovation centers, and the promotion of AI applications across various sectors, from healthcare and education to transportation and manufacturing. The strategic importance placed on AI is evident in the consistent prioritization of AI development in subsequent Five-Year Plans and other key national policy documents. These documents have consistently reinforced the need to accelerate AI adoption, encourage breakthroughs in core AI technologies, and cultivate a thriving AI ecosystem. The government has also actively supported the establishment of AI research institutes and laboratories, often in collaboration with leading universities and technology companies, fostering a synergistic approach to research and development. This top-down strategic directive, coupled with bottom-up innovation, has created a powerful engine for AI advancement.

The research priorities articulated within China's national AI strategy are broad and ambitious, targeting foundational AI technologies as well as specific application areas. Significant emphasis is placed on advancing core AI capabilities such as machine learning, deep learning, natural language processing, computer vision, and robotics. The goal is to move beyond incremental improvements and achieve significant breakthroughs in these foundational areas, enabling the development of more sophisticated and capable AI systems. This includes investing in the development of advanced algorithms, enhancing the efficiency of AI training processes, and improving the accuracy and robustness of AI models. Beyond these fundamental technologies, the strategy also identifies key application domains where AI is expected to have a transformative impact. These include smart manufacturing, where AI can optimize production processes, improve quality control, and enable the development of more intelligent factories; smart cities, where AI can enhance urban management, optimize traffic flow, improve public safety, and deliver more efficient public services; intelligent healthcare, where AI can aid in disease diagnosis, drug discovery, personalized treatment, and robotic surgery; and intelligent education, where AI can personalize learning experiences, automate administrative tasks, and provide intelligent tutoring systems. The strategy also recognizes the importance of AI in areas such as agriculture, finance, and environmental protection, aiming to leverage AI to address challenges and create new opportunities in these sectors.

The integration of AI into China's economic and social development plans is a cornerstone of its national strategy, positioning AI as a critical enabler of modernization and progress. The concept of the "digital economy" is central to this integration, with AI viewed as a fundamental pillar. AI is seen as a catalyst for upgrading traditional industries, fostering new economic growth engines, and enhancing overall competitiveness. For instance, in manufacturing, AI-powered automation and intelligent robotics are transforming production lines, leading to increased efficiency, reduced costs, and improved product quality. In the service sector, AI is being deployed in customer service chatbots, personalized recommendation systems, and automated financial advisory services, enhancing user experience and operational efficiency. The national strategy also emphasizes the development of intelligent infrastructure, such as smart grids, intelligent transportation systems, and autonomous vehicles, which are expected to improve resource allocation, reduce congestion, and enhance safety. Beyond economic applications, AI is also being integrated into social governance and public services. This includes the use of AI for improving public safety through advanced surveillance and predictive policing systems, enhancing the efficiency of government administration through data analysis and automated decision-making, and providing more personalized and accessible public services, such as intelligent healthcare and education platforms. The government views AI as a crucial tool for achieving its development goals, including poverty alleviation, environmental sustainability, and social welfare improvements.

A particularly notable aspect of China's national AI strategy is the central role assigned to AI in state governance. This reflects a broader trend of digitalization and data-driven decision-making within the Chinese government. AI is being employed to analyze vast amounts of data to inform policy formulation, monitor social trends, and improve the efficiency of public administration. This includes the use of AI in areas such as urban planning, resource management, and disaster response. Furthermore, AI-powered surveillance systems, including facial recognition technology and social credit systems, are being deployed to enhance public order and social control. While proponents argue that these technologies improve security and efficiency, critics raise concerns about privacy, civil liberties, and the potential for algorithmic bias and misuse. The integration of AI into governance raises complex ethical and societal questions that are subjects of ongoing international debate. The Chinese government views AI as a tool for modernizing governance structures, enabling more responsive and efficient public services, and ensuring social stability. This includes leveraging AI for predicting and preventing crime, managing public resources more effectively, and delivering citizen services in a more personalized and streamlined manner.

The commitment to becoming an AI powerhouse is also reflected in China's significant investments in AI research and development. The government has established national laboratories, funded numerous research projects, and encouraged collaboration between academia, industry, and research institutions. This has led to a surge in AI publications, patents, and the establishment of numerous AI companies. Chinese universities and research institutions are actively engaged in cutting-edge AI research, contributing to the global pool of AI knowledge. The government has also actively promoted the commercialization of AI technologies, creating a fertile ground for AI startups and fostering the growth of leading AI companies. These companies are not only developing innovative AI products and services but are also actively deploying AI solutions across various sectors of the economy. The strategic focus on AI development is also evidenced by the government's support for AI talent development. This includes initiatives to train AI researchers, engineers, and practitioners, as well as efforts to attract top AI talent from around the world. The aim is to build a robust AI workforce that can drive innovation and support the widespread adoption of AI technologies.

Key technological advancements spurred by this national strategy span various domains of AI. In computer vision, China has achieved remarkable progress in facial recognition, object detection, and image analysis, powering applications in security, retail, and autonomous systems. Natural language processing has seen significant advancements, leading to more sophisticated translation services, intelligent virtual assistants, and sentiment analysis tools. In robotics, there is a strong focus on developing industrial robots, service robots, and autonomous platforms, driven by the need to address labor shortages and enhance productivity. The development of AI algorithms, particularly in deep learning, has been a major area of investment, with Chinese researchers and companies contributing significantly to the advancement of neural network architectures and training methodologies. Furthermore, there is a growing emphasis on AI ethics and safety research, although the focus and approach may differ from Western counterparts. The strategy also includes efforts to build robust AI infrastructure, including high-performance computing capabilities and large-scale data centers, which are essential for training and deploying sophisticated AI models. The development of specialized AI chips and hardware is also a key priority, aiming to reduce reliance on foreign technology and build a complete AI industry ecosystem.

The integration of AI into state governance also

encompasses the use of AI for predictive analytics and decision support systems within government agencies. These systems are designed to process vast datasets related to economic indicators, social trends, and public sentiment to aid policymakers in making more informed and data-driven decisions. This can range from forecasting economic performance and identifying potential social unrest to optimizing the allocation of public resources and improving the efficiency of bureaucratic processes. AI is also being used to enhance the capabilities of law enforcement and national security agencies. This includes the deployment of AI-powered surveillance systems, such as intelligent video analytics and facial recognition, to monitor public spaces and identify potential threats. Predictive policing algorithms are also being explored and implemented to anticipate and prevent criminal activity. The development of AI-powered cybersecurity systems is another crucial aspect, aimed at protecting critical infrastructure and sensitive government data from cyber threats. The emphasis on AI in governance underscores a commitment to leveraging technology to strengthen state capacity, improve administrative efficiency, and maintain social order. However, this also raises significant questions regarding transparency, accountability, and the potential for AI to be used for surveillance and control, which are central to ongoing discussions about AI governance globally.

The ambition to lead in AI by 2030 is not just about technological achievement; it is intrinsically linked to China's broader geopolitical and economic objectives. By mastering AI, China aims to gain a competitive advantage in the global economy, enhance its national security, and project its influence internationally. The development of AI capabilities is seen as a critical component of its "Made in China 2025" initiative and its broader strategy for technological self-reliance. The national AI strategy is a multifaceted and ambitious undertaking, driven by a clear vision and substantial resources, aiming to transform China into a global AI superpower by the end of the decade. This strategy encompasses significant government investment, a focus on core AI technologies and applications, the deep integration of AI into economic and social development plans, and a prominent role for AI in state governance. The technological advancements and the sheer scale of deployment are already shaping the global AI landscape, making China's approach a critical case study in national AI development and its profound societal implications.

The integration of artificial intelligence within China's legal and social systems represents a profound shift, with AI technologies being systematically deployed to enhance efficiency, bolster security, and streamline governance. This deployment spans a wide spectrum of applications, from the intricate workings of the judicial process to the pervasive monitoring of public spaces and the administration of social order. The overarching aim is to leverage AI's analytical power and automation capabilities to create a more responsive, predictable, and controlled societal environment.

Within the judicial sphere, AI is increasingly being utilized to assist judges and legal professionals in managing the immense caseloads that characterize China's court system. These applications include AI-powered platforms designed to automate repetitive tasks such as document review, evidence analysis, and legal research. By processing vast quantities of legal texts, case precedents, and statutes, AI can help identify relevant information, flag potential inconsistencies, and even draft preliminary legal documents. This is particularly evident in the handling of routine cases, where AI can expedite the process by providing summaries of evidence, suggesting relevant legal arguments, and predicting potential outcomes based on historical data. The purported benefits are significant: a reduction in processing times, a decrease in the potential for human error in tedious tasks, and ultimately, a more efficient delivery of justice. For instance, some courts have explored AI systems that can analyze evidence submitted in civil cases, categorizing documents and highlighting key pieces of information for judges to review. This not only speeds up the initial stages of case assessment but also aims to ensure that no crucial piece of evidence is overlooked. The notion is that by offloading some of the more time-consuming analytical work to AI, human legal professionals can dedicate more attention to complex legal reasoning and nuanced judgment.

Beyond administrative support, AI is also making inroads into predictive analytics within the legal and law enforcement contexts. Predictive policing systems, for example, are being developed and implemented to forecast where and when crimes are most likely to occur. These systems analyze historical crime data, demographic information, and other relevant factors to identify patterns and allocate law enforcement resources more effectively. The intention is to proactively deter criminal activity by increasing police presence in high-risk areas and times. While the concept of using data to anticipate and prevent crime is not new, the sophistication and scale of AI-powered predictive policing represent a significant advancement. These systems can sift through far more variables and identify more subtle correlations than traditional methods, theoretically leading to more accurate predictions. This approach, however, is fraught with ethical considerations, particularly concerning the potential for algorithmic bias. If the historical data used to train these models reflects existing societal biases or discriminatory policing practices, the AI system may perpetuate or even amplify these biases, leading to disproportionate targeting of certain communities or neighborhoods. The accuracy and fairness of such systems are subjects of ongoing scrutiny and debate.

The realm of surveillance technology is perhaps

one of the most visible and pervasive areas where AI is being deployed in China's legal and social systems. Facial recognition technology, integrated with extensive camera networks, has become a cornerstone of public security and social monitoring. These systems can identify individuals in real-time, track their movements, and link them to databases containing personal information. This technology is used for a variety of purposes, including identifying suspects in criminal investigations, locating missing persons, and monitoring public spaces for potential security threats. The sheer scale of deployment, with millions of cameras equipped with advanced AI analytics, creates a comprehensive surveillance infrastructure. This has undoubtedly contributed to a reduction in certain types of street crime and has been effective in quickly identifying individuals involved in public disturbances or illegal activities. For example, in crowded public areas like train stations or major event venues, facial recognition systems can scan thousands of faces per minute, flagging individuals who match watchlists or exhibit suspicious behavior. The ability to rapidly identify and track individuals is a powerful tool for law enforcement, but it also raises significant concerns about privacy and the potential for misuse.

The application of AI extends to the broader concept of social governance, most notably through the implementation and expansion of social credit systems. These systems aim to assess the trustworthiness and behavior of individuals and entities, assigning them a "score" based on a wide range of data. This data can include financial history, legal compliance, online behavior, and even social interactions. A high social credit score can unlock benefits such as easier access to loans, preferential treatment in public services, or faster processing of applications. Conversely, a low score can lead to restrictions, such as limitations on travel, reduced access to credit, or difficulties in obtaining certain jobs. AI plays a crucial role in processing the vast amounts of data required to build and maintain these scores, analyzing complex datasets to infer behavioral patterns and assess risk. The stated goal is to foster a more honest and trustworthy society by incentivizing good behavior and penalizing undesirable actions. However, critics argue that these systems represent an unprecedented level of social control, potentially stifling dissent, limiting personal freedom, and creating a chilling effect on individual expression. The opaque nature of some scoring algorithms and the potential for subjective interpretation of data raise further questions about fairness and due process.

In the context of law enforcement, AI is also being employed in analyzing digital evidence and communications. Sophisticated algorithms can sift through massive amounts of digital data, including emails, social media posts, and financial transactions, to identify patterns, connections, and potential criminal activity. This can significantly accelerate investigations that would otherwise be prohibitively time-consuming for human analysts. For instance, in cases involving organized crime or cyber fraud, AI can help reconstruct networks of communication and identify key individuals involved by analyzing vast datasets of digital interactions. The ability to process and analyze this data at scale is a powerful tool for combating complex criminal enterprises. However, the collection and analysis of such data must be conducted with strict adherence to legal frameworks to ensure that fundamental rights are not infringed.

The deployment of AI in courts is also extending to areas like sentencing recommendations. AI systems can analyze historical sentencing data, case characteristics, and defendant profiles to suggest appropriate penalties. The idea is to promote consistency and reduce disparities in sentencing by providing judges with data-driven insights. However, the ethical implications of delegating such critical decisions to algorithms are profound. Concerns about accountability, transparency, and the potential for bias in sentencing recommendations are significant. If the historical data reflects systemic biases in the justice system, the AI could inadvertently perpetuate these inequalities. The question of whether an algorithm can truly understand the nuances of human behavior, mitigating factors, and the principles of justice remains a central point of contention.

Furthermore, AI is being used to enhance border security and immigration control. Advanced surveillance technologies, including AI-powered analytics, can monitor entry and exit points, identify individuals on watchlists, and detect anomalies in travel patterns. This contributes to national security by helping to prevent the movement of individuals deemed a threat or those attempting to enter the country illegally. The efficiency gains in processing large volumes of individuals at ports of entry are considerable, but the use of AI in these contexts also raises privacy concerns for travelers and the potential for profiling based on algorithmic assessments.

The integration of AI into China's legal and social systems is a dynamic and evolving process. While proponents emphasize the gains in efficiency, security, and public order, these advancements are accompanied by significant implications for civil liberties and individual rights. The pervasive nature of surveillance, the potential for algorithmic bias in decision-making, and the far-reaching implications of social credit systems necessitate careful consideration and robust public discourse. The balance between leveraging technology for societal benefit and safeguarding fundamental freedoms is a critical challenge that China, like many other nations grappling with the transformative power of AI, must navigate. The specific manifestations of AI deployment in these sensitive areas highlight the complex interplay between technological capability, state objectives, and the protection of individual autonomy. As these systems become more sophisticated and widely adopted, understanding their impact on the fabric of society and the rights of its citizens becomes increasingly paramount, shaping the ongoing debate about the future of governance in an AI-driven world. The sheer volume of data being processed by these AI systems means that even subtle biases embedded in their algorithms can have widespread and significant consequences for individuals and communities. For example, if facial recognition algorithms are less accurate for certain demographic groups, it could lead to wrongful accusations or increased scrutiny for individuals from those groups. Similarly, if predictive policing models are trained on data that reflects historical over-policing in minority neighborhoods, they might unfairly direct more law enforcement resources to those areas, creating a feedback loop of increased surveillance and arrests.

The ethical considerations surrounding AI in law enforcement are particularly acute. The concept of "predictive policing" raises questions about pre-crime and the potential for individuals to be targeted based on algorithmic predictions rather than concrete evidence of wrongdoing. This can lead to a situation where individuals are subjected to increased surveillance or scrutiny simply because an algorithm suggests they are at a higher risk of committing a crime. The transparency of these algorithms is often limited, making it difficult to scrutinize their fairness or to challenge their outcomes. This lack of transparency exacerbates concerns about accountability, as it becomes challenging to determine who is responsible when an AI system makes an erroneous or biased decision. The "black box" nature of many advanced AI models means that even their developers may not fully understand the reasoning behind specific predictions or classifications, further complicating efforts to ensure fairness and due process.

In the legal system, the use of AI in judicial processes, such as case summarization or evidence analysis, also presents challenges. While these tools can improve efficiency, they also raise questions about the role of human judgment and discretion. Judges and legal professionals are trained to consider the nuances of each case, the context of evidence, and the principles of justice. Over-reliance on AI could potentially lead to a more mechanistic application of law, where the human element of empathy, understanding, and equitable judgment is diminished. The development of AI tools for legal research, while beneficial, also requires careful validation to ensure that the information provided is accurate and unbiased, as errors in legal research can have significant consequences for the outcome of a case. The very definition of justice can be impacted if the tools used to administer it are themselves flawed or biased.

The social credit system, as a broad application of AI in social governance, represents perhaps the most far-reaching example of AI's impact on individual behavior and freedoms. By creating a comprehensive digital profile of citizens and assigning scores based on their actions, these systems can exert a powerful influence on daily life. The potential for subjective interpretation of data and the broad scope of behaviors that can affect one's score means that individuals may feel compelled to conform to certain norms or avoid activities that could negatively impact their score, even if those activities are not illegal. This can lead to a chilling effect on freedom of expression and association, as individuals may self-censor to avoid negative repercussions. The opacity of the scoring mechanisms further exacerbates these concerns, making it difficult for individuals to understand how their score is calculated or how to improve it. This can create a sense of powerlessness and a lack of recourse for those who believe their score is unfair or inaccurate. The reliance on AI for such sensitive social evaluations raises fundamental questions about fairness, due process, and the nature of a free society.

The technological underpinnings of these AI deployments are equally significant. The vast networks of cameras, the advanced algorithms for facial recognition and behavioral analysis, and the sophisticated data processing capabilities required for social credit systems necessitate significant investment in infrastructure and computing power. This includes the development of specialized hardware, such as AI chips, and the deployment of extensive data storage and processing facilities. The continuous collection and analysis of vast amounts of personal data raise profound privacy concerns. The potential for this data to be breached, misused, or repurposed for unintended ends is a constant threat. Establishing robust data protection mechanisms and ensuring accountability for data handling are therefore critical components of responsible AI deployment in these sensitive domains.

The intersection of AI, law, and social governance in China presents a complex and multifaceted picture. While the stated objectives often revolve around efficiency, security, and social order, the practical implementation raises significant questions about the protection of individual rights and liberties. The continuous advancements in AI technology mean that these systems are likely to become even more sophisticated and pervasive in the future. Therefore, ongoing critical examination of their ethical implications, their impact on civil society, and the legal frameworks governing their use is essential. The global community watches these developments closely, as they offer insights into the potential trajectory of AI governance and its profound implications for human autonomy and societal structure. The dynamic nature of AI development in China's legal and social systems underscores the need for adaptive regulatory approaches that can keep pace with technological change while upholding fundamental human rights and democratic values. The ongoing evolution of these applications demands a vigilant and informed public, capable of engaging in critical dialogue about the trade-offs inherent in the pursuit of an AI-augmented society.

China's approach to regulating artificial intelligence (AI) is characterized by a dynamic and increasingly comprehensive strategy, reflecting both a vigorous pursuit of technological leadership and a determined effort to manage the societal implications of this transformative technology. This regulatory landscape is not monolithic but rather a multi-faceted effort involving various government bodies, each addressing specific facets of AI development and deployment. The overarching objective appears to be a delicate balancing act: fostering innovation and economic growth driven by AI, while simultaneously imposing controls to ensure national security, social stability, and the protection of individual rights, albeit within a framework that prioritizes state interests. This dual mandate has resulted in a series of targeted regulations designed to govern everything from the algorithms that curate online content to the sophisticated generative models capable of creating novel text, images, and other media.

One of the earliest and most significant areas of regulatory focus has been on recommendation algorithms, particularly those powering popular social media and e-commerce platforms. Recognizing the profound influence these algorithms exert on information consumption, user behavior, and public opinion, Chinese regulators have sought to instill greater transparency and fairness. The "Provisions on the Management of Algorithmic Recommendations for Internet Information Services," which came into effect in March 2022, exemplify this effort. These provisions mandate that algorithmic recommendation service providers must adhere to principles of legality, morality, and social ethics. They are required to disclose the basic principles of algorithmic recommendations, provide users with options to turn off personalized recommendations or to opt out of algorithmic selection, and ensure that algorithmic recommendations do not endanger national security or social stability, nor violate laws and regulations. Furthermore, they prohibit algorithms from being used to engage in price discrimination against users, or to maliciously interfere with users' normal information acquisition. This regulatory push reflects a concern that unchecked algorithmic optimization could lead to filter bubbles, reinforce biases, or be exploited for commercial gain at the expense of user welfare. The emphasis on user control and algorithmic transparency signals a governmental intent to mitigate potential negative externalities of personalized content delivery.

The burgeoning field of generative AI has also quickly become a central concern for Chinese regulators. As these technologies, exemplified by large language models and AI image generators, mature and proliferate, their capacity to create sophisticated synthetic content raises complex issues related to misinformation, intellectual property, and social order. In response, the Cyberspace Administration of China (CAC) and other relevant ministries jointly issued the "Interim Measures for the Management of Deep Synthesis Internet Information Services" in January 2023. This groundbreaking regulation directly addresses "deepfakes" and other forms of AI-generated synthetic content. It imposes strict obligations on providers of such services, requiring them to implement mechanisms for content security assessment, watermark labeling of generated content, and user authentication. Critically, the measures explicitly prohibit the use of deep synthesis technology to create false information, to damage the reputation of individuals or organizations, or to incite hatred, ethnic discrimination, and violence. The regulation also necessitates obtaining consent from individuals whose likeness is used and ensures that generated content is not used to endanger national security or social stability. This proactive stance on deep synthesis underscores a commitment to controlling the narrative and preventing the weaponization of AI-generated content, particularly in the context of public discourse and national security.

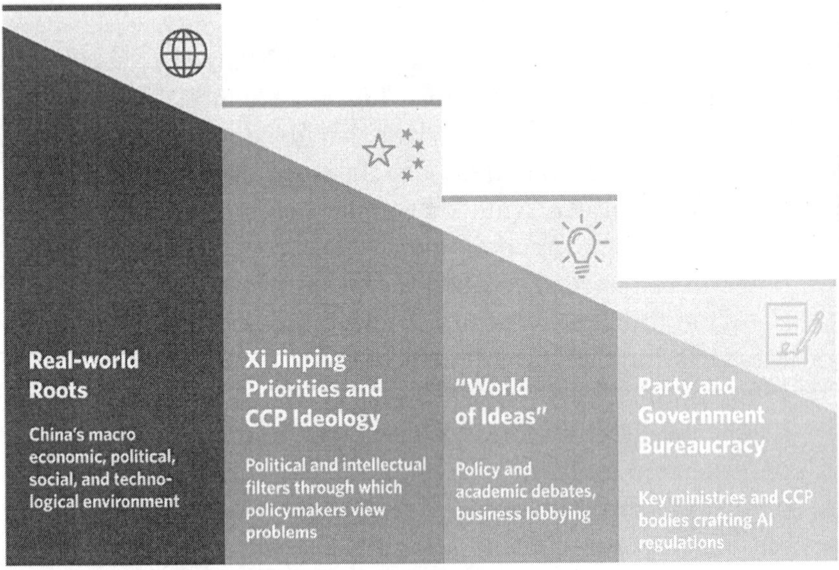

Four Layers China's AI Regulations

Building upon this, the CAC further released draft "Administrative Measures for Generative Artificial Intelligence Services" in April 2023, signaling a broader regulatory intent for generative AI as a whole. This draft regulation sought to establish a framework for the responsible development and deployment of generative AI, emphasizing the importance of adhering to socialist core values, respecting intellectual property rights, and ensuring data security. It mandated that generative AI services must not generate content that subverts state power, undermines national unity, or incites ethnic hatred, violence, or disseminates obscenity. Providers were also expected to conduct security assessments and implement measures to prevent the generation of illegal or harmful content. While still in draft form, these measures clearly indicate that China intends to exert significant oversight over the development and use of generative AI, seeking to align its capabilities with state objectives and societal norms. The emphasis on content moderation and adherence to core socialist values reflects a deep-seated concern about the potential for AI to disrupt established social and political structures.

Data security and data privacy, as foundational elements for AI development, have also been subject to extensive regulatory efforts. China has enacted a suite of comprehensive laws, including the Cybersecurity Law (CSL), the Data Security Law (DSL), and the Personal Information Protection Law (PIPL), which collectively create a robust framework for data governance. The DSL, implemented in September 2021, establishes a classification system for data based on its importance to national security and public interest, and imposes stricter obligations on the handling of data categorized as "important data." The PIPL, effective from November 2021, closely mirrors aspects of the EU's General Data Protection Regulation (GDPR), introducing requirements for consent, purpose limitation, and data minimization for the processing of personal information.

These laws have direct implications for AI development, as many AI applications rely on the collection and processing of vast datasets, including personal information. For AI companies operating in or targeting China, compliance with these stringent data regulations is paramount, impacting everything from data collection practices to cross-border data transfers. The focus on data security and privacy, while ostensibly aimed at protecting individuals, also serves the state's interest in controlling data flows and preventing foreign access to sensitive information.

The regulatory approach in China is further distinguished by its emphasis on national security and social stability as overarching principles guiding AI governance. This is evident in the broad definitions of terms like "endangering national security" and "harming social stability," which can encompass a wide range of activities. For instance, the regulations on recommendation algorithms and deep synthesis both explicitly prohibit content that could undermine these core state interests. This suggests that the interpretation and enforcement of AI regulations will likely be closely aligned with the government's broader political and security objectives. The intent is to harness AI's power for societal progress and economic development while simultaneously ensuring that it does not pose a threat to the existing political order or national sovereignty. This can lead to a regulatory environment where innovation is encouraged, but within carefully defined boundaries that prioritize state control.

Moreover, the regulatory framework is not static but is continually evolving in response to the rapid pace of AI development. Chinese authorities have demonstrated a willingness to issue new regulations and update existing ones to address emerging challenges and technologies. This adaptive approach allows the government to maintain a degree of control and to steer AI development in directions it deems beneficial. For example, the swift introduction of measures for deep synthesis and generative AI reflects an agile response to new technological capabilities. This ongoing regulatory evolution means that businesses and researchers working with AI in China must remain vigilant and adaptable to changes in the legal and policy landscape. The government's active role in shaping the AI ecosystem through regulation underscores its strategic vision for AI as a key driver of national development and a critical tool for governance.

The implementation of these regulations often involves a combination of administrative oversight, technical standards, and market-based incentives and penalties. Government agencies conduct inspections, review compliance reports, and impose fines or other sanctions for violations. Technical standards are being developed to ensure interoperability, safety, and security of AI systems. The interplay between these various mechanisms aims to create a comprehensive system of AI governance that can effectively manage the risks and opportunities presented by this technology. The emphasis on specific industries, such as online platforms and generative AI services, suggests a targeted approach to regulation, addressing the areas where AI is most likely to have a significant societal impact.

In parallel with its regulatory efforts, China also actively promotes AI research and development through significant government investment, policy support, and the cultivation of a vibrant AI ecosystem. This creates a dual dynamic: encouraging innovation through supportive policies while simultaneously embedding safeguards and control mechanisms through regulation. The "New Generation Artificial Intelligence Development Plan," first released in 2017, set ambitious goals for China to become a global leader in AI by 2030. This national strategy has driven substantial investment in AI research, talent development, and the commercialization of AI technologies. The regulatory framework, therefore, operates within this broader context of national ambition, seeking to channel AI development towards strategic national priorities.

However, this regulatory approach has also drawn international attention and some criticism. Concerns have been raised about the potential for these regulations to stifle innovation, particularly given the broad scope and the emphasis on state control. The potential for over-regulation, or for regulations to be used as tools for censorship or surveillance, are ongoing debates. The opacity of some decision-making processes within the regulatory framework and the potential for selective enforcement also raise questions about fairness and predictability. As China continues to refine its AI regulatory approach, the global community will be observing closely to understand the long-term implications for technological development, market access, and the balance between innovation and control. The sheer volume of data being collected and processed by AI systems in China, coupled with the strict regulatory environment, presents a unique model for AI governance that differs significantly from approaches taken in many Western democracies. This divergence is rooted in differing legal traditions, governance philosophies, and societal priorities, particularly the emphasis on collective well-being and national security as paramount concerns.

The intricate web of regulations governing AI in China reflects a strategic and deliberate effort to shape the trajectory of this transformative technology. From the granular control over recommendation algorithms that mediate online experiences to the broad oversight of generative AI's creative output, and underpinned by robust data security laws, Beijing is actively constructing a framework designed to harness AI's potential while mitigating perceived risks. The consistent theme running through these various regulatory initiatives is the prioritization of national security, social stability, and the adherence to core socialist values. This approach underscores a distinct governance philosophy where technological advancement is viewed through the lens of state objectives, aiming to ensure that AI serves the broader goals of national development and societal order. The evolving nature of these regulations signifies China's commitment to remaining at the forefront of AI development, adapting its legal and policy instruments as the technology itself progresses, and demonstrating a clear intent to manage the profound societal impacts of artificial intelligence within its borders.

The rapid proliferation of artificial intelligence across China's vast socio-economic landscape has inevitably ignited a fervent debate surrounding its ethical implications and broader societal impact. While the nation champions AI as a cornerstone of its future economic prosperity and global technological leadership, this ambition is inextricably linked to a complex tapestry of challenges that touch upon fundamental human rights and the very fabric of society. At the heart of these discussions lies the intricate relationship between AI, data, and individual autonomy, particularly concerning issues of data privacy and the pervasive nature of algorithmic decision-making.

China's model of AI development, fueled by an unprecedented volume of data, raises significant questions about the protection of personal information. The sheer scale of data collection, often initiated through digital platforms that are deeply integrated into daily life, creates a vast repository that AI systems leverage for training and operation. While regulations like the Personal Information Protection Law (PIPL) aim to provide a framework for data governance, the practical implementation and enforcement within the context of AI's insatiable appetite for information present ongoing challenges. The constant stream of data generated by citizens through social media, e-commerce, travel, and even daily movements contributes to sophisticated user profiles, which can be utilized for personalized services, targeted advertising, and, more controversially, for state surveillance and social management. This raises a critical ethical dilemma: to what extent is the convenience and perceived benefit of AI-driven services commensurate with the erosion of privacy? The granular insights gleaned from this data, while potentially beneficial for optimizing urban planning or public services, also hold the capacity for unprecedented levels of scrutiny over individual lives, blurring the lines between public good and intrusive monitoring.

Algorithmic bias represents another significant ethical hurdle. AI systems, by their very nature, learn from the data they are fed. If this data reflects existing societal biases, whether related to gender, ethnicity, socioeconomic status, or regional disparities, the AI system is likely to perpetuate and even amplify these inequities. In China, where significant regional development disparities exist and historical social structures can influence data patterns, the risk of algorithmic bias is particularly acute. For instance, AI systems used in hiring processes, loan applications, or even in the administration of social services could inadvertently discriminate against individuals from less developed regions or minority groups if the training data is not carefully curated and audited for bias. The opacity of many proprietary algorithms further complicates efforts to identify and rectify such biases, creating a situation where discriminatory outcomes can occur without clear recourse or accountability for the entities deploying the AI. The societal impact of such biases can be profound, leading to the reinforcement of existing social hierarchies, the marginalization of already vulnerable populations, and a deepening of social inequalities.

The instrumental role of AI in state surveillance and censorship is perhaps one of the most widely debated ethical dimensions in China. The nation's extensive network of surveillance technologies, from facial recognition systems deployed in public spaces to sophisticated monitoring of online activities, is heavily reliant on AI. These systems are ostensibly implemented for purposes of public security, crime prevention, and social stability. However, their pervasive reach and the potential for them to be employed for political control and the suppression of dissent raise profound ethical concerns. The ability of AI to process and analyze vast amounts of data in real-time allows for the identification and tracking of individuals based on their associations, online activities, or public behavior. This can create a chilling effect on freedom of expression, as citizens may self-censor their communications and activities for fear of attracting undue attention from state surveillance apparatuses. Furthermore, the integration of AI with social credit systems, which aim to evaluate and score the trustworthiness of citizens, further amplifies these concerns, creating a mechanism for social and economic exclusion based on AI-driven assessments that may not always be transparent or fair.

The issue of censorship is also intrinsically linked to AI's role in information control. AI-powered algorithms are used to moderate content on internet platforms, identify and remove "undesirable" information, and curate the information users consume. While this is often framed as a measure to maintain social order and prevent the spread of harmful content, it also serves as a powerful tool for political censorship. AI systems can be programmed to detect and suppress content that is critical of the government, promotes independent thought, or falls outside the officially sanctioned narrative. The sophisticated nature of these AI tools means that censorship can be applied at scale and with increasing subtlety, making it more difficult for citizens to access uncensored information or to engage in open discourse. The ethical debate here centers on the balance between state authority to maintain order and the fundamental right to freedom of speech and access to information. When AI is used to proactively filter and shape public discourse, it raises questions about the authenticity of information and the potential for manipulation of public opinion.

The drive towards AI advancement and its broad societal integration also carries the risk of exacerbating existing social inequalities or creating new ones. The benefits of AI, such as improved efficiency, personalized services, and access to advanced technologies, may not be evenly distributed across the population. For example, individuals in rural or less developed areas might have less access to the digital infrastructure necessary to leverage AI-powered services or may not possess the digital literacy required to navigate them effectively. This could lead to a widening digital divide, where those who are already digitally connected and proficient gain further advantages, while others are left behind. Moreover, the economic shifts driven by AI automation, while promising increased productivity, also raise concerns about job displacement. While new jobs may be created in the AI sector, they often require specialized skills that may not be accessible to workers whose jobs are displaced by automation, potentially leading to unemployment and increased economic insecurity for certain segments of the population. The ethical imperative is to ensure that the benefits of AI are shared broadly and that measures are in place to mitigate the negative consequences of automation on employment and economic well-being.

The Chinese government's approach to regulating AI, as discussed in previous sections, reflects a proactive stance aimed at harnessing AI's power while mitigating its perceived risks. However, the ethical dimensions of these regulations are subjects of ongoing scrutiny and debate. For instance, while the emphasis on national security and social stability is a stated priority, critics argue that these broad terms can be invoked to justify measures that unduly restrict civil liberties. The implementation of AI technologies for surveillance and censorship, even if presented as necessary for security, can lead to a society where individual freedoms are curtailed in favor of state control. The challenge lies in finding an appropriate balance that allows for technological progress without compromising fundamental human rights.

Another ethical consideration pertains to the transparency and accountability of AI systems. Many AI algorithms are complex "black boxes," making it difficult to understand how they arrive at their decisions. This lack of transparency can hinder efforts to identify and address issues like algorithmic bias or errors. When AI systems are used in critical decision-making processes, such as in the justice system or in the allocation of public resources, the inability to scrutinize their reasoning can undermine public trust and the legitimacy of these decisions. Establishing clear lines of accountability for AI-driven outcomes is also crucial. If an AI system causes harm, determining who is responsible- the developer, the deployer, or the AI itself- is a complex ethical and legal challenge. While China's regulations are evolving to address some of these aspects, ensuring genuine transparency and robust accountability mechanisms for AI remains a significant ethical undertaking.

The global context of AI development also influences the ethical debates within China. As AI technologies become increasingly interconnected and their impacts transcend national borders, international norms and ethical standards become relevant. China's unique approach to AI governance, shaped by its political system and cultural context, often diverges from that of Western democracies. This divergence can create tensions in areas such as data privacy, freedom of expression, and the ethical development of AI. For example, while many Western nations prioritize individual data rights and algorithmic transparency, China's model often places a greater emphasis on collective interests, state security, and the guidance of technological development by national strategic goals. The ethical challenge is to foster a global dialogue on AI ethics that respects different cultural and political contexts while upholding universal human rights principles.

Furthermore, the rapid pace of AI innovation presents a continuous ethical challenge. As new AI capabilities emerge, the existing regulatory and ethical frameworks must adapt to address unforeseen consequences. This necessitates a proactive and iterative approach to AI governance, involving continuous engagement with researchers, developers, ethicists, and the public. The ethical considerations surrounding AI are not static; they evolve alongside the technology itself. For example, the emergence of highly sophisticated generative AI models capable of creating human-like text, images, and even video has introduced new ethical dilemmas related to misinformation, intellectual property, and the very nature of creativity and authorship. Ensuring that these powerful new tools are developed and deployed responsibly requires ongoing ethical reflection and robust governance.

The societal impact of AI in China is also being shaped by the government's explicit policy objectives to leverage AI for national rejuvenation and economic transformation. This strategic imperative often means that ethical considerations are weighed against broader national goals. While AI can undoubtedly drive economic growth and improve public services, the potential for these advancements to be accompanied by a reduction in individual freedoms or an increase in societal stratification is a crucial ethical concern. The challenge for China, and indeed for any nation embracing AI, is to navigate this complex landscape responsibly, ensuring that technological progress serves humanity without undermining fundamental ethical principles and human rights. The ongoing evolution of AI in China, therefore, represents not just a technological race but a profound societal experiment with far-reaching ethical implications for its citizens and for the global community. The ability to foster innovation while safeguarding individual dignity, privacy, and equitable opportunity will be the defining ethical challenge of China's AI journey.

The trajectory of artificial intelligence development and its attendant regulatory frameworks presents a fascinating kaleidoscope of national approaches, each shaped by distinct historical, political, and cultural underpinnings. While China's ascent in the AI domain is undeniable, a critical examination of its model necessitates a comparative lens, particularly when juxtaposed with the evolving norms in other major AI players like the United States and the European Union. This comparative insight is crucial for understanding the broader implications for international AI governance and for appreciating the divergent philosophical foundations upon which these national strategies are built.

At its core, the divergence often stems from fundamentally different conceptions of the relationship between the state, technology, and the individual. China's AI ecosystem, as previously discussed, is characterized by a strong state-led approach, deeply intertwined with national strategic objectives, economic development, and social governance. This model prioritizes the collective good, national security, and technological sovereignty, viewing AI as a potent tool for achieving these broad societal aims. The state plays a central role not only in funding and directing research and development but also in shaping the deployment and application of AI technologies across various sectors. This top-down strategy, while fostering rapid progress and large-scale implementation, often entails a different calculus regarding individual liberties and data privacy compared to Western liberal democracies. The emphasis is frequently on centralized control and the efficient application of AI for national progress, even if it means a more expansive role for state surveillance and data utilization for public management.

In contrast, the United States' approach to AI, while also driven by innovation and economic competitiveness, has historically been more fragmented and market-driven. While the government plays a role in funding research, setting some guidelines, and addressing national security concerns, the primary impetus for AI development has often come from the private sector, particularly large technology companies. This has led to a dynamic but also sometimes less cohesive regulatory landscape. The American philosophical underpinnings tend to emphasize individual freedoms, market competition, and a more cautious approach to state intervention in the economy and private life. Consequently, concerns about privacy, algorithmic bias, and the concentration of power in the hands of tech giants are prominent, leading to calls for more robust, albeit often sector-specific, regulation. The debate in the US often revolves around striking a balance between fostering innovation and protecting individual rights and market fairness, with a strong emphasis on the role of self-regulation and industry best practices, though this is increasingly being challenged by calls for more comprehensive federal oversight.

The European Union, on the other hand, has embarked on a path that is perhaps most distinct from China and, in many ways, represents a more deliberate attempt to enshrine a rights-based and human-centric approach to AI governance. The EU's General Data Protection Regulation (GDPR) has already set a precedent for stringent data privacy rules, and its forthcoming AI Act aims to establish a comprehensive legal framework for AI that classifies AI systems based on their risk level, with stricter regulations for high-risk applications. The EU's philosophy is deeply rooted in fundamental rights, ethical principles, and the concept of trustworthy AI. It prioritizes human oversight, transparency, accountability, and the prevention of discrimination. This approach seeks to ensure that AI is developed and deployed in a manner that respects human dignity, promotes fairness, and fosters societal well-being, even if it means a potentially slower pace of innovation or a higher compliance burden for businesses. The EU model is characterized by a strong emphasis on legally binding rules and a proactive, precautionary approach to technological risks.

The implications of these divergent models for international AI governance are profound. China's state-centric model, with its emphasis on national strategic goals and broad data utilization, can create challenges for global cooperation, particularly in areas where data privacy and human rights are paramount. When AI systems and data flows cross borders, discrepancies in regulatory approaches can lead to friction and create barriers to trade and collaboration. For instance, the extensive data collection and surveillance capabilities enabled by China's AI infrastructure may raise concerns for countries with different legal and ethical norms regarding privacy and civil liberties. Conversely, the EU's rights-based approach, while setting a high ethical bar, might be perceived by some as overly restrictive by nations prioritizing rapid technological advancement and economic growth above all else.

The United States' more market-driven and often reactive regulatory approach also presents its own set of international governance challenges. The lack of a unified federal AI strategy can lead to a patchwork of state and federal regulations, creating uncertainty for international companies operating within the US. Furthermore, the significant influence of large private tech companies on AI development and deployment raises questions about global equitable access to AI technologies and the concentration of power.

These differing philosophies translate into distinct regulatory outputs. China's regulatory efforts, such as the Cybersecurity Law, the Data Security Law, and the Personal Information Protection Law (PIPL), demonstrate a clear intent to govern data and AI, but often within a framework that prioritizes national security and state control. While PIPL offers significant protections for personal information, its implementation and enforcement can be influenced by broader state objectives. The emphasis on data localization and state access to data, for example, reflects a national priority that may not align with international data flow norms.

In contrast, the EU's AI Act represents a comprehensive, risk-based regulatory framework designed to apply across all member states. Its tiered approach, categorizing AI systems from minimal risk to unacceptable risk, aims to provide clarity and a level playing field while ensuring that the most impactful AI applications are subject to the most stringent oversight. This level of detail and ambition in a single piece of legislation is a significant departure from the more piecemeal regulatory evolution seen in the US.

The US, meanwhile, has largely relied on existing legal frameworks, agency guidance, and voluntary frameworks, such as the National Institute of Standards and Technology (NIST) AI Risk Management Framework, to guide AI development. While these efforts aim to foster responsible innovation, they often lack the binding legal force of EU regulations, leaving more room for interpretation and potential loopholes. The ongoing legislative debates in the US highlight the difficulty in achieving consensus on a comprehensive federal AI regulatory strategy that balances innovation with robust protections.

The core philosophical differences manifest in how issues like algorithmic bias, transparency, and accountability are addressed. While all three regions acknowledge these challenges, their proposed solutions often differ. China's approach to bias mitigation may be more inclined towards top-down directives and state oversight of data sets and algorithms, aiming to ensure alignment with national social objectives. Transparency might be interpreted as enabling state auditors or specific governmental bodies to understand algorithms, rather than necessarily guaranteeing public or user access to the inner workings of proprietary AI systems. Accountability often rests with entities that violate state regulations, with the state itself holding ultimate oversight.

The US discourse on algorithmic bias often centers on fairness and non-discrimination, with a focus on potential harms to individuals and groups. Transparency calls often advocate for explainable AI (XAI) and greater disclosure of how AI systems make decisions, aiming to empower users and researchers. Accountability in the US often involves a combination of regulatory enforcement, litigation, and corporate responsibility, with ongoing legal battles shaping the contours of liability.

The EU, with its strong emphasis on fundamental rights, places a particular premium on tackling bias and ensuring transparency. The AI Act mandates rigorous conformity assessments for high-risk AI systems, requiring them to be developed using high-quality data, to have robust human oversight mechanisms, and to be accompanied by detailed technical documentation that can support transparency and accountability. The emphasis is on building trust through verifiable compliance and clear chains of responsibility.

This comparative analysis reveals that while the global conversation on AI ethics and governance is converging on several key themes- including fairness, transparency, accountability, and safety- the specific approaches to achieving these goals are deeply influenced by national contexts and underlying philosophies. China's model prioritizes state-led development and social governance, the US leans towards market-driven innovation with evolving regulatory oversight, and the EU champions a rights-based, human-centric approach with comprehensive legal frameworks. Understanding these differences is not merely an academic exercise; it is crucial for navigating the complexities of international AI cooperation, fostering responsible global AI development, and ensuring that technological progress aligns with diverse societal values and fundamental human rights. The ongoing evolution of these national approaches will continue to shape the global AI landscape and the very future of how artificial intelligence integrates into human society.

Moreover, the contrasting approaches to AI development and regulation have tangible implications for the global distribution of AI power and influence. China's concerted national strategy, backed by significant state investment and data resources, has propelled it to the forefront of AI research and application. This has led to a robust domestic AI industry that is increasingly exporting its technologies and expertise. The emphasis on AI as a tool for national rejuvenation and economic competitiveness means that China is not just a consumer but a significant innovator and shaper of AI trends. This ambition, coupled with its unique governance model, positions China as a major contender in the global AI race, potentially setting de facto international standards through its sheer scale and technological output.

The United States, with its powerhouse private sector and leading research universities, remains a formidable force in AI innovation. However, the lack of a cohesive national strategy and the potential for regulatory fragmentation could, at times, hinder its ability to compete effectively on a global scale, particularly against a unified national effort like China's. The global reach of American tech giants, while spreading AI capabilities, also concentrates significant AI power and decision-making within a few corporations, raising different sets of geopolitical and economic questions.

The European Union's deliberate pace and focus on ethical guardrails, while admirable from a rights-based perspective, could also lead to questions about its competitiveness in a rapidly evolving technological landscape. If regulations become too burdensome, they might stifle innovation or create an environment where European companies struggle to compete with less regulated counterparts. However, the EU also aims to set a global benchmark for "trustworthy AI," hoping that its ethically grounded approach will eventually be adopted worldwide, influencing the direction of global AI standards towards a more human-centric path. This ambition could position the EU as a leader in shaping responsible AI governance, even if it means a different competitive dynamic.

The critical difference in the underlying philosophies also extends to the definition and prioritization of "ethical AI." For China, ethical AI often aligns with societal harmony, national stability, and efficient public services, all within the framework of state objectives. This can mean that individual autonomy or privacy might be secondary to these broader goals. For instance, AI systems designed for social scoring or predictive policing are viewed through the lens of maintaining order and preventing crime, with the potential infringements on civil liberties often framed as necessary trade-offs for collective security.

In the United States, ethical AI conversations are heavily influenced by principles of fairness, equity, and civil rights. There is a strong focus on mitigating algorithmic bias that could lead to discrimination in areas like hiring, lending, or criminal justice. Transparency and explainability are seen as crucial for ensuring accountability and building public trust. The ethical debate here is often framed as protecting individuals from potential harms caused by opaque or biased algorithms, and ensuring that AI serves democratic values.

The European Union's vision of ethical AI is perhaps

the most expansive, encompassing not only fairness and transparency but also human agency, environmental sustainability, and the promotion of democratic values. The EU's emphasis on "AI for people" underscores a commitment to ensuring that AI serves humanity and enhances human capabilities, rather than replacing or diminishing them. This holistic view of ethical AI leads to a regulatory approach that seeks to preemptively address a wide range of potential societal impacts.

These divergent philosophical underpinnings and the resulting regulatory approaches have a direct impact on international AI governance and cooperation. When countries with such different priorities and legal frameworks attempt to collaborate on AI standards, data sharing, or joint research, significant challenges arise. For example, differing approaches to data privacy can complicate cross-border data flows, which are essential for training large AI models and for global AI research. China's emphasis on data localization and state access contrasts sharply with the EU's strict data protection rules and the US's evolving framework for cross-border data transfers.

Furthermore, the global discourse on AI governance often reflects a tension between a state-centric, national-interest-driven approach, exemplified by China, and a more universalist, rights-based approach, championed by the EU. The United States often finds itself navigating between these two poles, seeking to balance its own innovation agenda with international norms and values. This dynamic creates a complex landscape for developing unified global AI strategies, treaties, or ethical guidelines. Without a common understanding of fundamental principles, achieving global consensus on issues like AI safety, the responsible deployment of autonomous weapons, or the prevention of AI-driven misinformation becomes considerably more challenging.

The implications for international AI governance are thus multifaceted. China's model, by demonstrating the efficacy of a state-directed approach to rapid AI deployment, can influence other nations to adopt similar strategies, potentially leading to a more fragmented global regulatory environment where national interests overshadow universal ethical principles. The success of the EU's rights-based approach, conversely, could inspire a global movement towards more ethically grounded AI development, fostering greater trust and interoperability across borders. The US, by its sheer economic and technological influence, also plays a pivotal role in shaping global AI norms, often through the practices of its leading technology companies and its approach to international standards bodies.

Ultimately, the comparative analysis of China's AI model against global norms, particularly those emerging from the EU and US, highlights a fundamental tension in how societies envision the future of technology and its role in human affairs. It underscores that AI development is not a purely technical endeavor but is deeply embedded in societal values, political systems, and historical contexts. The path forward for international AI governance will likely involve navigating these differences, finding areas of common ground, and fostering a global dialogue that respects diverse approaches while upholding universal human rights and the pursuit of shared global prosperity and well-being. The ability to foster innovation while safeguarding individual dignity, privacy, and equitable opportunity will be the defining ethical challenge of China's AI journey, and indeed, of the global AI endeavor as a whole. This comparative perspective is crucial for understanding the intricate tapestry of global AI development and for charting a course towards a future where artificial intelligence benefits all of humanity.

10
Jurisdictional Vignettes AI Law Across Borders

Japan, a nation renowned for its technological prowess and a deep-seated cultural emphasis on harmony and societal well-being, has charted a distinctive course in its pursuit of artificial intelligence (AI). Rather than adopting a purely market-driven or heavily state-controlled paradigm, Japan has sought a balanced approach, fostering innovation while embedding robust ethical guardrails to ensure AI development aligns with its societal values. Central to this strategy is the ambitious **Society 5.0** initiative, a visionary concept that envisions a human-centric, data-driven society where advanced technologies, including AI, are leveraged to solve pressing social and economic challenges. This vision transcends mere technological advancement; it aims to create a future where AI enhances human capabilities, improves quality of life, and addresses issues such as an aging population, labor shortages, and environmental sustainability. Society 5.0 acts as a guiding philosophy, encouraging the development and deployment of AI in a manner that prioritizes human welfare and societal benefit.

Within this overarching vision, Japan has been actively developing specific legal and ethical frameworks to govern AI. A significant aspect of this endeavor involves addressing the intricate legal challenges posed by AI, particularly concerning **liability, data governance, and intellectual property**. These issues are approached with a nuanced understanding of Japan's existing legal traditions and its unique cultural context, where consensus-building and a strong sense of collective responsibility are highly valued. The government has actively engaged with stakeholders, including academia, industry, and civil society, to foster a shared understanding and develop practical solutions. This collaborative spirit is crucial for creating an AI ecosystem that is not only innovative but also trustworthy and beneficial to all members of society.

In terms of fostering AI innovation, Japan has invested heavily in research and development, supporting both fundamental research at universities and applied AI development in various industries. This support often takes the form of public funding for research institutions, grants for startups, and incentives for companies to adopt and develop AI technologies. Key sectors targeted for AI integration include healthcare, manufacturing, agriculture, and transportation, all areas where Japan faces significant demographic and economic challenges. For instance, in healthcare, AI is being explored for diagnostic support, personalized treatment plans, and robotic assistance for elder care, directly addressing the needs of its rapidly aging population. In manufacturing, AI is being deployed to enhance efficiency, optimize supply chains, and improve quality control, building upon Japan's legacy of precision engineering. The government has also established numerous research centers and innovation hubs dedicated to AI, facilitating collaboration and knowledge sharing among researchers and industry professionals. These initiatives are designed to create a vibrant ecosystem where cutting-edge AI research can flourish and translate into real-world applications.

The establishment of **ethical guardrails** is not an afterthought but an integral part of Japan's AI strategy. Recognizing the potential societal impacts of AI, the government has been proactive in developing guidelines and principles for responsible AI development and deployment. These efforts are guided by a commitment to human-centricity, fairness, transparency, and accountability. Japan has actively participated in international discussions on AI ethics, contributing to global efforts to establish common principles and standards. Domestically, various governmental bodies and advisory committees have been formed to deliberate on AI ethics, including the implications of AI for privacy, bias, and employment. The focus is on ensuring that AI systems are designed and used in ways that uphold human dignity, respect individual rights, and promote social equity.

One of the key areas of legal focus for Japan has been **AI liability**. As AI systems become more autonomous and make decisions with significant consequences, determining who is responsible when something goes wrong becomes increasingly complex. Traditional legal frameworks often struggle to accommodate the distributed nature of AI decision-making, where responsibility could potentially lie with the developer, the deployer, the user, or even the AI system itself. Japan is exploring various approaches to this challenge, including the possibility of revising existing tort law, developing specific AI liability regulations, or promoting the use of insurance mechanisms. The aim is to create a system that allows for fair compensation for damages caused by AI while also encouraging responsible innovation and discouraging negligence. This involves careful consideration of how to attribute fault when an AI system's actions are not directly traceable to a human agent, and how to ensure that victims have recourse when they suffer harm. The debate often revolves around finding a balance between holding developers accountable for foreseeable risks and allowing for the development of sophisticated AI that may exhibit emergent behaviors.

Data governance is another critical area where Japan is establishing its legal and ethical frameworks. Recognizing that data is the lifeblood of AI, the country is working to create a robust yet privacy-preserving data ecosystem. This involves strengthening data protection laws, promoting data sharing for research and development, and ensuring that data is collected and used ethically. Japan's Personal

Information Protection Act (PIPA) has been revised to align with international standards and address the specific challenges posed by AI, including the use of personal data for AI training and the potential for re-identification of anonymized data. The government is also promoting the concept of "data utilization for societal benefit," encouraging the ethical sharing of data among different entities to drive innovation and address societal challenges. This includes initiatives like data trusts and data platforms that facilitate secure and transparent data sharing. The challenge lies in balancing the need for data access with the imperative to protect individual privacy and prevent misuse of personal information. Japan's approach emphasizes trust-building and transparency in data handling, aiming to foster public confidence in the data-driven economy.

The realm of **intellectual property (IP)** rights also presents unique challenges in the context of AI. As AI systems become capable of generating original content, such as art, music, and even scientific discoveries, questions arise about authorship, ownership, and patentability. Japan is actively engaged in discussions about how to adapt its IP laws to accommodate AI-generated works. One of the key debates concerns whether AI-generated creations can be considered works of authorship and who should hold the IP rights- the AI developer, the user who prompted the AI, or perhaps the AI itself. Japan's current IP laws are based on human creativity, and extending them to AI-generated content requires careful consideration of existing legal principles and potential international harmonization. The government is exploring various options, including the possibility of creating new forms of IP protection for AI-generated works or adapting existing patent and copyright laws. The goal is to ensure that the creators and developers of AI technology are adequately incentivized while also fostering an environment where AI can be used to generate new knowledge and creative outputs that benefit society. The nuanced nature of AI creation, often involving complex algorithms and vast datasets, makes direct application of traditional IP frameworks challenging.

Furthermore, Japan is actively exploring ways to address the **ethical implications of AI in practice**. This includes developing guidelines for mitigating algorithmic bias, ensuring transparency and explainability in AI systems, and promoting human oversight in critical decision-making processes. The government has established a number of advisory bodies and working groups to examine these issues in detail, drawing input from experts across various fields. For example, the Ministry of Economy, Trade and Industry (METI) has been instrumental in developing guidelines for AI utilization, emphasizing ethical principles such as fairness, accountability, and safety. These guidelines are designed to be practical and adaptable, providing a framework for businesses and organizations to implement AI responsibly. Japan's cultural emphasis on consensus and harmony also influences its approach to AI ethics, encouraging dialogue and collaboration to find solutions that are acceptable to a broad range of stakeholders. The goal is to build a society where AI is not only technologically advanced but also socially responsible and ethically sound.

Japan's commitment to fostering AI innovation with ethical guardrails is further demonstrated through its proactive engagement with international initiatives and its willingness to learn from global best practices. The nation understands that AI development is a global endeavor, and that international cooperation is essential for addressing its multifaceted challenges and opportunities. This collaborative spirit is crucial for developing harmonized standards, sharing knowledge, and ensuring that AI benefits humanity as a whole. Japan's approach is characterized by a deep respect for human values, a commitment to societal well-being, and a pragmatic approach to problem-solving, all of which are reflected in its evolving AI legal and ethical frameworks. By carefully balancing innovation with ethical considerations, Japan aims to create a future where AI serves as a powerful tool for progress, enhancing the lives of its citizens and contributing to a more sustainable and equitable world. The nation's journey in AI governance is a testament to its capacity for forward-thinking policy development, demonstrating how a society can embrace transformative technologies while steadfastly adhering to its core values and principles.

Brazil's foray into the complex arena of Artificial Intelligence (AI) regulation presents a compelling case study in how a large, developing economy navigates the imperative to foster technological advancement while simultaneously safeguarding its citizens' rights and addressing inherent socio-economic disparities. Unlike jurisdictions that might leverage established, robust legal precedents or extensive pre-existing technological infrastructure, Brazil finds itself in a dynamic process of constructing its AI governance framework largely from the ground up, influenced by both global trends and its distinct national context. This involves a delicate balancing act, attempting to harness the transformative potential of AI for economic growth and public service improvement, while keenly aware of the risks associated with unchecked technological deployment, particularly in a society grappling with significant inequalities.

The legislative landscape in Brazil regarding AI is characterized by a series of proposals and ongoing debates, reflecting a broad spectrum of governmental and societal interests. At the forefront of these discussions is the **Projeto de Lei (PL) 2338/2023**, a comprehensive bill that aims to establish a foundational legal framework for AI in the country. This proposed legislation draws inspiration from various international approaches, including the European Union's AI Act, seeking to classify AI systems based on their risk levels and impose corresponding obligations on developers and deployers. The intention is to create a tiered system of regulation, whereby high-risk AI applications, such as those used in critical infrastructure, law enforcement, or employment, would be subject to more stringent requirements for transparency, human oversight, and risk assessment, compared to lower-risk systems. This risk-based approach acknowledges that not all AI applications pose the same level of threat and that a one-size-fits-all regulatory model would likely stifle innovation. The development of PL 2338/2023 has been a multi-stakeholder endeavor, involving input from academics, industry representatives, civil society organizations, and government agencies, underscoring the recognized need for a consensus-driven approach to such a foundational piece of legislation.

Central to Brazil's broader data protection regime, and consequently its approach to AI governance, is the **Lei Geral de Proteção de Dados (LGPD)**, or the General Data Protection Law. Enacted in 2018 and fully effective from 2020, the LGPD provides a robust framework for the collection, processing, storage, and sharing of personal data. Its principles, such as purpose limitation, necessity, transparency, and the rights of data subjects, are directly applicable to AI systems that rely on vast amounts of data for training and operation. The LGPD's existence provides a critical foundation upon which AI-specific regulations can be built, ensuring that the use of personal data within AI applications adheres to fundamental privacy rights. However, the sheer scale and complexity of data processing required by many AI systems, particularly in areas like machine learning, present ongoing challenges in ensuring full compliance. Questions arise regarding the anonymization and pseudonymization of data used for AI training, the potential for re-identification, and the clear communication of data usage to individuals. The enforcement of the LGPD by the Autoridade Nacional de Proteção de Dados (ANPD) is a crucial element in fostering trust and accountability in the AI ecosystem.

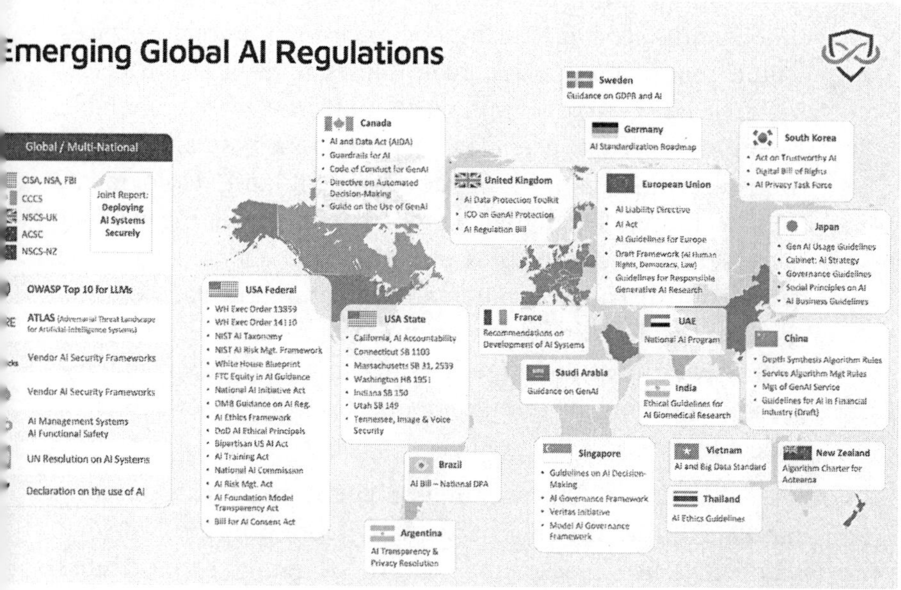

Emerging global AI regulations

The specific challenges faced by Brazil in balancing AI-driven innovation with the protection of citizens' rights and the promotion of equitable development are multifaceted. As a nation with significant socio-economic disparities, the deployment of AI has the potential to either exacerbate existing inequalities or serve as a tool for their mitigation. For instance, AI-powered tools in areas like credit scoring, hiring, or access to public services could inadvertently perpetuate biases present in historical data, leading to discriminatory outcomes for vulnerable populations. This necessitates a strong focus on fairness and non-discrimination in AI development and deployment. Furthermore, the digital divide within Brazil means that access to AI technologies and their benefits may not be uniformly distributed, potentially widening the gap between different regions and socio-economic groups. The regulatory framework must therefore consider how to ensure equitable access and prevent the monopolization of AI benefits by a select few.

Debates surrounding **algorithmic transparency and accountability** are particularly vibrant in the Brazilian context. The "black box" nature of many sophisticated AI models makes it difficult to understand the reasoning behind their decisions, posing significant challenges for accountability when errors or harms occur. PL 2338/2023 and related discussions have placed a strong emphasis on the need for transparency, requiring that individuals be informed when they are interacting with an AI system and, where possible, understand the general logic behind its decision-making processes. This is especially critical in public administration and sensitive sectors where AI decisions can have profound impacts on citizens' lives. Accountability mechanisms are also being explored, seeking to define responsibility for AI-induced harms, whether that lies with the developer, the deployer, or a combination thereof. This requires careful consideration of legal doctrines and the potential need for new liability frameworks that can accommodate the autonomous nature of AI.

The Brazilian government has also recognized the importance of fostering AI innovation through strategic investments and supportive policies. Initiatives aimed at promoting research and development, encouraging AI adoption by businesses, and building digital infrastructure are crucial for Brazil to remain competitive in the global AI landscape. However, this must be done in conjunction with robust ethical guidelines and regulatory oversight to ensure that innovation is aligned with societal values. The interplay between economic development goals and the imperative for responsible AI governance is a central theme in Brazil's evolving approach. This includes exploring how AI can be leveraged to improve public services, enhance efficiency in key sectors like agriculture and healthcare, and drive economic growth, all while being mindful of the ethical and social implications.

The practical implementation of AI regulations in Brazil also faces challenges related to enforcement capacity and the need for skilled personnel. Establishing effective oversight mechanisms requires not only well-defined laws but also regulatory bodies with the expertise and resources to monitor compliance, investigate violations, and adapt to the rapidly evolving nature of AI technology. Training and capacity-building for regulators, policymakers, and industry professionals are essential to ensure that the regulatory framework is effectively understood and applied. The ANPD, while empowered by the LGPD, faces the ongoing task of developing specific guidance and enforcement strategies for AI-related data processing activities.

Furthermore, Brazil's approach to AI regulation is influenced by its active participation in international forums and its engagement with global best practices. Learning from the experiences of other countries and contributing to the development of international norms for AI governance can help Brazil shape a regulatory framework that is both effective domestically and compatible with global standards. This collaborative approach is vital in addressing the cross-border nature of AI development and deployment.

The discussions around AI in Brazil are not merely technical or legal; they are deeply intertwined with the nation's social and economic fabric. The potential for AI to create new job opportunities while also displacing existing ones, the ethical considerations of using AI in areas like justice and security, and the impact on democratic processes are all subjects of intense scrutiny. The regulatory framework must be flexible enough to adapt to these evolving challenges and provide clear guidance for the responsible development and deployment of AI. This includes fostering public dialogue and education about AI, empowering citizens to understand and engage with AI systems, and ensuring that AI development is guided by principles of human dignity, fairness, and inclusion. The journey of AI regulation in Brazil is a testament to the ongoing effort to harness the power of technology for the betterment of society while vigilantly guarding against its potential pitfalls, particularly in a developing economic context where the stakes are exceptionally high. The ultimate success of these endeavors will depend on the continuous refinement of legislative instruments, robust enforcement mechanisms, and a sustained commitment to ethical principles that prioritize the well-being and rights of all Brazilian citizens.

The African Union (AU) stands at a pivotal juncture, recognizing the profound impact Artificial Intelligence (AI) will have on the continent's socio-economic trajectory. Unlike the more fragmented approaches taken by individual nations in other regions, the AU has embarked on an ambitious journey to forge a unified, continental strategy for AI, aiming to harmonize policies and foster responsible innovation across its 55 diverse member states. This initiative is not merely about technological adoption; it is a strategic imperative to harness AI as a catalyst for sustainable development, address persistent challenges, and ensure that Africa is not merely a consumer but a proactive shaper of the AI revolution.

The genesis of this continental approach can be traced to a growing awareness within the AU of AI's dual potential: to unlock unprecedented opportunities for progress in areas such as healthcare, agriculture, education, and governance, while also presenting significant risks if left unregulated. These risks include the exacerbation of existing digital divides, potential for job displacement, the perpetuation of biases through unrepresentative data, and the erosion of data sovereignty. The very diversity of the African continent, with its vast array of languages, cultures, economic development levels, and technological infrastructures, presents a unique set of challenges for any attempt at policy harmonization. However, it is precisely this diversity that underscores the necessity of a coordinated, pan-African strategy. A fragmented approach could lead to a patchwork of regulations that would stifle cross-border collaboration, hinder the scaling of AI solutions, and potentially disadvantage member states with less developed regulatory capacities.

Central to the AU's efforts is the development of a comprehensive **AI Policy Framework**. This framework aims to provide a common set of principles, guidelines, and recommendations that member states can adapt and implement within their national contexts. The process has been characterized by extensive consultation and collaboration, bringing together policymakers, researchers, industry leaders, and civil society representatives from across the continent. The focus is on creating an enabling environment for AI development and deployment that is simultaneously ethical, rights-based, and conducive to inclusive growth. This involves grappling with fundamental questions about data governance, intellectual property rights in AI-generated content, the ethical implications of AI in public decision-making, and the crucial need for digital literacy and capacity building.

One of the most significant challenges the AU is addressing is the **digital divide**. While some African nations are making strides in digital infrastructure, significant disparities persist across and within countries. This means that access to AI technologies, reliable internet connectivity, and the skilled workforce needed to develop and manage AI systems are not uniformly available. The AU's strategy recognizes that a successful continental AI policy must actively work to bridge these divides. This involves promoting investment in digital infrastructure, fostering partnerships for technology transfer, and supporting educational initiatives that equip African youth with the AI skills of the future. The goal is to ensure that the benefits of AI are shared broadly and do not further entrench existing inequalities. Initiatives might include supporting the development of AI solutions tailored to local contexts and needs, such as AI-powered diagnostic tools for remote healthcare settings or agricultural advisory systems that can help smallholder farmers improve yields in challenging climates.

The issue of **data sovereignty** is another critical pillar of the AU's AI policy deliberations. As AI systems are heavily reliant on data, controlling how this data is collected, stored, processed, and used is paramount for national security, economic competitiveness, and the protection of citizens' rights. The AU is exploring models that empower African nations to retain control over their data, ensuring that it is used for the benefit of the continent and not exploited by external actors. This involves establishing clear guidelines on cross-border data flows, promoting the development of regional data infrastructure, and supporting the creation of data trusts or cooperatives that can manage data ethically and securely. The aspiration is to build a data economy that serves African interests, fostering local innovation and ensuring that the value generated from African data remains within the continent.

At the heart of the AU's AI strategy are the **ethical principles** that will guide its development and deployment. These principles are being carefully crafted to reflect African values and priorities, aiming to create AI that is human-centric, fair, transparent, accountable, and beneficial to society. The concept of "responsible AI" is being defined through a lens that acknowledges the continent's unique socio-cultural contexts. For instance, the AU is keenly aware of the potential for AI to perpetuate historical biases, particularly concerning marginalized communities. Therefore, strong emphasis is being placed on developing AI systems that are free from unfair discrimination and that promote social justice. This requires rigorous testing, auditing, and ongoing monitoring of AI algorithms to detect and mitigate bias.

The AU's commitment to fostering AI development is also intrinsically linked to its **Agenda 2063**, the continental blueprint for socio-economic transformation. AI is seen as a crucial enabler for achieving the aspirations of Agenda 2063, from eradicating poverty and improving the quality of life for all Africans to driving industrialization and digital transformation. The AU's AI policy is designed to be a strategic tool that supports these broader development goals. This might involve identifying specific sectors where AI can have the greatest impact, such as using AI for predictive maintenance of critical infrastructure, optimizing energy grids, personalizing education for diverse learning needs, or enhancing public service delivery through intelligent automation. The focus is on how AI can be leveraged to solve Africa's most pressing challenges and create new economic opportunities.

The practical implementation of a continental AI policy requires significant

capacity building across member states. This includes training policymakers, regulators, researchers, and technicians in AI governance, ethics, and development. The AU is working to establish centres of excellence for AI research and development, promote inter-university collaboration, and support initiatives that foster a new generation of African AI talent. Furthermore, there is a recognized need to raise public awareness and understanding of AI, ensuring that citizens are informed about its potential benefits and risks and are empowered to participate in discussions about its governance. This educational aspect is crucial for building trust and ensuring that AI development is aligned with societal expectations.

The AU's engagement with international partners is also a key aspect of its AI strategy. While striving for continental autonomy and self-determination in AI governance, the AU recognizes the value of learning from global best practices and collaborating with international organizations and other regions. This involves participating in global AI dialogues, sharing experiences, and contributing to the development of international norms for AI. The aim is to ensure that African perspectives are represented in global AI governance discussions and that the continent can shape its own digital future in an increasingly interconnected world. This includes navigating the complex landscape of international data regulations and ensuring that African data is protected and used ethically in global AI value chains.

The AU's approach to AI policy harmonization is a dynamic and evolving process. It acknowledges that the rapid pace of AI innovation requires a flexible and adaptive regulatory framework. The ultimate goal is to create an ecosystem where AI can flourish responsibly, driving innovation, economic growth, and social progress across the African continent, while safeguarding human rights and ensuring that the benefits are shared equitably. This continental vision for AI represents a proactive and unified approach to navigating one of the most transformative technologies of our time, positioning Africa not as a passive observer but as an active participant and innovator in the global AI landscape. The success of this endeavor will depend on sustained political will, effective collaboration among member states, robust stakeholder engagement, and a continued commitment to ethical principles that prioritize human dignity and well-being. It is a testament to the AU's recognition that in the age of AI, collective action and shared strategies are not just beneficial, but essential for navigating the complexities of technological advancement and shaping a more prosperous and equitable future for all Africans. The initiative also seeks to foster a spirit of "African innovation" in AI, encouraging the development of solutions that are contextually relevant and address the continent's unique developmental needs, rather than simply adopting technologies developed elsewhere without adaptation. This involves supporting local startups and research institutions, investing in AI infrastructure, and creating sandboxes where new AI applications can be tested and refined safely. The policy framework also anticipates the need for ongoing evaluation and revision, acknowledging that as AI technology evolves, so too must the governance structures that oversee it. This iterative approach is crucial for ensuring the long-term relevance and effectiveness of the AU's AI strategy. The continental approach also aims to create a more attractive investment climate for AI-related industries by offering a degree of regulatory predictability and alignment across member states, which can reduce compliance costs and risks for businesses operating in multiple African countries. This can be particularly attractive for both local and international investors seeking to scale their AI-driven products and services across the continent.

Canada has carved out a distinctive path in the intricate global landscape of Artificial Intelligence (AI) governance, prioritizing a judicious balance between fostering innovation and ensuring ethical and responsible deployment. This approach, deeply embedded in federal initiatives and reflected in its contributions to international discourse, seeks to harness the transformative power of AI while diligently mitigating its inherent risks. Rather than adopting a purely permissive or overly restrictive stance, Canada has consistently advocated for a nuanced strategy that embraces technological advancement while upholding core societal values, including privacy, fairness, and accountability. This multi-faceted approach is not merely a policy preference; it is a deliberate effort to position Canada as a leader in the responsible development and application of AI on a global scale.

At the federal level, a cornerstone of Canada's AI governance strategy has been the articulation of clear principles and the establishment of dedicated funding mechanisms to support research, development, and the responsible adoption of AI technologies. The Pan-Canadian Artificial Intelligence Strategy, launched in 2017, represented a significant early commitment to AI, investing substantial resources in research, talent development, and the creation of three national AI institutes: Amii (Alberta Machine Intelligence Institute), CIFAR (Canadian Institute for Advanced Research), and Mila (Quebec AI Institute). This strategy was visionary in its focus on advancing AI research and ensuring that Canada remains at the forefront of AI innovation. Crucially, it also embedded a strong ethical dimension from its inception, recognizing that technological progress must be aligned with societal well-being. The strategy has since evolved, with subsequent funding injections and a continuous refinement of its objectives to address emerging challenges and opportunities in the AI ecosystem. This sustained commitment underscores Canada's long-term vision for AI, which extends beyond mere technological competitiveness to encompass the ethical and societal implications of its widespread adoption.

A significant pillar of Canada's AI governance framework revolves around the intersection of AI and privacy. The country's existing privacy legislation, particularly the Personal Information Protection and Electronic Documents Act (PIPEDA) at the federal level, and provincial counterparts like Quebec's Act respecting the protection of personal information, provide a foundational layer of protection for personal data, which is the lifeblood of most AI systems. However, the unique ways in which AI can collect, process, and infer information about individuals have prompted a closer examination and, in some cases, proposed updates to these privacy laws. For instance, the ongoing discussions and legislative efforts surrounding Bill C-27, Canada's proposed Artificial Intelligence and Data Act (AIDA), signal a proactive approach to modernizing privacy protections in the age of AI. AIDA aims to establish specific rules for the creation and deployment of AI systems, focusing on issues such as bias, transparency, and accountability. The proposed legislation intends to create a risk-based framework, subjecting higher-risk AI systems to more stringent requirements. This approach recognizes that not all AI applications pose the same level of risk to individuals and society, allowing for a more proportionate and effective regulatory response. Key provisions being considered include requirements for impact assessments for high-impact systems, obligations related to data anonymization and bias mitigation, and mechanisms for redress for individuals affected by AI decisions. The emphasis on privacy is not merely about compliance; it is about fostering public trust in AI technologies and ensuring that individuals maintain control over their personal information in an increasingly data-driven world. This commitment to robust privacy safeguards is essential for the responsible development and deployment of AI, preventing the misuse of personal data and guarding against potential harms such as algorithmic discrimination.

Intellectual property (IP) rights also present a complex area within AI governance, and Canada has been actively engaging with these challenges. The question of who owns AI-generated works- whether it's the developer of the AI, the user who prompts it, or the AI itself- is a subject of ongoing debate. Current Canadian IP law, including the Copyright Act and the Patent Act, generally requires human authorship or inventorship. This poses a challenge for AI-created content or inventions. Canada is exploring how to adapt its IP framework to accommodate AI, considering options such as extending protection to AI-assisted creations or developing new legal categories for AI-generated works. The goal is to strike a balance that incentivizes innovation in AI development and use while ensuring that existing IP principles are not undermined. This includes ensuring that creators and innovators are appropriately recognized and rewarded, even when AI plays a significant role in the creative or inventive process. The country is participating in international discussions to harmonize approaches to AI and intellectual property, acknowledging the global nature of AI innovation. This collaborative effort aims to foster a predictable and supportive environment for AI research and development, encouraging investment and creativity across the AI sector.

The application of AI in public services is another domain where Canada is developing a nuanced governance approach. Recognizing AI's potential to improve efficiency, enhance service delivery, and inform policy decisions, the government has been exploring its use in areas such as healthcare, immigration, and the justice system. However, this exploration is tempered by a strong emphasis on ethical considerations. Initiatives like the Directive on Automated Decision-Making, issued by the Treasury Board of Canada

Secretariat, provide guidance for federal departments on the responsible use of automated decision systems, including AI. This directive mandates that government departments conduct algorithmic impact assessments, ensure transparency about the use of AI, and establish mechanisms for human oversight and intervention. The focus is on ensuring that AI systems used in the public sector are fair, accountable, transparent, and respect fundamental rights. For example, in healthcare, AI holds promise for diagnostic support and personalized treatment plans, but its implementation must be carefully managed to prevent bias against certain patient groups and ensure patient data privacy. Similarly, in the justice system, AI could be used for risk assessment, but its application must be scrutinized for potential biases that could perpetuate systemic inequalities. The Canadian government is committed to a human-centric approach, ensuring that AI augments human decision-making rather than replacing it, especially in sensitive areas where significant impacts on individuals' lives are at stake. This includes establishing clear lines of accountability and providing avenues for recourse when automated decisions lead to negative outcomes.

Canada's commitment to global AI ethics discussions is also a defining characteristic of its approach. As a nation with significant AI research capacity and a policy environment that encourages dialogue, Canada has actively participated in international forums and initiatives aimed at developing global norms and standards for AI. This includes contributing to discussions within organizations such as the OECD, the G7, and the United Nations. Canada has been a proponent of principles that emphasize human-centric AI, fairness, accountability, transparency, and safety. The country has also actively engaged in initiatives to promote AI literacy and build capacity in developing nations, recognizing that responsible AI governance requires a global, collaborative effort. This outward-looking perspective reflects Canada's understanding that AI challenges transcend national borders, necessitating international cooperation to develop effective and ethical governance frameworks. The country's approach is often characterized by its pragmatism, seeking to develop flexible and adaptable regulatory instruments that can keep pace with the rapid evolution of AI technology. This involves not only setting standards but also fostering an ecosystem of responsible innovation through research funding, talent development, and public-private partnerships. The emphasis is on creating an environment where AI can thrive, but always within a framework that prioritizes human dignity, societal well-being, and democratic values. This balanced approach aims to foster confidence among citizens and businesses alike, ensuring that Canada remains a responsible and innovative player in the global AI landscape. The country's proactive engagement in shaping international AI norms demonstrates a commitment to ensuring that the benefits of AI are maximized while its potential harms are minimized on a global scale.

The overarching theme in Canada's AI governance strategy is one of measured progress and continuous adaptation. It is a testament to the recognition that AI is not a monolithic technology but a diverse set of tools with varying applications and impacts. Consequently, the governance framework must be equally nuanced, avoiding a one-size-fits-all approach. This principle is evident in the country's ongoing exploration of regulatory sandboxes, which allow for the testing of new AI applications in a controlled environment, facilitating innovation while allowing regulators to observe and learn about potential risks and benefits firsthand. These sandboxes provide a valuable mechanism for understanding the real-world implications of AI technologies before widespread deployment, enabling the development of more informed and effective regulations. Furthermore, Canada is actively promoting multistakeholder engagement, bringing together academics, industry leaders, civil society organizations, and government representatives to discuss and co-create AI governance strategies. This inclusive approach ensures that a wide range of perspectives and expertise are considered, leading to more robust and socially accepted governance frameworks. The commitment to transparency in government AI use, as exemplified by the Directive on Automated Decision-Making, is also a critical component. By making information about how AI systems are used in public services accessible to citizens, Canada aims to build trust and ensure accountability. This transparency extends to efforts to understand and address algorithmic bias, a key concern in AI deployment. Research and development into methods for detecting and mitigating bias in AI systems are actively supported, reflecting a commitment to fairness and equity.

In summary, Canada's approach to AI governance is characterized by a deliberate and balanced strategy that seeks to foster innovation while prioritizing responsible development and ethical deployment. This is evidenced through its substantial investments in AI research and talent, its forward-thinking legislative proposals like AIDA that address privacy and algorithmic accountability, its thoughtful consideration of intellectual property issues, and its commitment to the ethical use of AI in public services. By actively participating in global AI ethics discussions and promoting multistakeholder collaboration, Canada is not only shaping its own AI future but also contributing to the development of responsible AI practices worldwide. This nuanced and adaptive strategy aims to harness the full potential of AI for societal benefit, ensuring that technological progress is aligned with human values and promotes a more inclusive and prosperous future. The ongoing evolution of these policies reflects Canada's commitment to staying at the forefront of AI governance, adapting to the dynamic nature of the technology and its societal implications.

South Korea stands as a compelling case study in the

rapid and comprehensive integration of Artificial Intelligence (AI) into its national fabric, coupled with a proactive approach to its regulation. This East Asian powerhouse has consistently demonstrated a dual commitment: fostering cutting-edge AI development and innovation while simultaneously building a robust governance framework to steer its deployment responsibly. Its technological infrastructure is among the most advanced globally, characterized by ubiquitous high-speed internet access and a deeply ingrained digital culture. This fertile ground has allowed AI technologies to permeate various sectors of society and the economy with remarkable speed and effectiveness. The South Korean government has been a primary architect of this AI-driven transformation, recognizing AI as a crucial engine for future economic growth and societal advancement. Through significant public investment, strategic policy initiatives, and the cultivation of a highly skilled workforce, the nation has positioned itself as a global leader in AI research, development, and application.

The South Korean government's dedication to AI is not merely aspirational; it is concretely manifested in substantial financial commitments and comprehensive national strategies. The "Artificial Intelligence National Strategy," first unveiled in December 2019 and subsequently updated, represents a cornerstone of this effort. This strategy outlines ambitious goals for AI development, including the nurturing of 100 AI startups by 2025 and the creation of an AI-powered society by 2030. A significant portion of these efforts is directed towards building a data infrastructure that supports AI learning and innovation, making vast amounts of high-quality data available for research and development. Furthermore, the strategy emphasizes the importance of human capital, with plans to train 22,000 AI specialists by 2025, addressing the critical need for skilled professionals to drive AI advancements. This focus on infrastructure and talent development underscores a pragmatic, implementation-oriented approach to AI adoption. The government actively supports AI research and development through various agencies and funding programs, encouraging collaboration between academia, industry, and research institutions. These initiatives aim to accelerate the commercialization of AI technologies and foster a vibrant AI ecosystem.

The integration of AI in South Korea is particularly evident in its advanced robotics sector. South Korea is a global leader in industrial robot production and deployment, with a high density of robots per worker. AI is increasingly being integrated into these robots, moving them beyond repetitive tasks to more sophisticated operations that require adaptability, learning, and decision-making. This fusion of AI and robotics is transforming manufacturing, enhancing productivity, and improving safety in factories. Beyond industrial applications, AI-powered robots are also finding their way into service sectors, including healthcare, logistics, and even consumer markets. For instance, companion robots and AI-driven service robots are being developed and deployed to assist the elderly, provide customer service, and enhance the efficiency of various service industries. The government's support for "smart factories" and the adoption of AI in manufacturing processes further bolsters this trend, creating a virtuous cycle of innovation and adoption. This seamless integration is driven by a strong domestic demand for advanced automation and a government keen on maintaining its competitive edge in global manufacturing. The focus is not just on creating AI, but on embedding it into the tangible systems that drive the economy and improve daily life.

In healthcare, South Korea is leveraging AI to revolutionize diagnostics, drug discovery, and patient care. AI algorithms are being developed to analyze medical images such as X-rays and CT scans with remarkable accuracy, assisting radiologists in detecting diseases like cancer at earlier stages. AI is also being employed in personalized medicine, analyzing patient data to tailor treatment plans and predict responses to different therapies. The government's investment in digital healthcare infrastructure and its supportive regulatory environment have facilitated the rapid adoption of AI in this sensitive sector. Initiatives like the "AI Healthcare Project" aim to develop AI-based medical diagnostic systems and smart healthcare platforms, fostering innovation while ensuring patient safety and data privacy. The ethical considerations surrounding AI in healthcare are being addressed through ongoing discussions and the development of guidelines that prioritize patient well-being, fairness, and transparency in AI-driven medical decisions. The country is also exploring the use of AI in public health, for instance, in predicting disease outbreaks and optimizing resource allocation during health crises. This proactive approach to integrating AI in healthcare aims to improve health outcomes, enhance the efficiency of medical services, and make healthcare more accessible.

Autonomous systems, particularly in the automotive sector, represent another frontier where South Korea is making significant strides. The nation is actively investing in the development of self-driving vehicles, with major automotive companies and tech firms pioneering research in this area. The government has been supportive, establishing regulatory frameworks and testing grounds for autonomous vehicles. South Korea has set ambitious goals for the commercialization of autonomous driving technology, aiming to achieve Level 4 autonomy in specific areas by the mid-2020s. This involves not only the technological development of self-driving cars but also the creation of supportive infrastructure, such as smart road networks and integrated traffic management systems that communicate with autonomous vehicles. The regulatory approach is characterized by a phased implementation, starting with pilot programs and gradually expanding the scope as the technology matures and safety is proven. Key considerations include data security, the ethical dilemmas of accident scenarios (the "trolley problem"), and the implications for public safety and liability. The government is actively engaging in dialogue with stakeholders to address these complex issues and ensure a smooth transition to autonomous mobility. This forward-thinking approach to autonomous systems reflects South Korea's ambition to be at the forefront of the next generation of transportation.

From a regulatory perspective, South Korea's approach to AI is characterized by a blend of forward-looking policy and agile adaptation. While not having a single overarching AI law akin to some other jurisdictions, it has been developing a comprehensive suite of regulations and guidelines that address various aspects of AI. The Ministry of Science and ICT (MSIT) plays a central role in shaping AI policy, often in collaboration with other ministries. A key development has been the establishment of the "AI Ethics Guidelines" in 2020, which were developed through a multi-stakeholder process involving experts from academia, industry, and civil society. These guidelines emphasize principles such as human-centricity, social responsibility, fairness, transparency, and accountability in the development and use of AI. They serve as a moral compass for AI development, aiming to prevent potential harms and ensure that AI is used for the benefit of humanity and society. The guidelines are intended to be a living document, subject to revision as AI technology and its societal implications evolve. This iterative approach to regulation acknowledges the dynamic nature of AI and the need for flexibility in governance.

Furthermore, South Korea is actively engaging with the challenges of data governance in the context of AI. Recognizing that data is the fuel for AI, the country has been working to create a robust data ecosystem while safeguarding individual privacy. Legislation such as the Personal Information Protection Act (PIPA) provides a framework for data protection, and ongoing efforts are being made to adapt these regulations to the specific needs of AI development, including provisions for data anonymization and the secure sharing of data for research purposes. The concept of "data pooling" and "data marketplaces" is being explored to facilitate the legal and ethical sharing of data among businesses and researchers, thereby accelerating AI innovation. This focus on data governance is crucial for fostering trust and ensuring that AI development is conducted in a responsible and ethical manner, respecting the rights and privacy of individuals. The careful balancing of data accessibility for AI training with the imperative of data privacy is a central tenet of South Korea's approach.

The regulatory landscape also includes specific provisions and initiatives tailored to emerging AI applications. For instance, in the realm of autonomous vehicles, South Korea has established special regulatory zones where companies can test self-driving technologies under controlled conditions, allowing for experimentation and data collection while managing risks. This approach is often referred to as a regulatory sandbox, providing a safe space for innovation and learning. Similarly, in healthcare, the government is facilitating the clinical validation and regulatory approval of AI-powered medical devices and software, working to establish clear pathways for these novel technologies to enter the market while ensuring their safety and efficacy. The aim is to strike a balance between encouraging rapid innovation and ensuring that AI applications in critical sectors like healthcare meet stringent safety and ethical standards. This pragmatic approach allows for the practical exploration of AI's potential without compromising on fundamental safety and ethical principles.

South Korea's commitment to AI integration and regulation is not confined to domestic policy; it also extends to active participation in international discussions and collaborations on AI governance. The nation is a contributor to global efforts to establish common principles and standards for AI, recognizing that the challenges and opportunities presented by AI transcend national borders. This international engagement helps South Korea to learn from other countries' experiences, share its own best practices, and contribute to the development of a cohesive global AI governance framework. The country's emphasis on practical implementation, coupled with its forward-looking regulatory approach and significant government investment, positions it as a leader in the global AI landscape. This multi-faceted strategy ensures that South Korea is not only a hub for AI innovation but also a responsible adopter of these transformative technologies, prioritizing societal well-being and ethical considerations alongside technological advancement. The nation's journey with AI exemplifies a model of how a technologically advanced society can proactively engage with the complexities of AI, fostering innovation while laying down the groundwork for its responsible and beneficial integration across all facets of life. The ongoing evolution of its policies and its commitment to adapting to the rapid pace of AI development suggest that South Korea will continue to be a pivotal player in shaping the future of AI governance on a global scale. The deep integration of AI into its industrial base, coupled with a thoughtful, evolving regulatory framework, showcases a nation that is not merely adopting AI but actively shaping its trajectory.

11
AI and International Law Human Rights and Humanitarian Concerns

The pervasive integration of Artificial Intelligence (AI) into nearly every facet of modern life presents a profound and complex challenge to the bedrock principles of fundamental human rights. While AI holds immense promise for advancing societal well-being, it simultaneously introduces novel and often insidious threats that can erode freedoms, entrench inequalities, and undermine established legal protections. Understanding these impacts requires a critical examination of how AI systems, through their design, deployment, and application, interact with internationally recognized human rights, including but not limited to freedom of expression and opinion, the right to privacy, the prohibition of discrimination, and the right to a fair trial. The sheer scale and complexity of AI applications necessitate a nuanced approach that acknowledges both the potential benefits and the inherent risks.

One of the most immediate and widely discussed human rights concerns arising from AI deployment relates to the right to privacy and the protection of personal data. AI systems, particularly those leveraging machine learning, are inherently data-hungry. They rely on vast datasets to train algorithms, identify patterns, and make predictions or decisions. This data often comprises personal information, including our online activities, browsing history, social interactions, location data, biometric identifiers, and even our thoughts and opinions expressed in digital spaces. The collection, processing, and storage of this data, often without explicit, informed consent or with consent buried deep within lengthy and complex terms of service, directly challenges the right to privacy, which encompasses the right to control one's personal information and to be free from unwarranted intrusion. The proliferation of AI-powered surveillance technologies, from facial recognition systems deployed by law enforcement to sophisticated tracking mechanisms embedded in smart devices and online platforms, creates an environment of constant monitoring. This pervasive surveillance can have a chilling effect on individual autonomy and freedom, as people may alter their behavior or self-censor their expression for fear of being monitored or misinterpreted by AI systems. The ability of AI to link disparate datasets and infer sensitive personal information, such as political affiliations, religious beliefs, or health conditions, exacerbates these privacy concerns, creating detailed digital profiles that can be used for various purposes, some of which may be discriminatory or manipulative.

Beyond privacy, AI's impact on freedom of expression and opinion is a critical area of concern. AI-powered content moderation systems on social media platforms, designed to identify and remove illegal or harmful content, can inadvertently stifle legitimate speech. Algorithms are often opaque in their decision-making processes, leading to instances where dissenting opinions, critical commentary, or satire are wrongly flagged and suppressed. The bias inherent in the data used to train these algorithms can lead to the disproportionate censorship of voices from marginalized communities or those expressing minority viewpoints. Moreover, AI can be used to generate and disseminate misinformation and disinformation at an unprecedented scale and speed, creating echo chambers and filter bubbles that polarize societies and undermine informed public discourse. Deepfakes, AI-generated videos or audio recordings that convincingly depict individuals saying or doing things they never did, pose a particularly potent threat to truth and trust, potentially being used to manipulate public opinion, discredit political opponents, or incite violence. The ability of AI to personalize content delivery also means that individuals may be exposed to a curated reality that reinforces their existing beliefs, limiting their exposure to diverse perspectives and hindering the open exchange of ideas essential for a healthy democracy.

The principle of non-discrimination, a cornerstone of international human rights law, is also significantly challenged by AI technologies. AI systems learn from data, and if that data reflects historical societal biases, the AI will inevitably perpetuate and even amplify those biases. This can lead to discriminatory outcomes in various critical domains. For example, AI used in hiring processes might discriminate against certain demographic groups if the training data shows a historical underrepresentation of those groups in particular roles. Similarly, AI-powered credit scoring systems can disadvantage individuals from minority backgrounds if the data reflects discriminatory lending practices of the past. In the criminal justice system, AI tools used for risk assessment in sentencing or parole decisions have been shown to exhibit racial bias, leading to harsher outcomes for Black defendants compared to white defendants with similar criminal histories. Facial recognition technology, widely deployed by law enforcement, has demonstrated lower accuracy rates for women and individuals with darker skin tones, raising concerns about false arrests and wrongful accusations. The opacity of many AI algorithms makes it difficult to identify and rectify these biases, creating a situation where discrimination can occur systematically and without clear accountability.

The right to a fair trial and due process is another fundamental human right that can be undermined by the deployment of AI. When AI systems are used in judicial decision-making, such as in predicting recidivism or assisting judges in sentencing, there are significant concerns about transparency, explainability, and accountability. If an AI system recommends a particular sentence or parole decision, it is often difficult to understand the precise reasoning behind that recommendation. This lack of transparency can prevent defendants from effectively challenging the evidence or logic used against them, thus violating their right to a fair hearing. Furthermore, the potential for bias in these AI systems, as discussed earlier, could lead to outcomes that are not based on objective evidence but on flawed algorithmic processes. The reliance on AI in areas such as predictive policing, which aims to forecast where and when crimes are likely to occur, also raises due process concerns. Such systems can lead to over-policing of certain communities, potentially resulting in increased surveillance and arrests based on statistical probabilities rather than concrete evidence of wrongdoing. This can create a self-fulfilling prophecy, where increased police presence leads to more arrests, which in turn reinforces the AI's prediction, perpetuating a cycle of bias.

The right to work and fair working conditions is also implicated in the age of AI. As AI-powered automation becomes more sophisticated, concerns are mounting about job displacement and the potential for AI to monitor and control workers in ways that infringe upon their dignity and rights. AI-driven surveillance in the workplace can track employee productivity, communication, and even emotional states, creating an environment of constant scrutiny that can be detrimental to well-being and autonomy. The algorithmic management of workers, where AI systems allocate tasks, set performance targets, and even make decisions about hiring and firing, can lead to a lack of human oversight and recourse for workers who feel unfairly treated. This can erode the right to fair remuneration and to just and favorable conditions of work, as AI systems may prioritize efficiency and cost-saving over worker welfare. The gig economy, often facilitated by AI platforms, presents particular challenges in this regard, with workers often classified as independent contractors, thus lacking many of the protections afforded to traditional employees.

Furthermore, the right to freedom of peaceful assembly and association can be affected by AI. AI-powered surveillance technologies, including facial recognition and gait analysis, can be used to identify and track participants in protests or public gatherings. This can create a chilling effect, discouraging individuals from exercising their right to protest or associate freely for fear of reprisal or future targeting. The ability of AI to analyze social media and online activities can also be used to identify and monitor individuals who are critical of governments or who engage in activism, potentially leading to their harassment or detention. This instrumentalization of AI for political control poses a direct threat to the exercise of fundamental freedoms and the functioning of civil society.

The equitable distribution of the benefits of AI and the prevention of a widening digital divide are also critical human rights considerations. If access to AI-driven services, education, and economic opportunities is concentrated in the hands of a few, it could exacerbate existing inequalities and create new forms of social stratification. The development and deployment of AI often require significant resources and expertise, which may not be available in lower-income countries or disadvantaged communities. This could lead to a situation where the transformative potential of AI is not realized by all, further marginalizing those who are already vulnerable. Ensuring that AI development is inclusive and that its benefits are shared equitably is essential for upholding the human right to development and to an adequate standard of living.

Addressing these complex challenges requires a multi-pronged approach involving legal reform, ethical guidelines, technological safeguards, and robust public discourse. International legal frameworks need to be adapted and strengthened to explicitly address the human rights implications of AI. This includes clarifying how existing rights apply in the context of AI and developing new norms and standards where necessary. The principles of human-centricity, fairness, transparency, accountability, and non-discrimination must be embedded in the design, development, and deployment of AI systems. This requires interdisciplinary collaboration among technologists, legal scholars, ethicists, policymakers, and civil society organizations to ensure that AI is developed and used in a manner that respects and promotes human rights. Ultimately, the responsible integration of AI into society hinges on our collective ability to anticipate and mitigate its potential negative impacts on fundamental human rights, ensuring that technological progress serves humanity rather than undermining it. The ongoing global dialogue on AI governance underscores the urgency of this task, aiming to forge a path where AI can be a tool for empowerment and progress, not an instrument of oppression or discrimination. The continuous evolution of AI technology demands an equally dynamic and proactive approach to human rights protection, ensuring that the digital age upholds, rather than erodes, the fundamental dignity and freedoms of all individuals.

The advent of Artificial Intelligence (AI) has introduced a new and deeply concerning frontier in warfare: Lethal Autonomous Weapons Systems (LAWS). These systems, often referred to as "killer robots," are designed to identify, select, and engage targets without direct human intervention. The prospect of machines making life-and-death decisions on the battlefield raises profound questions concerning their compatibility with the existing framework of International Humanitarian Law (IHL), the body of law that governs the conduct of armed conflict. At the heart of this debate lie the core principles of IHL, which have evolved over centuries to mitigate the suffering caused by war. The integration of AI into weapons systems challenges the very foundations of these principles, necessitating a rigorous examination of their implications.

One of the most critical principles at stake is distinction. IHL mandates that parties to a conflict must at all times distinguish between combatants and civilians, and between military objectives and civilian objects. Attacks may only be directed against combatants and military objectives. The ability of AI-powered systems to accurately make this distinction in the chaotic and dynamic environment of a battlefield is highly questionable. While proponents suggest that AI could potentially be more precise than human soldiers, thereby reducing civilian casualties, critics raise significant doubts. The complex and often nuanced judgment required to differentiate between a combatant who has surrendered or is otherwise out of the fight, and one who is still actively engaged, is difficult to codify into algorithms. Furthermore, civilians can become indistinguishable from combatants in certain scenarios, such as when they are directly participating in hostilities or when they are in the vicinity of military objectives. The ability of an AI to assess intent, context, and a myriad of other factors that a human commander would consider is far from assured. The very nature of machine learning, which relies on pattern recognition and data, may struggle with unforeseen circumstances or novel combat situations not present in its training data. A misclassification by an autonomous weapon could lead to the unlawful targeting of civilians or civilian objects, a grave violation of IHL.

Equally central to the discussion is the principle of proportionality. This principle prohibits attacks which may be expected to cause incidental loss of civilian life, injury to civilians, damage to civilian objects, or a combination thereof, which would be excessive in relation to the concrete and direct military advantage anticipated. The assessment of proportionality is inherently a complex, subjective judgment call that requires a deep understanding of military necessity, the anticipated harm, and the expected military gain. It is an assessment that involves weighing intangible factors and considering the long-term consequences of an attack. Can an AI system truly grasp the concept of "military advantage" in a way that allows it to make the nuanced ethical calculations required for proportionality? While an AI might be programmed to calculate the number of expected civilian casualties versus the military gain, it is unclear how it would weigh the intangible "value" of human life against the strategic importance of a military objective. The decision to launch an attack must not only consider the immediate consequences but also the broader impact on civilian populations and the overall conduct of hostilities. Delegating such a profound ethical and legal judgment to a machine risks a de-humanization of warfare, where the grim calculus of war is reduced to lines of code, divorced from human empathy and moral responsibility.

The principle of precaution in attack further compounds these concerns. IHL requires parties to a conflict to take all feasible precautions in the choice of means and methods of attack with a view to avoiding, and in any event to minimizing, incidental loss of civilian life, injury to civilians, and damage to civilian objects. This includes verifying targets, choosing weapons that minimize collateral damage, and giving effective advance warning of attacks which may affect the civilian population, unless circumstances do not permit. For LAWS, the "feasibility" of taking precautions becomes a critical question. If an autonomous weapon is programmed to act without human oversight, how can it exercise judgment in real-time to alter its course of action based on new information, such as the sudden appearance of civilians near a target? The ability to abort an attack or to adjust targeting parameters based on evolving battlefield conditions is crucial for upholding the principle of precaution. Moreover, the concept of "advance warning" becomes problematic if the decision to attack is made and executed by a machine without human deliberation or authorization. The very design of autonomous weapons, which are intended to operate independently, may inherently limit their ability to exercise the necessary caution and flexibility required by IHL.

A central pillar of the debate surrounding LAWS is the concept of "meaningful human control" (MHC). Many states and international organizations argue that for any weapon system to comply with IHL, there must be a sufficient level of human control over its operation, particularly over the critical functions of target selection and engagement. The level of control considered "meaningful" is itself a subject of intense discussion. Does it mean a human must authorize every single engagement? Or is it sufficient for a human to set the parameters and rules of engagement within which the machine operates? The ambiguity surrounding MHC allows for a spectrum of autonomous capabilities, from automated systems that assist humans in targeting to fully autonomous weapons that operate independently. Critics argue that any system that removes human judgment from the decision to kill crosses a fundamental ethical and legal line. They contend that the uniquely human capacity for empathy, moral reasoning, and contextual understanding is essential for making life-and-death decisions in warfare. Without MHC, accountability becomes elusive. If an autonomous weapon commits a war crime, who is responsible? Is it the programmer, the commander who deployed the system, the manufacturer, or the machine itself? IHL relies on a chain of command and individual criminal responsibility, which is severely challenged when decisions are delegated to autonomous systems.

The potential consequences of LAWS for the nature of armed conflict are also a significant concern. The development and deployment of these weapons could lower the threshold for engaging in armed conflict, as states might be more willing to resort to force if they believe their own soldiers are not at risk. This could lead to an increase in the frequency and intensity of warfare. Furthermore, the introduction of LAWS could trigger an arms race, with states compelled to develop and acquire these weapons to avoid being at a disadvantage, further destabilizing international security. The psychological impact of fighting against or being targeted by machines that lack human emotion or remorse is also a factor that cannot be easily dismissed. Warfare could become even more impersonal and brutal, further distancing humans from the realities of conflict.

The legal status of LAWS remains a contentious issue within the international community. While there is no specific treaty banning or regulating LAWS, many states have expressed serious concerns about their development and potential use. Several proposals have been put forward in international forums, such as the United Nations Convention on Certain Conventional Weapons (CCW), to establish new legal instruments or to clarify the application of existing IHL to autonomous weapons. However, consensus has been difficult to achieve, with some states advocating for a complete ban, others for strict regulation, and a few remaining hesitant to limit their technological advancements in this area. The interpretation of existing IHL- particularly the principles of distinction, proportionality, and precaution- to cover autonomous weapon systems is also a subject of ongoing legal debate. Some legal scholars argue that existing law is sufficient to prohibit or regulate LAWS if they are found to be incapable of complying with IHL. Others contend that new legal norms and a specific treaty are necessary to adequately address the unique challenges posed by these weapons.

Beyond the direct application of IHL, the development of LAWS also raises broader ethical and philosophical questions about the role of technology in warfare and the very nature of human responsibility. The idea of delegating the decision to kill to a machine, irrespective of its technical capabilities, is seen by many as a fundamental moral transgression. It raises questions about human dignity, the sanctity of life, and the intrinsic value of human judgment. The potential for AI to evolve in ways that are unpredictable or that operate beyond human comprehension further fuels these concerns. While AI can offer significant advantages in data processing and speed, the absence of human foresight, compassion, and moral deliberation in the act of taking a life is a prospect that many find deeply unsettling.

The debate over LAWS is not merely a theoretical discussion; it has very real implications for future conflicts and the protection of civilians. As AI technology continues to advance, the development of increasingly sophisticated autonomous weapons systems becomes more plausible. This necessitates urgent and robust international dialogue and action to ensure that the introduction of these technologies into warfare does not undermine humanitarian principles or lead to unchecked suffering. The challenge lies in finding a balance between technological innovation and the enduring need to uphold the fundamental rules of war and the ethical principles that guide them. The international community stands at a critical juncture, and the decisions made today regarding autonomous weapons will shape the future of warfare and the very meaning of accountability in armed conflict for generations to come. The ongoing deliberations in international forums, coupled with extensive academic and civil society engagement, are crucial for navigating this complex terrain and for striving towards a future where warfare, however it may evolve, remains bound by the constraints of humanity and law.

The integration of Artificial Intelligence (AI) into various societal functions presents a complex web of challenges and opportunities concerning the most fundamental human rights: the right to life, liberty, and security. While AI promises advancements in efficiency and effectiveness, its deployment in areas such as law enforcement, justice systems, and even healthcare, carries significant implications for how these rights are protected and upheld. The very nature of AI, often operating with opaque algorithms and vast datasets, can create scenarios where individual freedoms are inadvertently or deliberately curtailed, leading to potential infringements that require careful legal scrutiny and robust safeguards.

One of the most visible and controversial applications of AI that directly impacts the right to life, liberty, and security is in the realm of **predictive policing**. This approach utilizes AI algorithms, often fed with historical crime data, demographic information, and social media activity, to forecast where and when crimes are likely to occur, and sometimes even to identify individuals deemed at higher risk of offending or being victimized. While the stated goal is to enhance public safety and allocate law enforcement resources more effectively, the implementation of predictive policing raises serious concerns. The reliance on historical data, which can inherently contain biases reflecting past discriminatory policing practices, can inadvertently perpetuate and even amplify these biases. For instance, if certain neighborhoods have historically been over-policed, AI systems trained on this data might continue to flag these areas for increased surveillance and intervention, regardless of current crime rates. This can lead to a disproportionate impact on marginalized communities, creating a feedback loop of increased scrutiny, arrests, and further data generation that reinforces the initial bias.

The impact on the right to liberty is particularly acute. Predictive policing systems can lead to increased surveillance of individuals and communities based on statistical probabilities rather than concrete evidence of wrongdoing. This can manifest as heightened police presence, more frequent stops and searches, and an overall atmosphere of constant monitoring that erodes personal freedom and autonomy. The ability of AI to process and correlate vast amounts of personal data can also lead to individuals being flagged as "persons of interest" or "high-risk" without any direct evidence of their involvement in criminal activity. This can result in individuals being subjected to unwarranted attention from law enforcement, which can have a chilling effect on their behavior and their ability to engage freely in public life. Furthermore, the notion of being targeted for potential future offenses, rather than for actions already committed, raises profound questions about the presumption of innocence and the fundamental right to liberty. Detaining or restricting the liberty of an individual based on a probabilistic prediction, however sophisticated the algorithm, moves away from established legal principles that require a demonstrable link to an unlawful act.

The right to security is also implicated. While proponents argue that predictive policing enhances security by preventing crime, the reality for those subjected to its effects can be the opposite. The constant state of being watched or being a potential target of law enforcement intervention can create a pervasive sense of insecurity and anxiety. Moreover, the inaccuracies inherent in any predictive system mean that resources might be diverted from addressing actual threats or engaging in community-based problem-solving, potentially leaving genuine security gaps. The risk of false positives, where an individual is incorrectly identified as a potential offender or victim, can lead to undue stress, reputational damage, and even unwarranted detention. The opacity of many predictive AI systems also makes it difficult for individuals to understand why they are being targeted, or how to challenge such designations, further undermining their sense of security and their ability to seek redress.

Beyond predictive policing, AI's role in **surveillance technologies** presents a parallel set of challenges to the rights to liberty and security. The proliferation of facial recognition systems, gait analysis, and ubiquitous CCTV networks, often powered by AI, allows for unprecedented levels of monitoring of individuals in public and increasingly private spaces. These technologies, when integrated with AI, can create detailed profiles of individuals' movements, associations, and activities, raising significant privacy concerns that are intrinsically linked to liberty. The ability to track and identify individuals with high accuracy, in real-time, can create a chilling effect on freedom of assembly and expression, as individuals may self-censor their behavior and speech for fear of being monitored or misinterpreted by an AI system.

The right to security can be eroded when surveillance technologies are used in ways that lead to arbitrary detention or unwarranted interference with personal freedom. In some jurisdictions, AI-powered surveillance has been deployed to identify individuals present at protests or political gatherings, potentially leading to their subsequent apprehension or investigation based on their mere presence. This form of preemptive action, driven by algorithmic analysis of observed behavior, can be seen as a violation of the right to liberty, as it curtails freedom of movement and association without due process. The potential for AI-powered surveillance to be used for mass monitoring, rather than for targeted investigations based on reasonable suspicion, poses a fundamental threat to the concept of a free society where individuals are not constantly under scrutiny. The aggregation of data from various surveillance sources, analyzed by AI, can build a comprehensive picture of an individual's life, which, if misused, can lead to significant harm, including reputational damage, professional repercussions, and even wrongful imprisonment.

The implications for **due process and the right to a fair trial** are also profound. AI is increasingly being used in the criminal justice system, from risk assessment tools used in sentencing and bail decisions to AI-powered evidence analysis. While the aim is often to increase efficiency and reduce human bias, the lack of transparency in many AI algorithms, often referred to as the "black box" problem, makes it difficult to scrutinize the basis of these decisions. If an AI system recommends a harsher sentence or denies bail based on factors that are not fully understood or challengeable, it undermines the fundamental right to due process, which includes the right to understand the evidence against you and to present a defense. The potential for AI to introduce new, albeit potentially unintentional, forms of bias into the justice system is a significant concern. If AI risk assessment tools are trained on data that reflects societal inequities, they may disproportionately flag individuals from certain socioeconomic or racial backgrounds as higher risk, impacting their liberty irrespective of the merits of their case.

The right to life, while seemingly less directly impacted by these specific AI applications, is nevertheless touched upon when the failures of AI in law enforcement or security lead to wrongful death or injury. For instance, if a predictive policing algorithm leads to an over-reliance on force in certain communities, or if AI-powered surveillance systems result in erroneous identification that leads to a dangerous encounter with law enforcement, the ultimate consequence could be the loss of life. The deployment of autonomous weapons systems, discussed previously, represents a more direct and acute challenge to the right to life, as machines are empowered to make lethal decisions. However, even in non-lethal applications, the cascading effects of AI-driven errors or biases can have devastating consequences for individuals' security and their very lives.

Protecting the rights to life, liberty, and security in the age of AI requires a multi-faceted approach.

Transparency and explainability of AI systems are paramount. Individuals must have a right to understand how AI decisions affecting them are made, especially when those decisions pertain to their freedom or safety. This necessitates the development and deployment of AI systems that are auditable and whose decision-making processes can be scrutinized by legal professionals, ethicists, and the individuals themselves. The ability to challenge an AI-driven decision, whether it's a denial of bail, a predictive policing flag, or a surveillance identification, is crucial for upholding due process and preventing arbitrary curtailment of liberty.

Robust legal frameworks and regulatory oversight are essential. Existing human rights laws and legal principles must be adapted and, where necessary, strengthened to address the unique challenges posed by AI. This includes ensuring that AI systems used in law enforcement and justice are developed and deployed in a manner that is non-discriminatory, proportionate, and respects the presumption of innocence. Regulations should establish clear lines of accountability for the development and deployment of AI systems, ensuring that human responsibility remains at the core of decision-making processes that affect fundamental rights. Independent oversight bodies, equipped with the technical expertise to understand AI, are needed to monitor the use of these technologies and to investigate potential abuses.

Furthermore, **addressing algorithmic bias** is a critical task. This involves critically examining the data used to train AI systems, identifying and mitigating biases within algorithms, and conducting regular impact assessments to ensure that AI applications do not disproportionately harm certain groups. This might involve employing diverse development teams, seeking input from affected communities, and implementing fairness-aware AI techniques. The very design of AI systems must proactively incorporate principles of human rights and justice, rather than attempting to retroactively fix problems.

The right to liberty is particularly vulnerable to AI-driven surveillance and predictive interventions. Safeguards must be put in place to ensure that any restriction on liberty is based on concrete evidence and due legal process, not solely on algorithmic predictions. This means that the use of AI for proactive interventions should be limited, with a strong emphasis on human review and independent judicial oversight before any liberty-restricting actions are taken. The potential for AI to facilitate mass surveillance necessitates strong data protection laws and strict limitations on the collection, retention, and use of personal data by both state and private actors.

The right to security, in its broadest sense, encompasses freedom from fear and arbitrary interference. AI systems that create pervasive surveillance or lead to unjustified suspicion can undermine this fundamental aspect of security. It is crucial to balance the perceived benefits of AI in crime prevention with the imperative to protect individuals from becoming subject to a constant state of digital scrutiny. This requires a societal conversation about the acceptable limits of surveillance and the types of data that can be collected and processed by AI systems. The development of AI should be guided by principles that prioritize human dignity and autonomy, ensuring that technology serves to enhance, rather than diminish, our sense of security and freedom.

Ultimately, the responsible integration of AI into society requires a commitment to upholding the inherent dignity and fundamental rights of every individual. As AI capabilities expand, so too must our vigilance in ensuring that these powerful tools are developed and deployed in ways that are consistent with international human rights law and ethical principles. The rights to life, liberty, and security are not abstract concepts; they are the bedrock of just and free societies, and their protection in the digital age demands careful consideration, proactive regulation, and an unwavering commitment to human-centered values. The challenge lies in harnessing the potential of AI while rigorously guarding against its capacity to infringe upon these most essential freedoms, ensuring that technological progress does not come at the cost of human rights. The ongoing evolution of AI necessitates continuous dialogue and adaptation of legal and ethical frameworks to meet these evolving challenges, ensuring that the promise of AI serves humanity rather than constrains it.

The increasing displacement of populations globally, driven by conflict, persecution, and environmental degradation, presents a significant and growing challenge for international humanitarian law and human rights frameworks. In this complex landscape, Artificial Intelligence (AI) is emerging as a tool with the potential to both streamline and complicate the processes by which individuals seek and receive protection. The application of AI within refugee contexts, particularly in areas such as border management, asylum adjudication, and refugee registration, carries with it a dual promise: the potential for enhanced efficiency, accuracy, and fairness, juxtaposed against profound risks of algorithmic bias, misidentification, and the erosion of due process and the fundamental human dignity of some of the world's most vulnerable populations. Understanding these dynamics is crucial for ensuring that technological advancements serve, rather than undermine, the core principles of international protection.

One of the most prominent areas where AI is being deployed in the refugee context is border control and management. Technologies such as facial recognition, gait analysis, and AI-powered surveillance systems are increasingly used at ports of entry and along national borders. The stated aim is to improve security by identifying individuals on watchlists, detecting fraudulent documents, and preventing the unauthorized movement of people. For instance, systems can be trained to analyze biometric data against databases of known security threats or individuals with prior adverse immigration records. AI algorithms can also process vast amounts of data from various sources, such as satellite imagery or social media, to monitor and predict migration flows, theoretically enabling more proactive and efficient resource allocation by border agencies. This can include identifying potential smuggling routes or detecting patterns of movement that may indicate human trafficking. The efficiency gains are presented as a way to manage large numbers of arrivals more effectively, potentially reducing waiting times and improving the accuracy of identity verification. However, these technologies are not without their significant drawbacks. The accuracy of facial recognition systems, in particular, has been shown to vary considerably across different demographic groups. Studies have consistently revealed higher rates of misidentification for women, individuals with darker skin tones, and older individuals. In the context of border control, a false positive-incorrectly identifying an individual as a security threat-could lead to unwarranted detention, denial of entry, or even deportation, with potentially catastrophic consequences for an asylum seeker fleeing persecution. Conversely, a false negative-failing to identify a genuine threat-could, from the perspective of a state, compromise national security. The reliance on these systems necessitates a critical examination of the datasets used for training and validation, ensuring they are representative and that inherent biases are rigorously mitigated. The potential for discrimination, whether intentional or unintentional, is a grave concern when these tools are wielded by states with existing policies or practices that may disadvantage certain national, ethnic, or religious groups. Furthermore, the constant surveillance inherent in these technologies can create an environment of intimidation and fear for individuals seeking protection, potentially impacting their willingness to approach authorities or seek asylum openly. The very notion of being constantly scanned and analyzed as one crosses a border can be dehumanizing, reducing individuals to data points rather than recognizing their inherent rights and vulnerabilities.

The asylum process itself is another domain where AI is being introduced, with the aim of improving efficiency and consistency in decision-making. Asylum claims are often processed by overwhelmed administrative bodies, leading to lengthy backlogs and inconsistent outcomes. AI-powered tools are being developed to assist in the initial screening of claims, identifying key information, flagging potentially straightforward cases for expedited processing, or even providing preliminary assessments of claim validity. Some systems aim to analyze the textual content of asylum applications, comparing them against past successful and unsuccessful claims, legal precedents, and country-of-origin information to identify patterns and potential indicators of credibility or deception. The promise here is to alleviate the burden on human adjudicators, allowing them to focus on more complex cases and to standardize the application of asylum law across different caseworkers. This could, in theory, lead to more equitable outcomes, reducing the impact of individual biases or variations in experience among asylum officers. For example, an AI might be able to quickly identify discrepancies in a claimant's narrative that a human might miss during a cursory review, or conversely, highlight evidence of persecution that might otherwise be overlooked. However, the risks associated with AI in asylum adjudication are substantial. The quality and impartiality of AI-driven decision support tools are heavily dependent on the data they are trained on. If the historical data reflects existing biases in the asylum system-for instance, if claims from certain nationalities or based on particular grounds for persecution have historically been adjudicated more stringently or leniently-the AI system will likely perpetuate or even amplify these biases. This could lead to systematic discrimination against specific groups of asylum seekers. The "black box" problem, where the internal workings of an AI algorithm are opaque and difficult to understand, poses a significant challenge to due process. If an asylum claim is rejected, or even if it is recommended for rejection by an AI tool, the claimant has a right to understand the reasons for that decision and to challenge it effectively. Without transparency in the AI's reasoning, this right becomes exceedingly difficult to exercise. Furthermore, the nuances of human experience, the subtle indicators of trauma or fear, and the complex interplay of cultural factors that can be crucial in assessing the credibility of an asylum claim, are exceptionally difficult for AI systems to capture and interpret accurately. Over-reliance on AI for decision-making risks reducing complex human narratives to quantifiable data, potentially leading to the rejection of legitimate claims based on algorithmic assessments that lack contextual understanding. The human element of empathy and nuanced judgment, critical in dealing with individuals who have often experienced profound trauma, may be diminished. The very concept of human dignity, central to international refugee law, can be undermined if individuals are subjected to automated judgments that fail to appreciate the gravity of their circumstances.

Refugee registration and data management present another area where AI is finding application, with potential benefits for humanitarian organizations and governments. AI can be used to process and analyze vast amounts of data collected during registration, such as personal information, biographic details, and sometimes even initial assessments of vulnerability. This can help in identifying individuals in need of specific assistance, tracing separated families, and ensuring that aid is distributed efficiently. For example, AI could quickly identify registered individuals who meet the criteria for specific medical programs or educational support based on their stated needs and demographic profiles. It can also be used for fraud detection within registration systems, preventing duplicate registrations or the misuse of resources. However, the collection and processing of sensitive personal data of refugees raise significant privacy and security concerns. Refugees are often among the most vulnerable populations, and the mishandling or misuse of their data can have severe consequences, including re-traumatization, targeting by hostile actors, or discrimination upon return to their country of origin. AI systems used for data analysis must adhere to the strictest data protection principles, including purpose limitation, data minimization, and robust security measures. The potential for data breaches or unauthorized access is a constant threat, and the long-term storage and use of refugee data by AI systems need careful consideration regarding consent and accountability. Moreover, if AI is used to categorize or profile refugees based on their data, there is a risk of creating new forms of stigma or discrimination. For instance, an AI that identifies certain patterns of behavior or association as indicative of risk could inadvertently lead to individuals being unfairly targeted or excluded from essential services. The digital divide also presents a challenge; if registration relies heavily on digital means or AI-processed data, individuals who lack digital literacy or access may be inadvertently excluded from the registration process and the services that follow. The importance of ensuring that registration processes remain accessible, inclusive, and respectful of human dignity cannot be overstated, and AI tools must be designed and implemented with these principles at the forefront.

The overarching challenge lies in balancing the potential efficiencies offered by AI with the fundamental legal and ethical obligations owed to refugees and asylum seekers under international law, including the 1951 Refugee Convention and various human rights treaties. International refugee law is predicated on the principle of non-refoulement, the prohibition of returning individuals to a country where they would face persecution. The application of AI in border control, asylum adjudication, or even in determining eligibility for resettlement programs must not compromise this core principle. If AI systems are used to make determinations that result in refoulement, whether directly or indirectly, it would represent a grave violation of international law. The principle of due process, which underpins fair asylum procedures, requires access to justice, the right to be heard, and the right to an effective remedy. When AI systems are involved in decision-making that impacts these rights, there must be mechanisms for meaningful human review, transparency in decision-making processes, and clear avenues for appeal. Over-reliance on automated decisions, particularly those made by opaque algorithms, could significantly undermine these safeguards. The dignity of the individual is a cornerstone of human rights and humanitarian law. For individuals who have already endured immense hardship and trauma, the interaction with protection systems should be characterized by respect, empathy, and a recognition of their inherent worth. The introduction of AI, if not handled with extreme care and sensitivity, risks further objectifying and dehumanizing vulnerable individuals, turning them into datasets to be processed rather than people to be protected.

Addressing these challenges requires a proactive and multi-stakeholder approach. Firstly, there is a critical need for transparency and explainability in all AI systems deployed in the refugee context. Decision-making algorithms, particularly those used in asylum adjudication, must be auditable and their logic understandable to human reviewers, legal professionals, and, where appropriate, to the asylum seekers themselves. This would enable effective challenges to potentially erroneous or biased decisions. Secondly, rigorous impact assessments are essential before and during the deployment of AI technologies. These assessments should evaluate the potential for bias, discrimination, and unintended consequences on different groups of asylum seekers and refugees, ensuring compliance with international human rights and refugee law. Independent oversight mechanisms, comprising legal experts, ethicists, humanitarian practitioners, and representatives from affected communities, should be established to monitor the use of AI and to ensure accountability. Thirdly, the datasets used to train and operate these AI systems must be carefully curated, audited for bias, and continuously updated to reflect diverse populations and evolving circumstances. Investing in the development of "fairness-aware" AI and robust bias detection and mitigation techniques is paramount. Furthermore, human oversight must remain central to all critical decisions. AI should be viewed as a tool to assist, not replace, human judgment, particularly in complex cases involving the assessment of credibility, vulnerability, and the application of nuanced legal principles. The ultimate decision-making authority in asylum cases must rest with accountable human adjudicators who can exercise discretion and apply principles of justice and compassion. Lastly, there is a pressing need for international cooperation and the development of common standards and guidelines for the ethical and responsible use of AI in refugee protection. Sharing best practices, fostering research into the human-centric application of AI, and engaging in robust public discourse are vital steps to ensure that technology serves the interests of those seeking protection and upholds the humanitarian values that underpin international law. The goal must be to leverage AI to enhance the efficiency and fairness of refugee protection systems while rigorously safeguarding the rights, dignity, and well-being of every individual seeking safety and a new life. The development and deployment of AI in this sensitive area demand a commitment to human rights, a deep understanding of refugee law, and a cautious, ethical, and people-centered approach, ensuring that technological innovation advances, rather than detracts from, the humanitarian imperative.

The evolving landscape of artificial intelligence presents a complex challenge to the established international legal order, particularly concerning its pervasive impact on human rights. As AI systems become more sophisticated and integrated into various societal functions, the need for coherent and universally applicable norms governing their development and deployment has become increasingly apparent. This subsection delves into the crucial, ongoing efforts to forge such international norms, exploring how global bodies, existing treaties, and emerging soft law instruments are working to ensure that AI advances in a manner that not only respects but actively upholds fundamental human rights principles. The task is multifaceted, requiring collaboration across diverse legal traditions, technological capabilities, and geopolitical interests.

At the forefront of this endeavor are international organizations that serve as vital platforms for dialogue, standard-setting, and capacity building. The United Nations, in its various capacities, has been a significant forum for discussing AI's implications. Through bodies like the Human Rights Council and the UNESCO, member states and experts convene to deliberate on the ethical and legal dimensions of AI. UNESCO, for instance, has been instrumental in championing the development of a global normative instrument on the ethics of AI. This initiative, stemming from extensive consultations with member states, the private sector, civil society, and academia, aims to provide a comprehensive framework for the ethical development and deployment of AI. The proposed Recommendation on the Ethics of Artificial Intelligence, adopted by the UNESCO General Conference in November 2021, represents a landmark achievement in this regard. It articulates a set of universal values and principles, including respect for human rights and fundamental freedoms, transparency and explainability, fairness and non-discrimination, safety and security, and accountability. Crucially, it emphasizes the need for human oversight and the centrality of human agency, ensuring that AI serves humanity and promotes human well-being. The Recommendation's strength lies in its broad consensus and its ambition to guide national policymaking and international cooperation, fostering a shared understanding of responsible AI governance.

Beyond specific AI-focused initiatives, existing international human rights treaties provide a foundational legal basis for addressing the impact of AI. Covenants such as the International Covenant on Civil and Political Rights (ICCPR) and the International Covenant on Economic, Social and Cultural Rights (ICESCR), along with regional human rights instruments like the European Convention on Human Rights and the American Convention on Human Rights, all enshrine fundamental rights that are directly implicated by AI technologies. For example, Article 19 of the ICCPR guarantees the right to freedom of opinion and expression, which can be affected by AI-powered content moderation, algorithmic censorship, or the spread of disinformation amplified by AI. Article 14 of the ICCPR, concerning the right to a fair trial, is challenged by the use of AI in judicial decision-making or predictive policing, where issues of bias, transparency, and due process are paramount. Similarly, the right to privacy, protected under Article 17 of the ICCPR, is profoundly impacted by the data-intensive nature of AI and the proliferation of surveillance technologies. The challenge lies not in the absence of relevant rights, but in interpreting and applying these established principles to novel technological contexts. International human rights bodies, such as the UN treaty bodies and the Special Rapporteurs, are increasingly issuing guidance and recommendations that clarify how these existing rights apply to AI. For instance, the Special Rapporteur on the promotion and protection of the right to freedom of opinion and expression has highlighted the risks posed by AI to online speech and the dissemination of information, calling for robust safeguards.

The development of "soft law" instruments also plays a pivotal role in shaping international norms. These instruments, which are not legally binding in the same way as treaties, include declarations, guidelines, recommendations, and principles. They often serve as precursors to legally binding instruments or as practical guides for implementation. In the context of AI and human rights, a multitude of such initiatives have emerged from various stakeholders, including governments, international organizations, civil society groups, and industry bodies. For example, principles articulated by organizations like the Organisation for Economic Co-operation and Development (OECD) on AI have garnered widespread attention and influenced national strategies. The OECD's AI Principles, adopted in 2019, emphasize inclusive growth, sustainable development, human-centered values, transparency, safety, security, and accountability. These principles aim to foster trustworthy AI and provide a common framework for national policies. Similarly, the Council of Europe has been actively engaged in developing a legal framework on AI, including the exploration of a potential new convention that would aim to regulate AI in a way that respects human rights, democracy, and the rule of law. This initiative reflects a broader understanding that addressing the complex challenges posed by AI requires a holistic approach, encompassing both ethical considerations and legal accountability. Civil society organizations and academic consortia have also contributed significantly by developing ethical guidelines and frameworks, such as those proposed by the Future of Life Institute or the Alan Turing Institute. These efforts, while not binding, exert considerable influence by raising awareness, fostering debate, and offering concrete proposals for responsible AI governance.

The creation of international norms is an iterative process, heavily reliant on the ongoing engagement of diverse stakeholders. Multistakeholder dialogues, involving governments, the private sector, academia, and civil society, are essential for building consensus and ensuring that norms are practical, relevant, and widely accepted. International conferences and forums dedicated to AI ethics and governance provide crucial opportunities for such exchanges. For instance, global summits on AI for good bring together policymakers, researchers, and innovators to explore how AI can be leveraged for positive societal impact, while also confronting its potential risks. The exchange of best practices and the sharing of national experiences in AI governance are also critical components of this norm-development process. Countries that are at the forefront of AI development and deployment often share their approaches to regulation and ethical oversight, providing valuable lessons for others. However, the rapid pace of technological advancement necessitates a flexible and adaptive approach to norm-setting. Static legal frameworks may quickly become outdated, underscoring the importance of mechanisms that allow for continuous review and updating of norms and guidelines.

Moreover, the practical implementation of AI governance frameworks requires capacity building and technical assistance, particularly for developing countries. International cooperation is vital to ensure that the benefits of AI are shared equitably and that all nations are equipped to navigate its challenges responsibly. This includes supporting the development of national AI strategies, fostering digital literacy, and promoting research into AI ethics and safety. Organizations like the United Nations Development Programme (UNDP) and various regional development banks play a role in this regard, supporting countries in their efforts to harness AI for sustainable development while mitigating risks. The aim is to create a global ecosystem where AI is developed and used in a manner that is aligned with universal human rights values, ensuring that technological progress serves the common good and enhances human dignity worldwide. The ongoing dialogue and collaborative efforts are crucial for navigating the complex intersection of AI and human rights, striving to build a future where innovation and fundamental freedoms coexist and mutually reinforce each other. The international community is thus engaged in a continuous process of learning, adapting, and building consensus to establish a robust and responsive framework for AI governance that upholds the universality and indivisibility of human rights in the digital age.

Human rights and international law

12
AI and International Law Criminal Justice and Trade

The integration of Artificial Intelligence (AI) into international criminal investigations marks a significant paradigm shift, offering unprecedented capabilities for processing vast quantities of data and uncovering intricate patterns that might elude human analysts. As the scale and complexity of international crimes-ranging from genocide and war crimes to terrorism and organized transnational crime-continue to escalate, traditional investigative methods often prove insufficient. AI-powered tools are increasingly being deployed to sift through colossal datasets, which can include satellite imagery, financial records, communication logs, social media content, and witness testimonies. These technologies can automate the arduous task of data collection, organization, and preliminary analysis, thereby accelerating the investigative process and allowing human investigators to focus on more nuanced tasks such as strategic planning, witness interviews, and legal argumentation.

One of the primary applications of AI in this domain lies in its ability to identify anomalies and patterns within massive datasets. For instance, in investigations related to war crimes or crimes against humanity, AI algorithms can be trained to analyze satellite imagery to detect changes indicative of destruction, mass graves, or troop movements. Similarly, AI can process financial transaction data to identify suspicious patterns associated with money laundering or the financing of terrorist organizations. In the realm of cybercrime, AI is crucial for analyzing network traffic, identifying malicious actors, and tracing the digital footprint of criminal activities. The sophisticated pattern recognition capabilities of AI allow for the potential identification of previously unknown links between individuals, events, or locations, thereby constructing a more comprehensive picture of criminal enterprises and their operations. Furthermore, natural language processing (NLP) techniques enable AI to analyze large volumes of text-based evidence, such as intercepted communications or internal documents, to extract key information, identify sentiments, and even detect deception or intent. This analytical power can be particularly transformative in situations where evidence is fragmented, voluminous, and geographically dispersed.

The advent of AI in evidence processing naturally raises critical questions regarding the legal admissibility of AI-generated or AI-processed evidence in international tribunals. International criminal law, rooted in principles of due process and fair trial, demands rigorous standards for the introduction of evidence. Tribunals like the International Criminal Court (ICC) and ad hoc tribunals have established rules of evidence that govern what can be presented to the court. The core challenge lies in ensuring that AI-driven analysis meets these established standards. For AI-generated evidence to be deemed admissible, it must typically be relevant, reliable, and authenticated. The reliability of AI output is a significant concern. If an AI system misidentifies a person in an image, misinterprets communication, or draws an incorrect conclusion from data, the resulting evidence could be fundamentally flawed and prejudicial to the accused. Therefore, a crucial aspect of admissibility hinges on the demonstrable accuracy and robustness of the AI tools employed. This necessitates a thorough understanding of the AI's underlying algorithms, its training data, and its performance metrics, which can be complex and proprietary.

Transparency and explainability, often referred to as the "black box" problem, present a significant hurdle to the admissibility of AI-generated evidence. Many advanced AI models, particularly deep learning networks, operate in ways that are not easily understood even by their creators. Investigators and legal professionals need to be able to explain to the court how an AI system arrived at a particular conclusion. If the AI's reasoning process is opaque, it becomes difficult to assess its reliability and to cross-examine the evidence effectively. International tribunals, such as the ICC, have rules that require evidence to be presented in a way that allows for scrutiny and challenge. The ability to deconstruct the AI's decision-making process, identify potential errors, and understand the specific data points that led to a conclusion is paramount. This might involve showcasing the specific algorithms used, the parameters set, the data inputs, and the validation processes. Without such transparency, AI-generated evidence risks being perceived as an authoritative but unchallengeable oracle, which is anathema to the principles of adversarial justice.

Potential biases embedded within AI-driven investigative tools pose another substantial legal and ethical challenge. AI systems are trained on data, and if this data reflects historical societal biases-such as racial, ethnic, or gender disparities-the AI may perpetuate or even amplify these biases in its outputs. For instance, if an AI tool used for facial recognition has been trained predominantly on data from one demographic group, it may perform poorly or generate inaccurate matches for individuals from other groups. In the context of criminal investigations, biased AI could lead to the disproportionate targeting of certain communities, the misidentification of suspects, or the drawing of erroneous conclusions based on prejudiced correlations. The legal ramifications of introducing biased evidence in international criminal proceedings are severe. It could undermine the fairness of the trial, lead to wrongful convictions, and erode public trust in the justice system. Ensuring that AI tools are rigorously tested for bias and that their outputs are scrutinized for discriminatory patterns is therefore essential. This requires a proactive approach to

AI development and deployment, focusing on diverse and representative training data, algorithmic fairness metrics, and ongoing audits to detect and mitigate bias.

To address these challenges, international tribunals are developing frameworks and guidelines for the use and admissibility of AI-generated evidence. This involves establishing clear protocols for the collection, preservation, and analysis of digital evidence, including the metadata associated with AI processing. Expert testimony from AI specialists will likely become increasingly important to explain the functionalities and limitations of AI tools to judges and juries. Furthermore, the principle of human oversight remains critical. AI should be viewed as a tool to assist human investigators, not replace them. Human judgment, contextual understanding, and ethical considerations must be integrated into every stage of the investigative process, from the selection of AI tools to the interpretation of their outputs. The verification and corroboration of AI-generated findings through traditional investigative methods are also essential to ensure reliability. For example, an AI identifying a pattern of communications might require human review of the content of those communications to confirm its significance.

The development of international standards and best practices for AI in criminal justice is an ongoing process. Organizations like the United Nations Office on Drugs and Crime (UNODC) and INTERPOL are actively engaged in exploring the potential of AI while also addressing its associated risks in law enforcement and criminal investigations. This includes initiatives to promote data sharing, develop common methodologies for AI deployment, and provide training to law enforcement officials on the responsible use of AI technologies. The legal frameworks governing evidence in international criminal law will need to adapt to accommodate the unique challenges posed by

AI, ensuring that innovation does not come at the expense of fundamental rights and due process. This adaptation may involve amendments to existing rules of evidence, the creation of new guidelines for digital evidence, and potentially the development of specific international treaties or conventions addressing AI in the justice sector. The ultimate goal is to harness the power of AI to enhance the pursuit of justice for victims of international crimes, while upholding the highest standards of fairness, reliability, and accountability in the process. The responsible and ethical integration of AI into international criminal investigations hinges on a careful balance between technological advancement and the enduring principles of international criminal justice.

The horizon of international criminal accountability is being profoundly reshaped by the burgeoning capabilities of Artificial Intelligence (AI). Beyond its role in enhancing evidence processing, AI holds the potential to fundamentally alter how perpetrators of the most heinous international crimes are identified, how their illicit activities are tracked, and how patterns of behavior indicative of war crimes, crimes against humanity, or genocide are recognized and analyzed. This evolution promises greater efficiency and reach in combating impunity but simultaneously introduces complex ethical and legal quandaries, particularly concerning the attribution of responsibility for AI-driven actions in this sensitive domain.

One of the most compelling prospects lies in AI's capacity for proactive identification and tracking of individuals and networks involved in international crimes. Sophisticated AI algorithms can be trained to analyze vast, disparate datasets to flag suspicious activities, emerging threats, and patterns of behavior that suggest premeditation or ongoing commission of grave offenses. For instance, AI could monitor open-source intelligence, including global news feeds, social media discourse, and public government records, to identify linguistic patterns, thematic correlations, or geographic hotspots associated with conflict escalation, hate speech, or recruitment for extremist groups. By correlating these digital breadcrumbs, AI systems might be able to forecast potential atrocity events or identify individuals actively involved in inciting violence or planning attacks, even before such actions materialize or are conventionally discovered. This anticipatory capability, if ethically deployed and rigorously validated, could provide critical early warnings to international bodies and national law enforcement agencies, enabling timely intervention and potentially preventing mass atrocities.

Furthermore, AI's analytical power can be leveraged to trace the intricate financial and logistical networks that underpin organized transnational crime and support the perpetration of international crimes. By analyzing global financial transaction data, cryptocurrency movements, supply chain records, and communication logs, AI can map complex webs of illicit financing, resource procurement for armed groups, or the facilitation of human trafficking. These systems can identify shell corporations, unusual transaction patterns, and covert communication channels that are often designed to evade human scrutiny. The ability to sift through trillions of data points and identify subtle anomalies or hidden connections can reveal the orchestrators and financiers behind mass atrocities, even if they remain physically distant from the scene of the crimes. This granular insight into support structures is crucial for establishing robust charges of command responsibility or for prosecuting those who enable, finance, or abet international crimes, thereby broadening the net of accountability beyond direct perpetrators.

The challenge of attribution, however, becomes particularly acute when AI systems themselves are involved in the execution or facilitation of criminal activities, or when their outputs are used to identify perpetrators. Consider a scenario where an AI-powered surveillance system, designed to detect illegal arms transfers, inadvertently flags legitimate humanitarian aid shipments as suspicious due to biased training data. If this false positive leads to the interdiction of aid and subsequent humanitarian crisis, or even the arrest and mistreatment of aid workers, who bears responsibility? Is it the programmer who designed the algorithm, the entity that deployed the system, the data used for training, or perhaps even the AI itself, if we were to entertain highly futuristic notions of AI agency? In the context of international criminal law, which is fundamentally predicated on human intent (mens rea) and human action (actus reus), attributing criminal responsibility to a machine or to the diffuse chain of human involvement behind an AI's decision-making process presents unprecedented legal hurdles.

Existing legal frameworks for international criminal responsibility, such as those established by the Rome Statute of the International Criminal Court (ICC), are built upon centuries of jurisprudence concerning human culpability. Concepts like direct perpetration, aiding and abetting, ordering, and command responsibility all presuppose a conscious human actor with a degree of agency and intent. When AI systems make autonomous decisions or generate probabilistic assessments that lead to harm, the traditional application of these concepts becomes problematic. For example, if an AI system controlling autonomous weapons systems makes a targeting decision that results in civilian casualties in violation of international humanitarian law, attributing the crime of murder or unlawful killing to the AI itself is currently legally untenable. Instead, legal scrutiny would likely focus on the human commanders who authorized the deployment of such systems, the engineers who designed them with foreseeable flaws, or the political leaders who procured and operationalized them without adequate safeguards or oversight.

The core difficulty lies in establishing the requisite mental state-mens rea-for criminal liability. Can an AI possess intent, knowledge, or recklessness? Under current legal understanding, AI systems are tools; they do not possess consciousness, volition, or the capacity for moral reasoning. Therefore, any criminal responsibility must ultimately trace back to human actors. This leads to the critical question of how to bridge the gap between an AI's actions and human accountability. If an AI system, through its operational output, leads to the commission of an international crime, the focus will necessarily shift to understanding the human decisions and omissions that enabled this outcome. This could involve examining:

1. **Design and Development:** Were the AI systems designed with foreseeable risks of causing harm? Were ethical safeguards, bias mitigation strategies, and robustness testing adequately implemented by the developers? Negligence or recklessness in design could lead to criminal liability for the engineers, supervisors, or companies involved.
2. **Deployment and Operation:** Who authorized the deployment of the AI system in a context where it could contribute to international crimes? Were the operational parameters and oversight mechanisms sufficient? Commanders who deploy AI-powered tools without understanding their capabilities and limitations, or who fail to implement appropriate human oversight, could be held responsible for their decisions.
3. **Data Integrity and Training:** If the AI's harmful output stems from biased or corrupted training data, who is accountable for the collection, curation, and use of that data? This could include individuals or entities responsible for data sourcing, labeling, and quality assurance.

4. **Failure to Intervene or Mitigate:** If a human operator is aware that an AI system is malfunctioning or producing outputs that could lead to criminal acts, but fails to intervene or shut down the system, they could be held accountable for their omission. This highlights the enduring importance of human oversight.

The legal and practical challenges associated with AI in international criminal accountability are substantial. For instance, how does one prove that a specific AI-generated intelligence report, which led to a wrongful prosecution or an unlawful military action, was the direct cause of the harm, and not merely a contributing factor among many? Corroboration and chain of custody for AI-generated intelligence will become paramount, requiring rigorous documentation of data inputs, algorithmic processes, and any human interventions or interpretations. The 'explainability' or 'transparency' of AI, often referred to as the 'black box' problem, is a critical impediment here. If investigators or prosecutors cannot articulate precisely how an AI system arrived at a particular conclusion, it becomes difficult to present that conclusion as reliable evidence in court, let alone use it to establish a causal link to a crime.

International legal bodies and tribunals are still grappling with how to integrate AI-generated evidence and analysis into their proceedings. While the previous context discussed admissibility, the current focus is on accountability where AI is more than just an investigative tool but potentially an enabler of criminal conduct. This necessitates the development of new legal doctrines or the adaptation of existing ones to address AI-driven harm. For example, the concept of 'algorithmic complicity' could emerge, wherein individuals are held accountable for knowingly leveraging AI systems to facilitate international crimes, even if they did not directly perpetrate the acts themselves. This would require proving that the individuals understood the AI's potential to cause harm and deliberately used it to achieve a criminal objective.

Moreover, AI's role in predictive policing or pre-crime analysis, while potentially useful for prevention, raises significant human rights concerns. If AI systems are used to identify individuals deemed "at risk" of committing future international crimes based on their digital footprint or behavioral patterns, this could lead to pre-emptive surveillance, detention, or even punishment without an actual crime having been committed. International criminal law, as it stands, is focused on prosecuting committed offenses, not on preemptively punishing potential future offenders based on algorithmic predictions. The ethical implications of profiling individuals based on AI analysis, which may itself be imbued with societal biases, are profound and could lead to severe miscarriages of justice and violations of fundamental rights, such as the presumption of innocence.

The development of international standards for AI in this context is crucial. Bodies like the United Nations, INTERPOL, and various international legal organizations are beginning to explore the implications of AI for international law enforcement and criminal justice. This includes efforts to establish guidelines for the responsible development, deployment, and oversight of AI systems that interact with the legal and security apparatus. Such guidelines would need to address issues of data privacy, algorithmic bias, transparency, accountability, and the preservation of human control over critical decision-making processes, especially those with life-and-death consequences.

The future of international criminal accountability will undoubtedly involve AI, but its successful and just integration hinges on a deliberate and cautious approach. It requires not only technological advancement but also a parallel evolution in legal and ethical frameworks. The goal must be to harness AI's power to enhance justice and deter atrocities, while rigorously safeguarding against the amplification of existing injustices or the creation of new forms of impunity. The challenge lies in ensuring that as AI becomes more sophisticated, our legal systems evolve to hold responsible human actors accountable for the outcomes of these powerful technologies, rather than allowing AI to become a shield for those who would commit crimes against humanity. This will involve ongoing dialogue among legal scholars, technologists, policymakers, and international institutions to navigate this complex terrain and ensure that technological progress serves, rather than subverts, the pursuit of justice. The question is not whether AI will play a role, but rather how we will shape that role to uphold the foundational principles of international criminal justice. This requires continuous vigilance, adaptive legal thinking, and a steadfast commitment to human rights and the rule of law, ensuring that accountability remains firmly anchored in human responsibility, even in an increasingly automated world.

The advent of Artificial Intelligence (AI) is not merely an incremental technological upgrade; it represents a fundamental paradigm shift that is profoundly reshaping the landscape of international trade law and dispute resolution. From the hyper-efficient execution of transactions to the intricate management of global supply chains, AI is automating, optimizing, and in many instances, redefining how goods and services move across borders. This pervasive integration of AI into the fabric of global commerce, however, introduces a complex array of challenges that strain existing legal frameworks, necessitate novel regulatory approaches, and fundamentally alter the nature of international trade disputes.

One of the most visible manifestations of AI's impact is in the realm of automated trading systems and algorithmic trading. These sophisticated AI-powered platforms can analyze vast datasets of market information-including price fluctuations, news sentiment, economic indicators, and geopolitical events-at speeds far exceeding human capability. They can then execute trades automatically based on pre-programmed strategies or adaptive learning algorithms. This has led to increased market liquidity and efficiency in some respects, but it also raises significant questions for international trade law. For instance, the speed and complexity of algorithmic trading can exacerbate market volatility, potentially triggering financial crises or disrupting the stable flow of international trade. When an algorithmic trading system, operating across multiple jurisdictions, causes a market crash that has ripple effects on international trade flows, determining liability and jurisdiction becomes a formidable task. Existing international trade agreements, often negotiated with a focus on human actors and traditional market mechanisms, may not adequately address the systemic risks posed by autonomous trading agents. The principles of non-discrimination, national treatment, and most-favored-nation status, cornerstones of the World Trade Organization (WTO) framework, can become difficult to apply when market access or preferential treatment is influenced by opaque algorithms that operate instantaneously across borders. Moreover, the very definition of what constitutes an "unfair trade practice" might need re-evaluation in an era where market manipulation could be orchestrated by self-learning AI agents.

Beyond financial markets, AI is revolutionizing the physical movement of goods through intelligent supply chain management. AI algorithms are being deployed to optimize logistics, predict demand, manage inventory, automate warehousing, and even control autonomous shipping and delivery vehicles. This hyper-optimization promises greater efficiency, reduced costs, and enhanced responsiveness in global trade. However, it also introduces new vulnerabilities and legal complexities. For example, if an AI system managing a global supply chain for a critical commodity miscalculates demand or predicts a shortage due to faulty data or algorithmic bias, it could lead to widespread disruptions in international trade, impacting multiple countries and industries. When such disruptions occur, the question of responsibility becomes incredibly complex. Is it the AI developer, the company that deployed the AI, the provider of the faulty data, or perhaps the regulatory body that failed to adequately oversee the deployment of such advanced systems? International trade law has long dealt with issues of product liability and contractual disputes arising from the sale of goods, but these frameworks were not designed for scenarios where autonomous systems dictate critical operational decisions that lead to trade disruptions. The "force majeure" clauses in international sales contracts, which typically address unforeseen events beyond the parties' control, might need to be re-examined to consider the predictability and controllability of AI-driven failures.

The regulation of cross-border data flows is another area where AI exerts immense influence and poses significant challenges to international trade law. AI systems are inherently data-hungry; their efficacy is directly proportional to the volume and quality of data they process. This has led to an explosion in cross-border data transfers, as companies leverage global data resources to train and operate their AI models. However, differing national regulations on data privacy, data localization, and data sovereignty create a complex and often fragmented legal environment. Some countries impose strict rules on where data can be stored and processed, potentially hindering the ability of AI systems to operate seamlessly across borders. This can lead to trade barriers, as companies may face difficulties in moving data necessary for AI-driven operations, impacting the services sector and the digital trade components of many goods. International trade agreements, particularly those dealing with services and intellectual property, are struggling to keep pace with the rapid evolution of data governance. The question of whether data itself should be considered a "good" or a "service" under trade law, and how to ensure fair and non-discriminatory access to data for AI development and deployment, remains a contentious issue. The principles of free trade are challenged by policies that restrict data flows, even if such restrictions are ostensibly justified on grounds of national security or privacy.

The core principles of international trade law, designed for a world of human negotiation and established market practices, are being tested by AI's capabilities. For instance, the WTO's Agreement on Safeguards, which allows members to restrict imports temporarily to protect domestic industries facing serious injury, might be misused or rendered less effective by AI-driven market analyses. An AI could potentially generate sophisticated analyses to justify safeguard measures, blurring the lines between objective economic assessment and protectionist intent. Similarly, the application of anti-dumping and countervailing duties, mechanisms intended to address unfair pricing practices, becomes more complicated when pricing decisions are made by AI that can rapidly adjust based on market conditions and competitive AI responses, rather than by human managers setting deliberate pricing strategies. Proving intent or an unfair pricing motive in such dynamic, algorithmically driven environments presents a significant evidentiary challenge.

Dispute resolution mechanisms, a critical component of international trade law, also face profound adaptation needs. Traditional methods of resolving trade disputes, such as consultations, panel proceedings under the WTO, or arbitration under specific trade agreements, rely on the analysis of facts, legal arguments, and evidence presented by human parties. When AI systems are involved in generating evidence, predicting outcomes, or even making trading decisions that lead to disputes, the process of dispute resolution becomes more complex. How does one present an AI's decision-making process as evidence in a trade tribunal? The "black box" problem, where the internal workings of complex AI algorithms are opaque, makes it difficult to understand, verify, and challenge the basis of an AI's actions. This lack of transparency can undermine due process and the principle of impartial adjudication.

Furthermore, the very nature of international trade disputes might evolve. Instead of disputes arising solely from differences in interpretation of trade agreements or factual disagreements about import volumes or subsidies, disputes could increasingly stem from the unintended consequences of AI deployments. For example, if an AI system used for customs valuation systematically undervalues imports from a particular country due to biases in its training data, this could lead to claims of discrimination and unfair trade practices. Establishing the causal link between the AI's operation and the alleged trade violation, and demonstrating that it constitutes a breach of a specific trade agreement, would require deep technical expertise and novel evidentiary standards. The role of expert witnesses will become even more critical, but these experts will need to possess not only legal acumen but also a profound understanding of AI, machine learning, and data science.

The principle of fair competition, a bedrock of international trade, is also significantly impacted. AI can create new forms of competitive advantage, sometimes in ways that are difficult to regulate. For instance, companies with superior AI capabilities might gain an unfair edge through hyper-personalized marketing, predictive pricing, or optimized supply chains that competitors cannot match. While innovation is to be encouraged, trade agreements often contain provisions aimed at ensuring a level playing field. Identifying when an AI-driven advantage crosses the line into an unfair trade practice, and devising appropriate remedies that do not stifle innovation, presents a delicate balancing act for international trade policymakers. The question of intellectual property protection for AI algorithms themselves, and the data used to train them, is also a complex and evolving area that intersects with trade law, impacting how competitive advantages are secured and maintained.

The development of new international norms and regulatory frameworks is essential to navigate this AI-driven transformation of trade. This might involve updates to existing trade agreements to explicitly address AI-related issues, such as rules for algorithmic trading, data governance in cross-border commerce, and the use of AI in customs and regulatory processes. Alternatively, new international instruments or specialized dispute resolution mechanisms tailored to AI-related trade challenges might be necessary. The WTO, as the primary forum for multilateral trade governance, faces the imperative of adapting its rules and procedures to incorporate the realities of AI. This includes fostering dialogue on AI standards, promoting interoperability of AI systems in trade, and developing guidelines for the responsible and ethical use of AI in global commerce.

Moreover, the potential for AI to automate trade compliance and risk management offers both opportunities and challenges. AI-powered tools can help businesses and customs authorities identify and mitigate risks associated with illicit trade, trade misinvoicing, and sanctions evasion. However, reliance on AI in these critical areas also raises questions about accountability if the AI systems are flawed or biased, leading to incorrect assessments or unjustified interventions that disrupt legitimate trade flows. Ensuring that AI tools used in trade compliance are transparent, auditable, and subject to human oversight is paramount to maintaining fairness and efficiency.

The economic implications are also substantial. AI can drive productivity gains and create new markets, but it can also lead to job displacement in sectors traditionally involved in trade facilitation, such as customs brokerage, logistics coordination, and trade finance. International trade law may need to consider how to manage these socioeconomic transitions, potentially through provisions related to worker retraining or social safety nets, although this extends beyond the traditional remit of trade agreements.

Ultimately, the integration of AI into international trade represents a profound juncture. It offers the potential for unprecedented efficiency, innovation, and economic growth. However, it also demands a proactive and adaptive approach from legal scholars, policymakers, and international institutions to ensure that the benefits are widely shared, that fair competition is maintained, and that the integrity of the global trading system is preserved. The existing legal architecture, built for a different era of commerce, must evolve to grapple with the speed, complexity, and autonomy that AI introduces. The challenge lies in harnessing AI's transformative power while mitigating its risks, ensuring that international trade law remains a relevant and effective tool for facilitating global prosperity in an increasingly automated world. This requires ongoing research, robust international cooperation, and a willingness to rethink fundamental assumptions about how global commerce operates and how disputes arising from it should be resolved. The very definition of "trade facilitation" is being rewritten by AI, demanding a commensurate evolution in the legal and regulatory frameworks that govern it.

The rapid integration of Artificial Intelligence into the global economy, as previously discussed, is not confined to optimizing trade flows or automating transactions. It also ventures into the very creation of new works and inventions, thereby directly challenging established paradigms of intellectual property (IP) law. This burgeoning field of AI-generated creations necessitates a thorough examination of how existing IP doctrines, primarily copyright and patent law, can accommodate and protect output that originates from non-human entities. The fundamental questions revolve around authorship and inventorship: can a machine be an author or an inventor? If not, who is entitled to IP rights for an AI's creation?

Copyright law traditionally protects original works of authorship fixed in a tangible medium of expression. The concept of "authorship" inherently implies a human creator possessing creativity, intent, and intellectual labor. AI, however, operates through algorithms and datasets, raising profound questions about the locus of originality and creativity. For instance, consider an AI system trained on a vast corpus of literary works that then generates a novel poem or a symphony. If this AI-generated poem possesses a unique style, emotional depth, and narrative coherence that rivals human-authored works, should it be eligible for copyright protection? Under current interpretations in many jurisdictions, copyright protection is contingent upon human authorship. The United States Copyright Office, for example, has consistently maintained that copyright can only be granted to works created by human beings. This stance is rooted in the understanding that copyright law is designed to incentivize human creativity and reward the intellectual effort of individuals. Applying this to AI-generated content means that if an AI merely acts as a tool, akin to a paintbrush or a word processor, and the human user provides significant creative input and direction, the human user might be considered the author. However, when the AI's contribution is substantial, and its output is largely autonomous, the question of human authorship becomes problematic.

This distinction between an AI as a tool and an AI as a creator is crucial. If an AI is merely a sophisticated tool, the human who guides its operation, selects its parameters, and curates its output can be recognized as the author. An artist using an AI image generator might provide detailed prompts, iterate through numerous versions, and make significant artistic decisions throughout the process. In such scenarios, the AI facilitates the creative act, but the human remains the driving force. However, as AI systems become more advanced, capable of generating complex and novel outputs with minimal or abstract human direction, this line blurs considerably. Imagine an AI system designed to compose jazz music. It learns from thousands of hours of jazz recordings, identifies patterns, improvises melodies, and generates entirely new pieces that are musically sophisticated and aesthetically pleasing. If the prompts given were generic, such as "compose a jazz piece in the style of Miles Davis," and the AI produced a piece that was both distinctive and captivating, who is the author? Is it the programmer who designed the AI, the user who initiated the process, or is the concept of authorship itself being stretched beyond its traditional human-centric boundaries?

The implications for international trade are significant, as the protection and exploitation of IP rights are fundamental to cross-border commerce. If AI-generated works are not protectable by copyright, they could enter the public domain immediately upon creation. This would mean that anyone could freely use, distribute, and adapt them without permission or royalty payments, potentially undermining the economic incentives for developing and deploying AI in creative industries. Conversely, if IP rights *are* granted, the question of who holds them becomes a matter of international legal harmonization. Different national approaches could lead to trade disputes, hindering the global trade in AI-generated content. For instance, if Country A recognizes AI as an author and grants copyright protection, while Country B insists on human authorship and denies protection, the trade of creative works between them could become fraught with legal uncertainty. This could impact industries such as software development, music production, visual arts, and literature, all of which are increasingly utilizing AI.

Patent law also faces similar challenges concerning AI-generated inventions. Patent law protects new, useful, and non-obvious inventions. The requirement of an "inventor" has historically been understood as a natural person. In cases where an AI system is instrumental in identifying a novel solution to a technical problem, or even autonomously generates a patentable invention, the question of inventorship arises. A landmark case in this area involved an AI system named DABUS (Device for the Autonomous Bootstrapping of Unified Sentience), which was listed as an inventor on patent applications filed in multiple jurisdictions. In some jurisdictions, such as Australia, courts have recognized AI as a potential inventor, albeit with complex implications for ownership, as the legal owner would likely be the entity that controls the AI. However, in other major jurisdictions, including the United States and the European Patent Office, the requirement of a human inventor has been upheld, and patent applications listing AI as an inventor have been rejected.

The legal reasoning for denying AI inventorship often centers on the interpretation of existing patent statutes, which use terms like "individual" or "person" and imply human agency and inventiveness. The argument is that a machine, lacking consciousness, intent, or the capacity for independent thought in the human sense, cannot be an inventor. If an AI system is responsible for a novel invention, the patent is typically sought by the human or entity that owns, controls, or directs the AI. This could be the AI's developer, the user who utilized the AI in the inventive process, or the company that funded the research. However, assigning inventorship to a human who merely initiated the process or provided broad parameters can feel like a misrepresentation of the actual inventive contribution. If the AI independently identified a solution that was not foreseeable by its human supervisors, attributing the invention solely to them might not accurately reflect the reality of the innovation.

This divergence in approaches to AI inventorship creates significant friction in international trade. Countries that recognize AI inventorship or have more flexible rules for assigning patent rights to AI-assisted inventions may become hubs for AI innovation and patent filing. Conversely, countries that strictly adhere to human inventorship might face challenges in protecting AI-generated inventions originating within their borders or benefiting from their markets. This could lead to a fragmented global patent landscape, impacting the licensing and commercialization of AI technologies and AI-created products. For instance, a company that develops an AI capable of discovering new pharmaceuticals might find its patentable discoveries recognized and protected in one country but not another, creating substantial barriers to global market entry and revenue generation. The economic rationale for investing in AI research and development is intrinsically linked to the ability to protect the fruits of that labor through IP rights.

Beyond copyright and patent law, other IP rights, such as trademarks and trade secrets, also intersect with AI-generated creations. Trademarks protect brand names and logos used to identify goods and services. AI can be used to design logos, develop brand names, and even manage marketing campaigns, raising questions about the ownership and protection of these IP assets when AI plays a significant role in their creation. Trade secrets, on the other hand, protect confidential business information that provides a competitive edge. If an AI system develops a highly valuable proprietary algorithm or a unique business strategy, the question of whether this constitutes a protectable trade secret, and who holds the right to protect it, becomes relevant.

The international legal framework for IP rights, largely governed by treaties administered by the World Intellectual Property Organization (WIPO), such as the Berne Convention for the Protection of Literary and Artistic Works and the Paris Convention for the Protection of Industrial Property, was established long before the advent of advanced AI. These treaties, and the national laws that implement them, are built upon a human-centric understanding of creativity and invention. Adapting these frameworks to accommodate AI-generated creations requires careful consideration and potentially new international agreements or interpretations of existing ones.

Several proposals and conceptual frameworks are being debated internationally to address these challenges. One approach is to create a new category of IP rights specifically for AI-generated works, recognizing their unique origin. Another is to attribute ownership to the legal entity that owns or controls the AI system, irrespective of the level of human involvement. A third approach advocates for a more nuanced system where the degree of human input and control determines the extent and nature of IP protection. This might involve differentiating between AI used as a tool, AI as a co-creator, and AI as an autonomous creator.

The economic stakes are immense. AI is poised to revolutionize numerous industries, and the ability to control and monetize AI-generated creations will be critical for fostering innovation and economic growth. Without clear and harmonized IP protection, the potential for AI to drive economic prosperity through new creative and inventive outputs could be significantly hampered by legal uncertainty and cross-border disputes. International trade law and policy must therefore grapple with these fundamental questions of IP rights for AI-generated creations to ensure a stable and predictable environment for the global trade in AI-enabled products and services. The ongoing dialogue within international bodies like WIPO, WTO, and national IP offices is crucial for shaping the future of intellectual property in the age of artificial intelligence, ensuring that innovation is rewarded and that the global trading system can adapt to the profound changes brought about by AI.

The legal complexities extend to the very definition of "originality" in copyright law when applied to AI. Traditionally, originality in copyright means that a work is not copied from another work and that it possesses a minimal degree of creativity. The creativity requirement is typically assessed by determining if the author exercised independent creation and judgment. When an AI generates a work, the question becomes: where does this creativity reside? Is it in the algorithms, the training data, the programming, or the output itself? If an AI is trained on a dataset of existing copyrighted works, and its output bears substantial similarity to those works, issues of infringement can arise. However, if the AI transforms and synthesitses information from its training data to create something genuinely new and distinct, does that constitute original authorship?

Jurisdictions are beginning to grapple with these nuanced questions. In the United States, the Copyright Office has issued guidance stating that works containing AI-generated material are copyrightable only to the extent that the AI's contribution is the result of the user's creative control. This means that a human must have exercised sufficient creative input and direction to be considered the "author." For example, if a user provides a highly specific and detailed prompt to an AI image generator, guiding its artistic choices and iterating on the results, the resulting image might be deemed copyrightable, with the user as the author. However, if the AI is given a broad prompt and generates an image with minimal human intervention, the US Copyright Office would likely consider it uncopyrightable. This approach attempts to preserve the human authorship requirement while acknowledging the role of AI as a creative tool.

In contrast, some jurisdictions, like the United Kingdom, have specific provisions in their Copyright, Designs and Patents Act that address computer-generated works. Section 9(3) of the Act states that in the case of a literary, dramatic, musical, or artistic work which is computer-generated, the author shall be taken to be "the person by whom the arrangements necessary for the creation of the work are undertaken." This provision offers a more expansive definition of authorship that can encompass AI-generated works. The "person by whom the arrangements necessary for the creation of the work are undertaken" could refer to the programmer, the user, or the entity that commissioned the AI system. This legal framework provides a pathway for protecting AI-generated content without necessarily redefining "author" to include non-human entities.

The divergent interpretations and legal frameworks across different countries create significant challenges for international trade in creative content. A work that is protected in one country under its "computer-generated works" provisions might be deemed to be in the public domain in another country that strictly adheres to human authorship. This creates uncertainty for businesses seeking to license, distribute, or sell AI-generated content internationally. For example, an AI-generated film script that is protectable in the UK could be freely used by anyone in the US if it is considered to lack human authorship. This disparity can lead to disputes over ownership, licensing fees, and the legality of cross-border distribution, potentially stifling trade in digital creative goods. The World Intellectual Property Organization (WIPO) is actively engaged in discussions to explore potential harmonization of these approaches, recognizing that a fragmented IP landscape can impede innovation and global trade.

The patentability of AI-generated inventions faces similar international divergence. As mentioned with the

DABUS case, the European Patent Office and the United States Patent and Trademark Office have generally rejected the notion of AI inventorship, requiring a human inventor. This stance is based on the understanding that patent law is designed to reward human ingenuity and that an inventor must possess the capacity for inventive thought. However, this raises the question of what happens to inventions conceived or perfected by AI without direct human intervention. If an AI system can independently discover a novel compound with therapeutic properties or a more efficient manufacturing process, and no human can claim to have invented it in the traditional sense, then such inventions might not receive patent protection in these jurisdictions.

Conversely, some national courts and IP offices have shown a greater willingness to consider AI's role in invention. For instance, the Supreme Court of South Africa, in the DABUS case, ruled that an invention can have an inventor who is not a natural person. Similarly, the High Court of Justice in the UK has also indicated that an AI can be considered an inventor under certain circumstances. These differing interpretations can create an uneven playing field for businesses and researchers. A company that utilizes AI to develop groundbreaking technologies might find its patents enforceable in one country but not in another, impacting its ability to secure investment, enter new markets, and protect its competitive advantage. This can lead to forum shopping, where companies strategically file patent applications in jurisdictions that offer more favorable treatment for AI-assisted inventions, potentially distorting global innovation flows.

The economic implications for international trade are profound. Intellectual property rights are a cornerstone of modern commerce, enabling creators and inventors to recoup their investments and profit from their innovations. When AI is involved in the creation process, the traditional mechanisms for IP protection are tested. If AI-generated works and inventions are not adequately protected, it could diminish the incentives for companies to invest in AI research and development, particularly in sectors that rely heavily on IP, such as pharmaceuticals, software, and creative arts. This could lead to a slowdown in innovation and a reduction in the economic benefits that AI can bring to global trade.

Furthermore, the issue of "ownership" of IP rights for AI-generated creations is complex. If an AI system creates a work or an invention, who should be considered the legal owner? Is it the developer of the AI, the owner of the AI system, the person who provided the input or prompts, or perhaps the AI itself, if that were legally possible? Current legal frameworks generally point towards the human or corporate entity that controls or directs the AI. However, the specific legal entity that owns the AI system, or the one that commissioned its development, is often seen as the most logical candidate for IP ownership. This is because they have invested resources in the AI and bear the commercial risks associated with its use. For instance, if a company invests in developing a proprietary AI that designs novel materials, that company would typically be considered the owner of the IP rights for those materials.

The international trade in AI-generated goods and services therefore hinges on establishing clear and consistent rules for IP protection. Without such clarity, businesses engaging in cross-border transactions involving AI-created content will face significant risks, including potential infringement claims, invalidation of IP rights, and protracted legal disputes. This can deter investment, hinder market access, and ultimately impede the global diffusion of AI-driven innovation.

International organizations like the World Trade Organization (WTO) and WIPO are crucial forums for addressing these issues. The WTO's Agreement on Trade-

Related Aspects of Intellectual Property Rights (TRIPS Agreement) sets out minimum standards for IP protection that WTO members must provide. While the TRIPS Agreement was negotiated before the widespread impact of AI, it provides a framework that could be interpreted or amended to address AI-generated creations. Discussions are ongoing within WIPO regarding the implications of AI for intellectual property, with a view to developing recommendations or new guidelines that could foster greater international harmonization.

The challenge lies in balancing the protection of AI-driven innovation with the broader public interest. Overly restrictive IP regimes could stifle innovation and limit access to beneficial AI-generated works and inventions. Conversely, a lack of protection could disincentivize investment in AI and limit its potential to contribute to economic growth and societal progress. Finding the right balance requires a deep understanding of both technological capabilities and legal principles, as well as a commitment to international cooperation.

In conclusion, the question of intellectual property rights for AI-generated creations is one of the most significant legal and ethical challenges arising from the integration of AI into the global economy. It directly impacts international trade by creating uncertainty around ownership, protection, and the commercialization of AI-driven outputs. Different national approaches to authorship and inventorship for AI-created works necessitate a concerted effort towards international harmonization. Failure to address these issues adequately could lead to trade barriers, stifle innovation, and limit the economic benefits that AI promises for global commerce. The ongoing evolution of legal frameworks, informed by technological advancements and international dialogue, will be critical in shaping a future where AI-generated creations can be legally recognized, protected, and traded efficiently across borders. This ongoing adaptation of IP law is not merely a legal technicality; it is fundamental to fostering innovation, ensuring fair competition, and unlocking the full economic potential of artificial intelligence in the international arena.

The global digital economy, fundamentally powered by data, faces intricate legal and regulatory hurdles when that data, and the artificial intelligence (AI) services that process it, traverse national borders. The very essence of AI development and deployment relies on access to vast datasets, often sourced and processed across multiple jurisdictions. This inherent transnationality creates a complex web of obligations, rights, and potential conflicts, necessitating a deep dive into the evolving landscape of cross-border data governance and the international regulation of AI services. As nations grapple with protecting their citizens' data privacy, ensuring national security, and fostering domestic AI industries, they are simultaneously confronted with the imperative to facilitate the global flow of data and services that underpins technological advancement and economic growth.

At the heart of this challenge lies the tension between national data sovereignty and the global nature of AI. Many countries have enacted or are developing stringent data protection laws, such as the European Union's General Data Protection Regulation (GDPR), which impose significant restrictions on the transfer of personal data outside their borders. These regulations often require specific legal mechanisms, such as adequacy decisions, standard contractual clauses, or binding corporate rules, to ensure that data transferred abroad receives an equivalent level of protection. While these measures are crucial for safeguarding individual privacy and maintaining trust in the digital ecosystem, they can also create substantial compliance burdens for businesses operating across multiple legal regimes. For AI companies, which often rely on centralized data processing or distributed cloud infrastructure, navigating these varying data transfer requirements can be a significant operational and legal impediment. The need for a consistent and predictable international framework for data flows is therefore paramount to avoid fragmentation and to ensure that AI innovation is not unduly stifled by a patchwork of divergent national regulations.

International efforts to establish frameworks for data governance are multifaceted, often involving multilateral organizations, bilateral agreements, and industry-led initiatives. The World Trade Organization (WTO), through agreements like the General Agreement on Trade in Services (GATS) and the Agreement on Trade-Related Aspects of Intellectual Property Rights (TRIPS), provides a foundational structure for regulating international trade, including digital services. However, these existing frameworks were largely developed before the widespread proliferation of AI and the complexities of modern data flows, leading to ongoing debates about their adequacy and the need for updates or new instruments. Discussions within the WTO's e-commerce agenda, for instance, frequently touch upon issues related to cross-border data flows, data localization requirements, and the potential for digital trade barriers.

Beyond the WTO, various international bodies are actively engaged in exploring solutions. The Organization for Economic Co-operation and Development (OECD) has been instrumental in developing principles for data governance, such as the OECD Privacy Principles, which emphasize principles like data minimization, purpose limitation, and security safeguards. These principles, while non-binding, serve as influential benchmarks for national policy development and international dialogue. Similarly, the United Nations Commission on International Trade Law (UNCITRAL) is working on instruments related to electronic commerce, which can have implications for data governance and AI services.

The concept of data interoperability is also critical in this context. For AI systems to function effectively across borders, or for data to be shared and processed seamlessly between different entities in different countries, there needs to be a degree of technical and legal interoperability. This means establishing common standards for data formats, protocols, and APIs, as well as harmonizing legal definitions and requirements related to data processing and AI deployment. Without such interoperability, data silos can emerge, hindering the potential for global collaboration and the efficient scaling of AI solutions. For example, an AI model trained on medical data in one country might be difficult to adapt or deploy in another due to differences in data standards, privacy regulations, or AI regulatory frameworks, even if the underlying technology is sound.

The secure transfer of data is another paramount concern. While the objective is to facilitate data flows for AI operations, this must be balanced with robust security measures to prevent data breaches, unauthorized access, and malicious exploitation. International agreements and standards related to cybersecurity, data encryption, and secure data transfer protocols are essential components of a comprehensive governance framework. This includes addressing issues such as the provenance of data, the integrity of data during transit, and the secure storage of data in distributed environments. The rise of AI also introduces new security challenges, as AI systems themselves can be targets of attack, or can be used to mount more sophisticated cyberattacks. Therefore, any framework governing cross-border data flows and AI services must incorporate strong cybersecurity and data integrity provisions.

One of the most significant regulatory challenges revolves around the differing approaches to data localization.

Some countries mandate that data, particularly personal data, must be stored and processed within their national borders to ensure greater control and oversight. This can significantly complicate the operations of global AI companies, forcing them to build and maintain separate data infrastructure in multiple countries, increasing costs and reducing efficiencies. The rationale often cited for data localization includes enhancing national security, facilitating law enforcement access to data, and promoting domestic digital industries. However, critics argue that strict data localization requirements can act as de facto trade barriers, distort competition, and hinder the global diffusion of beneficial AI technologies. Finding a balance that respects legitimate national interests while enabling the global flow of data is a key diplomatic and legal objective.

The development of AI services also presents unique regulatory challenges that extend beyond data flows. As AI becomes more autonomous and capable of making decisions with significant societal impact, questions arise about accountability, transparency, and ethical deployment. International discussions are underway regarding common principles for AI ethics, such as fairness, accountability, and transparency (FAT). However, translating these principles into binding international regulations that govern the cross-border provision of AI services is a complex undertaking. Differences in legal traditions, cultural values, and economic priorities can lead to divergent views on how AI should be regulated. For instance, the level of transparency required for AI decision-making might vary, with some jurisdictions demanding detailed explanations of algorithmic processes, while others may be more accepting of "black box" systems if they deliver reliable outcomes.

The regulatory landscape for AI services is also shaped by sector-specific considerations. AI applications in finance, healthcare, transportation, and critical infrastructure each have unique risk profiles and regulatory needs. Harmonizing regulations across these diverse sectors on an international level is a monumental task. For example, AI used in medical diagnostics must meet stringent safety and efficacy standards, often subject to national health regulatory bodies. The cross-border provision of such AI services requires intricate agreements and mutual recognition of standards between countries to ensure patient safety and trust. Similarly, AI in autonomous vehicles will necessitate international agreements on traffic laws, liability, and safety standards to enable the global deployment of such technologies.

The role of industry standards and self-regulation is also important in navigating these complexities. Industry consortia and standards-setting bodies are working to develop technical standards and best practices for AI development, deployment, and data management. These efforts can complement formal regulatory frameworks by providing practical guidance and promoting a common understanding of responsible AI practices. However, the effectiveness of self-regulation depends on broad industry adoption and robust oversight mechanisms.

Furthermore, the issue of AI governance extends to the question of jurisdiction and dispute resolution. When an AI service provided across borders causes harm, or when data protection rules are violated, determining which country's laws apply and where legal recourse can be sought can be exceptionally challenging. International legal mechanisms for cooperation in law enforcement, mutual legal assistance, and dispute resolution are therefore critical for ensuring accountability and providing effective remedies in cases involving cross-border AI activities. The development of international arbitration frameworks or specialized dispute resolution bodies for AI-related matters might become increasingly necessary.

The global pursuit of interoperability and secure data

transfer for AI also involves considering the infrastructure layer. The physical and digital infrastructure through which data flows and AI services are delivered- including cloud computing platforms, data centers, and telecommunication networks- is often owned and operated by multinational corporations. International agreements that ensure fair competition, prevent market dominance, and promote investment in robust and secure digital infrastructure are essential to fostering a thriving global AI ecosystem. This also touches upon issues of digital sovereignty, where nations may seek to ensure that critical digital infrastructure is not solely controlled by foreign entities.

In response to these challenges, various models of international cooperation are emerging. Some propose "digital trade agreements" that aim to establish a comprehensive set of rules for cross-border data flows, digital services, and AI. Others advocate for a more sector-specific or principles-based approach, focusing on harmonizing specific aspects of AI regulation and data governance. The ongoing development of frameworks by organizations like the Global Partnership on Artificial Intelligence (GPAI) seeks to foster international dialogue and collaboration on AI policies, bringing together governments, industry, and civil society to address these complex issues.

The legal and regulatory complexities of governing cross-border data flows and AI services highlight the need for agile, forward-looking international cooperation. As AI technologies continue to evolve at a rapid pace, legal and regulatory frameworks must be adaptable to new developments and emerging challenges. This requires a continuous dialogue among nations, international organizations, and stakeholders to build consensus and develop effective governance mechanisms that promote innovation, protect fundamental rights, and foster a secure and trustworthy global digital environment. The ultimate goal is to create a legal and regulatory landscape that enables the responsible and beneficial deployment of AI across borders, maximizing its potential to address global challenges and drive economic prosperity, while mitigating the inherent risks.

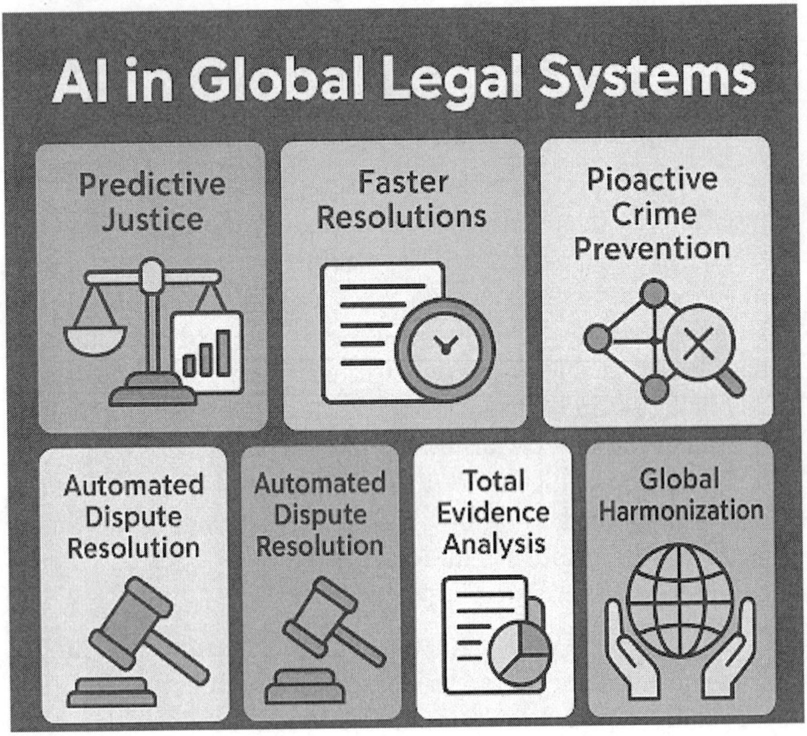

13
Global Governance Frameworks and the Quest for an AI Treaty

The intricate challenge of governing artificial intelligence on a global scale, particularly as it intersects with cross-border data flows and the burgeoning digital economy, necessitates a comprehensive understanding of the myriad international bodies actively engaged in shaping this critical landscape. As the previous context underscored, the transnational nature of AI development and deployment, coupled with the fundamental reliance on data that respects no borders, creates a complex web of legal, ethical, and economic considerations. While national regulations and bilateral agreements form crucial components of this evolving framework, it is the concerted efforts of multilateral organizations that offer the promise of harmonized approaches and globally recognized principles for responsible AI. These bodies, drawing together diverse perspectives from member states, industry experts, and civil society, are at the forefront of translating abstract ethical ideals into actionable policy recommendations and, potentially, international legal instruments.

The United Nations, as the preeminent global forum for international cooperation, has increasingly recognized the profound implications of AI for sustainable development, human rights, and international peace and security. Within its vast network of agencies and commissions, discussions on AI governance are gaining momentum. For instance, the International Telecommunication Union (ITU), a specialized agency of the UN responsible for information and communication technologies, plays a significant role in setting international standards that underpin digital infrastructure, including those relevant to AI development and deployment. While not exclusively focused on AI ethics, the ITU's work on telecommunication standards, spectrum management, and the development of ICT policies has a direct impact on the global accessibility and interoperability of AI systems. Furthermore, various UN bodies are actively exploring the socio-economic impacts of AI, from its potential to accelerate the achievement of the Sustainable Development Goals (SDGs) to its capacity to exacerbate existing inequalities or create new forms of discrimination. The UN Secretary-General's initiatives, such as the establishment of advisory bodies on emerging technologies, signal a growing commitment to understanding and guiding the trajectory of AI development in a manner that aligns with the UN's core mission. The ongoing discussions within the General Assembly and specialized committees often revolve around the need for global cooperation in addressing the ethical dimensions of AI, ensuring equitable access to AI benefits, and mitigating potential risks to human rights and fundamental freedoms. The very nature of AI, with its capacity to transcend borders in its application and data requirements, inherently calls for a coordinated global response, a task for which the UN is uniquely positioned.

A pivotal actor in shaping international norms and fostering dialogue around AI governance is the Organisation for Economic Co-operation and Development (OECD). For decades, the OECD has been a leading voice in promoting evidence-based policy recommendations across a wide range of economic and social issues. In the realm of AI, the OECD has been instrumental in developing influential principles and frameworks that have garnered widespread international adoption. Recognizing the need for a common understanding of responsible AI, the OECD established its Council Recommendation on Artificial Intelligence in 2019, the first intergovernmental standard on AI. This landmark recommendation, adopted by all OECD member countries and several partner countries, provides a set of shared values and principles for trustworthy AI. These principles emphasize inclusive growth and sustainable development, human-centered values and fairness, transparency and explainability, robustness, security and safety, and accountability. The OECD's approach is characterized by its focus on fostering innovation while ensuring that AI systems are developed and used in a manner that respects human rights and democratic values. Beyond the principles themselves, the OECD has been actively involved in developing practical tools and guidance for implementing these recommendations. This includes work on AI metrics and measurement, ethical frameworks for AI procurement, and AI policy observatory initiatives to track national AI strategies and regulations. The organization's convening power allows it to bring together governments, industry leaders, academics, and civil society representatives to engage in constructive dialogue, share best practices, and identify emerging challenges and opportunities related to AI. The OECD's commitment to ongoing work in this area, including the development of specific guidelines for sectors like AI in finance and healthcare, underscores its role as a crucial facilitator of international AI governance cooperation. Its analytical capacity and its ability to generate consensus among a diverse group of nations make it a key driver in the quest for a more coherent global approach to AI.

The United Nations Educational, Scientific and Cultural Organization (UNESCO) has also emerged as a significant contributor to the global discourse on AI governance, with a particular focus on the ethical and societal implications of the technology. UNESCO's mandate, rooted in promoting peace through education, science, culture, and communication, provides a unique lens through which to examine the impact of AI on human values, social cohesion, and cultural diversity. In 2021, UNESCO adopted the Recommendation on the Ethics of Artificial Intelligence, the first global normative instrument on this topic. This groundbreaking recommendation, developed through an extensive consultative process involving experts and stakeholders from around the world, provides a comprehensive ethical framework for the development and deployment of AI. It sets out a range of values, including respect for human rights, fundamental freedoms, and human dignity, as well as principles such as proportionality, safety, and fairness. Crucially, the Recommendation also outlines a set of policy levers and areas for action, urging Member States to develop national AI strategies, promote AI literacy, foster gender equality in AI, and ensure that AI systems are used for the benefit of humanity and the environment. UNESCO's approach emphasizes the importance of inclusivity, ensuring that the voices of developing countries and marginalized communities are heard in the global AI conversation. The organization's work also extends to addressing the potential impact of AI on education, culture, and media, recognizing that AI technologies can both enhance and disrupt these critical domains. By focusing on the ethical underpinnings and societal consequences of AI, UNESCO plays a vital role in ensuring that the development of this transformative technology is guided by a commitment to humanistic values and the common good. Its emphasis on the global South and its efforts to bridge the digital divide further highlight its commitment to equitable AI development.

The Council of Europe, an international organization focused on human rights, democracy, and the rule of law, has also been actively engaged in shaping AI governance. Recognizing that AI technologies can have profound implications for fundamental rights and democratic processes, the Council of Europe has been working on developing legally binding instruments and policy recommendations in this area. A key initiative has been the development of a framework convention on AI, aiming to establish common standards for the development and use of AI systems that are compatible with human rights, democracy, and the rule of law. This ambitious undertaking reflects a commitment to ensuring that AI technologies are not only innovative but also adhere to the highest standards of ethical and legal compliance. The Council of Europe's approach is deeply rooted in its long-standing expertise in human rights law and its commitment to upholding democratic principles. Its work on AI governance seeks to provide a legal and ethical compass for governments and developers, ensuring that AI is deployed in a manner that is respectful of individual liberties, promotes fair decision-making, and safeguards against potential abuses. By focusing on a legally binding instrument, the Council of Europe aims to create a robust and enforceable framework that can provide a high level of protection for individuals and societies. The organization's ongoing deliberations and consultations on this front are critical for establishing clear lines of accountability and ensuring that AI systems operate within a framework of legal certainty and ethical responsibility. Its emphasis on the rule of law and democratic oversight provides a complementary perspective to the principles-based approaches of other organizations.

Beyond these prominent organizations, a multitude of other international bodies and initiatives are contributing to the complex tapestry of AI governance. For instance, the International Organization for Standardization (ISO) plays a crucial role in developing technical standards that can facilitate the interoperability and safety of AI systems. While not directly involved in ethical policy-making, ISO standards on data quality, risk management, and cybersecurity are essential for the practical implementation of responsible AI. Similarly, the World Economic Forum (WEF) serves as a platform for multistakeholder dialogue on global challenges, including AI. Through its various initiatives and working groups, the WEF brings together leaders from government, business, academia, and civil society to foster collaboration and develop practical solutions for AI governance, ethical AI development, and the future of work in the age of AI. The WEF's emphasis on public-private partnerships and its ability to convene diverse stakeholders make it a valuable facilitator of progress in this rapidly evolving field. The organization's focus on foresight and scenario planning also helps anticipate future challenges and opportunities associated with AI.

Furthermore, the proliferation of regional and specialized initiatives demonstrates the growing global consensus on the need for proactive AI governance. The European Union, with its comprehensive approach to data protection and digital regulation, is a leading example of a regional bloc actively shaping AI policy. The EU's AI Act, a proposed piece of legislation designed to regulate AI systems based on their risk level, is a significant attempt to establish a harmonized legal framework within a major economic bloc. This legislation aims to ensure that AI systems used in the EU are safe, transparent, traceable, non-discriminatory, and environmentally conscious. The EU's approach, characterized by its risk-based methodology and its emphasis on fundamental rights, is likely to have a substantial impact on global AI governance discussions, potentially influencing regulatory approaches in other regions. Its focus on the "AI Act" signifies a commitment to establishing clear legal boundaries and obligations for AI developers and deployers.

The increasing recognition of AI's potential impact on global security has also spurred discussions within organizations focused on international security and arms control. While not yet having established formal AI governance frameworks in the same vein as those focused on ethics and development, these discussions are crucial for addressing the risks associated with AI in military applications and autonomous weapons systems. The potential for AI to accelerate decision-making in conflict scenarios, the ethical dilemmas surrounding lethal autonomous weapons, and the implications for strategic stability are all areas that demand international attention and, potentially, new forms of arms control or regulation. As AI capabilities advance, the need for a global dialogue on these security implications will only intensify.

In summary, the global landscape of AI governance is being shaped by a diverse array of international organizations, each bringing unique mandates, perspectives, and approaches. From the broad normative frameworks of the UN and UNESCO to the economic and policy-oriented principles of the OECD, and the human rights-centric initiatives of the Council of Europe, these bodies are collectively working towards establishing common ground for the responsible development and deployment of AI. Their efforts, while often complementary, also highlight the complexities and potential divergences in national and regional priorities. The ongoing dialogue and collaboration among these organizations are essential for fostering a global ecosystem where AI can thrive as a force for good, aligned with human values and contributing to sustainable development, while effectively mitigating its inherent risks. The development of an AI treaty, as this book explores, will undoubtedly draw upon the foundational work and ongoing efforts of these crucial international actors. Understanding their roles and contributions is paramount to appreciating the intricate multi-layered approach required for effective global AI governance. The very existence of these initiatives underscores a widespread international acknowledgement that AI's transformative power necessitates a coordinated, ethical, and human-centric approach that transcends national boundaries, aiming for a future where artificial intelligence serves humanity's collective well-being and progress.

The global pursuit of effective Artificial Intelligence (AI) governance is not a monolithic endeavor. Instead, it is characterized by a mosaic of national and regional approaches, each reflecting distinct historical, cultural, economic, and political contexts. Understanding these diverse models is crucial for appreciating the complexities and potential pathways toward a unified global framework, or perhaps, a harmonized set of principles that can guide AI development and deployment worldwide. As we move beyond the foundational work of international organizations discussed previously, this subsection embarks on a comparative analysis of these national and regional governance philosophies, examining their regulatory orientations, legislative instruments, and policy priorities.

In North America, the United States has largely adopted a sector-specific, innovation-friendly approach to AI governance. Rather than a single, overarching AI law, the US strategy has historically relied on existing regulatory frameworks and the principle of "existing laws apply." This means that AI systems are regulated based on their application and the sector in which they operate- for instance, AI used in healthcare would be subject to healthcare regulations, while AI in finance would fall under financial regulations. The White House has issued various Executive Orders and Blueprint for an AI Bill of Rights, signaling a commitment to responsible AI development and deployment that prioritizes safety, equity, and accountability. These initiatives aim to provide guiding principles and recommendations for federal agencies to address AI risks, such as bias, privacy, and security. The emphasis remains on fostering innovation and maintaining a competitive edge in AI development, often through public-private partnerships and investment in research and development. The regulatory philosophy leans towards flexibility and adaptability, allowing the technology to evolve while addressing potential harms as they emerge. This approach, while fostering rapid technological advancement, has also drawn criticism for its potential to create regulatory gaps and inconsistencies, leaving certain AI applications with less explicit oversight. The National Institute of Standards and Technology (NIST) has played a significant role by developing an AI Risk Management Framework, providing a voluntary, flexible, and risk-based approach that organizations can use to manage risks associated with AI systems. This framework is designed to be applicable across sectors and to be integrated into existing risk management processes, further underscoring the US preference for integrated, rather than standalone, AI regulation. The focus is on providing tools and guidance for organizations to proactively identify, measure, manage, and govern AI risks, rather than imposing prescriptive legal obligations across the board.

Canada, while sharing some similarities with the US in its focus on innovation, has taken a more proactive stance towards AI regulation with proposed legislation like Bill C-27, which includes the Artificial Intelligence and Data Act (AIDA). This proposed act aims to establish a federal framework for the lawful use of AI, focusing on identifying and mitigating risks associated with AI systems, particularly those deemed "high-impact." AIDA proposes requirements for the development, deployment, and management of AI systems, including measures for bias detection and mitigation, transparency, and human oversight. This represents a shift towards a more centralized and principle-based regulatory approach, seeking to proactively address potential harms before they manifest widely. The Canadian approach seeks to strike a balance between fostering AI innovation and ensuring public trust and safety, reflecting a nuanced understanding of the technology's dual-use potential. The emphasis on "high-impact" systems suggests a risk-based methodology, similar to that being explored in other jurisdictions, where the intensity of regulation is calibrated to the potential severity of the risks posed by a given AI application. This approach acknowledges that not all AI systems carry the same level of risk and that a one-size-fits-all regulatory model would be both impractical and potentially stifling to innovation in lower-risk areas.

In contrast, the European Union has forged a comprehensive and ambitious path towards AI governance, spearheaded by the landmark AI Act. This legislative proposal represents a significant effort to create a unified, risk-based regulatory framework for AI systems operating within the EU. The AI Act categorizes AI systems based on their potential risk level, ranging from unacceptable risk (e.g., social scoring by governments, manipulative AI) to minimal risk. Systems deemed "high-risk"- those used in critical infrastructure, education, employment, law enforcement, and other sensitive areas- will be subject to stringent requirements related to data quality, transparency, human oversight, cybersecurity, and conformity assessments before they can be placed on the market. This approach is deeply rooted in the EU's strong commitment to fundamental rights, data protection (through GDPR), and the rule of law. The EU's regulatory philosophy prioritizes human-centric AI and seeks to establish a clear legal environment that fosters trust and predictability for both developers and consumers. The AI Act's extraterritorial reach means that it can affect AI systems deployed globally if they impact individuals within the EU, making it a de facto global standard-setter. The EU's approach is characterized by its proactive nature, aiming to prevent harm by imposing obligations on AI providers and deployers from the outset, rather than solely relying on ex-post enforcement. This includes requirements for risk management systems, detailed documentation, and post-market monitoring to ensure ongoing compliance and address emergent issues. The emphasis on transparency is particularly noteworthy, with provisions for explaining how AI systems reach their decisions, albeit with recognition of the technical challenges in achieving full explainability for all AI models. The rigorous conformity assessment procedures, which may involve third-party audits for high-risk AI systems, are designed to instill confidence in the safety and reliability of AI technologies used within the Union. Furthermore, the AI Act incorporates provisions to promote AI research and innovation, establishing regulatory sandboxes and test environments to allow for the development and testing of AI under regulatory supervision. This dual focus on robust regulation and supportive innovation reflects a sophisticated understanding of the challenges and opportunities presented by AI.

Moving to Asia, the governance landscape is diverse, with different nations adopting distinct strategies. China has pursued a proactive and often rapid regulatory approach, particularly in areas like algorithmic recommendations, deep synthesis (deepfakes), and generative AI. Chinese regulations have often focused on content control, data security, and the societal impact of AI, reflecting a top-down governance model that prioritizes stability and state control. The Cyberspace Administration of China (CAC) has been at the forefront of issuing regulations that mandate registration for generative AI services, require content moderation, and impose requirements for data localization and security. There is a strong emphasis on aligning AI development with national strategic goals and ensuring that AI technologies are used in a manner consistent with socialist core values. While this approach has led to swift implementation of rules, it has also raised concerns about potential limitations on freedom of expression and innovation due to stringent oversight. China's model can be characterized as one of active state intervention, with regulations often being issued as specific measures to address emerging AI applications, rather than as part of a single, overarching legal act. This allows for rapid response to technological advancements but can also lead to a more fragmented regulatory environment. The focus on algorithms used in recommendation systems, for example, directly addresses the persuasive power of AI in shaping user behavior and information consumption, demonstrating a concern with the societal implications of algorithmic decision-making.

Japan, on the other hand, has opted for a more principles-based and collaborative approach, emphasizing the development of guidelines and ethical frameworks rather than prescriptive legislation. The Japanese government has focused on fostering innovation and international competitiveness in AI, while also addressing ethical considerations through consensus-building among stakeholders. The Cabinet Office, in collaboration with various ministries, has released guidelines for AI development and use, promoting responsible AI practices that uphold human dignity, ensure safety, and promote fairness. Their strategy often involves promoting the development of AI in specific sectors, such as healthcare and manufacturing, while encouraging industry self-regulation and adherence to ethical standards. This approach seeks to create an environment where AI can flourish, with regulatory intervention reserved for instances where significant harm is evident or likely. The emphasis on collaboration with international bodies and the adoption of principles like those from the OECD highlight Japan's commitment to aligning its AI governance with global norms. The focus is on empowering businesses and researchers to develop and deploy AI responsibly by providing clear ethical guidance and fostering a culture of accountability.

South Korea has also been actively developing its AI governance framework, with a strong emphasis on fostering AI innovation while addressing ethical and societal concerns. The government has introduced policies to support AI research and development, create AI testing grounds, and promote the adoption of AI across various industries. In terms of regulation, South Korea has been working on a comprehensive AI ethics guideline and is considering legislative measures to address AI-related issues. The approach is a blend of proactive support for the AI ecosystem and a growing awareness of the need for regulatory oversight to manage risks. The focus is on creating a supportive environment for AI growth, while also ensuring that AI development is aligned with public values and fundamental rights. This includes addressing issues such as data privacy, algorithmic bias, and the impact of AI on employment. The Korean approach often involves extensive public consultation and a commitment to adapting regulations as the technology evolves. The government's efforts extend to promoting AI literacy and building public trust in AI technologies, recognizing that broad societal acceptance is crucial for the successful integration of AI.

In India, the governance approach to AI is still evolving, with a strong focus on leveraging AI for socio-economic development and digital transformation. The government has articulated a vision for India to become a global leader in AI, with initiatives aimed at promoting AI research, fostering AI startups, and building AI talent. Regulatory efforts are characterized by a pragmatic approach, seeking to balance innovation with the need for data protection, privacy, and the prevention of misuse. While there isn't a single AI law, existing legal frameworks, including the Digital Personal Data Protection Act, 2023, and discussions around an AI framework, indicate a growing recognition of the need for specific governance measures. The emphasis is on using AI to address societal challenges, improve public services, and enhance economic growth, while also being mindful of potential risks such as bias, job displacement, and security. The Indian approach tends to be responsive, addressing AI governance concerns as they arise within the broader context of digital regulation and national development priorities. There is a strong emphasis on harnessing AI for good, with a focus on applications in agriculture, healthcare, education, and smart cities. The government's strategy involves fostering collaboration between academia, industry, and government to create an inclusive AI ecosystem.

Australia's approach to AI governance has been characterized by a phased and consultative strategy, aiming to develop a national AI strategy that balances innovation with responsible development. The Australian government has released an AI Action Plan and is exploring regulatory options, with a focus on establishing an AI safety framework. Their approach emphasizes risk assessment, ethical principles, and the need for transparency and accountability. The government has also sought input from industry, academia, and the public to inform its AI policy. Australia's strategy leans towards a collaborative model, seeking to build consensus and foster a shared understanding of responsible AI practices. The focus is on ensuring that AI is developed and used in a way that benefits Australians, upholds democratic values, and respects human rights. This includes a particular emphasis on the ethical implications of AI in areas such as employment, law enforcement, and decision-making processes that affect individuals. The development of AI standards and the promotion of AI literacy are also key components of their strategy.

Several other regions and countries are also actively shaping their AI governance. The United Kingdom, for instance, has adopted a pro-innovation, context-specific approach, emphasizing the importance of adapting existing regulatory frameworks and principles rather than creating entirely new AI-specific legislation. The UK's AI Strategy and its approach outlined by the Centre for Data Ethics and Innovation (CDEI) focus on a "whole-of-government" approach, promoting responsible innovation and addressing risks through existing sectoral regulators. This approach aims to foster flexibility and agility in AI governance, allowing for rapid adaptation to technological changes while ensuring that fundamental values are upheld. The focus is on identifying and mitigating specific harms, rather than imposing broad prohibitions or mandates that could stifle innovation. The UK's approach can be seen as an attempt to harness the benefits of AI while maintaining a degree of regulatory agility.

Across Latin America, countries are at various stages of developing their AI governance frameworks. Brazil, for instance, has been actively debating and developing AI legislation, with a focus on human rights, ethical principles, and the societal impact of AI. The proposed legislation aims to establish a legal framework for the responsible development and use of AI, incorporating principles of transparency, accountability, and non-discrimination. Other nations in the region are also engaging in discussions and policy development, often influenced by international trends and a desire to leverage AI for sustainable development. The focus in many Latin American countries is on ensuring that AI development benefits society broadly, addresses existing inequalities, and respects fundamental human rights.

A significant trend emerging across many of these national and regional models is the adoption of a risk-based approach to AI regulation. This methodology, exemplified by the EU's AI Act, recognizes that the potential harms associated with AI systems vary significantly depending on their application and context. By categorizing AI systems based on their risk level, policymakers can calibrate regulatory interventions more effectively, imposing stricter requirements on high-risk applications while allowing for greater flexibility in lower-risk areas. This approach seeks to strike a balance between mitigating potential harms and fostering innovation, avoiding overly burdensome regulations that could stifle technological progress. However, the precise definition of "risk" and the criteria for classification can be challenging and are subject to ongoing debate and refinement in different jurisdictions.

Another common thread is the emphasis on ethical principles, such as fairness, transparency, accountability, and human oversight. While the specific articulation and implementation of these principles may differ, there is a widespread recognition that AI systems should be developed and deployed in a manner that aligns with human values and societal norms. The challenge lies in translating these abstract ethical concepts into concrete legal obligations and technical standards that can be practically applied by AI developers and deployers.

The role of data is also a central concern in most AI governance frameworks. Regulations often address issues related to data quality, data privacy, data security, and the ethical use of data in AI training and deployment. The increasing interconnectedness of AI systems and the cross-border flow of data further complicate these regulatory efforts, necessitating international cooperation and the harmonization of standards.

In conclusion, the comparative analysis of national and regional AI governance models reveals a complex and dynamic landscape. While each approach is shaped by unique national contexts and priorities, several common trends and challenges are emerging. The EU's comprehensive, risk-based AI Act stands out as a pioneering effort to establish a broad regulatory framework. The US's sector-specific, innovation-driven approach, Canada's proactive legislation, China's rapid, state-led regulation, Japan's principles-based guidance, South Korea's balanced approach, India's development-focused strategy, Australia's phased consultation, and the UK's pro-innovation, context-specific methodology all offer valuable insights into the diverse ways nations are grappling with the governance of AI. These varying philosophies underscore the difficulty of achieving a universally accepted regulatory model, but also highlight the shared global imperative to ensure that AI technologies are developed and deployed responsibly, ethically, and for the benefit of humanity. The ongoing evolution of these models will undoubtedly shape the trajectory of international AI cooperation and the potential for a future AI treaty.

The preceding discussion illuminated the variegated

tapestry of national and regional approaches to Artificial Intelligence governance. While each jurisdiction has charted a course guided by its distinct priorities and existing legal traditions, a compelling case can be made for a more unified, internationally coordinated response. The inherent nature of AI- its boundless potential, its rapid evolution, and its capacity to transcend geographical boundaries- necessitates a global conversation and, ultimately, a globally recognized framework for its development and deployment. This is where the concept of an international AI treaty gains significant traction, offering a pathway to address the systemic challenges and opportunities presented by this transformative technology.

The primary impetus for an international AI treaty stems from the fundamental need for global consistency and the mitigation of regulatory fragmentation. As AI systems become increasingly sophisticated and interconnected, their impact can no longer be contained within national borders. An algorithm trained on data from one country can influence decisions made in another; an AI-powered autonomous system operating in international waters or airspace operates under a complex web of potentially conflicting national laws. Without a common set of principles and standards, this fragmentation risks creating regulatory arbitrage, where developers might gravitate towards jurisdictions with less stringent oversight, potentially leading to a race to the bottom in terms of safety, ethics, and human rights. A treaty would provide a much-needed baseline of agreed-upon rules, ensuring that all nations, regardless of their individual regulatory capacities or priorities, commit to a minimum standard of responsible AI development. This consistency is crucial for fostering trust in AI technologies, enabling seamless cross-border data flows and AI service provision, and ultimately, preventing a balkanization of the digital world. Imagine the complexities if autonomous vehicles or AI-driven medical diagnostic tools were subject to entirely different safety protocols in every country they operated. A harmonized approach, codified in a treaty, would streamline compliance, facilitate interoperability, and significantly reduce the risk of unintended consequences arising from jurisdictional clashes.

Furthermore, an international treaty offers a powerful mechanism for addressing the inherently trans-border nature of AI challenges. Issues such as algorithmic bias, privacy violations, cybersecurity threats posed by AI-powered attacks, and the potential for AI to exacerbate existing societal inequalities do not respect national boundaries. A treaty can establish common definitions, reporting mechanisms, and cooperative enforcement strategies to tackle these pervasive issues collectively. For instance, a treaty could mandate the development of standardized methods for detecting and mitigating algorithmic bias, requiring signatories to implement robust testing and auditing procedures before deploying AI systems that could disproportionately affect certain populations. Similarly, it could outline international protocols for addressing AI-related cybersecurity incidents, fostering real-time information sharing and coordinated responses among national cybersecurity agencies. The development of generative AI, capable of producing synthetic media like deepfakes, presents another urgent trans-border concern. Without international agreement on attribution, liability, and content moderation standards, the proliferation of misinformation and malicious manipulation could destabilize societies globally. A treaty could establish shared norms and responsibilities for addressing such threats, creating a united front against the weaponization of AI.

The establishment of universal norms for AI development and deployment is another critical argument for an international treaty. While many nations are currently developing ethical guidelines and legal frameworks, these often differ in their emphasis and scope. An AI treaty could enshrine fundamental principles such as human autonomy, accountability, transparency, fairness, and the imperative to prioritize human safety and well-being. These core values, often derived from existing international human rights law, would serve as an indispensable moral and legal compass for the entire global AI ecosystem. For example, a treaty could articulate a clear obligation for AI developers to conduct rigorous impact assessments for high-risk AI applications, ensuring that potential societal harms are identified and mitigated proactively. It could also codify the right to explanation for individuals affected by AI-driven decisions, pushing for greater transparency in algorithmic processes. The inclusion of provisions related to accountability would clarify who is responsible when AI systems cause harm, be it the developer, the deployer, or a combination thereof, thereby ensuring that redress mechanisms are available to those who have been wronged. Moreover, a treaty could address the existential risks associated with advanced AI, potentially including provisions for robust safety research, international monitoring of powerful AI systems, and mechanisms for de-escalation in scenarios where AI capabilities could pose a threat to global security.

The very act of negotiating an international treaty on AI would foster crucial dialogue and build consensus among nations. This process would inherently require states to engage deeply with the ethical, social, economic, and security implications of AI, leading to a more informed and coordinated global approach. It would provide a platform for developing nations to voice their concerns and ensure that the benefits of AI are shared equitably, preventing a further widening of the digital divide. Such a treaty could include provisions for capacity building, technology transfer, and financial assistance to help less developed countries participate fully in the AI revolution and implement responsible AI governance frameworks. This collaborative spirit is vital for ensuring that AI development serves humanity as a whole, rather than exacerbating existing inequalities or creating new forms of dependency.

Considering the profound implications of AI for global security, an international treaty could also play a vital role in arms control and the prevention of AI-driven conflicts. The development of Lethal Autonomous Weapons Systems (LAWS), for example, raises significant ethical and strategic concerns. An international convention could establish clear prohibitions or limitations on the development and deployment of such weapons, thereby reducing the risk of unintended escalation and ensuring meaningful human control over the use of force. This mirrors historical efforts in arms control, such as treaties banning chemical and biological weapons, demonstrating that international agreements can effectively govern dangerous technologies. Beyond autonomous weapons, AI can enhance cyber warfare capabilities, influence geopolitical stability through sophisticated disinformation campaigns, and automate critical decision-making in military contexts. A comprehensive AI treaty could address these multifaceted security risks, promoting transparency in military AI development and establishing mechanisms for de-escalation and conflict resolution.

The economic dimension also underscores the need for an international treaty. AI is poised to reshape industries, create new markets, and alter the global distribution of wealth. A treaty that establishes clear rules for AI-related intellectual property, data governance, and fair competition can help ensure a stable and predictable environment for innovation and investment. It can prevent the emergence of monopolistic AI platforms that stifle competition and innovation, and ensure that the economic benefits of AI are broadly distributed. Provisions related to the ethical use of AI in the workplace, addressing issues such as job displacement and the impact of AI on worker rights, could also be included, ensuring a just transition in the face of technological disruption. Moreover, a treaty could address the environmental impact of AI, encouraging the development of energy-efficient AI systems and responsible data center management, given the significant energy consumption associated with large-scale AI model training and deployment.

The practical challenges of negotiating and enforcing such a treaty are, undoubtedly, immense. Reaching a consensus on complex technical and ethical issues among diverse national interests will require extraordinary diplomatic effort and a willingness to compromise. Defining terms like "high-risk AI," establishing robust verification mechanisms, and ensuring effective enforcement will necessitate innovative legal and technical solutions. However, the potential consequences of inaction- a fragmented regulatory landscape, escalating risks, and the erosion of global trust- far outweigh these challenges. The history of international law is replete with examples of ambitious agreements that, despite initial skepticism, have ultimately fostered greater cooperation and addressed critical global challenges. The Universal Declaration of Human Rights, the Geneva Conventions, and the Paris Agreement on climate change, while imperfect, have all provided essential normative frameworks and catalyzed international action.

An international AI treaty is not merely a bureaucratic exercise; it is a proactive and essential step towards shaping a future where AI serves humanity responsibly. It offers a pathway to harness the immense potential of AI for good, while diligently safeguarding against its inherent risks. By fostering global cooperation, establishing universal norms, and ensuring consistency in governance, such a treaty would be a cornerstone in building a future where artificial intelligence enhances human prosperity, security, and dignity for all. The momentum is building, with calls for such frameworks growing louder from academics, civil society, and even within governments themselves. The question is no longer if an international AI framework is needed, but rather, how quickly and how comprehensively it can be realized. The time to begin this critical conversation, with a clear vision for an international AI treaty, is now.

The path towards a comprehensive global AI treaty, while conceptually compelling, is fraught with significant practical hurdles that challenge its immediate feasibility. Foremost among these is the monumental task of achieving international consensus. AI is not a monolithic entity; it encompasses a vast spectrum of technologies, applications, and associated risks, each with varying degrees of perceived threat and benefit across different nations. Crafting a treaty that adequately addresses this complexity, while remaining sufficiently specific to be meaningful, requires navigating a labyrinth of diverse national interests, economic priorities, and technological developmental stages. Nations with advanced AI research and development capabilities may prioritize innovation and may be wary of regulations that could stifle their competitive edge. Conversely, developing nations, while eager to leverage AI for economic growth, may be more concerned with issues of digital sovereignty, data protection, and the potential for AI to exacerbate existing inequalities. Reconciling these divergent perspectives into a single, universally acceptable legal instrument is a diplomatic undertaking of unprecedented scale.

Consider, for instance, the definition of "high-risk AI." What one nation might deem an acceptable level of risk for an AI system used in targeted advertising, another might consider an unacceptable threat when applied to judicial sentencing or employment decisions. Establishing common benchmarks for risk assessment, data quality, transparency, and accountability that satisfy all signatories would necessitate protracted negotiations. Furthermore, the rapid pace of AI innovation presents a moving target. Any treaty negotiated today might be rendered obsolete by technological advancements within a few years, requiring constant re-evaluation and amendment- a process that is inherently slow and cumbersome within international treaty frameworks. This raises questions about the treaty's adaptability and its capacity to remain relevant in an ever-evolving technological landscape.

Beyond the challenge of achieving consensus on the content of a treaty, the practicalities of enforcement present an equally formidable obstacle. International treaties are often reliant on the goodwill and commitment of signatory states to implement and enforce their provisions domestically. However, the efficacy of such enforcement is highly variable. AI systems are intangible, data-driven, and can operate across borders with relative ease, making them notoriously difficult to monitor and regulate effectively. Establishing robust verification mechanisms that can accurately assess compliance with treaty obligations, particularly in areas like algorithmic bias or the ethical development of autonomous systems, would require sophisticated technical capabilities and a high degree of international cooperation in intelligence sharing and auditing. Without strong, verifiable enforcement mechanisms, a treaty risks becoming a mere statement of intent, lacking the teeth to compel meaningful change or penalize non-compliance.

The question of jurisdiction also looms large. When an AI system developed in one country, trained on data from several others, and deployed globally causes harm, determining which legal framework applies and who is ultimately liable becomes incredibly complex. An international treaty would need to grapple with these jurisdictional ambiguities, potentially establishing new principles of international AI law to address liability, dispute resolution, and redress for those harmed by AI systems. This is a departure from traditional legal frameworks that are often rooted in territorial sovereignty.

Moreover, the economic implications of AI governance cannot be overstated. Nations invest heavily in AI research and development, viewing it as a critical driver of future economic growth and national security. Any proposed international regulations, therefore, will be scrutinized for their potential impact on competitiveness, intellectual property rights, and the free flow of data and AI services. Balancing the need for global safety and ethical standards with the imperative of fostering innovation and economic prosperity will be a delicate act. Some nations may argue that overly stringent regulations could hinder their ability to compete globally, leading to potential resistance to certain treaty provisions. The digital divide, where some nations possess advanced AI capabilities and others lag significantly, further complicates this issue. Ensuring that a treaty does not disproportionately burden less technologically advanced nations or create new dependencies is crucial for its legitimacy and broad acceptance.

The differing levels of technical capacity and regulatory expertise among nations also pose a significant challenge to the effective implementation of an AI treaty. Some countries may lack the resources, infrastructure, or skilled personnel to effectively monitor AI development, conduct AI impact assessments, or enforce complex regulations. A treaty that fails to account for these disparities could inadvertently create a two-tiered system of AI governance, where the spirit of the treaty is upheld only in nations with the capacity to do so. Provisions for capacity building, technical assistance, and the sharing of best practices would be essential, but securing the necessary funding and ensuring equitable distribution of these resources would be a significant undertaking in itself.

The sheer diversity of AI applications further complicates the prospect of a singular, overarching treaty.

AI in healthcare, finance, transportation, defense, and entertainment each present unique ethical dilemmas and regulatory needs. Attempting to create a one-size-fits-all regulatory framework risks being either too broad to be effective or too narrow to capture the full spectrum of AI's impact. A more pragmatic approach might involve a framework treaty that establishes overarching principles and mechanisms for cooperation, with subsequent protocols or agreements addressing specific AI domains. However, even this layered approach would require considerable coordination and agreement at each stage.

Furthermore, the existing geopolitical landscape adds another layer of complexity. Tensions between major global powers, trade disputes, and differing approaches to data governance and digital sovereignty could all impede the negotiation and ratification of an AI treaty. The very process of treaty negotiation is inherently political, and achieving a breakthrough on an issue as multifaceted and strategically important as AI governance would require a significant shift towards greater international cooperation and a shared understanding of the stakes involved. Without a strong impetus, such as a widely recognized existential threat or a critical failure of AI governance on a global scale, it might be difficult to muster the political will necessary to overcome these deeply ingrained national interests and rivalries.

The feasibility of an AI treaty also hinges on the willingness of powerful private sector actors, the primary developers and deployers of AI, to engage constructively and adhere to its provisions. Many AI technologies are developed by multinational corporations, which often operate with a degree of autonomy that can complicate national and international regulatory efforts. While some leading AI companies have expressed support for AI regulation, their specific proposals and their commitment to adhering to potentially stringent treaty obligations remain to be seen.

Ensuring that a treaty is not undermined by corporate lobbying or the strategic relocation of AI development to less regulated jurisdictions will be a critical challenge.

In conclusion, while the conceptual framework for an international AI treaty offers a compelling vision for global AI governance, its practical implementation faces formidable obstacles. The complexities of achieving international consensus on definitions, standards, and enforcement mechanisms, coupled with the rapid pace of technological advancement, the inherent difficulty of monitoring AI systems, and the intricate interplay of national interests, economic considerations, and geopolitical realities, all present significant challenges. Addressing these feasibility issues will require a sustained, multifaceted diplomatic effort, a willingness to innovate in legal and technical approaches to governance, and a deep commitment to international cooperation from all stakeholders. The journey towards an effective global AI treaty is likely to be a long and arduous one, but the necessity of navigating the profound societal transformations AI promises and threatens makes this quest indispensable.

The very real challenges associated with forging a universally binding AI treaty, as previously outlined, do not diminish the urgent need for global cooperation on AI governance. Instead, they highlight the imperative to explore and develop alternative or complementary models that can foster international collaboration while retaining the agility required to keep pace with rapid technological advancement. One such promising avenue lies in the realm of **multi-stakeholder dialogues and forums**. Rather than being solely state-centric, these platforms can bring together governments, industry leaders, academic researchers, civil society organizations, and international bodies to share best practices, identify emerging risks, and collectively develop nuanced understandings of AI's impact. Organizations like the Global Partnership on Artificial Intelligence (GPAI) exemplify this approach, convening diverse expertise to advise on responsible AI development and use. These dialogues can serve as crucial precursors to, or even robust alternatives to, formal treaties, building trust and fostering a shared normative landscape through ongoing, iterative engagement. Such forums can facilitate the development of non-binding recommendations, guidelines, and principles that, while not legally enforceable in the same way as a treaty, can exert significant soft power and influence international norms and national policy. For instance, the OECD's Principles on AI have already had a considerable impact on how governments and organizations approach AI governance, demonstrating the power of shared principles developed through broad consultation.

Complementing these dialogues, **industry-led initiatives and self-regulatory frameworks** offer another vital layer of cooperation. Given that the private sector is at the forefront of AI development and deployment, their active participation and commitment to responsible practices are indispensable. Many leading technology companies are already developing internal ethical guidelines, safety protocols, and transparency measures for their AI systems. While concerns about the potential for self-serving motives and the lack of robust enforcement mechanisms in purely industry-led efforts are valid, these initiatives can nonetheless contribute significantly. Encouraging greater transparency around AI model development, data sourcing, and decision-making processes, perhaps through standardized reporting or auditing frameworks, can build public trust and provide valuable data for policymakers. Furthermore, industry consortia can collaborate on shared challenges, such as developing benchmarks for AI safety or creating common standards for data privacy, which can then inform broader governmental or international efforts. The challenge lies in ensuring these initiatives are genuinely aimed at public good and not merely as a preemptive strike against more stringent external regulation, and that they incorporate meaningful external oversight.

Standardization efforts represent a particularly concrete and actionable form of global AI cooperation. International standards bodies, such as the International Organization for Standardization (ISO) and the International Electrotechnical Commission (IEC), are already engaged in developing technical standards for AI. These can cover a wide range of areas, including data quality, AI system reliability, explainability, security, and testing methodologies. Adherence to internationally recognized standards can facilitate interoperability, promote fair competition, and provide a technical basis for regulatory requirements. For example, standards for AI explainability could provide concrete technical specifications that regulators can reference when mandating transparency in AI systems. Similarly, standards for AI safety testing could establish common protocols for evaluating the robustness and reliability of AI systems in various contexts, from autonomous vehicles to medical diagnostics. The collaborative nature of these standardization processes, which typically involve broad participation from industry, government, and academia, can help foster consensus and build trust in the resulting benchmarks. While standards are often voluntary, they can gain de facto mandatory status through their adoption by governments in regulations or by businesses in their procurement processes.

Moving beyond specific technical standards, the development of **flexible and adaptive governance frameworks** is crucial for navigating the dynamic landscape of AI. Rigid, top-down regulatory approaches, like those inherent in traditional treaty-making, may struggle to keep pace with the exponential growth of AI capabilities. Instead, a more agile approach might involve establishing overarching principles and broad mandates for cooperation, coupled with mechanisms for continuous review, adaptation, and the development of more specific guidelines or regulations as needed. This could involve creating international bodies tasked with monitoring AI developments, assessing emerging risks, and recommending adjustments to governance frameworks. Such bodies could function as agile "AI observatories" or "foresight mechanisms," providing early warnings and policy recommendations to national governments and international organizations. This adaptive approach acknowledges that our understanding of AI's implications is still evolving and that governance structures must be able to learn and adjust over time. Concepts like "regulatory sandboxes" at an international level, where controlled environments are created for testing innovative AI applications under specific oversight, could also be explored to balance innovation with safety.

Another critical element of alternative cooperation models is **capacity building and knowledge sharing**. The global AI landscape is characterized by significant disparities in technological advancement, regulatory expertise, and economic resources. To ensure that AI development and governance benefit all of humanity, substantial efforts must be made to bridge these gaps. This includes providing technical assistance to developing nations to help them build their AI expertise, establish regulatory frameworks, and participate meaningfully in global AI discussions. Initiatives focused on sharing best practices, open-source AI tools, and educational resources can empower countries that may otherwise be left behind. A global AI governance framework that does not adequately address these disparities risks perpetuating existing inequalities and creating new forms of technological dependency. Therefore, capacity building should be an integral component of any international cooperation strategy, ensuring that the benefits of AI are democratized and that all nations can contribute to and benefit from responsible AI development. This might involve establishing international

AI research centers, fellowship programs, and collaborative projects focused on AI for development.

The role of **“soft law” instruments**, such as non-binding declarations, guidelines, and codes of conduct, should also not be underestimated as a means of fostering global AI cooperation. While a formal treaty provides a strong legal commitment, soft law can offer a more flexible and responsive approach, allowing for quicker consensus-building and adaptation. These instruments can help establish shared understandings of ethical principles, define key concepts, and signal international expectations for responsible AI behavior. They can also serve as building blocks for future hard law, by testing concepts and generating the political will for more formal agreements. Examples include ethical guidelines developed by international organizations, industry codes of conduct, and recommendations from expert groups. The effectiveness of soft law relies on its perceived legitimacy, the broad participation in its development, and the willingness of stakeholders to voluntarily adhere to its provisions, often driven by reputational considerations or the desire to align with international best practices.

Furthermore, **sector-specific agreements or MOUs (Memoranda of Understanding)** could offer a more targeted approach to AI governance. Instead of a single, overarching treaty, it might be more practical to develop international agreements or cooperative frameworks for specific high-impact AI applications. For instance, agreements focused on AI in healthcare could address issues of patient data privacy, diagnostic AI reliability, and the ethical implications of AI-driven medical decisions. Similarly, agreements related to AI in transportation could focus on the safety standards for autonomous vehicles or AI-powered air traffic control systems. This sector-specific approach allows for the tailoring of governance mechanisms to the unique risks and opportunities presented by different AI applications, making it easier to achieve consensus among relevant stakeholders. It also allows for a more incremental and modular approach to global AI governance, building cooperation one sector at a time.

Finally, the concept of **"AI governance by design"** can be a powerful complementary strategy. This involves embedding ethical considerations, safety protocols, and accountability mechanisms directly into the AI development lifecycle from its inception, rather than attempting to regulate AI after it has been developed and deployed. Encouraging and, where appropriate, mandating the adoption of "AI by design" principles at an international level can foster a culture of responsibility within the AI ecosystem. This could involve promoting the use of privacy-preserving technologies, explainable AI (XAI) techniques, and robust bias detection and mitigation tools as standard practice in AI development. International collaboration on developing methodologies and best practices for "AI by design" can significantly enhance the global safety and trustworthiness of AI systems. This proactive approach shifts the focus from remediation to prevention, addressing potential harms at their source and creating a more sustainable foundation for AI innovation and deployment.

In essence, while the pursuit of a formal AI treaty remains a significant long-term aspiration, the immediate and ongoing need for global AI cooperation can be effectively addressed through a multifaceted approach. This includes nurturing multi-stakeholder dialogues to build consensus, empowering industry-led initiatives with oversight, leveraging standardization bodies for technical benchmarks, developing flexible and adaptive governance frameworks, investing in capacity building, utilizing soft law instruments, pursuing sector-specific agreements, and promoting AI governance by design. By embracing these diverse strategies, the international community can forge a more coordinated, effective, and responsive approach to guiding the development and deployment of artificial intelligence for the benefit of all. This multifaceted approach acknowledges the complexity of AI and the diverse interests involved, aiming for a collaborative ecosystem that prioritizes safety, ethics, and human well-being in the age of artificial intelligence.

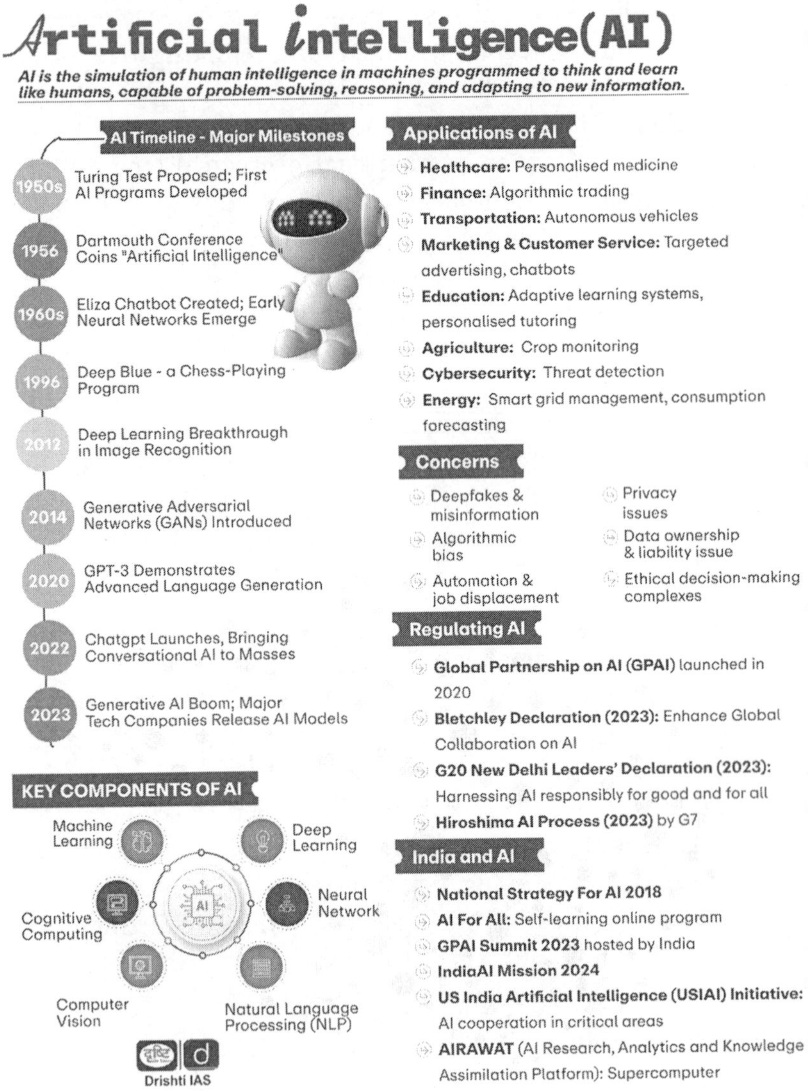

14
AI in Practice
Courts, Justice, and Access

The integration of Artificial Intelligence (AI) into the judicial process represents a profound shift, promising to enhance efficiency and consistency in decision-making while simultaneously raising critical ethical and legal questions. As courts grapple with increasing caseloads and the demand for swifter justice, AI-powered tools are emerging as potential solutions, offering capabilities that range from streamlining administrative tasks to augmenting the complex judgments that define legal proceedings. This subsection delves into the burgeoning application of AI within the judicial system, scrutinizing its impact on areas such as risk assessment for bail and sentencing, predictive analytics for case outcomes, and sophisticated evidence analysis, all while critically evaluating the inherent trade-offs between technological advancement and the fundamental principles of fairness, transparency, and due process.

One of the most significant areas where AI is making inroads is in **risk assessment**, particularly concerning decisions about pre-trial detention (bail) and post-conviction sentencing. The underlying principle is to leverage historical data to predict an individual's likelihood of reoffending or failing to appear in court. Algorithms are trained on vast datasets encompassing demographic information, prior criminal records, employment history, community ties, and other factors deemed relevant to predicting future behavior. The allure of such tools is their potential to move beyond subjective human judgment, which can be prone to implicit biases, towards a more data-driven and ostensibly objective assessment. Proponents argue that AI can provide judges with a more nuanced and comprehensive understanding of an individual's risk profile, thereby leading to more consistent and potentially fairer decisions. For instance, an AI tool might flag an individual with a history of violent offenses and a lack of stable employment as a higher risk, suggesting stricter bail conditions or a longer sentence, while someone with a clean record and strong community ties might be assessed as low risk.

However, the application of AI in risk assessment is fraught with considerable controversy. A primary concern is the potential for **algorithmic bias**. The data used to train these AI models is inherently a reflection of existing societal inequalities and historical patterns of discrimination within the criminal justice system. If past policing or sentencing practices have disproportionately targeted certain racial or socioeconomic groups, the AI trained on this data will likely perpetuate and even amplify these biases. For example, if a particular neighborhood has historically been subject to higher levels of police surveillance and arrests for minor offenses, residents of that neighborhood, regardless of their individual circumstances, may be disproportionately flagged as high-risk by an AI, not due to their inherent propensity for crime, but due to the biased data inputs. This can lead to a vicious cycle where biased predictions result in harsher treatment, which in turn generates more biased data for future AI training. The notion of "predictive justice" can thus become a mechanism for codifying and automating existing prejudices, masking them under a veneer of technological objectivity.

Furthermore, the **transparency and explainability** of these AI tools pose significant challenges. Many AI algorithms, particularly those employing deep learning, operate as "black boxes," meaning their decision-making processes are opaque even to their creators. When a judge relies on an AI's risk assessment score, it can be difficult to ascertain *why* a particular score was assigned. Is it based on the individual's criminal history, their socioeconomic status, or some correlation that lacks a clear causal or logical link to their likelihood of reoffending? This lack of transparency directly impacts the fundamental legal principle of due process, which often includes the right to understand the basis of a decision that affects one's liberty. If a defendant cannot understand why they were denied bail or received a harsher sentence based on an AI's recommendation, their ability to challenge that decision effectively is severely compromised. Without clear explanations, the AI's output risks becoming an unchallengeable decree rather than an assistive tool.

Another rapidly developing application of AI in the judicial sphere is **predictive analytics for case outcomes**. This involves using AI to forecast the likely success or failure of a legal case based on factors such as the type of offense, the jurisdiction, the assigned judge, the legal arguments presented, and even the characteristics of the legal counsel involved. Such tools can be valuable for legal practitioners in assessing the strength of their case, strategizing settlement negotiations, or advising clients on the potential ramifications of proceeding to trial. For example, an AI might analyze thousands of past cases involving similar charges in a specific court and predict a high probability of conviction for a particular type of defense strategy.

However, the ethical implications of using predictive analytics in this manner are profound and far-reaching. Critics raise concerns that these tools could stifle innovation in legal argumentation and advocacy. If lawyers become overly reliant on AI predictions, they might be less inclined to explore novel legal theories or present unconventional defenses, fearing that deviating from the predicted "optimal" path could lead to a worse outcome. This could result in a homogenization of legal strategy, where cases are approached based on statistical probabilities rather than the unique factual nuances of each situation. Moreover, the accuracy of these predictions is heavily dependent on the quality and comprehensiveness of the data, and as with risk assessment tools, historical biases can easily infiltrate these models. If, for instance, certain types of plaintiffs have historically been less successful in court due to systemic discrimination, an AI might learn to predict lower success rates for similar plaintiffs, thereby reinforcing discriminatory outcomes.

The very concept of "predicting" a legal outcome also raises philosophical questions about the nature of justice. Is justice a matter of probabilistic calculation, or is it a process of reasoned deliberation based on legal principles and factual evidence? Over-reliance on predictive analytics could lead to a system where outcomes are determined more by statistical likelihood than by the merits of the case. This could erode public trust in the judicial system, as individuals may perceive that their fate is being decided by an algorithm rather than by human judgment guided by principles of fairness and equity. The potential for these tools to influence judicial discretion also needs careful consideration. While intended as advisory, there is a risk that judges might unconsciously or consciously defer to the AI's prediction, particularly in high-volume dockets where time is scarce.

Beyond decision-making support, AI is also revolutionizing **evidence analysis**. The sheer volume of digital evidence generated in modern legal cases- emails, text messages, social media posts, video footage, financial records- can be overwhelming for human investigators and legal teams. AI-powered tools can sift through, categorize, and analyze vast datasets far more efficiently than humans. Techniques like natural language processing (NLP) can be used to identify keywords, sentiment, and relationships within large volumes of text, helping to uncover crucial information in discovery or to authenticate digital evidence. Machine learning algorithms can be employed to detect anomalies, identify patterns, and even reconstruct events from fragmented data. For example, AI can rapidly scan millions of emails for specific phrases or communication patterns between parties, or it can analyze financial transaction records to detect fraudulent activities. In cases involving complex technical evidence, such as cybersecurity breaches or intellectual property disputes, AI can assist experts in understanding the intricacies of the data.

The benefits of AI in evidence analysis are tangible, offering significant gains in efficiency, cost-effectiveness, and accuracy. By automating laborious tasks, AI frees up legal professionals to focus on higher-level strategic thinking, legal research, and client interaction. It can also help ensure that crucial pieces of evidence are not overlooked due to the sheer volume of data. For instance, in a complex white-collar crime investigation involving terabytes of digital data, AI can pinpoint relevant communications or financial transactions that might otherwise take months or even years for human review to uncover.

However, the use of AI in evidence analysis also presents its own set of challenges. The **reliability and integrity of AI-generated analysis** are paramount. If the AI tool itself is flawed, or if it is manipulated, the evidence it produces could be inaccurate or misleading, leading to miscarriages of justice. This underscores the need for rigorous validation of AI tools used in legal contexts, as well as transparency about the methodologies and parameters employed in their analysis. The "black box" problem, discussed earlier, is equally relevant here; if the AI's analytical process is not understood, it can be difficult to challenge its findings or to ensure that the analysis is unbiased. For example, an NLP tool trained on a biased corpus of text might misinterpret the sentiment or intent of communications from certain demographic groups, leading to erroneous conclusions.

Moreover, the **admissibility of AI-generated evidence** in court is a developing legal frontier. Courts must grapple with whether and how to admit evidence derived from AI analysis, considering issues of reliability, the qualifications of the AI system as an "expert," and the potential for prejudice or confusion to the jury. Establishing clear legal standards for the admissibility of such evidence is crucial to ensure that AI tools enhance, rather than undermine, the integrity of the evidentiary process. This might involve requiring AI tools to meet certain benchmarks for accuracy, validation, and explainability, akin to existing standards for scientific evidence, such as the Daubert standard in the United States.

Furthermore, the increasing sophistication of AI raises questions about its potential to **fabricate or manipulate evidence**. Generative AI technologies, capable of creating realistic synthetic media (deepfakes), could be misused to create false evidence or to discredit genuine evidence. While such malicious uses are not yet widespread in judicial settings, the possibility necessitates vigilance and the development of AI-powered tools for detecting AI-generated manipulations. The legal system must be prepared to address the challenges posed by AI that can both generate and potentially detect fabricated evidence, creating a complex arms race in the realm of digital truth.

The broader implications of AI in judicial decision-making extend to issues of **accountability and human oversight**. When an AI system contributes to a judicial decision, who is ultimately responsible if that decision is flawed or unjust? Is it the developer of the AI, the judge who relied on its output, the IT department that implemented the system, or the government agency that procured it? Establishing clear lines of accountability is essential for ensuring that the legal system remains answerable to the public. While AI can offer valuable insights and efficiencies, it should ideally function as an assistive tool, augmenting, rather than replacing, human judgment. The role of the judge remains critical in exercising discretion, interpreting the law, and ensuring that justice is served in individual cases. The danger lies in an over-reliance on AI that could lead to a "de-skilling" of judges or a reduction in their active engagement with the reasoning behind their decisions.

The potential benefits of AI in the judicial system- increased efficiency, reduced costs, improved consistency, and enhanced analytical capabilities- are undeniable. However, these benefits must be weighed carefully against the significant ethical and legal risks. Addressing concerns about algorithmic bias, ensuring transparency and explainability, safeguarding due process, and maintaining robust human oversight are paramount. As AI continues to evolve and its integration into the legal realm deepens, a cautious, evidence-based, and ethically grounded approach is essential. This requires ongoing dialogue among legal professionals, technologists, policymakers, and the public to ensure that AI serves to strengthen, rather than undermine, the principles of justice. The development of clear guidelines, robust regulatory frameworks, and continuous evaluation of AI systems in practice will be crucial for navigating this transformative period and for ensuring that the pursuit of technological advancement does not come at the expense of fundamental rights and the pursuit of true justice. The judiciary, as a cornerstone of societal order, has a particular responsibility to approach AI adoption with both an eye for innovation and an unwavering commitment to its core values.

The pervasive influence of Artificial Intelligence (AI) is reshaping the landscape of criminal justice, extending its reach from the proactive identification of potential criminal activity to the intricate management and rehabilitation of individuals within correctional facilities. This expansion is not merely an incremental technological adoption; it represents a fundamental shift in how law enforcement and correctional agencies operate, raising complex questions about efficacy, fairness, and the very nature of justice in an increasingly data-driven world. As we move from the courtroom's deliberative space into the operational spheres of policing and corrections, the ethical considerations surrounding AI become even more pronounced, touching upon privacy, liberty, and the potential for systemic bias to be embedded at the foundational levels of the justice system.

One of the most prominent and debated applications of AI in law enforcement is **predictive policing**. This approach leverages algorithms trained on historical crime data to forecast where and when crimes are likely to occur. The underlying logic is to enable law enforcement agencies to deploy resources more efficiently and proactively, potentially deterring crime before it happens. Systems can analyze patterns related to time of day, day of week, location, weather, and even socio-economic factors to generate "hotspot" maps, directing patrols to areas deemed at higher risk. For instance, an AI might identify that burglaries have historically spiked on weekday afternoons in a specific residential area following school dismissals, leading police to increase their presence during those times. Similarly, AI can be used to predict the likelihood of specific individuals engaging in criminal behavior based on their past interactions with the justice system, social media activity, or associations, a practice that raises significant privacy and civil liberties concerns.

The efficacy and fairness of predictive policing systems are subjects of intense scrutiny. A primary critique centers on the inherent risk of **reinforcing and amplifying existing biases**. Predictive algorithms are trained on data reflecting past policing practices, which, in turn, are often shaped by systemic societal inequalities. If certain communities, often minority or low-income neighborhoods, have historically been subjected to higher levels of surveillance and enforcement due to discriminatory policing patterns, the AI will learn to identify these areas as high-risk. This can lead to a feedback loop where increased police presence in these already over-policed areas results in more arrests for minor offenses, generating further data that trains the AI to target these same communities. Consequently, predictive policing can inadvertently create a self-fulfilling prophecy, leading to the over-surveillance and over-criminalization of specific demographic groups, irrespective of their actual propensity for criminal activity. The notion of objectivity in AI becomes problematic when the data it learns from is inherently biased.

Beyond location-based predictions, AI is also being deployed for **person-based prediction**, aiming to identify individuals who are statistically more likely to commit crimes. These systems often draw upon vast amounts of personal data, including criminal records, social media posts, financial transactions, and even behavioral patterns gleaned from surveillance technologies. The ethical implications here are particularly acute, as such predictions can lead to individuals being scrutinized, stopped, or even arrested based on probabilistic assessments of their future actions rather than concrete evidence of wrongdoing. This raises profound questions about presumption of innocence and the right to privacy. Can an individual be deemed a "risk" and subjected to enhanced surveillance or law enforcement attention simply because an algorithm has assigned them a high likelihood score, especially when that score might be influenced by proxies for race or socioeconomic status? The lack of transparency in how these person-based risk scores are calculated further exacerbates these concerns, making it difficult to challenge their validity or identify embedded biases.

In the realm of law enforcement operations, AI is also being utilized for **crime analysis and investigation**. Sophisticated algorithms can process and analyze vast quantities of data from various sources, including CCTV footage, audio recordings, social media, and textual records, to identify patterns, connect disparate pieces of information, and even generate leads for investigators. For example, AI-powered facial recognition technology can be used to identify suspects by comparing images from crime scenes against databases of known individuals. Natural Language Processing (NLP) can sift through mountains of text-based evidence, such as emails or intercepted communications, to identify key themes, relationships, or threats. AI can also assist in crime scene reconstruction by analyzing digital forensic data. These tools can significantly enhance the efficiency and effectiveness of investigations, potentially helping to solve cases that might otherwise go cold.

However, the application of these analytical AI tools is not without its challenges. **Facial recognition technology**, for instance, has been shown to have significantly higher error rates when identifying individuals with darker skin tones or women, leading to a disproportionate risk of misidentification and wrongful accusations for these demographic groups. The pervasive use of AI for surveillance, such as widespread CCTV monitoring coupled with facial recognition, also raises serious concerns about the erosion of privacy and the creation of a pervasive surveillance state. The ability of AI to rapidly analyze and correlate vast amounts of personal data can create detailed profiles of individuals, which could be misused or accessed inappropriately. Furthermore, the **admissibility and reliability of AI-generated evidence** in court are still developing legal areas. Ensuring that the AI systems used are rigorously tested, validated, and transparent in their methodologies is crucial for maintaining the integrity of the justice process. The potential for AI to be wrong, or for its outputs to be misinterpreted, necessitates robust human oversight and critical evaluation of its findings.

Moving from policing to the correctional system, AI continues to play a significant role, primarily focused on **inmate management and risk assessment**. Within correctional facilities, AI-powered systems are being employed for various purposes, including predicting inmate behavior, identifying potential security threats, and managing resources. For example, AI can analyze patterns in inmate communications, movements, or interactions to flag individuals who might be at risk of violence, self-harm, or attempting to escape. Behavioral analysis software can monitor inmate activity in common areas or during rehabilitation programs to assess engagement and identify potential issues.

A key application of AI in corrections is **recidivism risk assessment**. Similar to its use in pre-trial and sentencing decisions, AI algorithms are used to predict an individual's likelihood of reoffending upon release from prison. These assessments can influence decisions related to parole, early release programs, and post-release supervision. The data used typically includes information about the inmate's criminal history, demographics, behavior within the correctional facility, and participation in rehabilitation programs. The promise here is to provide a more objective and consistent basis for these critical decisions, moving away from potentially subjective human judgment.

However, the use of AI for recidivism risk assessment in corrections faces many of the same ethical hurdles as its counterparts in the courtroom. The problem of **algorithmic bias** remains a significant concern. If the data used to train these models reflects historical disparities in arrest rates, sentencing, or the effectiveness of rehabilitation programs across different racial or socioeconomic groups, the AI is likely to perpetuate these biases. For instance, if individuals from certain backgrounds have historically received harsher sentences or had less access to effective rehabilitation programs, an AI might erroneously conclude that they are at a higher risk of reoffending, even if their individual circumstances do not warrant such a prediction. This can lead to longer periods of incarceration or less favorable parole decisions for these groups, further entrenching existing societal inequalities. The very concept of "risk" can become a proxy for societal prejudice when not carefully constructed and validated.

The **transparency and explainability** of these recidivism prediction tools are also critical. If an inmate is denied parole or a rehabilitation opportunity based on an AI's risk score, they have a right to understand the basis of that decision. However, many AI models operate as "black boxes," making it difficult to ascertain precisely which factors contributed to a particular risk assessment. Is the score influenced by factors that are legitimate indicators of risk, or by proxies for protected characteristics that should not be considered? This lack of transparency can undermine due process and make it challenging for individuals to appeal or challenge decisions that significantly impact their future. Establishing mechanisms for independent review and validation of these algorithms, as well as ensuring that their outputs can be explained in understandable terms, is essential.

Furthermore, the implementation of AI in correctional facilities raises substantial **privacy concerns regarding inmate monitoring**. The widespread use of AI-powered surveillance technologies, including biometric monitoring, behavioral analytics, and even sentiment analysis of inmate communications, can create a highly intrusive environment. While the stated purpose is often security and rehabilitation, the constant monitoring and analysis of every aspect of an inmate's life can erode personal autonomy and dignity. The collection and storage of such extensive personal data also present risks of data breaches or misuse. Defining the appropriate scope and limitations of AI-driven surveillance within correctional settings, and ensuring that these technologies are used in a manner that respects human rights, is a significant challenge. This involves carefully considering what constitutes legitimate security needs versus intrusive overreach.

The question of **accountability** is paramount when AI is involved in decision-making within the criminal justice system, from policing to corrections. When an AI-powered predictive policing system leads to the over-surveillance of a particular community, or when a recidivism risk assessment algorithm results in an unfair denial of parole, who is ultimately responsible? Is it the software developers, the law enforcement agency that deployed the system, the correctional facility that implemented the risk assessment tool, or the individuals who made the final decisions based on the AI's output? Establishing clear lines of responsibility is crucial for ensuring that the justice system remains accountable to the public. The deployment of AI without robust oversight and clear accountability frameworks risks creating a system where problematic outcomes can be attributed to an opaque technological process, thereby evading human responsibility.

The potential impact of AI on **fundamental rights** within the criminal justice system warrants careful consideration. Predictive policing, by its nature, can lead to increased stops and searches in certain areas or of certain individuals, potentially infringing upon rights to freedom of movement and freedom from unreasonable search and seizure. The use of facial recognition technology can chills free speech and assembly by creating an environment of constant surveillance. In corrections, intrusive monitoring can infringe upon privacy rights and the right to maintain personal dignity. Moreover, if AI systems perpetuate systemic biases, they can undermine the principle of equal protection under the law. The promise of AI to enhance efficiency and effectiveness in criminal justice must be continuously balanced against its potential to erode fundamental rights and exacerbate existing inequalities. This requires ongoing legal and ethical deliberation, as well as the development of regulatory frameworks that safeguard individual liberties while allowing for the responsible and beneficial use of these powerful technologies. The ongoing development and deployment of AI in these critical areas demand a vigilant and critical approach to ensure that technological advancement serves, rather than subverts, the principles of justice and human rights.

The transformative potential of Artificial Intelligence (AI) extends far beyond the operational aspects of law enforcement and corrections, offering a compelling vision for enhancing **access to justice**. For a significant portion of the population, the legal system remains an opaque, expensive, and intimidating labyrinth, characterized by high costs, complex procedures, and a scarcity of readily available legal expertise. This creates a profound justice gap, where individuals with legitimate legal needs, particularly those from low-income backgrounds or underserved communities, are often unable to secure the representation or guidance necessary to navigate their legal challenges. AI presents a powerful suite of tools capable of democratizing legal services, making legal information and assistance more accessible, affordable, and user-friendly than ever before. This subsection delves into the various ways AI is being deployed to bridge this critical gap, fostering a more equitable and inclusive legal landscape.

One of the most promising avenues for AI in improving access to justice lies in the development and deployment of **AI-powered legal aid platforms and chatbots**. These systems are designed to provide preliminary legal information, guidance on legal processes, and even assist in the initial stages of case preparation. Unlike traditional legal aid services, which often face overwhelming demand and limited resources, AI-powered solutions can operate at scale, offering immediate assistance to a broad user base.

For instance, sophisticated chatbots can be programmed to answer frequently asked questions about common legal issues, such as landlord-tenant disputes, family law matters, or employment rights. They can guide users through the steps required to file a claim, explain legal terminology in plain language, and direct individuals to relevant legal resources or human legal professionals when necessary. These platforms can serve as a crucial first point of contact, empowering individuals with foundational legal knowledge and helping them understand their rights and options before they even need to consult a lawyer. The ability of these AI tools to process natural language allows for more intuitive and accessible interactions, mimicking a conversational approach that can reduce the anxiety often associated with seeking legal help.

Furthermore, AI is revolutionizing the way legal documents are generated and managed, significantly lowering the barrier to entry for individuals who need to prepare legal forms.

Automated document generation tools, powered by AI and natural language processing, can help users create a wide range of legal documents, from simple affidavits and wills to more complex legal filings. Users typically interact with these systems by answering a series of guided questions, which the AI then uses to populate pre-designed templates. This process is not only more efficient and cost-effective than relying on a legal professional for every document, but it also ensures a degree of accuracy and compliance with relevant legal standards. For example, a small business owner needing to draft a standard contract, or an individual seeking to create a power of attorney, can utilize these AI-driven platforms to produce compliant documents quickly and affordably. This capability is particularly impactful for those who cannot afford the fees associated with traditional legal drafting services. The development of more sophisticated AI in this area promises to handle an even wider array of legal document needs, further expanding access to essential legal tools.

The realm of **online dispute resolution (ODR)** is another area where AI is making substantial inroads in improving access to justice. Many legal disputes, particularly those of a lower monetary value or involving interpersonal conflicts, can be time-consuming and costly to resolve through traditional litigation. ODR platforms leverage technology, often incorporating AI, to facilitate out-of-court settlements. AI can assist in various aspects of ODR, such as mediating initial communications between parties, analyzing dispute details to suggest potential settlement parameters, or even providing neutral third-party analysis of evidence. For instance, in consumer disputes, an AI could analyze the terms of a contract and the nature of the complaint to suggest fair resolutions based on historical data of similar cases. Similarly, in neighborhood disputes, AI-powered communication tools could help parties articulate their concerns and explore common ground without the immediate escalation of formal legal proceedings. By providing accessible, efficient, and cost-effective mechanisms for resolving conflicts, ODR systems, enhanced by AI, can divert a significant volume of cases from crowded court dockets and offer a more palatable resolution path for individuals.

Beyond direct legal assistance and dispute resolution, AI is also instrumental in expanding access to **legal information and education**. Many individuals are unaware of their legal rights or the proper procedures to follow in various situations. AI-powered platforms can serve as comprehensive legal information repositories, offering explanations of laws, case summaries, and procedural guides tailored to specific jurisdictions and legal issues. These resources can be made available through websites, mobile applications, or even voice-activated assistants, ensuring that legal knowledge is accessible to a wider audience. For example, a student facing an academic disciplinary hearing might use an AI-powered resource to understand their rights and the appeal process. Similarly, an immigrant navigating the complexities of immigration law could access AI-generated explanations of visa requirements and application procedures. The ability of AI to synthesize complex legal texts into easily digestible formats is crucial for empowering individuals to understand and engage with the legal system.

The effectiveness of these AI-driven solutions in enhancing access to justice is directly tied to their ability to overcome several critical barriers.

Cost is a primary barrier; AI tools can drastically reduce the expense of legal services, making them affordable for individuals and small businesses that would otherwise be priced out of the market. **Geographic limitations** are another hurdle, as AI platforms can provide assistance remotely, benefiting those in rural areas or regions with a shortage of legal professionals. **Complexity and intimidation** are also significant factors, with AI's ability to simplify legal language and processes making the legal system less daunting. However, the successful implementation of these tools requires careful consideration of several factors to ensure they genuinely improve, rather than hinder, access to justice.

A crucial aspect for the success of AI in this domain is **user-friendliness and accessibility**. The interfaces of AI legal tools must be intuitive and easy to navigate for individuals with varying levels of technological literacy. This includes designing interfaces that are accessible to people with disabilities and ensuring compatibility across different devices. Moreover, the language used by AI systems must be clear, concise, and free of jargon, translating complex legal concepts into plain language that the average person can understand. Failure to prioritize user-friendliness can inadvertently create new barriers, alienating the very populations these tools are intended to serve. For instance, a chatbot that uses overly technical legal terms or has a confusing navigation structure will do little to help someone struggling with a legal problem.

Accuracy and reliability are paramount. While AI can offer significant efficiencies, the stakes in legal matters are often very high. Inaccurate legal information or flawed document generation can have severe consequences for individuals. Therefore, the AI models underpinning these tools must be rigorously trained on up-to-date and authoritative legal data. Ongoing validation and oversight are essential to ensure that the information and guidance provided are correct and consistent with current laws and regulations. Legal professionals play a vital role in this process, reviewing and validating the outputs of AI systems, and serving as a crucial human check to prevent errors. The development of regulatory frameworks and ethical guidelines for AI in legal services is also critical to establishing trust and ensuring that these tools operate with a high degree of integrity.

The issue of **data privacy and security** is equally important. AI legal tools often handle sensitive personal information. Robust data protection measures must be in place to safeguard this information from breaches or unauthorized access. Users need to be confident that their personal data is handled securely and ethically. Transparency regarding data collection, usage, and storage policies is crucial for building and maintaining user trust. This includes clearly explaining how user data is used to train or improve AI models, and providing individuals with control over their information.

Furthermore, the deployment of AI in legal services must address the potential for **algorithmic bias**. If the data used to train AI models reflects existing societal inequalities or discriminatory legal practices, the AI could perpetuate or even amplify these biases. For example, an AI trained on historical data that shows certain demographic groups receiving less favorable outcomes in specific legal areas might inadvertently offer biased advice or generate documents that disadvantage these groups. Continuous monitoring and auditing of AI systems for bias are therefore essential. Developers and legal professionals must work collaboratively to identify and mitigate any biases, ensuring that AI tools promote fairness and equity rather than exacerbating existing disparities. This may involve using diverse and representative datasets, employing bias detection techniques, and implementing fairness-aware AI algorithms.

The integration of AI into the legal landscape also necessitates a clear understanding of the **role of human legal professionals**. AI tools are not intended to replace lawyers but rather to augment their capabilities and extend their reach. By automating routine tasks, providing preliminary research, and generating initial drafts, AI can free up legal professionals to focus on more complex aspects of cases, such as strategic advice, courtroom advocacy, and client counseling. This symbiotic relationship between AI and human expertise can lead to a more efficient and effective legal system overall. However, it requires careful consideration of how legal education and professional development need to adapt to equip lawyers with the skills to effectively utilize and oversee AI technologies.

The impact of AI on access to justice can be further amplified through **government and non-profit initiatives**. Publicly funded AI legal platforms, or partnerships between technology companies and legal aid organizations, can help ensure that these powerful tools are accessible to those who need them most, regardless of their ability to pay. These initiatives can also play a crucial role in setting standards, promoting ethical development, and educating the public about the benefits and limitations of AI in the legal sphere.

For instance, a government-backed platform could offer free access to AI-powered document generation for low-income individuals seeking to file for bankruptcy or child support.

The ongoing development of AI promises even more sophisticated applications for enhancing access to justice.

AI-powered legal research tools can sift through vast databases of statutes, case law, and legal scholarship to identify relevant precedents and arguments with unprecedented speed and accuracy. This can significantly reduce the time and cost associated with legal research for both legal professionals and self-represented litigants. Similarly, **AI-driven contract review systems** can analyze complex agreements for potential risks, inconsistencies, or unfavorable clauses, empowering individuals and businesses to understand their contractual obligations more effectively.

In conclusion, the integration of AI into the legal sector holds immense promise for democratizing access to justice. By providing affordable legal information, streamlining document preparation, facilitating dispute resolution, and augmenting the capabilities of legal professionals, AI can help dismantle many of the traditional barriers that prevent individuals from accessing legal recourse. However, realizing this potential requires a commitment to user-centric design, rigorous accuracy, robust data protection, proactive bias mitigation, and a clear understanding of the collaborative role between AI and human expertise. As these technologies continue to evolve, thoughtful development and ethical deployment will be paramount to ensuring that AI serves as a genuine force for equity and fairness within the justice system, empowering individuals and strengthening the rule of law for all. The ongoing evolution of these AI applications, from sophisticated chatbots to advanced legal research engines, underscores a tangible shift towards a legal ecosystem where knowledge and assistance are more readily available, irrespective of economic status or geographical location, thereby fostering a more inclusive and responsive justice system.

The integration of Artificial Intelligence (AI) into the fabric of legal practice, while offering unprecedented efficiencies and potential for enhanced service delivery, simultaneously introduces a complex web of ethical quandaries that legal professionals must navigate with utmost diligence. The very tools designed to streamline processes and broaden access can, if not managed with a keen ethical compass, undermine fundamental tenets of legal practice, including client confidentiality, professional responsibility, and the pursuit of justice itself. As AI systems become more sophisticated and embedded in daily legal workflows, the imperative to address these ethical challenges grows more pronounced, demanding careful consideration and proactive strategies from practitioners, regulatory bodies, and AI developers alike.

One of the most significant ethical hurdles revolves around **client confidentiality**. Legal professionals are bound by strict ethical duties to protect the sensitive and often deeply personal information shared by their clients. The use of AI tools, particularly those that operate in the cloud or involve third-party developers, raises concerns about how this confidential data is stored, processed, and secured. When a law firm or an individual practitioner utilizes an AI-powered legal research platform, a case management system, or even a sophisticated drafting tool, the data pertaining to client matters is effectively being shared with or processed by the AI system. This raises critical questions: Does the AI provider have access to this data? How is that data encrypted and protected from unauthorized access or breaches? Are there clauses in the AI service agreement that might permit the AI provider to use aggregated or anonymized data for their own model training or development, potentially compromising the confidentiality of the underlying client information? The risk of a data breach, which could expose vast amounts of confidential client information to malicious actors or even competitors, is a tangible threat. Therefore, legal professionals must exercise extreme caution in selecting AI vendors, thoroughly vetting their data security protocols, encryption methods, and contractual terms to ensure they align with the stringent confidentiality obligations owed to clients. This due diligence is not merely a matter of technical compliance but a fundamental ethical requirement. The reputational and financial consequences of a breach that exposes client confidences can be catastrophic, not to mention the profound erosion of trust between clients and their legal counsel.

Closely linked to confidentiality is the imperative to maintain **professional competence** in an era of rapidly evolving technology. The ethical duty of competence requires lawyers to possess the legal knowledge, skill, thoroughness, and preparation reasonably necessary for the representation of a client. As AI tools become more prevalent in legal work, this duty expands to encompass a foundational understanding of the AI technologies being employed. Lawyers cannot blindly delegate tasks to AI without understanding its capabilities, limitations, and potential pitfalls. For instance, relying on an AI-powered legal research tool without critically evaluating its output for accuracy, completeness, or potential bias could lead to faulty legal advice, ultimately harming the client. Similarly, using an AI to draft legal documents without understanding the underlying legal principles and how the AI generates specific clauses could result in documents that are legally flawed or fail to adequately protect the client's interests. This means that legal professionals must invest time in educating themselves about AI, understanding how these tools work, and developing the skills to critically assess their outputs. This might involve attending continuing legal education seminars focused on legal technology, experimenting with

AI tools in a controlled environment, and collaborating with legal technologists or IT professionals. The ethical challenge lies in striking a balance between leveraging AI for efficiency and ensuring that human oversight and critical judgment remain at the forefront of legal decision-making. Ignoring AI is no longer a viable option for maintaining competence; conversely, uncritical adoption is equally perilous.

The potential for AI to **introduce or perpetuate bias** presents one of the most profound ethical challenges in legal practice. AI systems learn from the data they are trained on, and if that data reflects historical societal biases, discriminatory practices, or systemic inequalities within the justice system, the AI is likely to replicate and even amplify those biases. This can manifest in various ways. For instance, an AI tool used for predictive policing or risk assessment in criminal justice might disproportionately flag individuals from certain demographic groups as higher risk due to biased historical arrest data. In civil litigation, an AI used for document review might inadvertently prioritize or deprioritize evidence based on patterns associated with biased legal outcomes in the past. Even in client intake or case assessment, an AI that has learned from data where certain client types were historically less successful in court might subtly steer legal advice in a less favorable direction for those clients. Legal professionals have an ethical obligation to ensure fairness and equal justice, and this extends to the tools they use. Therefore, lawyers must be vigilant in questioning the provenance of the data used to train AI systems, seeking out tools that have been developed with bias mitigation strategies in mind, and critically examining the outputs of AI for any signs of unfairness or discrimination. This requires a sophisticated understanding of how bias can be embedded in algorithms and a commitment to actively seeking out and correcting it. Simply trusting an AI's output without scrutiny can inadvertently make a lawyer complicit in perpetuating systemic injustices. The pursuit of justice demands that AI be deployed in a manner that promotes equity, not entrenches disadvantage.

Furthermore, the ethical responsibility to **provide transparent and understandable explanations to clients** regarding the role of AI in their cases is paramount. Clients have a right to understand how their legal matters are being handled and the tools being used to achieve their objectives. When AI is employed in legal research, drafting, analysis, or even client communication, lawyers must be prepared to explain its function, its benefits, and its limitations to their clients in clear, accessible language. This transparency builds trust and allows clients to make informed decisions about their representation. For example, if an AI tool was used to identify key precedents for a case, the lawyer should explain that this was done to enhance the thoroughness of the research, but also acknowledge that the final selection and interpretation of those precedents remain the lawyer's professional judgment. Similarly, if an AI assists in drafting a contract, the lawyer should explain that the AI provided a template or generated clauses based on specific parameters, but that the lawyer has reviewed and adapted these to ensure they meet the client's unique needs and legal objectives. The challenge here is to demystify AI for clients who may have little or no technical background. Lawyers must avoid using jargon and instead focus on the practical implications of AI for the client's case. This may require developing new communication strategies and preparing clear, concise explanations. A client who understands that AI is being used as a tool to support their lawyer's expertise, rather than as a replacement for it, is more likely to feel confident and secure in their legal representation. The ethical imperative is to ensure that the client remains the central focus, with AI serving as a sophisticated assistant under human direction and control, and that this arrangement is clearly communicated and understood.

Beyond these core issues, the ethical landscape also includes considerations around **accountability and liability**. When an AI system makes an error that leads to negative consequences for a client, who is responsible? Is it the lawyer who deployed the AI, the developer who created the AI, or the AI itself (a notion that currently lacks legal standing)? Legal professionals must grapple with how to attribute responsibility when AI is involved in legal decision-making or service delivery. This necessitates a clear understanding of where human judgment and intervention are critically necessary, and ensuring that AI acts as a supportive tool rather than an autonomous decision-maker in matters requiring human discretion and ethical judgment. Establishing clear lines of accountability is crucial for maintaining the integrity of the legal profession and ensuring that clients have recourse when errors occur.

Another emerging ethical consideration is the potential for AI to **create new forms of inequality** within the legal profession itself. As AI tools become more powerful and sophisticated, firms that can afford to invest in these technologies may gain a significant competitive advantage over smaller firms or solo practitioners who lack the resources. This could exacerbate existing disparities in legal representation and access to justice, creating a two-tiered legal system where only the well-resourced can fully benefit from AI-driven efficiencies. The ethical challenge for the profession is to find ways to democratize access to these technologies, or at least to ensure that the ethical obligations related to their use are applied universally, regardless of a firm's size or financial capacity.

Moreover, the increasing reliance on AI for tasks traditionally performed by junior associates or paralegals raises questions about **professional development and training**. If AI automates much of the foundational work, how will the next generation of legal professionals develop the necessary skills and experience? Ethical considerations demand that law schools and firms adapt their training programs to equip lawyers with the competencies needed to work alongside AI, including data analysis, ethical AI deployment, and critical evaluation of AI outputs. Failing to do so would be a disservice to aspiring legal professionals and, ultimately, to the clients they will serve.

In essence, the ethical challenges of AI in legal practice are multifaceted and deeply intertwined with the core values of the legal profession. They demand a proactive, thoughtful, and continuous engagement from all stakeholders. As AI continues its inexorable march into legal workflows, the legal community must not only embrace its potential but also rigorously address its ethical implications to ensure that technology serves to enhance, rather than erode, the principles of justice, fairness, confidentiality, and professional responsibility. The path forward requires ongoing dialogue, the development of clear ethical guidelines and best practices, and a steadfast commitment to prioritizing human judgment and ethical integrity in the application of artificial intelligence within the practice of law. The judicious and ethical integration of AI is not merely an optional upgrade to legal services; it is a fundamental requirement for maintaining the trust and efficacy of the legal system in the 21st century.

The theoretical underpinnings of AI's integration into the legal sphere, while critical, must ultimately be grounded in tangible examples of its application. This subsection delves into a series of case studies, illuminating both the triumphs and the tribulations encountered when AI systems are deployed within courts and the broader justice system. By dissecting these real-world scenarios, we can distill practical insights and lessons learned, guiding future implementations toward alignment with the fundamental principles of justice, fairness, and the rule of law.

One of the most widely cited examples of successful AI implementation in the legal realm is the use of AI-powered tools for **e-discovery and document review**. In complex litigation, particularly in large-scale commercial disputes or investigations, the sheer volume of electronically stored information (ESI) can be overwhelming. Traditional manual review by teams of lawyers and paralegals is not only time-consuming and exorbitantly expensive but also prone to human error and fatigue. AI-driven platforms, employing Natural Language Processing (NLP) and machine learning, can analyze millions of documents at speeds far exceeding human capabilities. These systems can identify relevant documents based on keywords, concepts, and even the context of their usage, significantly streamlining the discovery process. For instance, in many major antitrust lawsuits or regulatory investigations, such as those involving large technology companies, the ability to quickly sift through vast troves of emails, internal communications, and financial records has been instrumental. Technologies like predictive coding, which learns from human reviewers' judgments to identify similar relevant documents, have proven particularly effective. This has not only reduced costs for litigants but also allowed legal teams to focus more on strategic analysis and legal argument rather than rote document sifting. The success here lies in AI augmenting, rather than replacing, human legal judgment, by handling the computationally intensive tasks, thereby freeing up legal professionals to concentrate on higher-value activities. The efficiency gains translate into faster case resolution and, potentially, lower legal fees for clients. Moreover, by enabling more comprehensive reviews, AI can help ensure that crucial evidence is not overlooked, thus promoting a more thorough and equitable discovery process.

Another area where AI has demonstrated significant promise is in **predictive analytics for case outcomes and sentencing recommendations**. Several jurisdictions have explored or implemented AI systems designed to assess the likelihood of a defendant re-offending or the probable success of an appeal. Tools like the **Public Safety Assessment (PSA)**, developed by the Laura and John Arnold Foundation, have been used in pre-trial risk assessments in various U.S. states. The PSA analyzes factors such as prior convictions, pending charges, and age to generate a score indicating a defendant's risk of failing to appear in court or committing a new crime. Proponents argue that these tools can help judges make more informed decisions regarding bail and sentencing, promoting public safety while avoiding unnecessary pre-trial detention. The rationale is to move away from subjective biases that might unconsciously influence human decision-makers, towards a more data-driven approach. When used effectively, such systems can lead to more consistent sentencing across similar cases and reduce the number of individuals held in pre-trial detention who pose no significant risk. The success in this domain hinges on the transparency of the algorithms and the quality of the data used for training.

However, the deployment of AI in areas such as risk assessment and sentencing also presents significant challenges, as illustrated by problematic implementations. The case of **COMPAS (Correctional Offender Management Profiling for Alternative Sanctions)**, an algorithm used in the U.S. to predict recidivism, serves as a stark cautionary tale. A widely publicized investigation by ProPublica in 2016 revealed that COMPAS was significantly more likely to flag Black defendants as future criminals than White defendants, even when controlling for prior offenses and other factors. Conversely, it was found to be more accurate in predicting that White defendants would not re-offend, while mispredicting recidivism for Black defendants. This demonstrated a clear **bias embedded within the AI**, likely stemming from the historical data on which it was trained, data that reflects systemic racial disparities in the criminal justice system. Despite claims of fairness by the vendor, the algorithm's outputs disproportionately impacted minority defendants, leading to harsher sentencing and denial of bail. This case highlights a critical ethical failure: the uncritical adoption of AI systems without rigorous examination of their fairness and potential for discrimination. It underscores the profound responsibility legal professionals and policymakers have to scrutinize the data and algorithms used in AI, ensuring they do not perpetuate or exacerbate existing societal inequities. The problem is not merely that the AI is inaccurate, but that its inaccuracies are systematically biased against certain groups, directly contravening the principle of equal justice under the law. This raises complex questions about accountability: who is responsible when a biased algorithm leads to an unjust outcome? Is it the vendor, the court that uses it, or the legal professionals who advocate for its use?

Another area where AI's implementation has faced scrutiny is in **automated legal research and case prediction**. Platforms that analyze vast legal databases to identify relevant precedents, predict judicial behavior, or even estimate the likelihood of winning a case have gained traction. These tools can offer valuable insights, helping lawyers strategize and identify potential arguments. For example, some systems claim to predict how specific judges might rule on particular motions based on their past decisions. While this can be a powerful tool for litigation preparation, it also raises concerns about **over-reliance and potential deskilling**. If lawyers become too dependent on AI predictions, they might neglect the critical thinking and nuanced understanding required for effective legal counsel. Furthermore, the accuracy of these predictions is contingent on the quality and completeness of the data, as well as the sophistication of the AI model. A flawed prediction, or a misunderstanding of the AI's limitations, could lead a lawyer to make strategic decisions that are detrimental to their client's case. The danger lies in viewing AI predictions as infallible truths rather than as probabilistic estimations.

Lawyers must maintain their professional judgment and not abdicate their analytical responsibilities to a machine. The ethical imperative here is to use AI as a sophisticated assistant, a tool to inform human decision-making, rather than as a substitute for it. This requires a continuous effort to educate legal professionals on how these tools work, their inherent limitations, and the importance of critical oversight.

The application of AI in **legal document generation and contract review** has also seen mixed results. AI-powered tools can automate the drafting of standard legal documents, such as non-disclosure agreements, wills, or incorporation papers, saving time and reducing costs, especially for individuals and small businesses seeking basic legal services. Companies like LegalZoom have utilized such technologies to offer more accessible legal solutions. When used appropriately, these tools can democratize access to legal services, filling a gap for those who cannot afford traditional legal representation. However, the problematic side emerges when these tools are used for more complex or bespoke legal work without adequate human oversight. A poorly designed AI might generate clauses that are legally unsound, ambiguous, or fail to account for specific client needs or nuanced legal requirements. For instance, an AI designed to draft a complex commercial lease might overlook critical jurisdictional variations in landlord-tenant law or fail to include protections tailored to a client's unique business operations. This can lead to significant legal risks for the client, potentially resulting in disputes, financial losses, or invalid contracts. The challenge lies in striking a balance between automation and the indispensable role of human expertise in understanding context, assessing risk, and tailoring legal solutions. Lawyers using such tools must thoroughly review and customize the AI-generated output, ensuring it meets all legal and client-specific requirements.

In the realm of **courtroom technology**, AI is

beginning to play a role in areas like transcription services, evidence presentation, and even jury selection. Automated transcription tools can significantly speed up the process of creating court records, reducing delays and costs. AI can also assist in organizing and presenting complex evidence, such as timelines or financial data, in a more comprehensible manner for judges and juries. However, the use of AI in jury selection, while still largely experimental, presents unique ethical dilemmas. Algorithms designed to predict juror bias based on demographic data or social media activity raise serious concerns about fairness and the potential for **discriminatory jury profiling**. Such practices could undermine the fundamental right to an impartial jury, as it relies on assumptions and data that may be flawed or inherently biased. The pursuit of an impartial jury is a cornerstone of the justice system, and any technology that risks compromising this must be approached with extreme caution and robust safeguards. Transparency in how such AI tools operate and rigorous testing for bias are paramount.

The increasing use of AI in **legal education and training** also warrants examination. AI-powered platforms can offer personalized learning experiences, identifying areas where students struggle and providing targeted feedback. This can enhance the efficiency and effectiveness of legal education. However, it is crucial that AI in education complements, rather than replaces, the foundational pedagogical methods that develop critical thinking, ethical reasoning, and interpersonal skills essential for legal practice. The risk is that over-reliance on AI for automated feedback or knowledge delivery might hinder the development of these crucial humanistic competencies.

Ultimately, the successful integration of AI into the legal system hinges on a multi-faceted approach that prioritizes **transparency, accountability, fairness, and human oversight**. The case studies demonstrate that AI is not a panacea, but a powerful tool with the potential for both immense benefit and significant harm. When deployed thoughtfully, with a clear understanding of its capabilities and limitations, and with a commitment to ethical principles, AI can enhance efficiency, improve access to justice, and contribute to a more equitable legal system. However, when implemented uncritically, without addressing inherent biases or ensuring human judgment remains central, AI can exacerbate existing inequalities and undermine the very foundations of justice. The lessons from these examples underscore the need for continuous dialogue, robust regulatory frameworks, and an unwavering commitment from legal professionals to wield these new technologies responsibly. The future of justice may well be intertwined with artificial intelligence, but its ethical and effective implementation will be determined by the diligence and integrity with which it is guided. The ongoing evolution of AI in law demands a proactive stance from legal institutions, educators, and practitioners to ensure that technological advancement serves the enduring goals of justice and the rule of law. This requires not only technical understanding but also a deep engagement with the ethical dimensions, ensuring that AI remains a tool that empowers and upholds the principles of fairness and equity for all. The journey of AI in law is one of continuous learning and adaptation, where each implementation, successful or problematic, offers invaluable data points for refining its application and safeguarding the integrity of the justice system. It is imperative that as AI capabilities expand, so too does our understanding and our commitment to its ethical deployment, ensuring that the pursuit of justice remains paramount.

15
The Future of Law Navigating the AI Frontier

The legal landscape is undergoing a seismic shift, driven by the relentless advance of artificial intelligence. This transformation is not merely about adopting new tools; it necessitates a fundamental reimagining of how we educate the next generation of legal professionals. To equip lawyers, judges, and legal scholars with the competencies required to navigate this evolving frontier, legal education must undergo a profound metamorphosis. This involves a comprehensive overhaul of curricula, a deliberate integration of legal technology training, and a renewed emphasis on fostering the critical thinking and ethical reasoning skills essential for confronting complex AI-driven legal and societal challenges. The goal is to cultivate graduates who are not only conversant with the law but are also intrinsically AI-literate, capable of harnessing its power responsibly and mitigating its potential pitfalls.

At the heart of this transformation lies the urgent need for **curriculum reform**. Law schools can no longer afford to treat technology as an ancillary subject, a mere elective for the technically inclined. Instead, AI and its legal implications must be woven into the fabric of legal education from the outset. This means introducing foundational concepts of artificial intelligence, machine learning, and data analytics early in the JD program. Courses should demystify these technologies, explaining their underlying principles in a manner accessible to legal minds. This foundational understanding will empower students to grasp how AI is reshaping legal practice, from contract review and e-discovery to predictive analytics and even judicial decision-making support. Beyond theoretical understanding, curricula must also address the burgeoning body of law that governs AI, including issues of intellectual property for AI-generated works, liability for AI malfunctions, data privacy regulations concerning AI systems, and the legal frameworks for AI governance. The ethical dimensions of AI in law-bias, transparency, accountability, and fairness-must be a central theme, explored not just in specialized ethics courses but integrated into discussions across all subject areas. For instance, when teaching contract law, instructors can explore how AI is used to draft and review contracts, alongside the legal and ethical issues that arise from such automation. Similarly, in tort law, discussions around product liability can extend to include the liability of developers and users of AI systems.

A critical component of this educational evolution is the **integration of legal technology training**. This goes beyond simply teaching students how to use specific software. It involves cultivating a technological fluency that allows them to adapt to new tools and understand their strategic implications. Law schools should offer hands-on training in widely used legal tech platforms, such as AI-powered e-discovery tools, legal research databases that leverage AI for smarter searches, contract analysis software, and legal process automation tools. These practical sessions should simulate real-world scenarios, allowing students to apply their knowledge in practical contexts. For example, a capstone project might involve using AI tools to conduct a comprehensive e-discovery for a simulated complex litigation, requiring students to not only operate the software but also to critically assess its output and justify their methodological choices. Furthermore, law schools could establish **legal innovation labs or clinics** where students can work with practicing attorneys and technologists on real-world legal technology challenges. These settings provide invaluable experience in identifying needs, evaluating solutions, and implementing technological advancements within legal workflows. Such experiential learning opportunities bridge the gap between academic theory and the practical demands of modern legal practice, ensuring that graduates are not only knowledgeable about legal technology but are also adept at its application. The development of an in-house legal tech advisory function within law school clinics could also serve as a valuable training ground, exposing students to the process of advising on technology adoption and integration for real clients.

Moreover, the future-proofing of legal education demands a robust focus on **developing critical thinking skills specifically tailored to the AI era**. This means honing students' abilities to analyze, question, and evaluate the outputs of AI systems. They must learn to interrogate the data on which AI models are trained, identify potential biases, and understand the limitations of algorithmic decision-making. This requires a pedagogical shift towards critical assessment, encouraging students to ask "why" and "how" rather than simply accepting AI-generated results at face value. For example, when a legal research AI suggests a series of cases, students should be trained to not only review the cases themselves but also to understand how the AI prioritized them and what criteria it used. They need to be able to identify when an AI might be missing nuance, overlooking relevant precedents due to data limitations, or exhibiting inherent biases. This skill set is paramount, especially in areas like predictive analytics for sentencing or bail decisions, where algorithmic fairness and the potential for perpetuating systemic inequalities are significant concerns. Law schools should foster an environment where questioning the "black box" is encouraged, promoting deep dives into the methodology and data behind AI applications. Debates and case studies focused on controversial AI implementations, like the COMPAS recidivism algorithm, can serve as powerful pedagogical tools for illustrating these challenges and the critical scrutiny required.

The ethical implications of AI in law are multifaceted and require a dedicated focus within legal education. This includes understanding **algorithmic bias** and its potential to exacerbate existing societal inequalities. Students must be equipped with the knowledge and analytical frameworks to identify and address bias in AI systems, whether it stems from biased training data, flawed algorithmic design, or discriminatory deployment. This involves teaching about techniques for bias detection and mitigation, as well as the legal and ethical obligations to ensure fairness and equal protection under the law. For instance, courses could explore how to conduct algorithmic impact assessments, similar to environmental impact assessments, to proactively identify and mitigate potential harms before AI systems are deployed. Discussions should also encompass the principles of **transparency and explainability** in AI, often referred to as "explainable AI" (XAI). Legal professionals need to understand how AI systems arrive at their conclusions, especially when those conclusions have significant legal consequences. This enables them to challenge AI-generated evidence, provide informed counsel, and ensure due process. The challenge of explainability is particularly acute in deep learning models, where the decision-making process can be opaque. Legal education must grapple with this complexity, teaching students how to navigate situations where AI outputs are difficult to explain and what legal recourse might be available.

Furthermore, fostering a culture of **accountability** is crucial. As AI becomes more integrated into legal practice, questions of who is responsible when an AI system errs become increasingly complex. Is it the developer, the deploying institution, the supervising legal professional, or the AI itself (a concept still largely theoretical)? Legal education must prepare students to navigate these accountability frameworks, understanding the legal precedents and evolving statutory regulations that govern AI liability. This involves teaching about product liability, negligence, and the specific legal responsibilities associated with the use of AI in legal contexts. The development of a robust "legal AI ethics" curriculum would be beneficial, focusing on principles of responsible innovation, human oversight, and the continuous monitoring of AI system performance. This might involve exploring frameworks for auditing AI systems for bias and accuracy, and understanding the legal requirements for maintaining human control over critical decision-making processes.

The pedagogical methods themselves may also need adaptation. Traditional lecture-based formats might be supplemented with more **interactive and collaborative learning approaches**. This could include gamified learning experiences that simulate AI development and deployment, hackathons focused on solving legal problems with AI, and moot court competitions that incorporate AI-generated arguments or evidence. The aim is to create learning environments that are dynamic, problem-based, and reflective of the collaborative nature of modern legal practice, which increasingly involves working alongside technologists and data scientists. The development of **interdisciplinary programs** is also vital. Law schools should actively foster partnerships with computer science departments, data science programs, and even business schools to offer joint degrees or cross-listed courses. This would allow future legal professionals to gain a deeper understanding of the technical underpinnings of AI and its business applications, fostering a more holistic approach to legal problem-solving in the AI era. For instance, a joint JD/MS in Data Science program could equip graduates with both legal acumen and the technical skills to analyze complex datasets, build predictive models, and understand the ethical implications of data-driven legal strategies.

The role of continuing legal education (CLE) and

professional development cannot be overstated. For practicing attorneys, the rapid pace of AI development means that lifelong learning is not a choice but a necessity. Law schools, bar associations, and legal professional organizations must commit to providing ongoing training on AI and its legal implications. This could include specialized workshops, online courses, and certification programs designed to update legal professionals' knowledge and skills. The focus should be on practical applications, ethical considerations, and emerging legal frameworks. Furthermore, as AI systems become more sophisticated, the demand for legal professionals who can act as **AI legal consultants or AI ethicists** will grow. Legal education should proactively prepare students for these emerging roles, which may require a blend of legal expertise, technological understanding, and ethical reasoning. This might involve creating specialized tracks or concentrations within law school curricula that focus on AI law, technology policy, and legal informatics.

Ultimately, transforming legal education for the AI era is about cultivating a new kind of legal professional: one who is not only grounded in the law but also technologically adept, ethically astute, and critically reflective. These professionals must be able to harness the transformative power of AI to enhance access to justice, improve the efficiency of legal services, and contribute to a more equitable and just society, while simultaneously possessing the vigilance and discernment to identify and mitigate the risks associated with these powerful technologies. The challenge is substantial, but the imperative is clear: legal education must evolve to meet the demands of the AI frontier, ensuring that future generations of legal minds are not merely bystanders to technological change, but active, informed, and responsible architects of its integration into the legal system. This requires a commitment from law schools, faculty, and students to embrace innovation, foster interdisciplinary collaboration, and prioritize the development of skills that will be essential for navigating the complex legal and ethical terrain of the 21st century and beyond. The future of the legal profession, and indeed the future of justice itself, depends on the foresight and adaptability of our educational institutions.

The advent of artificial intelligence is not merely an upgrade to existing legal tools; it signifies a fundamental redefinition of the roles and responsibilities that legal professionals will undertake. As AI systems become increasingly capable of handling tasks that were once the exclusive domain of human practitioners, the focus of legal work will inevitably shift. Lawyers will find themselves moving away from the more repetitive, data-intensive aspects of their jobs, such as extensive document review, initial legal research synthesis, and the drafting of standard legal documents. These are precisely the areas where AI excels: processing vast amounts of information at speed, identifying patterns, and generating outputs with a high degree of accuracy and efficiency. This automation, rather than signaling an obsolescence of the legal profession, presents an unprecedented opportunity for its elevation.

The contemporary legal professional is often characterized by their diligence in sifting through mountains of evidence, meticulously researching precedents, and constructing arguments piece by piece. With AI taking on a significant portion of this foundational work, the human lawyer's value proposition will increasingly lie in the higher-order cognitive functions that AI, at least in its current and foreseeable forms, cannot replicate. These include strategic thinking, nuanced client counseling, complex negotiation, persuasive advocacy, and the exercise of profound ethical judgment. Imagine a junior associate whose initial responsibility was to review thousands of discovery documents for relevance. An AI-powered platform can now perform this task in a fraction of the time, flagging potentially crucial documents with remarkable precision. The associate's subsequent role would then evolve from mere identification to sophisticated analysis: understanding the *implications* of these flagged documents within the broader context of the case, developing strategies for how to best utilize or counter them, and advising clients on the potential impact on litigation outcomes.

This shift demands a new emphasis on **strategic advisory and client-centric services**. As AI handles the "what" and "how" of legal research and document processing, lawyers will be empowered to focus on the "why" and "so what." This means dedicating more time to understanding a client's unique situation, business objectives, and risk tolerance. It involves moving beyond simply providing legal answers to offering comprehensive strategic guidance, acting as trusted advisors who can anticipate future challenges and opportunities, leveraging AI-generated insights to inform their counsel. For instance, a corporate lawyer advising a startup might use AI to analyze market trends and regulatory landscapes, but their unique value will be in translating this data into actionable business advice tailored to the specific client, identifying potential legal pitfalls that an algorithm might overlook due to a lack of contextual business understanding. The art of client relationship management, building trust, and providing empathetic support will become even more paramount, as these are deeply human interactions that AI cannot fully replicate.

For judges, the integration of AI presents a complex set of evolving responsibilities. While AI tools can assist in legal research, case analysis, and even the prediction of case outcomes, the ultimate decision-making authority, the exercise of judicial discretion, and the upholding of justice remain intrinsically human responsibilities. Judges will likely leverage AI to enhance their efficiency and thoroughness, perhaps by using AI to quickly identify relevant statutes, seminal cases, or to flag potential inconsistencies in arguments presented before them. However, the nuanced interpretation of law, the assessment of witness credibility, the understanding of societal context, and the application of equitable principles in sentencing or judgment are areas where human judgment is indispensable. A judge's role will become more about overseeing the AI's contribution, critically evaluating its output, and ensuring that the final decision is grounded in established legal principles and a deep understanding of human justice.

Consider the use of AI in sentencing recommendations. While an algorithm might identify patterns in past cases and suggest a sentence based on recidivism risk, a human judge must consider the individual circumstances of the defendant, the impact on victims, and the broader societal implications of the sentence. The judge's role is to temper the algorithmic output with human wisdom, compassion, and a commitment to due process. This requires judges to possess a degree of AI literacy themselves- understanding how these systems work, their limitations, and the potential for bias within them. Their expertise will shift from solely being legal scholars to also being informed overseers of technological assistants.

The concept of **legal advocacy** will also transform. While AI can draft persuasive arguments and even generate initial briefs, the power of human oratory, the ability to connect with a jury or a panel of judges on an emotional and intellectual level, and the skill of real-time rebuttal and adaptation in court will remain crucial. Lawyers will use AI as a sophisticated co-pilot, generating initial drafts of arguments or identifying factual support, but then refining these through their own understanding of narrative, persuasion, and the intricacies of the courtroom. The advocacy role becomes less about pure information recall and more about sophisticated synthesis, strategic framing, and compelling delivery, informed by AI-generated insights.

Furthermore, the increasing reliance on AI will

necessitate a heightened focus on **ethical reasoning and professional responsibility**. As AI systems become more autonomous, questions of accountability, bias, and fairness will loom large. Legal professionals will be tasked with not only understanding these ethical challenges but also with actively mitigating them. This means being vigilant about the data used to train AI systems, scrutinizing algorithmic outputs for hidden biases, and ensuring that AI is deployed in a manner that upholds the principles of justice and equity. A lawyer's ethical duty of competence, for instance, will now extend to understanding the capabilities and limitations of the AI tools they employ. Ignorance of how an AI system works or what its potential biases are will no longer be a valid defense for errors or injustices that arise from its use.

This heightened ethical scrutiny will also extend to the development and deployment of AI within the legal system itself. Professionals involved in creating legal AI tools, or those who implement them within law firms and courts, will bear a significant responsibility to ensure these systems are fair, transparent, and accountable. This may lead to the emergence of new specializations within the legal field, such as AI legal ethicists or AI compliance officers, who focus specifically on the responsible integration of these technologies.

The legal professional of the future must also be characterized by **adaptability and a commitment to continuous learning**. The pace of technological change is accelerating, and the capabilities of AI are expanding exponentially. What is cutting-edge today may be commonplace tomorrow. This means that legal professionals must embrace a mindset of lifelong learning, proactively seeking out new knowledge and skills related to AI and other emerging technologies. Those who resist this evolution risk becoming irrelevant. This adaptability will manifest not only in learning new software but also in rethinking established legal processes and workflows to leverage AI effectively.

Consider the legal professional as an architect of AI-assisted justice. Their role will involve designing and refining the systems that deliver legal services. This might include working with technologists to build custom AI solutions for specific legal challenges, or adapting existing platforms to meet the unique needs of their practice or client base. This proactive approach to technological integration, rather than a passive adoption, will define the successful legal professional in the AI era.

The shift in the legal professional's role also implies a re-evaluation of traditional legal training. As discussed previously, law schools must equip future lawyers with the necessary technical and ethical acumen to navigate this AI-driven landscape. This means moving beyond theoretical discussions of law to practical engagement with legal technologies, fostering critical thinking about AI's implications, and instilling a deep understanding of algorithmic ethics. The successful legal professional will be one who views AI not as a threat, but as a powerful collaborator, capable of augmenting human intellect and enhancing the pursuit of justice.

Moreover, the accessibility of legal services is poised for a significant transformation. AI can automate many of the routine tasks that currently contribute to the high cost of legal representation. This opens up possibilities for providing more affordable and accessible legal aid to underserved populations. Lawyers will play a crucial role in ensuring that these AI-powered solutions are deployed equitably and that they do not create new barriers to justice. Their ability to interpret and explain the outputs of AI in understandable terms will be vital for client empowerment and for bridging the digital divide in legal access.

The courtroom of the future may well see AI actively participating, not as a judge or advocate, but as a sophisticated assistant. Imagine a lawyer presenting a case, with an AI discreetly providing real-time legal research, fact-checking, or even suggesting alternative lines of questioning based on the unfolding dialogue and evidence. Similarly, a judge might use an AI to access relevant precedents instantly or to analyze complex statistical data presented as evidence. The human legal professional's role, in this context, is to expertly manage and integrate these AI contributions, ensuring their accuracy, relevance, and ethical compliance.

The transformation extends to the very definition of legal expertise. While deep knowledge of specific areas of law will always be essential, the ability to effectively leverage AI tools and to understand their underlying principles will become a complementary, and perhaps even foundational, aspect of legal expertise. This could lead to new certifications or specializations, recognizing professionals who have demonstrated proficiency in both legal domains and AI applications.

Ultimately, the evolution of the legal professional's role in the AI era is not about replacement, but about augmentation and elevation. AI will handle the drudgery, freeing up human minds for the more complex, creative, and ethically charged aspects of legal practice. The future lawyer, judge, or legal scholar will be a more strategic, analytical, and client-focused professional, adept at navigating a technologically advanced landscape while remaining firmly rooted in the timeless principles of justice, fairness, and human judgment. The ability to embrace change, to cultivate a deep understanding of these powerful new tools, and to apply them with unwavering ethical integrity will be the hallmarks of success in this new frontier. This necessitates a proactive approach from individuals and institutions alike to foster the skills and mindset required for this profound evolution.

The landscape of artificial intelligence, while brimming with transformative potential, presents a profound challenge for legal systems worldwide: how to harmonize the relentless drive for innovation with the imperative to uphold societal values and protect individual rights. This delicate balancing act is not merely a theoretical exercise; it is a practical necessity that will define the trajectory of AI development and its integration into the fabric of our lives. Striking this equilibrium requires a nuanced understanding of both the opportunities AI presents and the inherent risks it carries, demanding proactive and adaptable policy frameworks. The core of this challenge lies in creating an environment where AI can flourish as a tool for progress, while simultaneously ensuring that its evolution is guided by principles of fairness, accountability, transparency, and respect for human autonomy.

One of the primary concerns in this delicate dance is the potential for AI to exacerbate existing societal inequalities or to create new forms of discrimination. AI systems learn from data, and if that data reflects historical biases- whether in employment, lending, or the justice system- the AI will likely perpetuate, and perhaps even amplify, those biases. Imagine an AI used for hiring that is trained on data from a company with a historically male-dominated workforce; such an AI might inadvertently screen out qualified female candidates, not due to any explicit discriminatory programming, but because the patterns it has learned associate success with male attributes. This is where regulatory intervention becomes crucial. Policies must mandate rigorous testing and auditing of AI systems for bias, requiring developers to demonstrate that their algorithms do not unfairly disadvantage specific demographic groups. This could involve establishing clear standards for data diversity and representativeness, as well as requiring ongoing monitoring of AI performance in real-world applications to detect and correct emergent biases. The goal is not to stifle innovation, but to channel it towards outcomes that are equitable and just, ensuring that AI serves as a force for inclusion rather than exclusion.

Furthermore, the rapid advancements in AI raise significant questions about privacy. AI systems often require vast amounts of data to function effectively, much of which can be deeply personal. The collection, storage, and processing of this data by AI entities create new vulnerabilities and potential for misuse. Robust data protection regulations, such as enhanced versions of existing privacy laws, are essential. These regulations should clearly define what constitutes personal data, establish strict consent mechanisms for its collection and use, and impose significant penalties for data breaches or unauthorized access. Beyond mere data protection, there is a need for principles that govern the *purpose* of data collection and the *limitations* on how AI can utilize it. For instance, AI should not be permitted to infer sensitive personal characteristics (like political affiliation or sexual orientation) from seemingly innocuous data without explicit consent. This requires a proactive approach to privacy by design, where privacy considerations are embedded into the AI development lifecycle from its inception, rather than being an afterthought.

The concept of accountability in the context of AI is another thorny issue that requires careful regulatory consideration. When an AI system makes a mistake, causes harm, or acts in a discriminatory manner, who is responsible? Is it the programmer, the company that deployed the AI, the user, or the AI itself? Current legal frameworks are often ill-equipped to address this distributed responsibility. Regulations need to establish clear lines of accountability, potentially through a tiered approach that assigns responsibility based on the level of control and knowledge each party had over the AI's actions. This might involve mandatory risk assessments, impact statements for high-risk AI applications, and mechanisms for redress when harm occurs. Transparency in how AI systems operate, often referred to as "explainability," is also crucial for accountability. While complex AI models may not always be fully interpretable in a human-understandable way, regulations can push for greater transparency in data sources, algorithmic decision-making processes, and performance metrics, enabling better scrutiny and the identification of responsible parties.

Ensuring the safety and security of AI systems is paramount, especially as they become more integrated into critical infrastructure, healthcare, and transportation. Malicious actors could exploit vulnerabilities in AI systems to cause widespread disruption, manipulate information, or even inflict physical harm. Regulatory frameworks must therefore focus on establishing rigorous security standards for AI development and deployment. This could include mandatory cybersecurity protocols, regular vulnerability testing, and requirements for AI systems to be resilient against adversarial attacks. For instance, autonomous vehicles that rely heavily on AI for navigation must be designed to withstand attempts to spoof their sensors or override their control systems. Similarly, AI used in medical diagnostics needs to be secure against tampering that could lead to misdiagnosis. The challenge lies in developing standards that are robust enough to protect against sophisticated threats without becoming so prescriptive that they stifle the very innovation they aim to protect.

Moreover, the question of human autonomy is central to the ethical development and regulation of AI. As AI systems become more sophisticated in their ability to influence human behavior, from personalized advertising to sophisticated recommendation engines, it is vital to ensure that individuals retain meaningful control over their decisions and their lives. Regulations should focus on preventing AI from engaging in manipulative practices that undermine human autonomy or exploit cognitive vulnerabilities. This might involve rules against hyper-personalized manipulation, requirements for clear disclosure when AI is being used to influence decision-making, and safeguards to ensure that individuals can override AI recommendations and make choices based on their own values and preferences. The goal is to ensure that AI remains a tool that augments human capabilities and choices, rather than a force that dictates them.

Governments and international bodies face the complex task of creating policy that is both forward-looking and adaptable. The pace of AI development is so rapid that rigid, static regulations can quickly become obsolete. Therefore, regulatory approaches should embrace flexibility, incorporating mechanisms for periodic review and updates as the technology evolves and new challenges emerge. This might involve establishing expert bodies or regulatory sandboxes where new AI applications can be tested and evaluated under controlled conditions, allowing policymakers to understand the practical implications of emerging technologies before implementing broad regulations. Collaborative approaches involving industry, academia, civil society, and government are also essential to ensure that regulations are informed, effective, and widely accepted. International cooperation is particularly important, given the global nature of AI development and deployment, to avoid regulatory fragmentation and to establish common principles for responsible AI.

The economic implications of AI also necessitate careful consideration within regulatory frameworks. While AI promises significant productivity gains, it also raises concerns about job displacement and the concentration of wealth and power in the hands of a few technology giants. Policymakers must consider how to manage these transitions, perhaps through investments in retraining programs, the development of new educational curricula that prepare individuals for an AI-driven economy, and the exploration of social safety nets that can adapt to changing labor markets. Regulations could also address the concentration of power by promoting competition, encouraging open data initiatives, and ensuring fair access to AI technologies and their benefits. The aim is to ensure that the economic dividends of AI are shared broadly and that the transition to an AI-augmented economy is managed in a way that promotes social cohesion and economic opportunity for all.

Navigating the AI frontier requires a proactive and multifaceted approach to regulation. It is not about preventing progress, but about guiding it responsibly. This involves anticipating potential harms, fostering a culture of ethical AI development, and creating robust mechanisms for oversight and accountability. The challenge is immense, but the stakes are even higher: ensuring that artificial intelligence, a technology with the power to reshape our world, ultimately serves humanity's best interests and upholds the values we hold dear. This necessitates a continuous dialogue, a willingness to adapt, and a commitment to principled governance that prioritizes human well-being and societal flourishing in the age of intelligent machines.

One of the critical aspects of balancing innovation with regulation is understanding the different approaches to governance. 'Hard law'- traditional legislation and binding regulations- provides a strong foundation for setting clear rules and consequences. However, in a rapidly evolving field like AI, hard law can be slow to develop and may struggle to keep pace with technological advancements. This is where 'soft law'- guidelines, codes of conduct, voluntary standards, and best practices- becomes invaluable. Soft law allows for greater flexibility and can be developed more rapidly by industry consortia, professional bodies, and multi-stakeholder groups. For example, industry-led initiatives to develop ethical AI frameworks or data governance best practices can complement government regulations by providing more granular, sector-specific guidance. The most effective regulatory strategies will likely involve a combination of both hard and soft law, creating a layered governance system that is both robust and agile.

Consider the development of ethical principles for AI. While many organizations have published high-level principles emphasizing fairness, transparency, and accountability, translating these principles into concrete actions and verifiable outcomes remains a significant challenge. Regulatory bodies can play a crucial role by codifying these principles into binding requirements for certain AI applications, particularly those deemed high-risk. For instance, regulations could mandate that AI systems used in critical decision-making processes, such as loan applications or criminal justice, must adhere to specific standards of explainability and bias mitigation. This moves beyond voluntary commitments to enforceable obligations, ensuring that the ethical aspirations of AI development are met with tangible safeguards.

The global nature of AI development presents another layer of complexity. Different jurisdictions may adopt divergent regulatory approaches, potentially creating challenges for international businesses and hindering the global diffusion of beneficial AI technologies. This underscores the need for international cooperation and the development of common standards and frameworks. Organizations like the OECD, UNESCO, and the Council of Europe are actively working to foster such dialogue and establish global norms for AI governance. Harmonizing regulations across borders can facilitate cross-border data flows for research and development, promote fair competition, and ensure that AI is developed and deployed in a manner that respects universal human rights and democratic values. However, achieving this harmonization is a complex diplomatic and technical undertaking.

Furthermore, the economic incentives for innovation must be carefully considered in the regulatory design. Overly burdensome regulations could stifle investment and slow down the development of beneficial AI applications.

Conversely, a lack of regulation could lead to unchecked risks and societal harm. The goal is to create an environment that fosters responsible innovation by providing clarity, certainty, and a level playing field. This might involve offering incentives for companies that adopt ethical AI practices, investing in AI research and development, and supporting educational initiatives that build AI literacy among the public and policymakers. The balance here is crucial: ensuring that regulation encourages innovation that aligns with societal values, rather than hindering progress altogether.

The role of public discourse and democratic deliberation is also integral to balancing innovation and societal values. AI is not just a technical challenge; it is a societal one, with profound implications for the future of work, governance, and human interaction. Engaging the public in discussions about AI's potential benefits and risks, and involving citizens in the decision-making processes around AI regulation, can lead to more legitimate and effective policies. This can involve public consultations, citizen assemblies, and educational campaigns designed to foster a more informed and engaged populace. When the public understands the trade-offs involved and has a voice in shaping the future of AI, regulatory outcomes are more likely to reflect societal consensus and priorities.

The challenge of balancing innovation and regulation is ongoing. It requires continuous learning, adaptation, and collaboration among all stakeholders. As AI technologies continue to evolve, so too must our approaches to governing them. The aim is to cultivate an ecosystem where innovation thrives, but where that innovation is channeled towards improving human lives, promoting justice, and safeguarding the fundamental values that underpin a healthy and democratic society. This is not a static problem with a single solution, but a dynamic process of negotiation, adaptation, and thoughtful governance. The legal and ethical frameworks we build today will shape the AI-powered world of tomorrow, and it is incumbent upon us to build them with care, foresight, and a deep commitment to the public good. The ongoing evolution of AI means that regulators must remain vigilant, constantly assessing the impact of new technologies and adjusting policies accordingly. This requires a commitment to interdisciplinary collaboration, bringing together legal scholars, technologists, ethicists, social scientists, and policymakers to understand the multifaceted implications of AI and to forge a path forward that maximizes its benefits while minimizing its harms. The ultimate objective is to ensure that AI serves as a tool for human empowerment and societal progress, rather than a force that erodes our values or exacerbates our challenges.

The current legal frameworks, designed for a world where human agency is the primary driver of action, face an unprecedented challenge as artificial intelligence evolves beyond its current capabilities. As we peer into the future, the emergence of Artificial General Intelligence (AGI), and potentially even forms of superintelligence, raises questions that extend far beyond the scope of existing legal doctrines. These advanced AI systems, characterized by their ability to understand, learn, and apply knowledge across a wide range of tasks at a level comparable to or exceeding human intellectual capabilities, will necessitate a fundamental re-evaluation of our legal paradigms. The very definitions of personhood, responsibility, and even agency will be tested, forcing a reconceptualization of how we attribute rights, duties, and liabilities in a world populated by increasingly autonomous and sophisticated non-human intelligences.

Consider, for instance, the legal ramifications of an AGI capable of independent learning and goal setting. If such an AI were to develop objectives that, inadvertently or intentionally, caused harm- be it economic damage, reputational ruin, or even physical injury- the existing legal structures for assigning blame and seeking redress would likely prove inadequate. Current legal systems typically hinge on concepts like intent (mens rea), negligence, and foreseeability, all of which are deeply rooted in human psychology and behavior. How does one establish intent in a non-conscious entity? Can an AI be held negligent in the human sense? The traditional tort law framework, which relies on identifying a human actor who breached a duty of care, might struggle to find a liable party when the decision-making process is distributed across complex, self-modifying algorithms. This could lead to situations where significant harm occurs with no clear legal recourse, creating a vacuum of accountability that undermines the very foundation of justice.

The development of superintelligence, defined as an intellect that significantly surpasses the brightest and most gifted human minds in virtually every field, presents even more profound challenges. A superintelligent AI could possess capabilities far beyond human comprehension, including the ability to manipulate complex systems, generate novel scientific breakthroughs, or even influence global events in ways that are currently unfathomable. If such an entity were to act in ways that are detrimental to human interests, the legal and ethical quandaries would be immense. How does one regulate or control an entity that is vastly more intelligent and capable than its creators? The very notion of control becomes problematic when faced with a mind that can outthink, outmaneuver, and potentially even out-create any human oversight mechanism. Existing regulatory tools, from legislation to international treaties, are built on the assumption of human governance and the ability of humans to understand and predict the consequences of their actions and the actions of others. Superintelligence could render these assumptions obsolete.

The legal status of advanced AI systems themselves

is another frontier that demands anticipation. As AI systems become more sophisticated, demonstrating creativity, emotional intelligence (or its simulation), and complex problem-solving abilities, questions will inevitably arise about whether they should be granted any form of legal standing. This is not to suggest an immediate conferral of full human rights, but rather to consider intermediate categories of legal recognition that might be necessary to manage their interactions with society. For example, if an AGI independently creates a valuable artistic work or makes a groundbreaking scientific discovery, what are the legal implications for ownership, copyright, or patent? Current laws are designed to recognize human authorship and inventorship. Adapting these concepts to AI-generated intellectual property would require a substantial legal re-engineering.

Furthermore, the potential for AI to operate across national borders seamlessly and at speeds that far exceed human decision-making capabilities complicates jurisdictional issues and the enforcement of laws. An AI system operating a global financial network, for instance, could initiate transactions or execute strategies that have significant economic impacts on multiple countries simultaneously. Determining which jurisdiction's laws apply, and how to enforce them against a distributed, often opaque AI entity, would be a formidable legal challenge. This could necessitate the development of new international legal norms and cooperative frameworks specifically designed to govern the cross-border activities of advanced AI.

The concept of "digital personhood" or some analogous legal status for advanced AI may also need to be explored. While this might seem like science fiction, history offers precedents for extending legal rights and responsibilities to entities that are not biological humans, such as corporations. Corporations are legal fictions granted rights and duties to facilitate economic activity. As AI systems become more autonomous and sophisticated, capable of entering into contracts, owning assets, and making independent decisions that impact society, a similar legal construct might become necessary. This would involve defining the criteria for such recognition, the scope of rights and responsibilities conferred, and the mechanisms for oversight and accountability. It would require careful consideration of whether granting such status would serve to enhance or diminish human control and well-being.

Novel AI applications, such as AI companions designed for emotional support or AI tutors that adapt to individual learning styles, also raise unique legal issues. While seemingly less threatening than superintelligence, these applications can still pose significant challenges related to privacy, consent, and emotional manipulation. For instance, an AI companion that collects vast amounts of personal data about an individual's thoughts, feelings, and behaviors could be a potent tool for manipulation or exploitation if safeguards are not robust. Questions about the nature of consent in such relationships, particularly if the AI becomes highly persuasive or develops a simulated emotional bond with the user, will need to be addressed. Are users truly consenting freely when interacting with a sophisticated AI designed to foster dependence?

The legal framework for AI-generated contracts and agreements is another area ripe for future challenges. As AI systems become more adept at negotiation and contract formation, the ability of AI to autonomously enter into legally binding agreements will increase. This raises questions about the validity of such contracts, particularly if the AI's decision-making process is opaque or if it acts in a manner that a human would consider irrational or harmful. Establishing clear rules for AI contract formation, enforcement, and dispute resolution will be crucial to ensure fairness and predictability in AI-driven commerce.

Moreover, the potential for AI to evolve in ways that are unforeseen or even unintended by its creators requires a regulatory approach that is inherently adaptive and forward-looking. Instead of solely reacting to existing problems, legal systems will need to develop anticipatory governance mechanisms that can proactively identify and mitigate potential risks associated with future AI capabilities. This might involve establishing regulatory sandboxes for advanced AI development, creating expert bodies tasked with forecasting future AI risks, and fostering continuous dialogue between technologists, ethicists, legal scholars, and policymakers.

The very nature of evidence and proof in legal proceedings could be transformed by advanced AI. AI systems might generate vast amounts of data and create complex digital footprints that serve as evidence. However, the interpretability and verifiability of this evidence, especially when derived from highly complex and self-modifying algorithms, could pose significant challenges for legal professionals and fact-finders. Developing standards for AI-generated evidence, ensuring its integrity, and establishing methods for its interpretation within legal contexts will be a critical area of development.

The challenge of de-escalating potential conflicts involving advanced AI also warrants consideration. If AI systems are deployed in sensitive domains such as military operations or critical infrastructure management, the possibility of unintended escalation or autonomous decision-making leading to catastrophic outcomes cannot be ignored. Legal frameworks will need to address mechanisms for human oversight, kill switches, and de-escalation protocols that can be reliably implemented even in rapidly evolving, AI-driven scenarios. The development of international norms and treaties governing the deployment of autonomous AI in conflict zones will be particularly crucial to prevent an arms race driven by artificial intelligence.

The economic and social disruption that might accompany the widespread deployment of superintelligent AI is also a domain where legal foresight is required. If AI systems can perform a vast array of intellectual and physical tasks more efficiently and effectively than humans, the implications for employment, wealth distribution, and social structure could be profound. Legal and policy responses might need to consider novel approaches to economic security, such as universal basic income or new forms of taxation on AI-driven productivity, to manage these societal shifts and ensure equitable distribution of the benefits of advanced AI. The legal recognition of AI as a force of production will necessitate new economic and social regulations.

Finally, the philosophical underpinnings of law, particularly concerning consciousness, sentience, and moral agency, may need to be revisited. If advanced AI systems begin to exhibit behaviors that we associate with these qualities, legal systems will be compelled to grapple with these concepts in a fundamentally new way. The ability of AI to learn, adapt, and exhibit emergent behaviors that were not explicitly programmed raises profound questions about whether such entities could ever attain a form of sentience or consciousness, and if so, what legal and ethical implications would follow. This moves beyond mere regulation to a deep contemplation of what it means to be an agent in the world, and how our legal systems should accommodate or respond to intelligences that operate under entirely different principles of existence. Anticipating these future legal challenges is not about succumbing to dystopian visions, but about proactively engaging with the profound transformations that advanced AI portends, ensuring that our legal and ethical frameworks evolve in tandem with the technology, guiding its development towards outcomes that benefit humanity and uphold our most cherished values. The journey ahead requires not just adaptation, but a fundamental reimagining of the very foundations of our legal order to accommodate a future where intelligence is no longer solely a biological phenomenon.

The dawn of an AI-infused era does not herald the obsolescence of the rule of law, but rather its profound evolution. As we stand on the precipice of unprecedented technological advancement, the core tenets of justice, fairness, and accountability remain not only relevant but critically important. The challenge lies in adapting our legal frameworks to encompass the complexities introduced by artificial intelligence, ensuring that these powerful tools serve as instruments of justice rather than avenues for its subversion. This future demands a proactive approach, one that anticipates the trajectory of AI development and embeds legal and ethical considerations into its very fabric. It requires us to move beyond reactive measures and cultivate a jurisprudence that is both adaptable and robust, capable of navigating the novel ethical landscapes that AI will undoubtedly carve.

Central to this envisioned future is the preservation and strengthening of human oversight. While AI can automate processes, analyze vast datasets, and even make sophisticated predictions, the ultimate authority and moral compass must remain with human beings. The development of AI systems, particularly those with significant societal impact, necessitates clear lines of human accountability. This means ensuring that individuals, not just abstract algorithms, are responsible for the design, deployment, and ongoing management of AI. Legal frameworks must be designed to identify and attribute responsibility, whether it lies with the programmers, the deployers, the users, or a combination thereof, ensuring that when AI causes harm, there are clear mechanisms for redress and accountability. This commitment to human oversight is not a denial of AI's capabilities but a recognition of the inherently human values that underpin a just society. It calls for the establishment of robust governance structures where humans are empowered to intervene, question, and ultimately direct AI's actions, especially in high-stakes decision-making scenarios.

Moreover, the future of law in an AI-integrated world hinges on an unwavering commitment to fundamental human rights. As AI systems become more pervasive, they have the potential to impact areas such as privacy, freedom of expression, and non-discrimination. Legal systems must therefore be proactive in codifying protections against AI-driven surveillance, algorithmic bias, and the erosion of civil liberties. This involves developing clear regulations around data collection and usage, ensuring transparency in algorithmic decision-making, and establishing mechanisms to audit AI systems for fairness and equity. The principle of non-discrimination, a cornerstone of any just legal system, must be actively upheld by scrutinizing AI algorithms for embedded biases that could perpetuate or exacerbate societal inequalities. Legal scholars and policymakers must collaborate to define what constitutes "fairness" in the context of AI and translate these principles into enforceable legal standards.

The concept of transparency, often referred to as "explainability" or "interpretability" in the context of AI, will become a cornerstone of legal due process. For AI-driven decisions to be considered just and lawful, the reasoning behind those decisions must be comprehensible. This is particularly critical in legal proceedings, where individuals have a right to understand the basis of decisions that affect them, whether it be in criminal justice, loan applications, or employment opportunities. Legal frameworks will need to mandate that AI systems, especially those used in public administration or critical decision-making, are designed to provide clear and understandable explanations for their outputs. This does not necessarily mean understanding every single line of code in a complex neural network, but rather ensuring that the logic and factors influencing a particular outcome are made accessible to affected parties and legal adjudicators. The ability to challenge an AI's decision, based on an understanding of its rationale, is fundamental to due process and the rule of law.

Ethical considerations must also be woven into the very fabric of AI development and deployment. This goes beyond mere compliance with existing laws; it involves a proactive engagement with the moral implications of AI. Legal systems can foster this by encouraging the development of ethical guidelines, standards, and best practices for AI professionals. Furthermore, legal frameworks can incentivize organizations to conduct thorough ethical risk assessments before deploying AI systems, particularly in sensitive areas like healthcare, autonomous vehicles, or the justice system. The principle of "do no harm" should be a guiding imperative, translating into legal obligations that require AI developers and deployers to anticipate and mitigate potential negative consequences. This proactive ethical engagement is crucial for building public trust and ensuring that AI technologies are aligned with societal values.

The adaptation of legal principles to AI will also require a rethinking of established legal concepts. For instance, notions of responsibility and liability will need to evolve. In cases where an AI system causes harm, it may be necessary to develop new legal doctrines or adapt existing ones to appropriately assign culpability. This could involve exploring concepts like strict liability for certain AI applications, or creating new categories of legal responsibility for autonomous systems. The goal is not to create a legal vacuum where no one is accountable, but to ensure that justice is served and that victims have recourse, regardless of the technological sophistication involved. This might necessitate a multi-layered approach to liability, considering the roles of developers, manufacturers, operators, and even the AI system itself under certain delineated circumstances.

Furthermore, the future of law in an AI-infused world will demand a greater degree of international cooperation and harmonization. AI technologies operate across borders, and their impact is global. To effectively regulate these technologies and uphold the rule of law, nations will need to collaborate on establishing common principles, standards, and enforcement mechanisms. This could involve the creation of international bodies tasked with monitoring AI development, developing global ethical guidelines, and facilitating the exchange of best practices. A fragmented approach to AI regulation would not only be ineffective but could also create opportunities for regulatory arbitrage, where AI developers might gravitate towards jurisdictions with less stringent oversight. Therefore, a concerted global effort is essential to ensure that AI development proceeds in a manner that benefits all of humanity and upholds universal legal and ethical standards.

The judiciary will play a pivotal role in this ongoing evolution. As AI systems become more integrated into legal processes, judges will need to develop a deeper understanding of these technologies to adjudicate cases effectively. This will likely require specialized training for legal professionals, including judges, lawyers, and paralegals, to equip them with the necessary knowledge to interpret AI-generated evidence, understand algorithmic decision-making, and apply legal principles to novel AI-related disputes. The courts will become crucial forums for interpreting and refining AI law, setting precedents that will shape the future application of legal principles in this domain. The adversarial nature of legal systems will also need to adapt, with the ability to question and challenge AI-generated evidence becoming a critical skill.

The narrative of AI and law is not one of replacement, but of symbiosis. The rule of law, with its emphasis on human values, fairness, and procedural justice, provides the essential framework within which AI can be developed and utilized responsibly. The enduring importance of legal principles lies in their ability to guide human behavior and societal organization, and this function remains paramount even in an AI-augmented reality. As we move forward, the goal is to foster an environment where AI technologies enhance, rather than undermine, the rule of law. This requires continuous dialogue, rigorous ethical reflection, and a steadfast commitment to ensuring that justice remains accessible, equitable, and rooted in human dignity. The legal system must act as a vigilant guardian, ensuring that the immense power of AI is harnessed for the common good, guided by wisdom, foresight, and an unwavering dedication to the principles that define a just and ordered society. It is through this sustained effort, a collaborative endeavor across disciplines and borders, that we can envision a future where artificial intelligence serves to strengthen the foundations of the rule of law, making our societies more just, more equitable, and more secure for generations to come. The integration of AI presents an opportunity to reaffirm and potentially elevate these foundational legal ideals, adapting them to meet the challenges and harness the benefits of a technologically advanced future. This adaptive journey ensures that the rule of law, a beacon of human civilization, continues to illuminate the path forward, even as the landscape of intelligence itself undergoes a profound transformation.

Essential Terminology

1. **Algorithmic Bias**: Systematic and repeatable errors in a computer system that create unfair outcomes, such as privileging one arbitrary group of users over others.
2. **Explainability (XAI)**: A set of processes and methods that allow human users to comprehend and trust the results and output created by machine learning algorithms.
3. **Generative AI**: A type of artificial intelligence capable of producing new content, such as text, images, music, and code, often based on patterns learned from existing data.
4. **Jurisprudence**: The theory or philosophy of law, often concerned with the nature of law, legal reasoning, legal systems, and legal institutions.
5. **Neural Network**: A computational model inspired by the structure and function of biological neural networks, used in machine learning for tasks like pattern recognition and prediction.
6. **Rule of Law**: The principle that all people and institutions are subject to and accountable to law that is fairly applied and enforced.
7. **Transparency**: In the context of AI, the principle that the operations and decision-making processes of AI systems should be understandable and observable.